Civil War in Syria

In 2011, hundreds of thousands of Syrians marched peacefully to demand democratic reforms. Within months, repression forced them to take arms and set up their own institutions. Two years later, the inclusive nature of the opposition had collapsed, and the PKK and radical jihadist groups rose to prominence. In just a few years, Syria turned into a full-scale civil war involving major regional and world powers. How has the war affected Syrian society? How does the fragmentation of Syria transform social and sectarian hierarchies? How does the war economy work in a country divided between the regime, the insurgency, the PKK, and the Islamic State? Written by authors who have previously worked on the Iraqi, Afghan, Kurd, Libyan, and Congolese armed conflicts, this book includes extensive interviews and direct observations. This is a unique book, which combines rare field experience of the Syrian conflict with new theoretical insights on the dynamics of civil wars.

Adam Baczko is a Ph.D. candidate in Political Science at the School for Advanced Studies in the Social Sciences (EHESS, Paris). His research focuses on the implementation of justice by armed groups and its political implications, with a particular focus on Afghanistan. He has carried out fieldwork in Afghanistan, the Democratic Republic of Congo, Iraq, and Syria.

Gilles Dorronsoro is Professor of Political Science at Pantheon Sorbonne University and the Principal Investigator of the ERC Social Dynamics of Civil Wars. He has researched on civil wars throughout his career, making significant contributions through his books on Afghanistan, Turkey, and Syria. He is the author of *Revolution Unending: Afghanistan, 1979 to the Present*.

Arthur Quesnay is a Ph.D. candidate in Political Science at the Pantheon-Sorbonne University. His research centers on the political dynamics of the sectarian conflicts in Iraq, where he has conducted extensive fieldwork since 2009. In a comparative perspective, he also carried out fieldwork in Libya (2011–2012) and Syria (2012–2016) with insurgent groups.

Problems of International Politics

Series Editors

Keith Darden, *American University*

Ian Shapiro, *Yale University*

The series seeks manuscripts central to the understanding of international politics that will be empirically rich and conceptually innovative. It is interested in works that illuminate the evolving character of nation-states within the international system. It sets out three broad areas for investigation: (1) identity, security, and conflict; (2) democracy; and (3) justice and distribution.

Civil War in Syria

Mobilization and Competing Social Orders

Adam Baczko
EHESS, Paris

Gilles Dorronsoro
Université Paris 1 Panthéon-Sorbonne

Arthur Quesnay
Université Paris 1 Panthéon-Sorbonne

CAMBRIDGE
UNIVERSITY PRESS

CAMBRIDGE
UNIVERSITY PRESS

University Printing House, Cambridge CB2 8BS, United Kingdom

One Liberty Plaza, 20th Floor, New York, NY 10006, USA

477 Williamstown Road, Port Melbourne, VIC 3207, Australia

314–321, 3rd Floor, Plot 3, Splendor Forum, Jasola District Centre, New Delhi – 110025, India

79 Anson Road, #06–04/06, Singapore 079906

Cambridge University Press is part of the University of Cambridge.

It furthers the University's mission by disseminating knowledge in the pursuit of education, learning, and research at the highest international levels of excellence.

www.cambridge.org
Information on this title: www.cambridge.org/9781108420808
DOI: 10.1017/9781108355322

First published 2018

Printed in the United Kingdom by Clays, St Ives plc

A catalogue record for this publication is available from the British Library.

ISBN 978-1-108-42080-8 Hardback
ISBN 978-1-108-43090-6 Paperback

There is only the trying. The rest is not our business

T.S. Eliot

Contents

Tables

Maps

Acronyms

ACU	Assistance Coordination Unit
AKP	Justice and Development Party
AQAP	al-Qaida in the Arabian Peninsula
AQM	al-Qaida in Mesopotamia
CAP	Communist Action Party
Daesh	Arabic acronym for ISIL
FARC	Revolutionary Armed Forces of Colombia
FSA	Free Syrian Army
HDI	Human Development Index
IS	Islamic State
ISI	Islamic State in Iraq
ISIL	Islamic State in Iraq and the Levant
KDP	Kurdistan Democratic Party
KNCS	Kurdish National Council in Syria
KRG	Kurdish Regional Government
NCDC	National Committee for Democratic Change
OPCW	Organization for the Prohibition of Chemical Weapons
PJAK	Party for a Free Life in Kurdistan
PKK	Kurdistan Workers Party
PUK	Patriotic Union of Kurdistan
PYD	Democratic Union Party
RUF	Revolutionary United Front
RWB	Reporters Without Borders
SCPR	Syrian Center for Policy Research
SIF	Syrian Islamic Front
SILF	Syrian Islamic Liberation Front
SNC	Syrian National Council
TCK	Kurdish Youth Movement
TEV-DEM	Democratic Kurdish Movement
UNDP	United Nations Development Program
UNHCR	United Nations High Commissioner for Refugees
YPG	People's Protection Units

Acknowledgments

We could not have done this work without the support of our respective institutions, CESSP (The European Center for Sociology and Political Science) at the University of Paris 1 Panthéon Sorbonne and CESPRA (The Raymond Aron Center for Sociological and Political Studies) at The School for Advanced Studies in the Social Sciences (EHESS). Our research was made possible by the support provided by the TEPSIS Laboratory of Excellence and, in particular, Elisabeth Sieca. The research on the Islamic State was sustained by The Program on Governance and Local Development (housed in Yale University and the University of Gothenburg), the Richard Lounsbery Foundation, and Noria. This project has received funding from the European Research Council (ERC) under the European Union's Horizon 2020 research and innovation program (grant agreement No 669690). An earlier version of the prolegomena and of Chapter 2 were published in the *Revue française de science politique* and of Chapter 11 in *Actes de la recherche en sciences sociales*.[1]

Of the many researchers and analysts who encouraged, supported, and critiqued us, we owe a special debt of gratitude to Amin Allal, Adèle Blazquez, François Burgat, Myriam Catusse, Gérard Chaliand, Nathalie Fustier, Olivier Grojean, Boris James, Bassma Kodmani, Salam Kawakibi, Steven Lukes, Ellen Lust, Kate Miller, Elizabeth Picard, Matthieu Rey, Laura Ruiz de Elvira Carrascal, and the anonymous reviewers for their constructive comments. The theoretical framework, developed in the prolegomena, owes to the collective discussions with our ERC "Social Dynamics of Civil Wars" Thursday seminar: Yohanan Benhaïm, Adèle Blazquez, Denia Chébli, Lola Guyot, Romain Le Cour

---

[1] See, respectively, Adam Baczko and Gilles Dorronsoro, "Pour une approche sociologique des guerres civiles," *Revue française de science politique* 67 (2), 2017, pp. 309–327; Adam Baczko, Gilles Dorronsoro, and Arthur Quesnay, "Mobilisations as a Result of Deliberation and Polarising Crisis: The Peaceful Protests in Syria (2011)," *Revue française de science politique* 63 (5), 2013, pp. 815–839; Adam Baczko, Gilles Dorronsoro, and Arthur Quesnay, "Le capital révolutionnaire," *Actes de la recherche en sciences sociales* 211–212, 2016, pp. 24–35.

Grandmaison, Victor Louzon, Claude Mbowou, Cléa Pineau, Camille Popineau, Candice Raymond, Emmanuelle Veuillet, and, finally, Tanya Karagyozova for her outstanding job in managing us. We are grateful to Klaus Schlichte, Anastasia Shesterinina, and Dennis Rodgers for their stimulating remarks on the theory. Ian Shapiro, who heads the International Studies Series at Cambridge University Press, supported our project and the book benefited from Cambridge University Press editors Lew Bateman and John Haslam's work. Louise Rosen first translated the manuscript, including the quotations from the French sources, and Henry Randolph then translated the prolegomena and revised the entire text.

We benefited equally from questions by the audience at IFEA (French Institute of Anatolian Studies) in Istanbul, IFPO (French Institute for the Middle East) in Erbil, Beirut, and Amman, and IREMAM at the University of Aix-Marseille, and at Columbia University, the Yale Law School, and the University of Paris 1 Panthéon Sorbonne. Remarks by Thomas Pierret, Hélène Michalak, and Patrick Haenni helped us to greatly improve certain chapters. We also wish to thank Felix Legrand, Robin Beaumont, and Aurélie Daher for rereading a first version of the manuscript. Maaï Youssef took part in the Iraq interviews and in writing the working paper, which provided the basis for Chapter 10 on the Islamic State.[2] Finally, we would like to thank Myriam Rubiano for her work on the site www.facebook.com/Syrian.Revolution.

In Syria, an extremely difficult environment on occasion, numerous individuals took the time to tell us their story, guide us through their neighborhood, invite us into their homes, and often put us up. Some are now dead, others refugees, and all experienced dramatic changes in their lives. The former mayor of Aleppo, Ahmed Azuz, inestimably aided our research in the summer of 2013. An electrician who hosted us in Aleppo, a militant Kurdish journalist in Kobane, some students turned fighters on the frontlines of the Salaheddin quarter (Aleppo), youngsters in Al-Bab, a Kurdish doctor at Afrin, a Damascene woman living between Turkey and Egypt – so many people who would deserve being named in a work filled with their stories but who must for good reason remain anonymous. Finally, the Syrian situation led us to conduct a portion of our interviews in Turkey, Egypt, Lebanon, Jordan, France, and Iraq. We are especially grateful to the Iraqis recently escaped from regions held by the Islamic State who recounted their experiences for us, frequently with humor and always with dignity, when their likely fate in the coming years is life in exile or in a refugee camp.

---

[2] Adam Baczko, Gilles Dorronsoro, Arthur Quesnay, and Maaï Youssef, "The Rationality of an Eschatological Movement: The Islamist State in Iraq and Syria," *The Program on Governance and Local Development Working Paper* 7, 2016.

A Note on Transcription

For this work, we opted for a hybrid transliteration system so that non-Arab speaking readers may familiarize themselves with the retranscribed concepts without too much difficulty, but also that the proficient Arab speaker might easily find the corresponding Arabic terms.

The Arabic consonants will be transliterated as shown in the following table of correspondences:

ا	a	ض	d
ب	b	ط	t
ت	t	ظ	dh
ث	th	ع	'
ج	J	غ	gh
ح	H	ف	f
خ	kh	ق	q
د	d	ك	k
ذ	dh	ل	l
ر	r	م	m
ز	z	ن	n
س	s	ه	h
ش	sh	و	w, u
ص	s	ي	y, i

As the table shows, we chose not to indicate the emphatic consonants. The same holds for the difference between long vowels and short vowels. Therefore, ا, و et ي and the short vowels have been transliterated equally by a, u, and i (instead of â/a, û/u, and î/i).

The *hamza*, regardless of its spelling (أ, إ, ؤ, ذ, ئ, ء), will be retranscribed simply by the apostrophe " ' ," not to be mistaken for the inverted apostrophe " ' " that in the table corresponds to the letter ع. The *hamza* will only be shown inside a word or at its end, not at the word's beginning. Thus, we write *hay'a* and *liwa'* but *intiqad* and not *'intiqad*.

The *shadda* will be reproduced by a doubling of the preceding consonant(s), as in *hurriyya*.

Arabic Names and Titles

Arabic names for persons, places, and institutions as well as titles and technical terms peculiar to the Arabic language will be reproduced without marks (and not according to the transliteration code spelled out above) when they are normally encountered in the written Anglo-Saxon media. Hence, we write "Bashar" and not "Bashshar" and "Deir ez-Zor" and not "Dayr al-Zur."

How We Handle Plurals

To keep from disconcerting the non-Arabic speaking reader, for words taken from the Arabic we will resort to an Anglicized plural, including for the irregular plurals. This means forming the plural from the singular by adding the letter "s" to the latter. Thus, the plural of "sheikh" will be rendered as "sheikhs" and not as "shuyukh." Following the same logic, we will use "ulama" and not a "'alim" for the singular of "ulama."

Prolegomena
For a Sociological Approach to Civil Wars

December 2012, a house in a village in the North of Syria, we are guests for the night, the meal is finished, and the mood is relaxed. Children are in our midst. One of our hosts brings out his mobile phone and starts to show us some videos: summary executions, desecrated bodies, a man buried to his neck and then run over by a car, a head, shot off by a missile fragment, then held at arms' length. We are about to see signs of individual and collective trauma on a massive scale. Objective figures later confirm our first impressions: since 2011, out of 22 million Syrians, nearly 500,000 were reported killed, around 6 million are in exile, close to 7 million have been displaced, hundreds of thousands of people have been tortured in the regime's prisons. These numbers include the 11,000 deaths between 2011 and 2013, documented by a photographer codenamed "Caesar," a defector from the Syrian Army.[1] Not to be forgotten are the repeated gas attacks on civilians by the Syrian army, the persecution of religious minorities by Islamic groups (kidnappings, seizure of goods, assassinations, rapes), and the dozens of journalists and aid workers kidnapped or killed.

Beyond the destruction of Syrian society, this crisis represents a pivotal moment in the transformation of the Greater Middle East, from Sahel to Afghanistan. Since the end of the cold war, the American interventions in Iraq (1991 and 2003–2011) and in Afghanistan (since 2001), the failure of authoritarian regimes, and the Arab revolutions are the cause or the symptom of an instability that affects a long list of countries to different degrees: Afghanistan, Yemen, Syria, Iraq, Egypt, Lebanon, Bahrain,

---

[1] The 2014 report is available at www.carter-ruck.com/images/uploads/documents/Syria_Report-January_2014.pdf. More can be found in the December 2015 Human Rights Watch Report, "If the Dead Could Speak: Mass Deaths and Torture in Syria's Detention Facilities," available at www.hrw.org/report/2015/12/16/if-dead-could-speak/mass-deaths-and-torture-syrias-detention-facilities. A French journalist carried out hours of interviews with the turncoat photographer. Garance Le Caisne, *Opération César: Au cœur de la machine de mort syrienne*, Paris, Editions Stock, 2015.

Libya, Somalia, Mali, Nigeria. The violent turn of the "Arab Spring," except in Tunisia so far, has strengthened radical jihadist movements that are challenging borders established in the Near East since the First World War. To make matters worse, regional competition between Saudi Arabia and Iran exacerbates the cleavage between Sunnis and Shias. Increases in war crimes, massacres, ethnic cleansing, extrajudicial executions, and indiscriminate bombings of civilians, including in schools and hospitals, make Syria the most violent of our contemporary conflicts. In addition, the flow of refugees and the spectre of terrorism bring a global dimension to the crisis and provide the impetus for foreign involvement. The presence of armed forces from Russia, Lebanon (Hezbollah), Iran, Iraq, Turkey, the United States, and other NATO countries and of foreign fighters from all over the world makes Syria's one of the most internationalized civil wars. It has also precipitated some surprising strategic realignments that, for example, have the United States arm the PKK, classified as a terrorist movement by its agencies, which is fighting Turkey, a NATO member country; or there is Israel taking care of fighters of Jabhat al-Nusra, a movement affiliated with al Qaida.

Yet qualifying the events taking place in Syria since 2011 as a "civil war" fails to carve out a natural object from the continuum of history[2]; as is the rule in all research, how we account for reality depends on the theoretical perspective we adopt. However, the prevailing theories reveal themselves as unsuited because they prevent us from understanding, or even simply posing, the questions that hold the most interest for us. We will lay out our definition of civil wars, namely the coexistence on the same national territory of competing social orders engaged in a violent relationship, and the questions that form the outline of a research program. Yet, first we must dissect the aporetic propositions of the dominant paradigm. The readers less interested in the following theoretical development might skip the prolegomena and proceed directly to the introduction.

The Limits of Neopositivism

Beginning in the 1990s, publications in political science and economics multiplied that were intent on accounting for the emergence and dynamics of civil wars by mathematical formalizations associated with

---

[2] As do the quasi-totality of actors in contemporary civil wars, the Syrians widely reject the term "civil war". Nevertheless, we use it; for us, it has no moral connotation and does not signal siding with one party to the conflict but indicates instead a desire to come within the scope of an academic sub-field, that of the theories of civil wars. Using the term enables us to think about this conflict in general categories that are open to comparison.

quantitative studies. This led to an academic field organized around several research centers (Stanford, Yale, MIT, Harvard, PRIO, Oxford, ETH Zurich) that can be qualified as neopositivist. It is an approach distinguished by its partiality to rational choice theory (RCT), naturalization of research objects, limiting studied objects as a function of their statistical measurability, and an epistemic closure that translates into a refusal to regard other paradigms as scientific.[3] This return to positivism points to the possibility of theoretical regression in social sciences. Today, it is essential to engage in a debate with this paradigm that goes beyond discussions on the technical aspects of collecting data or its mathematical treatment. The triviality of the published results, despite an ever more labored mathematical formalization, and the repetitive nature of the subjects discussed in fact raise questions about neopositivism on three levels: the conception of rationality, the methodology, and the choice of objects.

The Exhaustion of a Paradigm

By adopting RCT, the neopositivist works execute a theoretical power grab whose radicalism has several consequences. First, this way of thinking explicitly rejects a century's worth of social science research on the pretext that the works it produced do not tally with scientific criteria. Rejecting this intellectual heritage has created the conditions for a sort of professional amnesia that translates into a tendency to reinvent extant concepts, as demonstrated by certain recent works on transnationalism and socialization.[4] Next, the lion's share of studies on civil wars these days is produced by researchers with limited or no direct on-the-ground knowledge or even of the secondary literature dealing with the countries in question. Young researchers are explicitly discouraged from gathering data by observation and non-structured interviews. The result is that the neopositivists, bereft of contextual knowledge, frequently are incapable of putting forward sociologically relevant causes to explain the correlations found. The *American Political Science Review* recently furnished an example in the form of a disastrous study on the demarcation line during the German occupation of France, in which the authors failed to account for the presence of a railroad line as

---

[3] The RCT does not necessarily involve quantitative data processing and these techniques are not the exclusive domain of a particular paradigm or discipline, see, for instance, Durkheimian and Marxist approaches, the Annales School or Social Movement Theory.

[4] Jeffrey Checkel, *Transnational Dynamics of Civil War*, Cambridge, Cambridge University Press, 2015; Jeffrey Checkel, "Socialization and Violence: A Framework Essay," *Simons Papers in Security and Development* 48, 2015.

the, one would have thought, obvious reason for the Resistance's sabotage actions.[5] Beyond this one questionable article, the more general problem is that leaving historians out of the referee process leads to texts being vetted strictly based on the formal validity of the methodology employed.

Then, the epistemic closure of the neopositivist movement has the effect of shielding its findings against all substantive criticism. It has been pointed out for a long time, by Donald Green and Ian Shapiro in the United States or Raymond Boudon in France among others, that RCT, the anthropological model favored by the neopositivists, suffers from a design flaw.[6] The neopositivists shut off the discussion by challenging the validity of critiques that do not accept their premises, at the risk of making them look highly partisan. Thus, in 1996, Robert Bates, professor of political science at Harvard and president of the Comparative Politics section of APSA (American Political Science Association), called for drawing a distinction between "*social scientists*" who line up behind RCT and "*area specialists*" whose output is reduced to a literary form.[7] With respect to civil wars, recurrent critiques have been leveled against RCT since the late 1990s. Here, the debate over greed vs. grievances, growing out of the studies by Paul Collier and Anka Hoeffler as well as by James Fearon and David Laitin, exemplifies this epistemic closure.[8] Despite the theoretical and empirical criticisms leveled at these works,[9] their categories are regularly revived, for instance by Jeremy Weinstein when he contrasts predatory rebellions (oriented toward greed) with politically engaged rebellions (mobilized

---

[5] Jeremy Ferwerda and Nicholas L. Miller, "Political Devolution and Resistance to Foreign Rule: A Natural Experiment," *American Political Science Review* 108 (03), 2014, pp. 642–660. Matthew Kocher and Nuno Monteiro in a detailed critique highlighted the many problems with this article: Matthew Kocher and Nuno Monteiro, "What's in a line? Natural Experiments and the Line of Demarcation in WWII Occupied France (July 31, 2015)." Available at SSRN: http://ssrn.com/abstract=2555716.

[6] Raymond Boudon, *Raison, bonnes raisons*, Paris, PUF, 2003; Donald P. Green and Ian Shapiro, *Pathologies of Rational Choice Theory: A Critique of Applications in Political Science*, New Haven, Yale University Press, 1994.

[7] Robert Bates, "Letter from the President: Area Studies and the Discipline," *APSA-CP: Newsletter of the APSA Organized Section in Comparative Politics* 7 (1), 1996, pp. 1–2.

[8] Paul Collier and Anke Hoeffler, "On the Economic Causes of Civil War," *Oxford Economic Papers* 50, 1998, pp. 563—73; James Fearon, David Laitin, "Ethnicity, Insurgency, and Civil War," *American Political Science Review* 97 (1), 2003, pp. 75–90.

[9] Christopher Cramer, "Homo Economicus Goes to War: Methodological Individualism, Rational Choice and the Political Economy of War," *World Development* 30 (11), 2002, pp. 1845–1864; Roland Marchal and Christine Messiant, "De l'avidité des rebelles: l'analyse économique de la guerre civile selon Paul Collier," *Critique internationale* 16, 2002, pp. 58–69; Mike McGovern, "Popular Development Economics – An Anthropologist Among the Mandarins," *Perspectives on Politics* 9 (2), 2011, pp. 345–355.

by grievances).[10] Similarly, most of the analyses put forward to explain the duration and occurrence of civil wars follow the same pattern of opposing poverty and institutional weakness[11] to inequalities.[12]

Finally, and this is probably the crucial point, the advances made in understanding civil wars thanks to research that relies on the RCT paradigm have been remarkably limited, particularly considering the scale of the resources expended.[13] Specifically, game theory has only very marginally contributed to clarifying the reality of the conflicts. Barbara Walter, in applying game theories to civil wars, reworks three factors previously proposed by James Fearon in his 1995 paper on the occurrence of international conflicts: asymmetric information, commitment problems, and issue indivisibilities.[14] From this, she concludes that governments confronted with separatist movements employ violence as a means of snuffing out other secessionist demands. This conclusion, which has limited scientific interest, is – more importantly – impervious to proof. Indeed, unfazed by this *non-sequitur*, the author extrapolates the strategies of States from the observation of individual behaviors in laboratory settings.[15] Even research that is more empirically based presents similar limitations. In his classic book, Stathis Kalyvas examines the spatial distribution of violence in civil wars as a function of the degree of microscale control exerted by the insurgents.[16] His theory of a joint production

---

[10] Jeremy Weinstein, *Inside Rebellion: The Politics of Insurgent Violence*, Cambridge, Cambridge University Press, 2007.

[11] Douglass C. North, John J. Wallis, and Barry R. Weingast, *Violence and Social Orders: A Conceptual Framework for Interpreting Recorded Human History*, Cambridge, Cambridge University Press, 2009; Sylvain Chassang and Gerard Padro i Miquel, "Economic Shocks and Civil War," *Quarterly Journal of Political Science* 4 (3), 2009; Daron Acemoglu, Davide Ticchi, and Andrea Vindigni, "Persistence of civil wars," *Journal of the European Economic Association* 8, 2010.

[12] Joan Esteban and Gerald Schneider, "Polarization and Conflict: Theoretical and Empirical Issues," *Journal of Peace Resolution* 45 (2), 2008; Lars-Erik Cederman, Kirstian Skrede Gleditsch, and Halvard Buhaug, *Inequalities, Grievances and Civil Wars*, Cambridge, Cambridge University Press, 2013.

[13] Similar comments have been made in the past about the vote and international security. See, respectively, Raymond Wolfinger, "The Rational Citizen Faces Election Day, or What Rational Choice Theories Don't Tell You About American Elections," in M. Kent Jennings and Thomas E. Mann (eds.), *Elections at Home and Abroad: Essays in Honor of Warren E. Miller*, Ann Arbor, University of Michigan Press, 1993; Stephen Walt, "Rigor or Rigor Mortis: Rational Choice and Security Studies," *International Security* 23 (4), 1999, pp. 5–48.

[14] Barbara Walter, "Bargaining Failures and Civil War," *Annual Review of Political Science* 12, 2009, pp. 243–61; James Fearon, "Rationalist Explanations for War," *International Organization* 49 (3), 1995, pp. 379-414.

[15] Barbara Walter, *Reputation and Civil War: Why Separatist Conflicts are so Violent*, Cambridge, Cambridge University Press, 2009.

[16] Stathis N. Kalyvas, *The Logic of Violence in Civil War*, Cambridge, Cambridge University Press, 2006.

of selective violence by fighters and civilians rests on a radical reductionism derived from his hypotheses about rationality. Notably, because of "urge to survive" the individual is supposed "to be good at" calculating threats and opportunities but unaffected by emotions and the past and incapable of anticipating.[17] Kalyvas very well perceives that his hypotheses are extremely restrictive but suggests, based on anecdotal evidence, that civilians overestimate the stability of control of armed groups and that they make their decisions essentially according to local information and events. It therefore follows that violence produces obedience among those who suffer it.[18] However, there are many examples of resistance to violence, of the porosity between civilians and militaries, of the importance of governance of armed actors, of a capacity for anticipation or the importance of national or international information.[19] In fact, any consideration of the sociohistorical context implies a renunciation of the RCT. Thus, Elisabeth Wood argues that, in El Salvador, the long-term mobilization of peasants in the armed movement does not depend on the economic situation, but on the political culture produced during and by the struggle. Unable to get around the Olsonian paradox inherent in the RCT paradigm, she draws on the theory of social movements. Hence, in a specific case she revisits the findings of Tarrow, McAdam, and Tilly.[20] The attempt to revert to the RCT in the appended formal model forces a non-operationalizable definition of personal interest: "defiance, an intrinsic motivation, and/or pleasure in agency."[21]

The Obsession with Quantification

The neopositivist investment in the RCT paradigm explains the obsession with quantification mistaken for scientificity that runs through their work. Since the 1990s, neopositivist studies of civil wars have been

---

[17] op. cit., p. 207.

[18] op. cit., pp. 207–208.

[19] op. cit., pp. 27–28 and 91–104. For cases of resistance against a disproportionately stronger opponent, see for Afghanistan, Gilles Dorronsoro, *Revolution Unending: Afghanistan, 1979 to the Present*, New York, Columbia University Press, 2005; for Abkhazia, Anastasia Shesterinina, "Collective Threat Framing and Mobilization in Civil War," *American Political Science Review* published online 24 October, 2016; concerning Syria, see chapters 2 and 3.

[20] Elisabeth Wood, *Insurgent Collective Action and Civil War in El Salvador*, Cambridge, Cambridge University Press, 2003, p. 20. Furthermore, Sydney Tarrow, in reviewing the book, reminds us that "*Wood is not the first to argue that political culture matters, or that the attribution of injustice is necessary to produce collective action*," recalling especially the classic works on this subject by E. P. Thompson, Barrington Moore Jr., or David Snow. Sydney Tarrow, "Inside Insurgencies: Politics and Violence in an Age of Civil War," *Perspective on Politics* 5 (3), 2007, p. 593.

[21] Elisabeth Wood, *op. cit.*, p. 267.

structured around quantitative techniques whose mastery confers a badge of legitimacy in the field. While, during the 1980s, the work of historians and sociologists (Theda Skocpol, Charles Tilly, Barrington Moore) dominated the interpretations of civil wars, a number of economists and political scientists changed the nature of the debate with mathematical modeling of quantitative data, thus expanding the area for application of the neopositivist paradigm.[22] Since then, the body of works that can be considered relevant has shrunk drastically and crucial theoretical choices are buried under methodological questions. The systematic use of quantified data, of mathematical and statistical formalizations obscures serious methodological problems.

Indeed, far from the image of cumulative scientific progress enabled by a rigorous accumulation of data, the reality is much more disappointing. During the mid-2000s, most of the research relied on the same American database inaugurated in 1963, one that is regularly updated with the same methodological options: "Currently, about a dozen research projects have produced civil war lists based on apparently divergent definitions of civil war, but there is less pluralism here than one might think. Most projects do not conduct original historical research and depend heavily on COW [Correlates of War]. The result may be replication of errors due to the original COW coding rules and uncertainty about whether different definitions generate different results."[23] COW is of decisive importance, because it has imposed definitions, thresholds, and criteria that all the studies of the ensuing years incorporated. Subsequently, certain researchers, confronted by the repetitive nature of the results, focused on producing alternative databases (PRIO/UPCD dataset) and on accessing databases of international institutions (World Bank) or national ones (American army). Then, methodological innovations, including the use of surveys in war zones, field experiments, and process-tracing ended up largely monopolizing the debate.[24]

Collectively, these studies pose numerous problems of data selection and category definition. To begin with, fundamental to how this corpus is constituted, we find unscientific empiricist definitions of civil war through the setting of thresholds (25 or 1,000 dead, without taking into account

---

[22] Paul Collier and Anke Hoeffler, *op. cit.;* James Fearon and David Laitin, *op. cit.*

[23] Nicholas Sambanis, "What is Civil War," *Journal of Conflict Resolution* 48 (6), 2004.

[24] Concerning these methodologies, James Druckman, Donald Green, James Kuklinski, and Arthur Lupia (eds.), *Cambridge Handbook of Experimental Political Science*, Cambridge, Cambridge University Press, 2011; Macartan Humphreys and Jeremy M. Weinstein, "Field Experiments and the Political Economy of Development," *Annual Review of Political Science* 12, 2009, 367–378; Andrew Bennett and Jeffrey T. Checkel (eds.), *Process Tracing: From Metaphor to Analytic Tool*, Cambridge, Cambridge University Press, 2014.

the size of the population). However, only theoretical hypotheses ought to define a series of empirical situations to be retained as a function of a question derived from a research program. Next, the "variables" are defined in a simplistic manner. The notion of identity, frequently reduced to that of ethnicity, is pegged to fixed criteria and an objective membership despite anthropological works that for decades have demonstrated the opposite to be true.[25] Finally, badly constructed quantitative data can lead to contradictory conclusions as a function of the dependent and independent variables chosen. Thus, the quantitative works have managed to show correlations *both* between resource scarcity and civil war, on the one hand, and resource abundance and civil war, on the other.[26]

Add to this that the twin obsessions with measurability and with innovative methodology produce data sets that are increasingly problematic. First, while qualitative approaches may not be entirely lacking, they remain in the minority, serve as window dressing, and are denied legitimacy. Hence, Paul Collier, Anke Hoeffler, and Stathis Kalyvas repeatedly insist on the impossibility of alternative approaches because the discourses are not reliable and because the actors, consciously or not, may hide their "true motives."[27] Yet databases do not solve this issue: they aggregate facts that have already been interpreted, which – contrary to neopositivist practice – calls for a critical analysis of how they are produced.[28] The coding categories thus are seldom explicit, which leads to ignoring the theoretical and, at times, normative options of the authors, while on the other hand the practical work of coding is left to students or jobbers. Repeatedly, specialists on conflicts have cast serious doubt on the quantitative data collected in their fields.[29] The most serious problem appears to be that a number of interviews (structured or semi-structured)

---

[25] See, for instance, the Minority at Risk and All Minorities at Risk databases. For a critical perspective of such a static understanding of identity, following the seminal work Fredrik Barth, see Rogers Brubaker and Frederick Cooper, "Beyond 'Identity'," *Theory and Society*, 29 (1), 2000, pp. 1–47; Fredrik Barth, *Ethnic Groups and Boundaries: The Social Organization of Culture Difference*, Long Grove, Waveland Press, 1969.

[26] Stormy-Annika Mildner, Gitta Lauster, and Wiebke Wodni, "Scarcity and Abundance Revisited: A Literature Review on Natural Resources and Conflict," *International Journal of Conflict and Violence* 5 (1), 2011.

[27] Paul Collier and Anke Hoeffler, "Greed and Grievance in Civil War," *The World Bank Policy Research Working Paper* 2355, 2000, Stathis Kalyvas, *op. cit.*

[28] Yoshiko Herrera and Devesh Kapur, "Improving Data Quality: Actors, Incentives, and Capabilities," *Political Analysis* 15 (4), 2007, pp. 365–386; Christian Davenport and Patrick Ball, "Views to a Kill: Exploring the Implications of Source Selection in the Case of Guatemalan State Terror, 1977–1995," *The Journal of Conflict Resolution* 46 (3), 2002, pp. 427–450.

[29] Roland Marchal and Christine Messiant, *op. cit.;* Ibrahim Abdullah, "Man Does Not Live by Bread Alone," *African Review of Books* 2 (1), 2006, pp. 12–3. The same holds true in Afghanistan and in Iraq, where data collection conditions also lack rigor.

are not done by the researchers themselves but are subcontracted to local interviewers or private firms that use badly trained or untrained local staff under conditions that make it impossible to check the quality of the data collection. Finally, a significant share of the studies relies on databases produced by large national and international institutions without any critical reflection on the bureaucratic and ideological biases that mathematical rigor camouflages. One of the most striking examples in recent years is the use of internal data of the American army in Iraq and Afghanistan by researchers around Jason Lyall at Yale, at Princeton around Jacob N. Shapiro, and around Eli Berman at UC San Diego. Not only are conditions under which these data were produced unknown, but they have also not been compared with other sources, which prevents any possible biases surfacing. In the same vein, Andrew Beath, Fotini Christia, and Ruben Enikopolov, respectively a World Bank employee and two academics contracted by the World Bank, solely use the evaluation of a rural development program's impact in their work to describe the transformations of Afghan society.[30]

An Arbitrary Reduction of Legitimate Objects

A deceptively rigorous methodology and problematic conception of rationality translate into a naturalization of research objects and an arbitrary discounting of legitimate subjects. Generally, the neopositivists claim that their categories objectively describe actions. Thus, acts of violence are often subsumed under the category of homicides, excluding injuries and despite the difficulties that the social qualification of these acts poses. In practice, the neopositivists generally adopt the classifications produced by international and Western institutions. The literature on refugees is particularly instructive in this regard, since the statistics and hence the definitions of the international agencies (HCR, IOM) are adopted without debate.[31] Similarly, the distinction between civilian and combatant is a reification of categories taken from international

---

[30] See especially Andrew Beath, Fotini Christia, and Ruben Enikolopov, "Empowering Women through Development Aid: Evidence from a Field Experiment in Afghanistan," *American Political Science Review* 107 (3), 2013, pp. 540–57. Their final audit report is available at www.nsp-ie.org/reports/finalreport.pdf. Conversely, Alessandro Monsutti researches the design and implementation of this program; see Alessandro Monsutti, "Fuzzy Sovereignty: Rural Reconstruction in Afghanistan, between Democracy Promotion and Power Games," *Comparative Studies in Society and History* 54 (3), 2012, pp. 563–591.

[31] For a critique of the notion of refugees, see Anthony Richmond, "Sociological Theories of International Migrations: The Case of Refugees," *Current Sociology* 36 (2), 1988, pp. 7–26.

law. In the real world, a man fights for part of the day, an individual shelters a fighter, a judge serves the insurrection: in a civil war context are they then civilians? It is telling that these questions, ignored by the neopositivists, do not escape the actors: thus, the Taliban movement and UN Office of Human Rights in Afghanistan engage in repeated discussions on the status of policemen when the latter are not engaged in combat operations. Here, too, the uncritical adoption of categories injects a normative bias in lockstep with the institutions that produce them.

Legitimate research objects are reduced depending on how feasible quantification is and are co-produced with the institutions that provide the data. Thus, after Kalyvas, works multiplied that dealt with the occurrence of violent civilian deaths and the degree of control over territory based on their measurability rather than their intrinsic interests. Similarly, the forming of armed groups is reduced to inquiries into cohesion and the process of engagement to a mere decision.[32] In addition, access to institutional databases (World Bank, American army) most often presuppose a co-definition of the research object.[33] Publications are legion that pose questions directly inspired by these institutions: for instance, the effects of aerial bombardment on the support for Western intervention in Afghanistan and the role of cell phones in the insurgent attacks in Iraq – both studies funded by the U.S. Air Force.[34] Similarly, the conclusions drawn by Andrew Beath, Fotini Christia, and Ruben Enikopolov – to wit that involving women in the distribution of aid has a partial effect on their social position; that bypassing the local elites in aid distribution gives villagers a sense of participation without increasing effectiveness; and

---

[32] Paul Staniland, *Networks of Rebellion: Explaining Insurgent Cohesion and Collapse*, Ithaca, Cornell University Press, 2014; Ana Arjona and Stathis N. Kalyvas, "Recruitment into Armed Groups in Colombia: A Survey of Demobilized Fighters," in Yvan Guichaoua (ed.), *Understanding Collective Political Violence: Conflict, Inequality and Ethnicity*, New York, Palgrave-Macmillan, 2011, pp. 143–171; Eli Berman, Michael Callen, Joseph H. Felter, and Jacob N. Shapiro, "Do Working Men Rebel? Insurgency and Unemployment in Afghanistan, Iraq, and the Philippines," *Journal of Conflict Resolution* 55 (4), 2011, pp. 496–528; Macartan Humphreys and Jeremy Weinstein, "Who Fights? The Determinants of Participation in Civil War," *American Journal of Political Science* 52 (2), 2008, pp. 436–455.

[33] The American army's biases are evident, especially the fact that the reports in part are bureaucratic artefacts for the hierarchy justifying itself internally. For an analysis of World Bank biases, see Béatrice Hibou, "The Political Economy of the World Bank's Discourse: from Economic Catechism to Missionary Deeds (and Misdeeds)," *Etudes du CERI* 39, 2000.

[34] Jason Lyall, Graeme Blair, and Kosuke Imai, "Explaining Support for Combatants during Wartime: A Survey Experiment in Afghanistan," *American Political Science Review* 107 (4), 2013, pp. 679–705; Jacob Shapiro and Nils Weidmann, "Is the Phone Mightier Than the Sword? Cellphones and Insurgent Violence in Iraq," *International Organization* 69 (2), 2015, pp. 247–274.

that distribution of aid does not help win "hearts and minds" except where violence is low-level and of short duration only – are those of an audit of a World Bank program.[35] Besides the ethical questions that a *de facto* participation in counterinsurgency programs can raise, this alignment with institutional objectives discourages theoretical discussions in favor of a normative and technicist approach.

Finally, these works leave the impression that they systematically disregard the most interesting sociological enigmas in favor of objects whose main interest lies in their being quantifiable. Emotions and values are treated at the margin and in maladapted analytical frameworks. Hence, Kalyvas and Walter relegate norms and emotions to prediction errors in their models.[36] Roger Petersen highlights the importance of emotions and social norms, but ignores their social construction and reduces them to their measurable consequences, thus emptying the initial observation of all relevance.[37] Another failing of neopositivist works is the refusal to take an interest in ideologies, storytelling, and, more broadly, imaginaries. This results in the key articles and papers in the field skipping over these questions, as if one could analyze moves by the PKK, the Islamic State, and the LTTE without considering their universe of meaning. We had to wait until 2014 to see an article conceding in very general terms that ideas and ideologies do play a role in civil wars.[38] In summary, everything points to an exhaustion of the paradigm: a sub-field that is more and more technicist, rarely contributes to general sociology, fails to revisit its hypotheses, and, moreover, whose outputs are frequently repetitious and trivial.

What Constitutes a Civil War?

The limitations of the neopositivist approach lead us to reaffirm the necessity of approaching contemporary civil wars sociologically, starting with a discussion of the state in relation to the international system.

---

[35] Andrew Beath, Fotini Christia, and Ruben Enikolopov, *op. cit.;* Andrew Beath, Fotini Christia, and Ruben Enikolopov, "Direct Democracy and Resource Allocation: Experimental Evidence from Afghanistan," *Policy Research Working Papers* 6133, 2012; Andrew Beath, Fotini Christia, and Ruben Enikolopov, "Winning Hearts and Minds through Development: Evidence from a Field Experiment in Afghanistan," *Policy Research Working Papers* 6129, 2012.

[36] Stathis Kalyvas, *op. cit.*, p. 302; Barbara Walter, *op. cit.*, pp. 133–134.

[37] Roger Petersen, *Understanding Ethnic Violence: Fear, Hatred, Resentment in Twentieth Century Eastern Europe*, Cambridge, Cambridge University Press, 2002.

[38] Francisco Gutiérrez Sanín and Elisabeth Wood, "Ideology in Civil War: Instrumental Adoption and Beyond," *Journal of Peace Research* 51 (2), 2014, pp. 213–226.

The Economy of Violence and the International System

Most often, the definitions of civil war rest, explicitly or not, on a Weberian conception of the State as holding a monopoly on legitimate violence within a given territory.[39] Civil war therefore would be the loss of that monopoly following a violent challenge that ends in a situation of divided sovereignty. Without denying the heuristic interest of this definition, it is based on a conception of the state that can obscure the complexity of the objects it subsumes. We propose to introduce an alternative conceptualization in terms of the economy of violence, defined by the relatively stable interactions (competition, cooperation, delegation) between actors capable of using violence or threatening it. These actors differ (individuals, clans, criminal organizations, state institutions, militias) and encounter one another around social, economic, and political stakes. The economy of violence as we conceive it does not presuppose an economic rationality of the actors and, moreover, says nothing about this social order being functional or legitimate. This definition departs from the Weberian approach in three aspects: legitimacy, monopoly, and the role of the international.

First, this definition does not assume that state violence is legitimate, an empirical and theoretical impasse.[40] In particular, discovering why individuals obey the state in routine situations is often impossible. Empirical work under authoritarian regimes is generally fraught with difficulty and it is scarcely possible to decide between different hypotheses (fear of repression, interiorization of dominance, a more or less negotiated equilibrium between the state and social groups). Moreover, crisis situations do not reveal the individual's "real" preferences because these are not stable.[41]

Second, no state disposes of a complete monopoly on violence. Some states coexist with an important level of private military capital: tribes, private companies, vigilantes, criminal organizations, etc.[42] In certain

---

[39] Max Weber, *Economy and Society: An Outline to Interpretative Sociology*, Berkeley, University of California Press, 1978. For perspective, see Catherine Colliot-Thélène, "La fin du monopole de la violence légitime?" *Revue d'études comparatives Est-Ouest* 34 (1), 2003, pp. 5–31.

[40] We can only agree with Tilly when he says that the legitimacy of violence is not definitive in the functioning of the state monopoly, "War-Making and State-Making as Organized Crime," in Peter B. Evans, Dietrich Rueschmeyer, and Theda Skocpol (eds.), *Bringing the State Back in*, Cambridge, Cambridge University Press, 1985, p. 171.

[41] Charles Kurzman, *The Unthinkable Revolution in Iran*, Cambridge, Harvard University Press, 2005; Karl-Dieter Opp, Christiane Gern, and Peter Voss, *Origins of a Spontaneous Revolution: East Germany, 1989*, Ann Arbor, University of Michigan Press, 1996.

[42] Military capital is defined by the entirety of the cumulative resources (including bureaucratic skills and financing) that make it possible to exert organized violence.

countries, there is even a trend toward developing private military capital (Mexico and Central America). Political parties may field an armed wing, as was the case in Lebanon well before 1975.[43] Certain types of violence are also accepted or tolerated: against women, children, marginalized populations, etc. Add to this that the state is never a unitary actor and conflicts between state institutions on occasion are anything but anecdotal. Nevertheless, institutions of the state play a key role in how the economy of violence is organized, including by confinement of the actors, for instance, in the illegal economy or in the territorial margins.[44] From this perspective, a collective work in progress shows how, in situations of high levels of violence in Mexico and Central America, the existence of informal rules allow a reproduction of social routines.[45] Criminal actors that challenge the state directly are punished severely, for example, the Medellin Cartel in Colombia or the Cosa Nostra in Italy. Furthermore, an armed group may employ violence to grab power or as a tactic in negotiating with the regime in place. In the case of the post-Goma Agreement Democratic Republic of Congo (2003), the armed groups regularly entered the political system during negotiations that functioned as sites for converting military capital into political or economic capital. The opposition followed a different logic than during the preceding period when overthrowing the regime in reality was the issue. More broadly, this case can be understood as a variation on certain historical cases, notably the Ottoman Empire, where armed dissidence by fringe elements is the opening gambit in the process of negotiation.[46]

For our part, we choose to limit ourselves to situations where the existing economy of violence is at stake (regime change or secession). Hence, it is not the level of violence that characterizes civil wars for us – unlike the thresholds defined by the databases – but the attempt to install a different economy of violence. This leads us to two observations. On the one hand, these are political actors explicitly organized as such, which differentiates them from the more informal practices of resistance that

---

[43] Kemal S. Salibi, *Crossroads to Civil War: Lebanon, 1958–1976*, New York, Caravan Books, 1976.

[44] For the case of Mexico, Adèle Blazquez, "Négocier dans une marge criminalisée. L'application de la loi agraire de 1992 dans la sierra de Badiraguato (Sinaloa, Mexique)," *Cahiers des Amériques latines* 81 (1), 2016, pp. 73–91.

[45] See Adèle Blazquez and Romain Le Cour Grandmaison, "Armed Groups and Criminals Organizations. The Political Dimension of Violent Practices in Mexico and Central America," unpublished draft, available at http://civilwars.eu/project/mxac/. For similar cases, see Laurent Gayer, *Karachi: Ordered Disorder and the Struggle for the City*, London, Hurst, 2014; Jean-François Bayart, Stephen Ellis, and Béatrice Hibou, *The Criminalization of the State in Africa*, Bloomington, Indiana University Press, 1999.

[46] Karen Barkey, *Bandits and Bureaucrats: The Ottoman Route to State Centralization*, Ithaca, Cornell University Press, 1994.

partake in an economy of violence.[47] On the other hand, we should not presuppose fixity of intentions and goals. The aims of an armed group are mutable; at times global as contrasted with parochial, the same movement can transform its goals over time or pursue several simultaneously. Yet, there are few examples of passing from a logic of political contestation to a logic of economic accumulation – or the reverse – even though certain cases (Sierra Leone, Liberia, Democratic Republic of Congo) seem ambiguous in this regard. Indeed, the 1990s thesis of a criminalization/depoliticization of armed groups, as distinct from their utilization of illegal financial sources to achieve their political goals, smacks more of ideological discourse than rigorous research.[48]

Third, Max Weber conceptualizes the formation of the state fundamentally as an individual trajectory, whereas we consider it to be conceivable only within a historically situated international state system where both coproduce each other. Civil war is too often thought of as an ahistorical phenomenon, an "internal war," whence the frequent juxtaposition in the literature of examples drawn from the Peloponnesian War, the English Civil War, the Thirty Years War, with those from Vietnam or Iraq. We assume, on the contrary, that civil war is an object to be historicized according to the nature of states, and therefore, inextricably, of the international system. The stakes and dynamics in a civil war depend on the international system at a given time, from which stems the difficulty of making comparisons over extended historical periods. The effects of the international system on civil war can be difficult to isolate for a single case, but they become visible when civil wars are examined in series. In other words, contemporary civil wars exhibit structural resemblances that indissociably are effects of the international system and of the nature of contemporary sovereignty. It is therefore prudent to confine our study, at least tentatively, to a distinct state of the international system, namely the specific relationship to territory and international borders following the waves of decolonization.

What are the effects of the international system on contemporary civil wars? The first is that they are transnational phenomena: the quasi-totality of armed movements make use of a sanctuary in a neighboring country, refugees are the universal products of these conflicts, and the non-military actors (IOs, NGOs) step in systematically. The existence of a sanctuary, the role of transnational political organizations, and the management of refugee camps play key roles in the perspectives of an armed movement.

---

[47] See, for example, James Scott, *Domination and the Arts of Resistance: Hidden Transcripts*, New Haven, Yale University Press, 1990.

[48] Pascal Chabal and Jean-Pascal Daloz, *Africa Works: Disorder as a Political Instrument*, Oxford, James Currey, 1999.

The second trait is that the stakes orienting the practices of the parties in conflict are broadly defined by the international system. In fact, contemporary civil wars do not entail, as a rule, a modification of international borders; annexations, rare as they are, in practice are never internationally recognized, and secessions remain infrequent.[49] Since the end of decolonization, territories are more stable than states. In fact, contrary to the Eliasian model, in which the political center progressively defines its territorial spread,[50] borders today have largely stabilized. Therefore, the state, even if absent, imposes itself as the key stake in the struggle, including for secessionist projects. In a much more structuring manner than commodities, resources linked to state formation such as control of the capital city, of currency, customs duties, and international recognition are critical. Even if they have little chance of success, authentically transnational dynamics (the Islamic State) are the more interesting to analyze in that *a contrario* they permit understanding the dominant logic.

This set of constraints and resources largely conditions the interactions of the actors battling for the state. Any stabilization of the relations between armed groups, barring an external guarantee, can only be temporary, since the survival of one actor ultimately depends on it controlling or neutralizing the political center, which implies the elimination or assimilation of its competitors. The economic interests of military actors are not enough to create the necessary conditions for a stable division of the territory and its resources, which confirms the criticism levelled at theories that reduce civil war to the predatory exploitation by violent actors who avoid or, at least, minimize confrontation. On the contrary, anticipation of a durable reconstruction of the state brings with it an intensification of violent competition for control of territory, state institutions, and international recognition. The development of a bureaucracy is a key element in this struggle, since the ability to accumulate resources strongly impacts the probability of an armed group's survival.

Attempt at a Definition

What do the social sciences tell us about situations of political violence that deeply affect the social fabric? Faced with multiplying civil wars during the 1990s, some researchers turned – perhaps more than before – to studying

[49] Mark Zacher, "The Territorial Integrity Norm: International Boundaries and the Use of Force," *International Organization* 55 (2), 2001, pp. 215–250; Boaz Atzili, "When Good Fences Make Bad Neighbors: Fixed Borders, State Weakness, and International Conflict," *International Security* 31 (3), 2006/2007, pp. 139–173.

[50] Norbert Elias, *The Civilizing Process, Vol. II. State Formation and Civilization*, Oxford, Blackwell, 1982.

societies at war. This is especially true of anthropologists who saw the conflicts play out on their fields in Mozambique, Sri Lanka, Sierra Leone, or Bosnia.[51] Sociologists and political scientists tried to account for the transformations in societies confronted with political violence, for instance, in Algeria, Afghanistan, the Democratic Republic of Congo, Bosnia, or in Angola.[52] Numerous works on specific aspects of the transformations of societies rent by civil wars are extant, for example, on socialization, violence, land, gender relations, segmentary organizations, and on migrations.[53] However, the fertility of these approaches should not obscure the difficulty of generalizing from them, since the cases are not connected in a systematic manner. A methodologically based comparison does not result from parallelizing cases, however many in number, or from a one-off theoretical borrowing, but from discussing them in a general theoretical framework. In this regard, Georgi Derluguian, Klaus Schlichte, and Koen Vlassenroot's careful attention to practices, discourses, and social processes lay the foundations of a comparatist approach.[54]

In this perspective, revisiting Bourdieu's conception of the state could constitute a productive enterprise.[55] The state can be understood

---

[51] Christian Geffray, *La cause des armes au Mozambique: anthropologie d'une guerre civile*, Paris, Karthala, 1990; Carolyn Nordstrom, *A Different Kind of War Story*, Philadelphia, University of Pennsylvania Press, 1997; Paul Richards, *Fighting for the Rain Forest: War, Youth and Resources in Sierra Leone*, Portsmouth, Heinemann, 1996; Ivana Macek, *Sarajevo Under Siege: Anthropology in Wartime*, Philadelphia, University of Pennsylvania Press, 2009.

[52] Xavier Bougarel, *Bosnie, anatomie d'un conflit*, Paris, La Découverte, 1996; Luis Martinez, *The Algerian Civil War 1990–1998*, New York, Columbia University Press, 2000; Koen Vlassenroot and Timothy Raymaekers, *Conflict and Social Transformation in Eastern DR Congo*, Gent, Academia Press, 2004; Gilles Dorronsoro, *op. cit.*; Teresa Koloma Beck, *The Normality of Civil War: Armed Groups and Everyday Life in Angola*, Frankfurt, Campus Verlag, 2012.

[53] See among others, Carolyn Nordstrom, *Girls and Warzones: Troubling Questions*, Uppsala, Life and Peace Institute, 1997; Stephen C. Lubkemann, *Culture in Chaos: An Anthropology of the Social Condition in War*, Chicago, Chicago University Press, 2008; Christopher Cramer and Paul Richards, "Violence and War in Agrarian Perspective," *Journal of Agrarian Change* 11 (3), 2011; Marielle Debos, *Living by the Gun in Chad: Governing Africa's Inter-Wars*, London, Zed Books 2016; Kee Kooning and Dirk Kruijts (eds.), *Societies of Fear: The Legacy of Civil War, Violence and Terror in Latin America*, London, Zed Books, 1999; Sverker Finnström, *Living with Bad Surroundings: War, History and Everyday Moment in Northern Uganda*, Durham, Duke University Press, 2008; Henrik Vigh, *Navigating Terrains of War: Youth and Soldiering in Guinea-Bissau*, New York, Berghahn, 2006.

[54] Georgi M. Derluguian, *Bourdieu's Secret Admirer in the Caucasus*, Chicago, University of Chicago Press, 2005; Koen Vlassenroot, "Societal View on Violence and War: Conflict & Militia Formation in Eastern Congo," in Preben Kaarsholm (ed.), *Violence, Political, Culture & Development in Africa*, Oxford, James Currey, 2006, pp. 49–65; Klaus Schlichte, *The Shadow of Violence: the Politics of Armed Groups*, Frankfurt, Campus Verlag, 2009.

[55] Pierre Bourdieu, *On the State: Lectures at the College de France, 1989–1992*, Polity Press, Cambridge, 2015.

as a central authority for defining the relative value of various species of capital and relationships between fields.[56] Its retreat therefore entails a revaluation of the relative value of capitals, which draws our attention to alternative institutions that may guarantee them and to the reorganization of certain fields. For example, the religious field may restructure itself around transnational institutions; the institutions linked to an armed group may (or may not) guarantee the value of economic capital and impose a new legal order. Let it be noted that the societies researched may be structurally different from the Western societies in and for which the fundamental concepts of sociology were originally formulated.[57] For instance, Bourdieu's list of capitals (cultural, economic, and social) can be expanded by adding identity capital (see below).[58] The relative weighting of capitals – made visible in their conversion – is not identical from one society to the other. Likewise, while the specialization of fields is practically universal (Niklas Luhmann, Pierre Bourdieu, Anthony Giddens), we do not assume any specific degree of independence for them vis-à-vis the rest of society.[59] Particularly, the degree of autonomy of fields in non-democratic regimes is conditioned by the transversal role of the security apparatus and party-state relationships. In communist regimes, for example, the ubiquitous nature of the party limits the autonomy of fields. In Turkey, at different periods, the symbiotic relationship between the ruling party

[56] We use Pierre Bourdieu's concept of field, which refers to a social space based on specific practices and norms; however, we do not suppose that each field is built on a related capital. In addition, capital must be thought of as the decontextualized analog of a resource, which notably allows thinking about accumulation (of a capital) and conversion (of one capital to another). Moreover, resources – capital in action – relate to a context and an intentionality; they let a social agent produce or reproduce power or exert influence on relationships. Finally, schemes of thought define the resources that can be used in a specific social context. The dynamic of social systems derives from multiple, contradictory schemes of thought, which are used creatively by social agents. Schemes of thought that do not allow using resources tend to disappear. For developments on the concepts of field, capital, and scheme of thought, see, respectively, Pierre Bourdieu, *Sociologie générale, Volume 1: Cours au Collège de France 1981–1983*, Paris, Seuil, 2015, p. 531; Pierre Bourdieu and following; Pierre Bourdieu, *The Logic of Practice*, Stanford, Stanford University Press, 1990, p. 122 and following; William H. Sewell Jr., "A Theory of Structure: Duality, Agency, and Transformation," *The American Journal of Sociology* 98 (1), 1992, pp. 1–29.

[57] Dipesh Chakrabarty, *Provincializing Europe: Postcolonial Thought and Historical Difference*, Princeton, Princeton University Press, 2000.

[58] Membership (ethnic or religious) has the properties of a collective capital. In effect, objectivized identities are not solely principles of territorial or social affiliation, categories of ethnographic description or popular perception, but they also signal a ranking in access to different resources under a framework of competition or unequal competition between groups, Gilles Dorronsoro and Olivier Grojean (eds.), *Identity, Conflict and Politics in Turkey, Iran and Pakistan*, Hurst, London, 2017.

[59] Bernard Lahire, *Monde pluriel: penser l'unité des sciences sociales*, Paris, Seuil, 2012, p. 63.

and the state created a comparable situation.[60] In Libya, the Gaddafi regime deliberately weakened institutions to the point where society operated on a largely informal basis.[61]

Ultimately, we define civil war as the coexistence on the same national territory of competing social orders engaged in a violent relationship. By "social order" we mean an economy of violence, relative values of capitals, and relations between fields at varying degrees of institutionalization. The national territory therefore sees the coexistence of different identity regimes, legal systems, and property rights. Competing social orders are most visible when armed movements control a territory, yet other modalities may prevail, such as day/night division of population control.[62]

The Outlines of a Research Program

Our definition points us to three topics that we believe can provide the basis for a program of research: the fluctuations in relative values of capitals, the emergence of competing institutional systems producing alternative social orders, and, finally, the transformation of individual dispositions and decision-making processes.

A New Economy of Capitals

The existence of competing social orders on a national territory implies the emergence of several economies of capitals. Civil war thus affects social structure in three ways: by the appearance of new capitals, an often-severe fluctuation in the value of existing capitals and, finally, new circuits for converting capitals. To begin with, the state's withdrawal engenders the (re)formation of certain capitals, notably the development of military capital, made possible by the conversion of preexisting competences and capitals. The new centrality of military capital changes the value of all the capitals, especially the modes of economic accumulation and the identity regime.

Second, economic capital, social capital, and identity capital are particularly affected during civil wars. In these three instances, the retreat of

---

[60] Gilles Dorronsoro and Benjamin Gourisse, "Une clé de lecture du politique en Turquie : les rapports État-Partis," *Politix* 107 (1), 2015, pp. 195–218.

[61] Luis Martinez, *The Libyan Paradox*, New York, Columbia Press, 2007.

[62] Colonial situations and local counter-hegemonic situations, in which an official order coexists with a de facto order, display similar characteristics, Gilles Dorronsoro and Nicole Watts, "The Collective Production of Challenge: Civil Society, Parties, and pro-Kurdish Politics in Diyarbakir," in Elise Massicard and Nicole Watts (eds.), *Negotiating Political Power in Turkey: Breaking up the Party*, London, Routledge, 2013; Emmanuel Terray, "Le climatiseur et la véranda," in Alfred Adler (ed.), *Afrique plurielle, Afrique actuelle: hommage à Georges Balandier*, Paris, Karthala, 1986, pp. 37–44.

the state *a contrario* shows its role in what is routinely ascribed to spontaneous social functioning. To start with, the fighting changes the value of economic capital, especially because of currency and real estate price fluctuations. Next, territorial control by an armed group translates into a change in social capital,[63] for example, because gender relations or the performativity of the affiliation with segmentary groups (families, clans, tribes) are transformed. In general, individual social capital fluctuates widely in opposite directions: on the one hand, the majority sees its social capital shrink and, consequently, its ability to interact. On the other hand, the militants, inserted into highly mobilized networks, increase their social capital. Last, identity capital is impacted by a brutal denaturalization of hierarchies between groups. To be Hazara in Afghanistan, Hutu in the eastern Democratic Republic of Congo, or Zaghawa in Sudan does not imply the same thing before and after the outbreak of civil war and by regions.

Third, the withdrawal of the state shifts the circuits for converting capitals. Save for the presence of a network of institutions, barriers of various kinds (economic, legal) that prohibit or impose a cost on crossing from one field to another tend to disappear, thus easing the conversion of capitals. For example, in Afghanistan, starting in the 1980s, religious capital was converted into leading positions within political parties.[64] Elsewhere, new conversion circuits appear. For instance, armed actors can accumulate economic capital through predation, taxation, and alliances with notables. Additionally, the division of the national territory engenders the emergence of internal borders, which poses the problem of the differing value of capitals between regions. On the economic level, while internal barriers often become more constraining than the international borders, channels between territories can develop around certain resources (food, oil, gas, drugs, etc.). Specific individuals or groups can reap considerable profits simply due to price differences. Also, the existence of identity regimes orients migration channels, as in the case of Afghanistan's Hazaras.[65]

---

[63] "Social capital is the aggregate of the actual or potential resources which are linked to possession of a durable network of more or less institutionalized relationships of mutual acquaintance and recognition – or in other words, to membership of a group – which provides each of its members with the backing of the collectively-owned capital, a 'credential' which entitles them to credit, in the various senses of the word," Pierre Bourdieu, "The Forms of Capital," in John Richardson (ed.), *Handbook of Theory and Research for the Sociology of Education*, New York, Greenwood, p. 249.

[64] Gilles Dorronsoro, "Dynamiques entre champs religieux et politique. Le cas de l'Afghanistan," *Purusartha* 30, 2012.

[65] Alessandro Monsutti, *War and Migration: Social Networks and Economic Strategies of the Hazaras of Afghanistan*, London, Routledge, 2005.

Competing Networks of Institutions

Control over a population by armed groups opens a space for setting up new institutions.[66] The prevailing perspective (rebel governance) treats these institutions from the perspective of controlling the population and providing public services.[67] We shift our attention toward the formation of fields – rather than an individual history of institutions– and the production of society, especially through law.

To begin with, the reconstruction of sectors of activity – health, education, justice, religion, economy, security – runs up against three limits: objectivization, a dearth of resources, and competition. First, the objectivization of new institutions happens through recruiting specialized personnel and implementing set procedures often copied from state institutions (forms, maps, uniforms, official IDs). This can be observed among armed groups as disparate as the Taliban, the PKK, the RCD-Goma, and the LTTE.[68] The courts can rely on preexisting institutions, including religious ones in case of Islamist movements, or notables. Next, the dearth of available resources creates conditions of dependency on the outside (diaspora, foreign countries, transnational networks). Also, putting in place new institutions is complicated by the presence of competing institutions (linked to other armed groups), which alters the usually monopolistic functioning of sectors like the currency, security, and the law. Local monopolies may form, but, unless exclusive control is achieved, complex situations arise that compel forms of cooperation (formal or not) and accommodation, as in operating certain indivisible goods like electricity, water, or the recognition of legal documents between otherwise competing legal systems. Furthermore, beyond a single institution or even a specific sector, some movements succeed in reestablishing differentiated fields. This network of institutions consolidates itself by cross recognitions between sectors that favor their objectivization and, perhaps, their legitimacy. Justice here appears as a defining element due to its structural effects on other fields. Indeed, relatively sophisticated and independent legal systems affect the entire administration and activities in the territory controlled by the armed movement.

---

[66] We hypothesize that under certain conditions, notably the lasting division of the national territory, the regime is severely affected and tends to align its practices with those of other armed actors.

[67] Ana Arjona, Zacharia Mampilly, and Nelson Kasfir, *Rebel Governance in Civil War*, Cambridge, Cambridge University Press, 2015; with a different perspective, Koen Vlassentroot, Ken Menkhaus, and Timothy Rayemaekers, "State and Non-State Regulation in African Protracted Crises: Governance Without Government," *Afrika Focus* 21 (2), 2008, pp. 7–21.

[68] Zachariah Mampilly, *Rebel Rulers: Insurgent Governance and Civilian Life During War*, Ithaca, Cornell University Press, 2011.

To cite an example, the Taliban courts – because they enjoy functional autonomy and have, in part, achieved their enterprise of objectivization – legitimize the administration and military organization, which, in turn, helps them function.[69]

Next, the institutions diffuse modes of governance and so participate in producing society. First, the administration of armed movements redefines the social fabric. For example, in handling conflicts over land or marriages, the courts affect property and relationships between genders.[70] More generally, the institutions transform social hierarchies by the classifications they use during their daily activities. Who will get priority treatment in a hospital – children or the aged, fighters or civilians, men or women? Then also, civil wars generally occasion the penetration by external models of governance. Given a lack of resources, armed groups generally welcome outside organizations (or homegrown ones organized on the same principles). Some armed groups allow, or facilitate, the presence of NGOs and IOs that can take over entire swaths of everyday administration (SPLM in South Sudan, Afghan commanders in the 1980s). Other movements, like the PKK or the LTTE, mobilize their network of sympathizers abroad for collecting resources and organizing the NGOs that are active where armed movement, population, and international actors interface.[71] Even the movements that *a priori* appear to be closed maintain contact with transnational networks, such as the madrasas with the Taliban, diverse Salafist preaching organizations with the Islamic State. The policies of these organizations can have important effects; for example, the physical layout of refugee camps induces changes in the status of women and in the modes of authority and notability. Moreover, the decentralized functioning and competition between these actors hinder the attempts at monopolization by armed movements, leading to recurring tensions. These dynamics explain in part how government by armed movements at times can be out of step with local history.

Dispositions, Skills, and Decisions

Against the neopositivist model of the isolated individual, we will stack up an agent that is socially grounded (gender, class, dispositions

---

[69] Adam Baczko, "Judging in the Midst of Civil War: The Taliban Courts in Afghanistan (2001–2013)," *Politix* 104 (4), 2013, pp. 25–46.

[70] Adam Baczko, "Legal Rule and Tribal Politics: The US Army and the Taliban in Afghanistan (2001–2013)," *Development and Change* 47 (6), 2016.

[71] Olivier Grojean, *La révolution kurde: enquête sur une utopie en actes*, Paris, La Découverte, 2017; Øivind Flugerud, *Life on the Outside: Tamil Diaspora and Long Distance Nationalism*, London, Pluto Press, 1999.

to act,[72] and body hexis) and involved in daily interactions. We distinguish three aspects: socialization, the political context, and the interaction setting. The agent calculates the risks and odds of success, but this strategic aptitude depends on his socialization and available resources (information, time, money), which allow him to interpret the context and, more immediately, the interaction setting. He deliberates, meaning that he generally makes his decisions following interactions during which he forms his judgment. Furthermore, he referees different ends, which, regardless of whether they are collective or individual, altruistic, or egoistical ones, imply an ethic and values. Finally, in contrast to a static vision of individuals and their preferences, we assert that the context transforms the agent's dispositions, competences, and decision-making processes. We therefore analyze successively the transformation of his dispositions to act, the learning of competences, and, finally, the transformation of decision-making processes.

First, the emotional intensity of commitments, the multiplying traumatic experiences, and the participation in total institutions work to modify the initial dispositions of agents.[73] To begin with, the exercise of violence, not only suffered but also committed and witnessed, has a transformative effect on the psychic economy,[74] as do total institutions, armed movements (PKK, LTTE, FARC, ISIS), prisons, or, to a lesser extent, refugee camps.[75] Next, the denaturalization of most mundane categories of daily life (religious or ethnic affiliations, gender, etc.) leads individuals to reassess their identity. These transformations translate into biographical ruptures that are difficult to predict from the social positions actors occupied before the war.

However, all individuals do not experience such radical transformations of their dispositions as certain habitus survive the institution itself, for example, some judges or military people, who continue to a certain degree

---

[72] Taking up the distinction between these two terms proposed by Bernard Lahire, a "disposition" is an "inclination or an appetency interiorized in the course of an individual's trajectory via the different locales and stages of his socialization," while "competence" designates "highly circumscribed knowledge and know-how linked to a circumstance or a highly specific practice." Bernard Lahire, *Portraits sociologiques: Dispositions et variations individuelles*, Paris, Nathan, 2002, p. 415.

[73] Erving Goffman, *Asylums: Essays on the Social Situation of Mental Patients and Other Inmates*, Garden City, Anchor Books, 1961, pp. 1–125.

[74] Beyond the civil war context, here we find a parallel with the effects of torture. Gilles Dorronsoro, "La torture discrète: capital social, radicalisation et désengagement militant dans un régime sécuritaire," *European Journal of Turkish Studies* 8, 2008.

[75] On the role of armed movements, see Olivier Grojean, "La production de l'Homme nouveau au sein du PKK," *European Journal of Turkish Studies* 8, 2008; Laurent Gayer, "Faire l'amour et la guerre: le problème des 'relations physiques' au sein de la People's Liberation Army (PLA) du Népal," *Politix* 107 (3), 2014, pp. 85–115.

to conduct themselves as professionals (hexis, manner of speech, vocabulary, etc.). Perhaps the most striking examples of this are doctors or members of the clergy whose social recognition of competence persists even after the health sector or religious field has collapsed. Moreover, certain individuals, less involved or less exposed to violence, essentially maintain their dispositions to act, which draws our attention to highly contrasted experiences dependent on time and place. One can doubt that the inhabitants of Kabul before and after 1992 or those of Latakia and Aleppo experienced the same war. Civil wars produce radically new interactions, in which the existing dispositions to act prevent a "natural" adjustment to varied situations. Thus, this phenomenon is a generalized and brutal form of hysteresis, which usually originates from socioeconomic changes (such as rural exodus) frequently found in civil wars, which are also times of mass-migration and accelerated urbanization.[76]

Second, the war leads to, and sometimes compels, competences differentiated by the frequently changing positions of agents: body techniques,[77] mastery of objects and tools, specific social skills, and interpretations of situations. This is evident in the case of civilians turned fighters (knowing, handling, maintaining weapons), tactical skills, and physical discipline,[78] but, in reality, it affects the entire society. Indeed, belt-tightening, for example, affects ways of cooking; fighting compels concealment in order to move and to protect oneself, to interpret sounds and smells;[79] the incidence of casualties leads to learning simple first aid techniques (possibly in a structure of care), militancy leads to mastering specific communication and administrative tools. Some agents such as smugglers, gang- or secret-society members, or ex-military personnel can reinvest preexisting skills. More generally, organizational capabilities, external to or directed against incumbent institutions, are regularly mobilized during crises situations.

Third, decisions are social processes that are impacted in crisis situations. These processes are complex, but we can approach them via three dimensions – calculation, emotional investment, and collective deliberation – all of them affected by the outbreak of civil war.[80] Here it is worth emphasizing that situations can vary significantly between disorganized

---

[76] Pierre Bourdieu, *The Logic of Practice*, Stanford, Stanford University Press, 1980.

[77] In this regard, see the classic work by Marcel Mauss, "Techniques of the body," *Economy and Society* 2 (1), 1973, pp. 70–88.

[78] Stéphane Audoin-Rouzeau, *Combattre: une anthropologie historique de la guerre moderne (XIXe-XXe siècle)*, Paris, Seuil, 2008.

[79] Sverker Finnström, *Living with Bad Surroundings: War, History and Everyday Moment in Northern Uganda*, Durham, Duke University Press, 2008.

[80] Henrik Vigh, *Navigating Terrains of War: Youth and Soldiering in Guinea-Bissau*, New York, Berghahn, 2006.

phases with inclusive discourses and front line war between territorialized armed groups relying heavily on a network of institutions. The hypotheses we suggest clearly do not apply in all circumstances; we aim primarily to characterize non-routine situations in which institutions are weakened. First, incertitude is heightened when institutions are no longer capable of playing their role as reducers of uncertainty. Yet, routines are an important dimension of daily life: most actions in fact are nonstrategic behaviors.[81] Faced with uncertainty, the agents, short of exiting, may accept to rely heavily on an institution (armed movement, refugee camp). In the reverse case, agents are caught up in a calculating hyperactivity, because the risks are mounting and institutional routines, which act to dampen uncertainty on the individual level, attenuate, or disappear. The actors are forced to anticipate the consequences of their actions and to inquire. The most mundane actions, like sending the children off to school, going shopping, or quarreling with a neighbor can have serious consequences.[82] For example, which jurisdiction do you appeal to for filing a complaint? Then also, the emotional investment is especially intense: agents may adhere to a cause and the stakes are existential (personal or family safety). Finally, individual decisions generally have a more pronounced collective dimension than they do in routine situations. Group dynamics become key to exchanging information, to assessing risk and reward, and making sense of events. In addition, in certain phases of a civil war, routines are resumed and uncertainty is reduced. Indeed, agents can decide to surrender to an institution (armed group, refugee camp), and the building of new institutions (or the stabilization of frontlines) might also let them again anticipate the future.

---

[81] Peter Berger and Thomas Luckmann, *The Social Construction of Reality: A Treatise in the Sociology of Knowledge*, Garden City, Anchor Books, 1966.
[82] Linda Green, *Fear as a Way of Life: Mayan Widow in Rural Guatemala*, New York, Columbia University Press, 1999.

Introduction

The situation in Syria beginning in 2012 fits our definition of a civil war as the coexistence on the same national territory of competing social orders engaged in a violent relationship. Before we introduce the argument of our book, we will review the literature and then turn to our methodology.

The sheer quantity of source material available on the Syrian civil war poses difficulties: millions of videos, a profusion of newspaper articles, reports by experts, journalists' narratives, and eye witness accounts. The fact remains that the research on Syria prior to 2011 is essential for understanding current developments,[1] especially as published by the network of researchers centered on the French Institute of the Near East (IFPO).[2] Some of these researchers have, in addition, expanded on their own analyses: Fabrice Balanche, Thomas Pierret, Cécile Boëx, Laura Ruiz de Elvira Carrascal, and Souhair Belhadj, respectively, have worked on the role played in the current crisis by sectarian dynamics, religious elites, artistic circles, civil society, and the security apparatus.[3] Finally, certain websites provide core information and follow recent publications, especially *Syria Comment*,

---

[1] For a recent panorama of research on the eve of the protest movements, see Raymond Hinnebusch and Tina Zintl (eds.), *Syria from Reform to Revolt: Volume 1, Political Economy and International Relations*, Syracuse, Syracuse University Press, 2015; Christa Salamandra and Leif Stenberg (eds.), *Syria from Reform to Revolt, Volume 2, Culture, Society, and Religion*, Syracuse, Syracuse University Press, 2015.

[2] A significant proportion of academic research on Syria has been conducted by researchers who were members of the IFPO. We used in particular the many publications on urbanization, the city of Aleppo, real estate, the ulama, the economy, and civil society. Although its institutes in Damascus and Aleppo had to be shut down, the IFPO continues to conduct research on Syria from its centers in Erbil, Beirut, and Amman.

[3] Fabrice Balanche, "Géographie de la révolte syrienne," *Outre-Terre* 29 (3), 2011, pp. 437–458; Thomas Pierret, *Religion and State in Syria: The Sunni Ulama from Coup to Revolution*, Cambridge, Cambridge University Press, 2013; Cécile Boëx, "Ce que la révolution fait à la création cinématographique en Syrie," *Revue des mondes musulmans et de la Méditerranée* 133, 2013, pp. 145–156; Souhail Belhadj, *La Syrie de Bashar al-Assad: anatomie d'un système autoritaire*, Paris, Belin, 2013; Laura Ruiz de Elvira and Tina Zintl, "The End of the Ba'thist Social Contract in Bashar al-Asad's Syria: Reading Sociopolitical Transformations through Charities and Broader Benevolent Activism," *International Journal of Middle Eastern Studies* 46, 2014, pp. 329–349.

the site run by Joshua Landis, *Syria in Crisis*, the webpage of the Carnegie Endowment for International Peace, and Ignace Leverrier's blog *Un œil sur la Syrie* on *Le Monde* site.[4]

The output extant on the post-2011 period is characterized by a scarcity of original sources due to a quasi-absence of investigations in Syria. Starting in 2014, the intensifying war (bombing, besieging of pockets of the opposition) complicated going into the field even more, with this distancing only partly compensated for by interviewing refugees or by Skyping.[5] Moreover, because of police surveillance and risks to Syrians contacts, it is impossible to do research on the regime side; and access is equally precluded with the radical groups (Jabhat al-Nusra and the Islamic State). Still, participants in the protest movement and journalists put pen to paper to relate what they have seen, and their accounts constitute indispensable sources.[6]

The difficulties of access limit the issues tackled (geopolitical, refugees, international aid) to the detriment of, for example, studying Syria's internal dynamics, the functioning of municipal institutions, or of alliances between armed groups. Thus, the first two summaries on the conflict, *Syria's Uprising* by Emil Hokayem and *La révolution orpheline* by Ziad Majed, suffer from the difficulties inherent in works based on secondary sources.[7] Two years later, with *Burning Countries*, Robin Yassin-Kassab and Leila al-Shami offered one of the rare works based on a series of interviews that are both detailed and rigorous. Finally, the scholarly field is politically polarized, which tends to compartmentalize the environment and make discussion more difficult. Just as in other civil wars,[8] the academic field, far from being a space for transcending divisions, has been strongly affected by the crisis, which at times becomes evident in the edited volumes and journals devoted to the subject.[9]

---

[4] See, respectively, www.joshualandis.com/blog/; http://carnegie-mec.org/diwan/issue/155 8?lang=en; and http://syrie.blog.lemonde.fr/.

[5] Thierry Boissière "L'anthropologie face au conflit syrien: replacer la société au coeur de l'analyse," *Revue d'étude des mondes musulmans et de la Méditerranée* 138, 2015, pp.117–130.

[6] Among several published works, see especially Samar Yazbek, *The Crossing: My Journey to the Shattered Heart of Syria*, London, Ebury Publishing 2016; Majd Al-Dik, *A l'est de Damas, au bout du monde: Témoignage d'un révolutionnaire Syrien*, Paris, Editions Don Quichotte, 2016. See also the filmed diaries of six Syrians continuously gathered since 2012 by Caroline Donati, http://syria.arte.tv/mosaic/journal/fra.

[7] Emile Hokayem, *Syria's Uprising and the Fracturing of the Levant*, Adelphi Papers 438, 2013; Ziad Majed, *Syrie, la revolution orpheline*, Paris, Actes Sud, 2014.

[8] For the Lebanese case, Candide Raymond, *Réécrire l'histoire au Liban. Une génération d'historiens face à la période ottomane, de la fin des années 1960 à nos jours*, Thesis, EHESS, 2013.

[9] See, for instance, François Burgat and Bruno Paoli (eds.), *Pas de Printemps pour la Syrie, Les clés pour comprendre les acteurs et les défis de la crise (2011–2013)*, Paris, La Découverte, 2013; Nader Hashemi and Daniel Postel (eds.), *The Syrian Dilemma*, Cambridge, MIT Press, 2013; Barah Mikaïl (ed.), "La tragédie syrienne," *Confluences Méditerranée* 89 (2), 2014.

The combination of fieldwork constraints and political agendas explains the research corpus being organized around five themes. First, the interpretation of the 2011 mobilization is structured around two positions. On one side of the literature is the search for etiological macrosocial causes. Thus, Fabrice Balanche interprets the revolution as an expression of identitarian cleavages, a thesis that echoes Emil Hokayem.[10] Climate change and the government's failure to respond to repeated droughts and the ensuing rural exodus get equal billing for causing the uprising.[11] To escape monocausality, Samer Abboud mobilizes a series of macrosociological factors by way of explanation.[12] On the other side, the 2011 uprising is construed as a social movement, initially of an inclusive nature, as an extension of the Arab revolutions. This perspective, which is more attentive to the unfolding of the events, is notably developed by Reinoud Leenders and Wendy Pearlman.[13] Parenthetically, Lise Weeden points out the complex role of neoliberalism, as much in the emergence of the protest movement as in the response by the Syrian regime.[14]

Second, a significant number of works endeavor to unravel the jihadist nature of the insurgency, singling out two of the most radical groups – the Islamic State and the Jabhat al-Nusra. The most frequently cited works, *ISIS* by Hassan Hassan and *The Syrian Jihad* by Charles Lister, describe funding, preaching, or treatment of minorities, but their sources are mostly uncheckable (such as the former's regular reference to Western intelligence officers).[15] In the end, what is known of the Islamic State's governance is therefore based mostly on press accounts, Internet sources, and policy reports.[16] This focus on Jabhat al-Nusra and the Islamic State comes at

[10] Fabrice Balanche, "Géographie de la révolte . . . *op. cit*; Emil Hokayem, *op. cit.*

[11] Francesca de Châtel, "The Role of Drought and Climate Change in the Syrian Insurgency: Untangling the Triggers of the Revolution," *Middle Eastern Studies* 50 (4), 2014, pp. 1–15; Francesco Femia and Caitlin Werrell, "Climate Change Before and After the Arab Awakening: The Cases of Syria and Libya," in Caitlin Werrell, Francesco Femia, and Anne-Marie Slaughter (eds.), *The Arab Spring and Climate Change*, Center for American Progress, Stimson, The Center for Climate and Security, pp. 23–32; Shahrzad Mohtadi, "Climate Change and the Syrian Uprising," *Bulletin of the Atomic Scientists*, 2012.

[12] Samer Abboud, *Syria*, Cambridge, Polity Press, 2016.

[13] Leenders, Reinoud, "Collective Action and Mobilization in Dar'a: An Anatomy of the Onset of Syria's Popular Insurgency," *Mobilization* 17 (4), 2012, pp. 419–434; Wendy Pearlman, "Moral Identity and Protest Cascades in Syria," *British Journal of Political Science*, forthcoming.

[14] Lisa Wedeen, "Ideology and Humor in Dark Times: Notes from Syria," *Critical Inquiries* 39, 2013, pp. 841–873.

[15] Michael Weiss and Hassan Hassan, *ISIS: Inside the Army of Terror*, New York, Regan Arts, 2016; Charles Lister, *The Syrian Jihad: Al-Qaeda, the Islamic State and the Evolution of an Insurgency*, Oxford, Oxford University Press, 2016.

[16] International Crisis Group, the Soufan Group and the Institute for the Study of War published the most informative reports on the Islamic State. "Iraq: Falluja's Faustian

the expense of the rest of the insurgency and the subjacent social dynamics. In the end, it is recent works by Thomas Pierret on the militancy at the core of the insurgency that number among the rare works based on interviews.[17]

Third, various works deal with the position of the Syrian Kurds after 2011. Works by Harriet Allsopp, Michael Gunter, Cyril Roussel, and Eva Savelsberg and Jordi Tejel thus provide accounts of the Kurds' engagement in the 2011 protests and of the history and the tensions between and within the different Kurdish political movements in Syria.[18] In addition, a number of studies focus on the Syrian branch of the PKK, especially its political model and the role of female fighters. However, most works are characteristically aligned politically with the PKK, which reflects proximity to the extreme left in support of the Kurdish cause or the fight against the Islamists. Too often, the quest for a revolutionary model possibly transplantable to other countries obscures the Syrian reality.[19]

Fourth, the refugees are studied intensively, for one thing because they offer a way of approaching the armed conflict without entering Syrian territory and for another because funding is available. Published since 2012, these works bear especially on the social transformations prompted by exile, the impact on the receiving countries, or on medical issues.[20] The

Bargain," *Middle East Report* 150, International Crisis Group, 2014, www.crisisgroup.o rg/en/regions/middle-east-north-africa/iraq-iran-gulf/iraq/150-iraq-falluja-s-faustian-bar gain.aspx; Charles C. Caris and Samuel Reynolds, "ISIS Governance in Syria," *Middle East Security Report* 22, Institute for the Study of War, 2014; Richard Barett, "The Islamic State," November, 2014, http://soufangroup.com/wp-content/uploads/2014/10 /TSG-The-Islamic-State-Nov14.pdf.

[17] Thomas Pierret, "Salafis at War in Syria: Logics of Fragmentation and Realignment," in Francesco Cavatorta and Fabio Merone (eds.), *Salafism After the Arab Awakening: Salafism After the Arab Awakening: Contending with People's Power*, London, Hurst, 2015; Thomas Pierret, "Fragmentation et consolidation de l'opposition armée," *Confluences Méditerranée* 89 (2), 2015, pp. 45–51; Thomas Pierret, "Crise et déradicalisation : les rebelles syriens d'Ahrar al-Sham," *Confluences Méditerranée* 94 (3), 2015, pp. 43–49; Thomas Pierret and Mériam Cheikh, "'I Am Very Happy Here': Female Jihad in Syria as Self-Accomplishment," *Journal of Women of the Middle East and the Islamic World* 13, 2015, pp. 241–269.

[18] Harriet Allsopp, *The Kurds of Syria: Political Parties and Identity in the Middle East*, London I.B. Tauris, 2014; Michael Gunter, *Out of Nowhere: The Kurds of Syria in Peace and War*, Oxford, Oxford University Press, 2014; Olivier Grojean, *La révolution kurde : enquête sur une utopie en actes*, Paris, La Découverte 2017; Roussel Cyril, "Les Kurdes de Syrie et le projet du Rojava : rêve éphémère ou espoir durable ?" *Maghreb-Machrek* 222 (4), 2014, pp. 75–97; Jordi Tejel and Eva Savelsberg, "The Syrian Kurds in Transition to Somewhere," in Michael Gunter and Mohammed Ahmed (eds.), *The Kurdish Spring: Geopolitical Changes and the Kurds*, Costa Mesa, Mazda Publishers, 2013, pp. 189, 2013.

[19] For instance, Anja Flach, Ercan Ayboga, Michael Knapp, *Revolution in Rojava: Democratic Autonomy and Women's Liberation in the Syrian Kurdistan*, Chicago, University of Chicago Press, 2016.

[20] Among many, Jonathan Hassine, *Les réfugiés et déplacés de Syrie: Une reconstruction nationale en question*, Paris, L'Harmattan, 2016; Lewis Turner, "Explaining the (Non-)

parallel asserts itself with 1980s Afghanistan, when the refugee problem rapidly became a prime lens through which to appraise the war.[21]

Finally, the conflict's international dimension has been scrutinized in an abundance of publications that frequently resemble current events commentaries. Numerous articles thus have been written to account for the foreign policies of the countries involved in the Syrian crisis, although the data remain highly uncertain, including with respect to the scale of outside assistance. Moreover, attention is focused on the question of Sunni jihadism, including foreign militants and their regional supporters (Turkey, the Gulf countries) when we still know little about the role, decisive as it is, of Iran and Hezbollah siding with the regime.[22] Finally, the confessional dimension of the regional competition centered on Syria often comes down to an unnuanced Sunni-Shiite confrontation without being put in the larger perspective of the complex alliances formed.[23]

The Investigation

This book is based on fieldwork conducted in a Syria at war. How is research conducted in a situation of armed conflict?[24] How reliable are the data? And what is the stance of the authors?

We travelled to areas beyond the control of the Damascus regime. There, we generally conducted semi-structured or nondirective interviews with individuals or groups and observed the front lines organization, the civil institutions, social interactions, and economic life. We favored an approach based on interviews and direct observation, which, due to the difficult terrain, could not be complemented by other methodologies (statistics, questionnaires) in a context of war. We employed snowball sampling, focusing on people in charge of various civilian and military institutions inside the insurgency and the local branch of the PKK (Partiya Karkeren

Encampment of Syrian Refugees: Security, Class and the Labour Market in Lebanon and Jordan," *Mediterranean Politics* 20 (3), 2015, pp. 386–404.

[21] Pierre Centlivres and Micheline Centlivres-Demont, "The Afghan Refugee in Pakistan: An Ambiguous Identity," *Journal of Refugee Studies* 1 (2), 1988, pp. 141–152; Alessandro Monsutti, *War and Migration . . . op. cit.*

[22] Emile Hokayem, "Iran, the Gulf States and the Syrian Civil War," *Survival* 56 (6), 2014, pp. 59–86; Will Fulton, Joseph Holliday, and Sam Wyer, *Iranian Strategy in Syria*, Washington: Institute for the Study of War and American Enterprise Institute's Critical Threats Project, 2013.

[23] For an exception in this regard, see Frederic Wehrey, *Sectarian Politics in the Gulf: From the Iraq War to the Arab Uprisings*, New York, Columbia University Press, 2016.

[24] Anthropologists provide particularly interesting perspectives on these issues, especially Carolyn Nordstrom and Antonius Robben, *Fieldwork under Fire*, Oakland, University of California Press, 1996.

Kurdistan, Kurdistan Workers Party). We also interviewed participants in the 2011 demonstrations as well as Syrians without any stated political involvement.[25] For the book, we used 162 interviews of the more than 250 we took notes on. In addition to this corpus, many informal conversations played a decisive role in the treatment and control of our data.[26] An analysis *a posteriori* of our list of interviewees shows that the personnel from institutions in insurgent zones and participants in the initial peaceful demonstration occupy a central place (see "Interviews" in the Annex). Carrying a letter from an insurgent official, we would introduce ourselves as researchers in political science from the Sorbonne. To protect our interviewees, we did not record them, but two of us took comprehensive notes during each interview.[27] In general, we were welcomed readily; the most reticent, perhaps predictably, were the radical Islamist groups (we have only three interviews with fighters from the al-Nusra Jabhat, including two with former members, and none with al-Dawla al-Islamiyya fil-'Iraq wal-Cham, the Islamic State in Iraq, and the Levant (ISIL)).[28] Finally, the work continued with refugees and Syrian activists in Turkey and France with Arthur Quesnay carrying out further fieldwork in Iraq, Lebanon, Jordan, and Egypt. Unlike in other civil war circumstances, speech was unfettered and criticism of armed groups was voiced in public. The only exception concerned the Islamic State (al-Dawla al-Islamiyya, the Islamic State, formerly ISIL): In the summer of 2013, in rebel-held areas in the North, people we spoke with opted to express in private – or outside Syria – their opposition to a group known for its mastery of political assassinations. To complete our research on the Islamic State, in January-February 2015 with Maaï Youssef we did some forty interviews in Northern Iraq and by Skype with Iraqis and Syrians living or having lived under the caliphate.

Our work has several limitations. Essentially, our data were collected either in areas controlled by the insurgency, those controlled by the local

---

[25] For a relatively similar methodology set out in detail, see Jeffrey Sluka, "Participant Observation in Violent Social Contexts," *Human Organization* 49 (2), 1990, pp. 114–126; Koen Vlassenroot, "War and Social Research: The Limits of Empirical Methodologies in War-Torn Environments," *Civilisations* 54, 2006, pp. 191–198.

[26] Especially repetition and triangulation, see Jean-Pierre Olivier de Sardan, "La politique du terrain," *Enquête* 1, 1995, pp. 71–109.

[27] The specific conditions in the field forced us to work without retranscribing our interviews, by anonymizing them, see the list of interviews in the appendix.

[28] We have chosen to use the self-denominations, "Islamic State in Iraq" (ISI – Dawlat al-Iraq al-Islamiyya), "Islamic State in Iraq and Levant" (ISIL – Dawlat al-Islamiyya fi al-Iraq wa-al-Sham), and "Islamic State" (Dawlat al-Islamiyya), in use during the period (Chapters 9 and 10). In some interviews, we also encountered the term "Daesh," the Arabic acronym for ISIL, carrying a pejorative connotation aimed at negating the caliphate's claims.

branch of the Kurdish PKK, or from Syrians in exile.[29] Our information regarding the regime comes from secondary sources. In addition, for security reasons our time on the ground in Syria was limited. Conditions varied from one trip to the next, and we worked mostly in the Aleppo governorate. The first field trip from December 2012–January 2013 was physically challenging due to the cold, and the bombardments by the Syrian army created a palpable sense of insecurity. That said, travel by bus, taxi, or car inside insurgent areas of the North required neither escorts or special planning. Families would welcome us into their homes or, if nothing else was available, civil institutions and insurgent groups would give us shelter. During our second visit, in August 2013, we cut our stay short due to the risk of kidnapping, and we continued our interviews in Turkey.[30] As is often the case, the transformation of the research context is symptomatic of the political evolution that we were there to observe.[31]

Although incomplete, our fieldwork was nevertheless essential in several respects.[32] From the fieldwork to the writing, these interviews proved indispensable.[33] We have used them to provide information (the functioning of an institution or a personal trajectory), to construct a hypothesis, or to express a protagonist's perspective (ideological engagement, subjective view of a situation). To begin with, the accounts available outside Syria do not match what we observed on the ground. The creation of civil institutions in northern Syria has been all but forgotten by the media, by the experts, and, more surprisingly, by the Syrian activists outside Syria. To our knowledge, no more than a handful of reports have been published on this subject and no academic work. As these structures have since largely mutated or dissolved, the second part of the book aims to provide a methodical – though not exhaustive – description of them. The fieldwork also allowed us to test *in situ* certain assumptions that form the backbone of this book. Such research requires *a fortiori* a degree of theoretical reactivity.

[29] For the sake of clarity, we have treated the Islamic State separately; the term "insurgency" in this book refers then to all the other groups fighting the Damascus regime.

[30] For thoughts on these issues, see Jeffrey Sluka, "Reflections on Managing Danger in Fieldwork: Dangerous Anthropology in Belfast," in Jeffrey Sluka and Antonius Robben (eds.), *Ethnographic Fieldwork: An Anthropological Reader*, Hoboken, Wiley-Blackwell, 2012, pp. 283–296.

[31] See Olivier Grojean, "Les aléas d'un terrain comme révélateurs de sa structuration: gestion et objectivation d'une relation d'enquête sur une mouvance radicale et transnationale," *Revue internationale de politique comparée* 17 (4), 2010, pp. 63–76.

[32] Too often reduced to an illustrative or anecdotal capacity, fieldwork is an inherent part of the theoretical work. See Lisa Wedeen, "Reflections on Ethnographic Work in Political Science," *Annual Review of Political Science* 13, 2010, pp. 255–272 and Daniel Bizeul, "Que faire des expériences d'enquête? Apports et fragilité de l'observation directe," *Revue française de science politique* 57 (1), 2007, pp. 69–89.

[33] Stéphane Beaud, "L'usage de l'entretien en sciences sociales: plaidoyer pour l'"entretien ethnographique'," *Politix* 9 (35), 1996, pp. 226–257.

We work in conditions that preclude the scheduling of interviews and often exclude the possibility of meeting our interviewees a second time.[34] Finally, these interviews provide a rich body of material for examining the subjectivity of the actors. In this sense, the 162 interviews, which we have reproduced in extract form, are all the more precious for having been gathered face to face.

Our working as a team played a defining role in interpreting the interviews and field observations and in the writing. First, working as a trio allows us to take on different roles during the interviews or the observations (e.g., questioning, note-taking, observing). Next, interpreting the interview or observation passes through the, at times, tight and exacting crucible of three perspectives that reflect different knowledge, interests, empathies, prior learning – or simply divergent attention during the interaction. In cases where the disagreements about part or all of an interview persisted, we discarded it. Having worked solo in other venues, we are convinced of the superiority of this mode of collective work.[35]

Conducting research in war-torn Syria can leave no one indifferent. The relationship between the researchers and their subjects is particularly fraught in such situations due to the emotional intensity of the experience.[36] Science differs from other forms of knowledge to the extent that it does not presuppose a transformation of the self, but such fieldwork undeniably affects those who undertake it. It is probably not possible or desirable for it to be otherwise: not to be morally repelled by the targeting of schools and hospitals by the regime, by the evident signs of torture on the bodies of our interviewees, or the extrajudicial execution of a prisoner seen alive and well only a few hours earlier. Reflexivity was therefore at a premium. Previous research, work as a trio, and our interactions with other researchers, activists, journalists, and humanitarians all facilitated this process. But the

---

[34] Limited space makes it impossible to list all the disappointments, failures, and surprises we encountered in the field. But it would have been impossible to imagine *a priori* what was feasible and what was not. In the words of Daniel Bizeul, "we made do with disappointments" ("nous avons fait avec les déconvenues"), see Daniel Bizeul, "Faire avec les déconvenues: une enquête en milieu nomade," *Sociétés contemporaines* 33–34, 1999, pp. 111–137.

[35] Our thanks go to Anastasia Shesterinina for having prompted us to explain our mode of working as a trio.

[36] Such environments inevitably affect the researcher, especially when he himself is a member of the community at war, and may feel inclined toward a combatant group. See, respectively, Elisabeth Wood, "The Ethical Challenges of Field Research in Conflict Zones," *Qualitative Sociology* 29 (3), 2006, pp. 373–386; Abderrahmane Moussaoui, "Du danger et du terrain en Algérie," *Ethnologie française* 37 (2), 2001, pp. 51–59; Philippe Bourgois, "La violence en temps de guerre et en temps de paix," *Cultures & Conflicts* 47, 2002; Dennis Rodgers, *Making Danger a Calling: Anthropology, Violence and the Dilemmas of Participant Observation*, London, LSE Development Research Centre, 2001.

process of writing is the decisive moment of distancing, as it is here that a theoretically and empirically based argument admissible by the research community is constructed.

We subscribe to Max Weber's definition of value neutrality,[37] namely – and the formula is often misunderstood – by explicitly distinguishing between our sociological work and our political positions. In practice, we have produced two distinct types of publication: first, reports for think tanks, public talks, editorials, and, second, articles in scholarly journals that have laid the foundations for parts of this book. The distinction, necessary because of the controversial nature of the issues covered, does not preclude the two approaches from enriching each other. Our policy recommendations are grounded in our sociological analysis. Attracting attention as we did in the spring of 2013 to the importance of building civil institutions in Aleppo, or a few months later, to the dangers of ISIL, did indeed stake out political positions, but these were based on thorough fieldwork and our analysis so far has proved to be reasonably accurate. That our warnings, along with those of others, went unheeded demonstrates once again the huge difficulty of translating knowledge into action.[38]

The Argument of the Book

Given the research program outlined in the prefatory remarks and our previous experiences in other civil wars, three topics seem to be especially interesting for understanding the social dynamics of the war in Syria: the entry into civil war, the constituting of distinct territories with their institutional networks, and, finally, the fluctuating values of capitals within the territorialized social orders. Other questions would have been just as pertinent but, if it must be stated, this first attempt at comprehending the conflict has, in the mind of its authors, a calling to be completed, countered, and surpassed in the coming years.

Why Syrians Rebel

To account for civil war breaking out in Syria presupposes supplying answers to three linked questions: What was the situation in Syria and how did the regime function before 2011? How did a mass protest movement emerge? And how, finally, did it turn into generalized violence?

Interpretations of the 2011 crisis largely depend on understanding the Syrian regime, especially its transformation during the 2000s. Did we see,

[37] Max Weber, *From Max Weber: Essays in Sociology,* New York, Oxford University Press, 1946.
[38] Jean-François Revel, *The Flight from Truth: The Reign of Deceit in the Age of Information,* New York, Random House, 1992.

as many experts suggest, a transition toward a less directly coercive, more accommodating power? And what was the level of support and acceptance of this domination within the population? The Baathist State is one of the most violent contemporary regimes. In 1982, the Hama massacre (between 10,000 and 40,000 killed) had clearly shown a power waging war on its people.[39] The tracking down, imprisonment, and systematic torture of its opponents were the routine practices of an insecure regime. On the international scene, Damascus had a track record of colluding with violent networks (the terrorist Carlos, Palestinian factions, jihadists in Iraq) and of engaging in political assassinations (of the French ambassador Louis Delamare in 1981, the former Lebanese Prime Minister Rafic Hariri in 2005). Yet, the coming to power of Bashar al-Assad in 2000 had seemed like a turning point, at least on the socioeconomic level. As part of a process of adapting to economic realities, the regime had initiated a relative liberalization, leading, as some would have it, to a control of society through a new political economy.[40] In addition, various academics detected a contract (albeit implicit) that allowed certain social fields including the religious one a degree of autonomy.[41] The prevailing hypothesis held that this was a form of control at once more indirect and more targeted in its violence.

Consequently, the question of the acceptance of this regime was framed in new terms. The mechanisms by which this authoritarian regime penetrated and controlled society – well described in other contexts – gave the impression of a stabilized system.[42] Thus, the transgressive acts of the 1980s and 1990s described by Lisa Wedeen – derision, diversion, or escapism – that continued under the presidency of Bashar al-Assad rarely excited active opposition.[43] It could therefore be assumed that the regime had found a degree of acceptance and that the population co-produced the power that oppressed it. However, empirical verification of these hypotheses was problematic, since authoritarian societies are notoriously difficult to research and the internalization of domination is a complicated hypothesis to demonstrate in routine situations. A rational choice-based approach could explain the absence of challenge as stemming

---

[39] Michel Seurat, *L'Etat de Barbarie*, Paris, Presses universitaires de France, 2012.

[40] Steven Heydemann, *Upgrading Authoritarianism in the Arab World*, Washington, Brooking's Institute, 2007.

[41] Thomas Pierret and Kjetil Selvik, "Limits of 'Authoritarian Upgrading' in Syria: Private Welfare, Islamic charities, and the Rise of the Zayd Movement," *International Journal Middle Eastern Studies* 41, 2009, pp. 595–614.

[42] Béatrice Hibou, *Anatomie politique de la domination*, Paris, La Découverte, 2011.

[43] Lisa Wedeen, *The Ambiguities of Domination: Politics, Rhetoric, and Symbols in Contemporary Syria*, Chicago, Chicago University Press, 1999. The same phenomenon was seen in the Eastern countries in the 1970s, see Jay Rowell, *Le totalitarisme au concret. Les politiques du logement en RDA*, Paris, Economica, 2006.

instead from an analysis of the risks created by repression. The theories of hegemony and rational choice converged for different reasons to reach the same conclusion. A revolt was unlikely in 2011, either because the regime and society had managed to find a *modus vivendi*, the State had established a hegemonic domination, or resistance was simply too risky. This was the consensus of Syria specialists on the cusp of the Arab spring.[44]

Ultimately, the 2011 crisis allows *a posteriori* a better understanding of the functioning of the Syrian regime. Indeed, we witnessed mobilizations on a remarkable scale: Hundreds of thousands of people marched for months in the face of repression, but, unlike other Arab Springs, the regime did not fall. This leads us to several observations. First, the rapid development of the protests shows that the regime had failed to impose a hegemonic relationship on the population.[45] It also leads us to question the assumption of the regime's domination via the political economy. In fact, the repressive apparatus did retain a primary role, but as a deterrent. A rational choice theory would therefore seem a better explanation for the lack of opposition. However, this approach fails to account for the mobilization of the protesters in 2011 despite the heavy risks confronting them.

Which approach then better reflects the events in both their genesis and their development? From our point of view, the peaceful protests and the transition to civil war can be explained *via* two models: "mobilization through deliberation" explains the genesis of the protests and is followed by the "polarizing crisis," which accounts for the transition to civil war. Both models derive from the specific organization of prerevolutionary Syrian society.[46] Indeed, the autonomy of the various fields – political, trade union, economic, religious – was overwhelmingly restricted by a transversal dynamic: the all-pervasive grip of the security apparatus and patronage networks. Government control of the collective actors (unions,

---

[44] See Joshua Landis, "Will 'Day of Rage' Rock Syria?" *Syria Comment*, February 2, 2011; Bassam Haddad, "Why Syria is Unlikely to Be Next . . . for Now," *Sada* (Formerly known as Arab Reform Bulletin), March 9, 2011. Specialist correspondents made the same analyses, for example, see Aryn Baker, "Syria Is Not Egypt, but Might It One Day Be Tunisia?" *Time*, February 4, 2001, http://content.time.com/time/world/article/0,8599,204 6426,00.html; Lina Sinjab, "Syria: Why is There No Egypt-Style Revolution?" *BBC*, March 4, 2011, www.bbc.com/news/world-middle-east-12639025.

[45] Alternatively, reflecting on his 2008–2009 fieldwork in Aleppo after the 2011 demonstrations, Paul Anderson argues that the recurrent expressions of scorn and cynicism that he encountered among its interlocutors constitute acts of political agency, by which Syrians detached themselves from the regime, preparing the ground for revolt. Paul Anderson, "The Politics of Scorn in Syria and the Agency of Narrated Involvement," *Journal of the Royal Anthropological Institute* 19 (3), 2013, pp. 463–481.

[46] Those two models were previously developed in an article by the co-authors, Adam Baczko, Gilles Dorronsoro, and Arthur Quesnay, "Mobilisations as a Result of Deliberation and Polarising Crisis: The Peaceful Protests in Syria (2011)," *Revue française de science politique* 63 (5), 2013, pp. 815–839.

parties, associations) was therefore too restrictive for them to play a role in the genesis of the protests. Consequently, the first protests neither started in a specific field (union or political) nor were they relayed by any institution in particular.

The initial mobilizations were primarily the result of *personal engagement* and were relatively independent of social position and sectarian affiliations (both religious and ethnic). Informal discussions triggered by events in Tunisia and Egypt were at the root of the mobilization. These discussions led to a transformation in the perception of political opportunities,[47] regardless of the actual evolution of the Syrian regime. The term "Arab Spring," jointly constructed by the media and the protesters, promoted the identification of the Assad regime with other Arab regimes that were overthrown. Even if this term glossed over significant differences between the regimes,[48] it was performative and played an important role in individual engagement. Moreover, many of the debates took place in private or semi-private spaces (small groups, over the Internet) providing some degree of security. This site of deliberation was strategic, as it created not only spaces for exchanging information, but also for assessing risk and building a collective project. The continuous reevaluation of the context of any action, the emotional intensity of the discussions, and the definition of collective good melded in a circular relationship. This model also explains how the protests could persist for months, with informal groups transforming over time into revolutionary networks.

During these deliberations, stakeholders defined the meaning of the conflict, often incorporating ideas and arguments from the Tunisian and Egyptian revolutions. These exchanges created a shared vision as to legitimate means and the nature of the claims. First, the agendas were nationwide, inclusive, and humanist, transcending any local or sectarian solidarity. Refusal to accept socioeconomic concessions from the regime, as well as the political and moral slogans and symbols, suggest that the protesters were engaged in a "struggle for recognition" that for a time transcended sectarian and social divides.[49] Personal or sectional interests faded from mobilizing rhetoric in favor of quite abstract collective goals. As in other revolutionary situations (Afghanistan in 1979 and Libya in 2011), sectarian and ethnic oppositions temporarily lose power because

---

[47] Olivier Fillieule, "Requiem pour un concept. Vie et mort de la notion de structure des opportunités politiques," in Gilles Dorronsoro (ed.), *La Turquie conteste*, Paris, Presses du CNRS, 2006.

[48] Michel Camau, "Un printemps arabe? L'émulation protestataire et ses limites," *L'année du Maghreb* 8, 2012, pp. 27–47.

[49] Axel Honneth, *The Struggle for Recognition: The Moral Grammar of Social Conflicts*, New York, Polity Press, 1995.

of individual commitments to universal ideas. The deliberation on ends is inextricable from a discussion of means. The reference to the Arab Spring assumed peaceful demonstration, a stance that would continue for months despite the violence of the repression.

Far from negotiating, ceding, or managing the repression *a minima*, the regime exacerbated the crisis with a strategy of unbridled violence. This polarizing approach was made possible by the cohesion of institutions dominated by the security apparatus, which was tightening its grip on all fields. By designating the protesters as internal enemies, the regime legitimized its use of violence. By contrast, in Tunisia and Egypt, the protests succeeded in paralyzing institutions and toppling regimes.[50] In Syria, lacking any institutional relay and faced with increasingly violent repression, the protesters were forced into armed struggle.

The Formation of Competing Territories and Administrations

The acephalous mobilization described earlier produced a decentralized, fractured insurgency despite the inclusive ideology. But, when compared with other cases, the Syrian insurgency has one unexpected feature: the lack of exclusive control of territories by its armed groups. The coexistence of armed, nonhierarchically organized groups could have led to immediate fragmentation, territorial as well as political, along the lines of the Somali or Congolese cases.[51] Instead, we observe the fluidity with which the fighters shift from one group to another and the low incidence of armed conflict between them, despite the absence of hierarchy or arbiters. Furthermore, these improvised units often merged to tackle more ambitious goals. The first explanation for this unusual situation lies in the absence of political parties, practically nonexistent inside Syria before 2011, and that the protestors rejected as a source of division. Moreover, the armed groups – even if they often had the same geographical origins – did not represent a specific community, which explains the relative mobility of fighters between units. Until the spring of 2013,

[50] See Amin Allal, "'Revolutionary' trajectories in Tunisia : Processes of political radicalization 2007–2011," *Revue française de science politique* 62 (5), 2012, pp. 821–841; Youssef El-Chazli, "On the road to revolution : How did 'depoliticised' Egyptians become revolutionaries?" *Revue française de science politique* 62 (5), 2012, pp. 843–865.

[51] For the Democratic Republic of the Congo, Koen Vlassenroot and Timothy Raeymaekers, "New Political Order in the D.R. Congo? The Transformation of Regulation," *Afrika Focus* 21 (2), 2008, pp. 39–52; for Somalia, Ken Menkhaus, "Governance without Government in Somalia: Spoiler, State-Building and the Politics of Coping," *International Security* 31 (3), 2006/7, pp. 74–106.

insurgent groups advancing with the front line regarded themselves as the forerunners of a national army.

This phenomenon created the conditions for the rapid reconstitution of civil institutions distinct from military actors. The relative lack of fighting between the armed groups in 2012–2013 allowed the formation and growth of an administrative apparatus. Indeed, in areas that fell to the insurgents, a rapid process of institutionalization began that affected many areas of daily life. It started after the first improvised military groups, uncoordinated and unstructured, merged progressively into units composed of several thousand men. The Syrian revolutionaries proceeded to set up civil and military institutions as well as external representation based on an explicitly state-like model. In areas beyond regime control, new institutions backed by military units emerged in a few scant months. They grew because of social demands that were asserted via informal channels and demonstrations and thanks to a certain level of external funding. The activist networks formed during the phase of peaceful protest also played a role in this process. Indeed, these networks, initially informal, became more institutionalized with the organization of elections and the beginnings of a bureaucracy. With a quasi-monopoly on political representation and bureaucracy, the new institutions in the insurgent territories appear as an objectivization of the activist's social capital. This process draws our attention to the structural impact of events, in this case the transformation of informal networks into institutions.

However, a countervailing dynamic asserts itself as the advancing transnational movements, the PKK and the Islamic State, eliminate all competing groups on their territory and produce their own institutional system strongly integrated with their military structure. Better organized and fielding experienced fighters, these groups espoused alternative political agendas and fought the other groups to gain exclusive control of a territory. This fragmented the insurgency and led to the formation of territories with divergent political models and administration systems controlled by the PKK and the Islamic State. In June 2014, the latter proclaims a caliphate over parts of Iraq and Syria, with a global claim. Its specific rationality, deriving from an eschatological ideology, set it apart from Syrian society. For its part, despite a participative rhetoric, the PKK develops a centralized and ethnonationalist political model with essentially transnational objectives.

This competitive logic accelerates the conflict's sectarian dimension. Indeed, the communitarian dimension, largely absent from the 2011 demonstrations, became dominant through the regime's strategy and the rise of identity discourses. From the start, Damascus' policy was to bolster the most radical groups (informal agreements with the PKK, the release of radical jihadists from the Iraq war) as a tactic for dividing the opposition. In addition, the rhetoric within the insurgency gradually took on a more religious connotation; martyrology linked to the violent conflict tended to exclude non-Sunnis. The sectarianization was furthered by external actors providing funding and fighters. So, while the regime showed a marked "Shiitization" due to its dependence on Iran and Lebanese Hezbollah, the insurgents espousing an Islamist ideology (sometimes for purely tactical reasons) were receiving significant funding from the Gulf, particularly in the period 2012–2013. This weakened the secular protest groups, which only received token support from the West.

In the end, polarization and political fragmentation, rather than a product of the Syrian society, reflect the influence of external actors. International or transnational dynamics affected the insurgency even more because of its disorganization. On the one hand, the regime army's breakdown and the insurgency's decentralization led to a high degree of dependence on outsiders, including the diaspora, foreign countries, and transnational actors. On the other hand, the PKK and the Islamic State grew through their superior ability to accumulate and use resources. This enabled their holding, even extending, territory in which to gradually build an increasingly complex administrative apparatus. In Syria, as in other contexts of increased political and military competition (Afghanistan, Iraq, Angola, or the Democratic Republic of Congo), the ability to centralize, to accumulate, and to use resources strategically is crucial to survival.

The Variation of Capitals

With the division of the country between competing territorialized political actors, the value of capital (economic, social, cultural, identity) differs from one region to another. Within the framework developed in the prolegomena, we address three dimensions of this phenomenon for the Syria case: social capital, economic capital, and the identity regime.

First, in the context of a generalized decline in social relations, small groups of activists increase their social capital. Indeed, impoverishment, insecurity, and communication problems directly affected the ability of a large majority of Syrians to maintain relationships. The extreme conditions of this situation allow for a clearer reading of how social capital relates to other forms of capital and to the State, disproving the idea that the ability to create and maintain social relationships depends purely on individual capabilities. In this context of increasing individual isolation, the minority of Syrians involved in the 2011 protests increased their social capital because of their membership in revolutionary networks. This then becomes a practical requirement for access to institutional positions in the insurgency's reconstituting administration. Despite a scarcity of sources, women's militancy appears to remain rare and seems to require the women to make a more radical personal break than the men, inasmuch as the former's public expression challenges the boundaries between the public and the private.

Second, the civil war facilitates the accumulation of military capital unregulated by the State and causes Syria to disappear as an integrated economic market. Instead, internal borders are drawn that demarcate differing values for goods and labor. Moreover, violence becomes the chief means of economic accumulation, via both taxation and extortion. A superficial reading of the Syrian situation is consistent with the market-based theories formulated in the late 1990s, which characterized civil wars as competitions for the accumulation of the means of violence and their subsequent use for economic benefit.[52] This conception, while it accounts for an economic rationality that is indeed present, is nevertheless misleading. The formation of military groups and the conversion of military means into economic resources cannot be modeled as a market. The accumulation of military power is a quest for domination. Contrary to what these theories assume, the military actors in Syria do not reinvest their wealth in line with a purely economic rationality. On the contrary, the accumulation of economic resources leads to an intensification of violence aimed at reconstructing the State. Indeed, no mechanism can ensure either the security of the actors or the partitioning of territory. Cases where the actors cooperate on an economic stake are explained by the existence of indivisible goods (electricity, water) and where shared economic interests are both rare and easily called into question. This dynamic is also apparent in the Afghan and Iraqi conflicts: the economic use of military capital does not *per se* create the necessary conditions for a stable division of territory and resources.

Third, the previous identity regime of Syrian society has disappeared for good. By "identity regime" we mean a set of practices and positions that prioritize, define, and organize the relationship between ethnic and religious groups. Their hierarchization depended largely on the political system, which played a central role in the definition of relative status and power. The withdrawal of the state led to a violent denaturalization of the

---

[52] Jean-Christophe Rufin and François Jean (eds.), *L'économie des guerres civiles*, Paris, Hachette, 1996; Elwert Georg, "Market of Violence," in Georg Elwert, Stephan Feuchtwang, and Dieter Neuvert (eds.), *Dynamics of Violence: Processes of Escalation and De-Escalation in Violent Group Conflicts*, Berlin, Duncker & Humblot, 1999, pp. 85–102; David Keen, *The Economic Functions of Violence in Civil Wars*, Adelphi Paper 320, 1998. Paul Staniland proposed a model along similar line, Paul Staniland, "States, Insurgents, and Wartime Political Orders," *Perspectives on Politics* 10 (2), 2012, pp. 243–264. For an application of these models in Syria, Abboud Samer, *op. cit.*

hierarchies between groups. The emergence of several political entities – the government, the Kurds, the insurgency, and the Islamic State – created coexisting but competing identity regimes. Indeed, being Alawite, Druze, Christian, and Sunni did not mean the same thing in the government zone in Latakia, the rebel-held part of Aleppo, Islamic State-dominated Raqqa, or in the Kurdish town of Ayn al-Arab controlled by the local PKK branch. This transformation in the value of identities causes individuals to react in two ways. On the one hand, memberships are simplified in an atmosphere of extreme polarization, for example, for someone born of mixed couples. On the other hand, individuals learn to manipulate their identity markers when moving around in physical (road checkpoints, for example) or social space (interacting with different institutions or armed actors.)

***

To investigate these three issues and equip the reader for understanding the genesis of the actors and the successive engendering of configurations, we have organized the book into four parts. We present the regime and society on the eve of the initial demonstrations (Chapter 1), followed by the genesis of the protests (Chapter 2) and the transition to civil war (Chapter 3). We then analyze the creation of military institutions (Chapter 4), civil institutions (Chapter 5), and representation abroad (Chapter 6). Third, we examine the fragmentation of the insurrection starting from the international dimension (Chapter 7), the Kurdish movements (Chapter 8), the growth of radical Islam (Chapter 9), and the case of the Islamic State (Chapter 10). In the fourth and final part, the focus shifts to exploring the mutations within Syrian society from three angles: social capital (Chapter 11), the war economy (Chapter 12), and the identity regime (Chapter 13).

Part I

Genesis of a Revolution

1   The al-Assad System

Instead of presenting an illusorily exhaustive study of Syrian society, the following analyses seek to identify the elements necessary for understanding the crisis that started in March 2011.[1] Nor will we try to set out a causal model from independent variables, but rather to describe a preliminary state that defines the conditions of possibility and probabilities of occurrence. Especially decisive for understanding the events that transpired starting in 2011 appear to be three issues: the new political economy of the 2000s, the identity regime, and the depoliticization of society.

The Political Economy of the Syrian Regime

On the eve of the 2011 revolution, Syria was plagued by social and economic tensions that affected its political system. The Syrian regime had essentially evolved from a "socialist" system, which characteristically included land reform, the marginalization of the bourgeoisie, and nationalization of the economy, to a neoliberal system that privatized entire sections of the economy for the benefit of those close to power at the expense of the middle and lower classes. The regime had also implemented delegated ("discharged" in Weber's meaning of the term) basic governmental functions, sparing itself from having to structurally reform the state apparatus but fostering divisions and sectarianism.[2]

---

[1] For a general presentation of Syria, see Baudouin Dupret, Zouhair Ghazzal, Youssef Courbage, and Mohammed al-Dbiyat (eds.), *La Syrie au présent: Reflets d'une société*, Paris, Actes Sud, 2007; Fred H. Lawson, *Demystifying Syria*, London, Saqi Books, 2010; Chiffoleau Sylvia (ed.), "La Syrie au quotidien: cultures et pratiques du changement," *Revue des mondes musulmans et de la Méditerranée* 115–116, 2006.

[2] Here we use the concept of "discharge" as defined by Béatrice Hibou, that is the use of private actors by the State as the dominant mode of governmentality, see "Retrait ou redéploiement de l'Etat," *Critique internationale* 1, 1998, p.154. On discharge in Syria, see Thomas Pierret and Kjetil Selvik, *op. cit.* On community-based management, see Fabrice Balanche, *La région alaouite et le pouvoir syrien*, Paris, Karthala, 2006; Cyril Roussel, *Les Druzes de Syrie: Territoire et mobilité*, Beirut, Presses de l'Ifpo, 2011.

The nationalization of the economy starting in the 1960s allowed marginalizing the old economic and social elites. When Hafez al-Assad took power in 1970, he relied initially on the urban petty bourgeoisie, notably by enlarging the civil service.[3] A connection to the ruling clique, as it were, conditioned the access to resources;[4] for example, economic elites would be recruited from networks where top regime officials mixed with members of the security services.[5] In the 1980s, Michel Seurat thus wrote that the "new bourgeois classes [. . .] grow not by controlling the means of production, but like parasitic classes attached to the bureaucratic bourgeoisie. As for the latter, by definition it does not exist independently of the State at any level related to production."[6] In the perspective of a general theory of practices, a form of social capital (belonging to networks close to the government) is the direct means for economic accumulation. While, in contemporary Western societies social capital is often analyzed as secondary or derivative with respect to economic capital, here it comes first. The relationship to politics is that much more important in constituting the economic elites since Syria was a rentier society in the 1970s and 1980s, which derived its revenues from oil, from aid by the Gulf States, and from pillaging the Lebanese economy.

However, the economy on which this system was based began to weaken during the 1990s as the regime saw these sources of revenues shrink. First, the Gulf countries stopped sharing their oil revenues with Syria, solidarity between Arab countries and the confrontation with Israel no longer being a priority for them. In addition, Syrian oil production peaked in 1996, so much so that it became a net importer starting in 2006.[7] Finally, the withdrawal of the Syrian army from Lebanon in 2005 deprived the regime of $750

---

[3] Bassam Haddad, *Business Networks in Syria: The Political Economy of Authoritarian Resilience*, Stanford, Stanford University Press, 2012.

[4] The term "clique" refers to John A. Barnes, who used graph theory to describe groups founded on personal relations rather than similar status. John A. Barnes, "Class and Committees in a Norwegian Island Parish," *Human Relations* 7, 1954, pp. 39–58.

[5] For members of the Syrian security apparatus, see Souhaïl Belhadj, "L'appareil sécuritaire syrien, socle d'un régime miné par la guerre civile," *Confluences Méditerranée* 89 (2), 2014. For the economic elite, see Ali El Salah, "Les bourgeoisies syriennes," in Baudouin Dupret, Zouhair Ghazzal, Youssef Courbage, and Mohammed al-Dbiyat (eds.), *op. cit.*, p. 771–778; Élizabeth Picard, "Syrie: la coalition autoritaire fait de la résistance," *Politique étrangère* 4, 2005, pp. 755–768 and Bassam Haddad, *Business Networks in ...*, *op. cit.*, 2012.

[6] Michel Seurat, "Les populations, l'Etat et la société," in André Raymond, (ed.), *La Syrie d'aujourd'hui*, Paris, Editions du CNRS, 1980, p. 128. Volker Perthes picks up the same theory fifteen years later, Volker Perthes, *The Political Economy of Syria under Asad*, London, I.B. Tauris, 1995.

[7] Samir Aita, "L'économie de la Syrie peut-elle devenir sociale? Vous avez dit: 'économie sociale de marché'?" in Baudouin Dupret, Zouhair Ghazzal, Youssef Courbage, and Mohammed al-Dbiyat (eds.), *op. cit.*, p. 570.

million in annual revenues from smuggling along the so-called "Military road." Army officers stationed in Lebanon lost several thousand euros of income per month. Money laundering through Lebanese banks ended, as did controlling drug production in the Bekaa, an activity the Damascus regime had subcontracted to the military in exchange for its loyalty.[8]

As explained by Elizabeth Picard, the Syrian regime in the 2000s experienced a profound transformation: "To reprise a comparison with other authoritarian regimes, in particular in the Arab region, the Syrian regime has entered a 'post–populist' phase where maintaining the privileges of the ruling group outweighs promises of growth."[9] The decrease in income in effect pushed the regime to liberalize its economy. The rise to power of Bashar al-Assad therefore coincided with an acceleration of reforms, initiated in 1991 with Law No. 10, which aimed to liberalize the Syrian economy and facilitate foreign investment.[10] In 2000 and 2001, a series of laws paved the way for the emergence of a private banking system, a stock exchange, and private universities. In addition, the regime created special economic zones based on the Chinese model to attract foreign investment. It privatized many public enterprises, so that in 2007 the private sector accounted for 70 percent of economic activity.[11] Its share of imports rose from one-fifth in 1981 to four-fifths in 2003.[12]

Nevertheless, in Caroline Donati's words, "the infitah process (liberalization) was always done with the utmost restraint and under supervision, the regime being anxious to keep control of the economic resources."[13] Thus, in the 1990s and 2000s, those close to power took control of entire sectors of the economy.[14] "The regime liberalized the economy sector by sector. That way its members were able to maintain control" explained a businessman from Aleppo who had fled to Turkey, "one family, one of whose members was the Minister of Health, was able to develop a large pharmaceutical company, because part of its revenue was diverted directly to the clan in power."[15] Similarly, the establishment of the largest industrial zone in the country, Sheikh Najjar, on the outskirts of Aleppo,

---

[8] Caroline Donati, *L'exception syrienne: entre marchandisation et résistance*, Paris, La Découverte, 2011, p. 149 and p. 171; Glenn Robinson, "Elite Cohesion, Regime Succession and Political Instability in Syria," *Middle East Policy* 5 (4), 1998, pp.171–172.
[9] Elisabeth, Picard, *op. cit.*, p. 761.
[10] Raymond A. Hinnenbusch, "The Political Economy of Economic Liberalization in Syria," *International Journal of Middle East Studies* 27 (3), 1995, pp. 305–310 and "Syria: The Politics of Economic Liberalization," *Third World Quarterly* 18 (2), 1997, pp. 249–265.
[11] Caroline Donati, *op. cit.*, pp. 211–244.
[12] Samir Aita, *op. cit.*, p. 562.
[13] Caroline Donati, *op. cit.*, p. 89.
[14] Elizabeth Picard, *op. cit.*, pp. 759–761.
[15] I-1, in Antakya, September 2014.

was accompanied by zoning manipulations benefiting important investors in the project that included the mayor and his allies.[16] The economic opening resulted in widespread corruption with increased blurring of the distinction between public and private assets.[17] Rami Makhlouf, a cousin of Bashar al-Assad, personifies these new arrangements. He controls SyriaTel, the largest mobile phone network, airport duty-free shops, the Syrian border posts, most of Byblos Bank; he has interests in oil and gas, cigarette imports, and garbage collection. Additionally, he heads up two consortia, Al Cham and Al Suriyya. The first brings together seventy members of influential families, who subscribed for a total $350 million, the second grouping twenty-five heirs of the great families with a capital of $80 million.[18] Most State contracts were awarded to these companies, and foreign companies doing business in Syria had to make them shareholders. The Egyptian company Orascom Telecom eventually abandoned its 25 percent stake in SyriaTel because of excessive demands by Rami Makhlouf.[19] Only international corporations were able to invest in the most profitable sectors (finance, luxury, tourism, land) in return for paying off people close to Bashar al-Assad.[20] In 2001, Riyadh Saif, owner of the Adidas franchise in Syria, was imprisoned for competing with Rami Makhlouf for the mobile phone franchise. Similarly, the Sankar family was forced into exile after a dispute involving award of the Mercedes franchise.[21]

By hijacking the benefits of economic reform, the regime abandoned public policies that had favored the lower classes.[22] From the 1990s on, due to the economic difficulties and failure of the collectivization of the 1960s and 1970s,[23] the Syrian government was no longer investing sufficiently either in the newly urbanized or the rural areas.

[16] Samir Aita, *op. cit.*, 541–580.
[17] Bassam Haddad, "The Formation and Development of Economic Network in Syria: Implications for Economic and Fiscal Reforms, 1986–2000," in Steven Heydemann (ed.), *Networks of Privilege in the Middle East: The Politics of Economic Reform Revisited*, New York, Palgrave Macmillan, 2004, pp. 53–66.
[18] Caroline Donati, "The Economics of Authoritarian Upgrading in Syria: Liberalization and the Reconfiguration of Economic Networks," in Steven Heydemann and Reinoud Leenders (eds.), *op. cit.*, pp. 41–42.
[19] Volker Perthes, *Syria under Bachar al-Asad: Modernisation and the Limits of Change*, Adelphi Paper 366, 2004, pp. 37–38.
[20] Caroline Donati, *op. cit.*, p. 229.
[21] Fabrice Balanche, "Communautarisme en Syrie: lorsque le mythe devient réalité," *Confluences Méditerranée* 89, 2014, p. 33.
[22] Ignace Leverrier, "Les ressources sécuritaires du régime," in François Burgat and Bruno Paoli (eds.), *op. cit.*, p. 41.
[23] See Myriam Ababsa, "Agrarian Counter-Reform in Syria," in Raymond Hinnenbusch (ed.), *Agriculture and Reform in Syria*, Boulder, Lynne Rienner, 2011, p. 96 and "Le démantèlement des fermes d'Etat syriennes: une contre-réforme agraire (2000–2005),"

Unemployment, the regime's mismanagement of the drought of 2006–2010, and the lack of an urbanization policy were aggravated by the weak redistribution mechanisms.[24] On the eve of the revolution, the regime's presence in the villages and small towns were attenuated, particularly when compared to the 1960s and 1970s.[25] The influence of the Baath Party's satellite institutions, which had held sway over the population in the 1970s, three decades later was now diminished.[26] The party ceased to be a vector of social mobility[27] and its structures were no longer an essential resource for the political elites. Fabrice Balanche held that "Membership in the Baath is a prerequisite for access to the administration, [. . .] but it is no longer an honor."[28] In the same vein, a resident of Maraa, a small town in the north of the Aleppo governorate, states: "We officials, we were all Baath members. It was an effective way to be promoted within the administration. What mattered most was not to be political."[29] Thus, Damascus, with its population of 4.5 million in 2004, only had 29,000 active militants.[30] In the 2000s, Baath still had the members but few were believers.

The Syria of the 1990s and 2000s thus presented a paradox: an authoritarian regime pursuing the neoliberal policy of shrinking the State. However, as in Egypt and Turkey, Syrian cities were experiencing rapid growth.[31] The continued impoverishment of the countryside that started in the 1980s and the droughts of the 2000s had accelerated a rural exodus whose effects were multiplied by an annual population growth of 2.5 percent projected to double the population every twenty

in Baudouin Dupret, Zouhair Ghazzal, Youssef Courbage, and Mohammed al-Dbiyat (eds.), *op. cit.*, pp. 739–745.

[24] Francesca de Châtel, "The Role of Drought and Climate Change in the Syrian Insurgency: Untangling the Triggers of the Revolution," *Middle Eastern Studies* 50 (4), 2014, pp. 1–15.

[25] Hanna Batatu, *Syria's Peasantry, the Descendants of Its Lesser Rural Notables, and Their Politics*, Princeton, Princeton University Press, 1999; Alasdair Drysdale, *Center and Periphery in Syria: A Political Geographic Study*, Thesis, University of Michigan, 1977; Raymond A. Hinnenbusch, "Local Politics in Syria: Organization and Mobilization in Four Village Cases," *Middle East Journal* 30 (1), 1976, pp. 1–24.

[26] Raymond A. Hinnenbusch, *Revolution from Above*, New York, Routledge, 2002.

[27] Eberhard Kienle, "Entre jamaa et classe: le pouvoir politique en Syrie contemporaine," *Revue des mondes musulmans et de la Méditerranée* 59–60, 1991, pp. 211–239.

[28] Fabrice Balanche, *op. cit.*, p. 152.

[29] I-2, in Maraa, December 2012.

[30] Caroline Donati, *op. cit.*, p. 155.

[31] The same phenomena are observed in Turkey, see Jean-François Pérouse (ed.), "Les tribulations du terme *gecekondu* (1947–2004): une lente perte de substance. Pour une clarification terminologique," *European Journal of Turkish Studies* 1, 2004, http://ejts.revues.org/117, viewed January 7, 2016, and in Egypt, Patrick Haenni, *L'ordre des caïds: Conjurer la dissidence urbaine au Caire*, Paris, Karthala, 2005. An edited volume by Myriam Ababsa, Baudouin Dupret, and Eric Denis compares the Egyptian, Syrian, Jordanian, Lebanese, and Turkish cases, *Popular Housing and Urban Land Tenure in the Middle East*, Cairo, The American University in Cairo Press, 2012.

years.[32] This growth primarily affected small rural towns,[33] whose populations have multiplied by five or even ten times since the 1980s. "The
population of our city [al-Bab] has significantly increased, but no reforms
have been made to accommodate the new people from the countryside. We
lack schools, hospitals, and the electricity supply has not kept pace."[34] The
informal neighborhoods that sprang up in large cities like Aleppo and
Damascus covered almost half their respective areas.[35] Finally, the influx
of Iraqi refugees, with nearly 1.5 million recorded in 2007, accelerated
urban growth and the rise in real estate prices.[36]

The regime was incapable of implementing an urban planning
policy,[37] leaving the new city dwellers to settle in overcrowded, often
substandard, housing with limited access to public services.[38] In the
informal neighborhoods, the regime assured itself in principle of the
population's docility by playing on their need to regularize the title to
their self-built property and regulating their access to public utilities.[39]
The strategy was not new, the regime since the 1960s having made
use of manipulating administrative boundaries to assure itself of local
support.[40] However, back then it could still guarantee creation of administrative jobs, which, forty years later, was no longer the case. Finally,

[32] Myriam Ababsa, Cyril Roussel, and Mohammed al-Dbiyat, "Le territoire syrien entre
intégration nationale et métropolisation renforcée," in Baudouin Dupret, Zouhair
Ghazzal, Youssef Mujahidin, and Mohammed al-Dbiyat (eds.), *op. cit.*, pp. 37–78.

[33] Robert Goulden, "Housing, Inequality, and Economic Change in Syria," *British Journal
of Middle Eastern Studies* 38 (2), 2011, p. 195.

[34] I-3, leader of the al-Bab revolutionary city council, in al-Bab, December 2012.

[35] Franziska Laue, "Vertical Versus Horizontal: Constraints of Modern Living Conditions
in Informal Settlements and the Reality of Construction," in Myriam Ababsa, Baudouin
Dupret, and Eric Denis (eds.), *op. cit.*, p. 112.

[36] Reinoud Leenders, "Iraqi Refugees in Syria: Causing a Spill-over of the Iraqi Conflict,"
Third World Quarterly 29 (8), 2008, p. 1567.

[37] Cha'ban Abboud, "Les quartiers informels de Damas: une ceinture de misère," in
Baudouin Dupret, Zouhair Ghazzal, Youssef Mujahidin, and Mohammed al-Dbiyat
(eds.), *op. cit.*, pp. 169–176.

[38] On the informal neighborhoods in Aleppo, see Balsam Ahmad, "Neighborhood and
Health Inequalities in Formal and Informal Neighborhoods in Aleppo," in Balsam
Ahmad and Yannick Sudermann (eds.), *Syria's Contrasting Neighborhoods: Gentrification
and Informal Settlements Juxtaposed*, Boulder, Lynne Rienner, 2012; Fadi Hammal,
Jeremiah Mock, Kenneth D. Ward, Fouad M. Fouad, Bettina M. Beech, and Wasim
Maziak, "Settling With Danger: Conditions and Health Problems in Peri-Urban
Neighborhoods in Aleppo, Syria," *Environment and Urbanization* 17 (2), 2005, pp.
113–125.

[39] Fabrice Balanche, "L'habitat illégal dans l'agglomération de Damas et les carences,"
Revue géographique de l'Est 49 (4), 2009.

[40] Fabrice Balanche, "La région côtière: d'une périphérie délaissée à une périphérie
assistée," in Baudouin Dupret, Zouhair Ghazzal, Youssef Mujahidin, and Mohammed
al-Dbiyat (eds.), *op. cit.*, p. 89.

during the 2000s, informal crime control by neighborhood networks was another sign of the weakening State.[41]

From the 1990s onward, the economic crisis brought permanent impoverishment to the middle and working classes who had already suffered not only from the sudden liberalization of the economy but also from the stagnant private sector undermined by corruption.[42] State employee salaries ranged from $150 to $300 a month: a factory worker earned approximately $70. However, in 2007, the monthly living expenses in Damascus for a couple without children averaged over $600.[43] Most men had a second or even a third job in the informal economy. Likewise, hundreds of thousands of Syrians each year poured into Lebanon looking for work.[44] The informal economy played a vital role for a large part of the population, which helps to explain why 60 percent of transactions were settled in cash. Nearly half of all agricultural jobs were illegal,[45] and smuggling (cigarettes, textiles) that often mobilized ethnic or tribal allegiances was rife in border areas,[46] while non-monetized barter of goods or services grew. If the informal economy allowed the population to survive, it put an additional strain on the state budget by reducing the tax base. At the same time, corporate taxation remained largely token.[47]

In the end, it is clear a clique close to the regime purloined the national wealth.[48] The inequalities were even more strongly felt, given the conspicuous consumption by the elite[49] that paralleled them, and the increased access of the middle class to the Internet and mobile phone access to foreign media. The social gap was both wider and more obvious.[50] On the one hand, the internationalized elites close to the regime had passports, studied abroad, and were free to purchase

---

[41] Zouhair Ghazzal, "Shared Social and Juridical Meanings in Aleppo Neighborhood," in Myriam Ababsa, Baudouin Dupret, and Eric Denis (eds.), *op. cit.*, pp. 169–202.

[42] Raymond Hinnenbusch, "Syria: From Authoritarian Upgrading to Revolution?" *International Affairs* 88 (1), 2012, pp. 95–113.

[43] For workers' salaries, Myriam Ababsa, Cyril Roussel, and Mohammed al-Dbiyat, *op. cit.*, p. 51; for civil servants', Caroline Donati, *op. cit.*, p. 264.

[44] Fabrice Balanche, "La région côtière ...," *op. cit.*

[45] Samir Aita, *op. cit.*, p. 568.

[46] Cyril Roussel, "Reconfiguration des espaces transfrontaliers dans le conflit syrien," Noria-research, February 19 2014, www.noria-research.com/la-reconfiguration-des-espaces-transfrontaliers-dans-le-conflit-syrien/, viewed February 25, 2014.

[47] Bassam Haddad, "The Formation and Development ...," *op. cit.*, pp. 53–66.

[48] Caroline Donati, *op. cit.*, 2013, pp. 55–56.

[49] Leïla Vignal, "La 'nouvelle consommation' et les transformations des paysages urbains à la lumière de l'ouverture économique: l'exemple de Damas," *Revue des mondes musulmans et de la Méditerranée* 115–116, 2006, pp. 21–41.

[50] Leila Hudson, "Le voile et le portable: l'adolescence sous Bachar al-Assad," in Baudouin Dupret, Zouhair Ghazzal, Youssef Mujahidin, and Mohammed al-Dbiyat (eds.), *op. cit.*, pp. 303–304.

imported goods. By contrast, the children of the middle classes, often with diplomas but without economic capital, and the working classes living in informal settlements, saw their standard of living fall.[51]

The Identity Regime

The civil war is often presented as resulting from the multisectarian structure of Syrian society, a topic we will return to. Yet the undeniable importance of ethnic and religious memberships in any number of everyday situations did not imply *ipso facto* that communities were established political actors or that the State represented any one group despite its being perceived as Alawite. In reality, the Syrian regime perpetuated, or even aggravated, ethnic and religious divides as a means for ensuring its own survival.

Ethnic or sectarian identity played an important role in specific contexts, starting with marriage. Within communities, endogamy was indeed strong and perhaps growing. Catherine Dupret-Schepens shows that, in the mid-2000s, from a sample of thirty-three families or 3,332 individuals belonging to different ethnic and religious communities, intermarriage made up only 2.1 percent of all marriages, with 1.5 percent of intermarriages entered into abroad.[52] Moreover, these couples, and even more so their children, faced rejection, often from their own families.[53] More generally, "in daily practices, mixing is far from the rule: a Christian will see a Christian doctor."[54] Likewise, even the transportation system showed signs of sectarianism in Syria (Table 1.1, Map 1.1).[55]

This endogamy is accompanied by each group in some way being concentrated in specific areas: the Druze in the south of the country, the Alawites to the west, the Kurds in the north and east and the Christians and Ismailis in the towns. These historical concentrations had, however, been turned upside down by urbanization. As an example, in 2011, most Kurds lived in Damascus and Aleppo, i.e., outside the predominantly Kurdish areas of the governorates of Aleppo and Hasaka where they had traditionally been concentrated. The significance of trans-sectarian interactions and the degree of ethnic or confessional homogeneity varied by

---

[51] Caroline Donati, *op. cit.*, pp. 335–342.

[52] Catherine Dupret-Schepens, "Les populations syriennes sont-elles homogènes?" in Baudouin Dupret, Zouhair Ghazzal, Youssef Mujahidin, and Mohammed al-Dbiyat (eds.), *op. cit.*, p. 220.

[53] I-4, a Sunni woman married to an Alawite man, in Antakya, September 2013. For other examples, see A. M. Kastrinou Theodoropoulou, "A Different Struggle for Syria: Becoming Young in the Middle East," *Mediterranean Politics* 17 (1), 2012, pp. 68–73.

[54] Caroline Donati, *op. cit.*, p. 295.

[55] Fabrice Balanche, "Transports et espace syrien," *Annales de Géographie* 112, n°630, 2003, p.165.

Table 1.1 *Ethnic and religious affiliation*[56]

Group	Population in 1953 (000)	% in 1953	Population in 2004 (esti-mated) (000)	% in 2004 (estimated)	Multiplier between 1953 and 2004	Annual growth rate (‰)	Population in 2012 (projected) (000)	% in 2012 (projected)
Arab Sunni	2,259	61.8	12,765	71.7	5.7	3.40	15,800	72.8
Arab Alawi	399	10.9	1,846	10.4	4.6	3.00	2,200	10.2
Kurds	248	6.8	1,450	8.1	5.8	3.46	1,800	8.3
Arab Christians	479	13.1	946	5.3	2.0	1.33	1,000	4.6
Arab Druzes	113	3.1	350	2.0	3.1	2.22	400	1.8
Arab Ismaelis	37	1.0	171	1.0	4.6	3.00	200	0.9
Turkmens	49	1.3	114	0.6	2.3	1.66	100	0.6
Arab Shiites	15	0.4	69	0.4	5.6	3.00	80	0.4
Cherkessians	23	0.6	68	0.4	3.0	2.13	80	0.3
Yazidis	3	0.1	14	0.1	4.7	3.02	20	0.1
Total	3,657	100.0	17,793	100.0	4.9	3.10	21,600	100.0

[56] The 1953 figures come from work by Etienne de Vaumas, used by Youssef Courbage. Those for 2004 come from the "evaluations carried out by specialists of Syria" and "the deduction of certain demographic parameters based on regional data." The 2012 extrapolations are Youssef Courbage's projections, based on the estimated figures for 2004. See, respectively, Etienne de Vaumas, "La population de la Syrie," *Annales de géographie* 64 (341), 1955, pp. 74–80; Youssef Courbage, "La population de la Syrie: des réticences à la transition (démographique)," in Baudouin Dupret, Zouhair Ghazzal, Youssef Mujahidin, and Mohammed al-Dbiyat (eds.), *op. cit.*, p. 189; Youssef Courbage, "Ce que la demographie nous dit du conflit syrien," *Slate*, October 15, 2012, www.slate.fr/story/62969/syrie-guerre-demographie-minorites, viewed November 19, 2014.

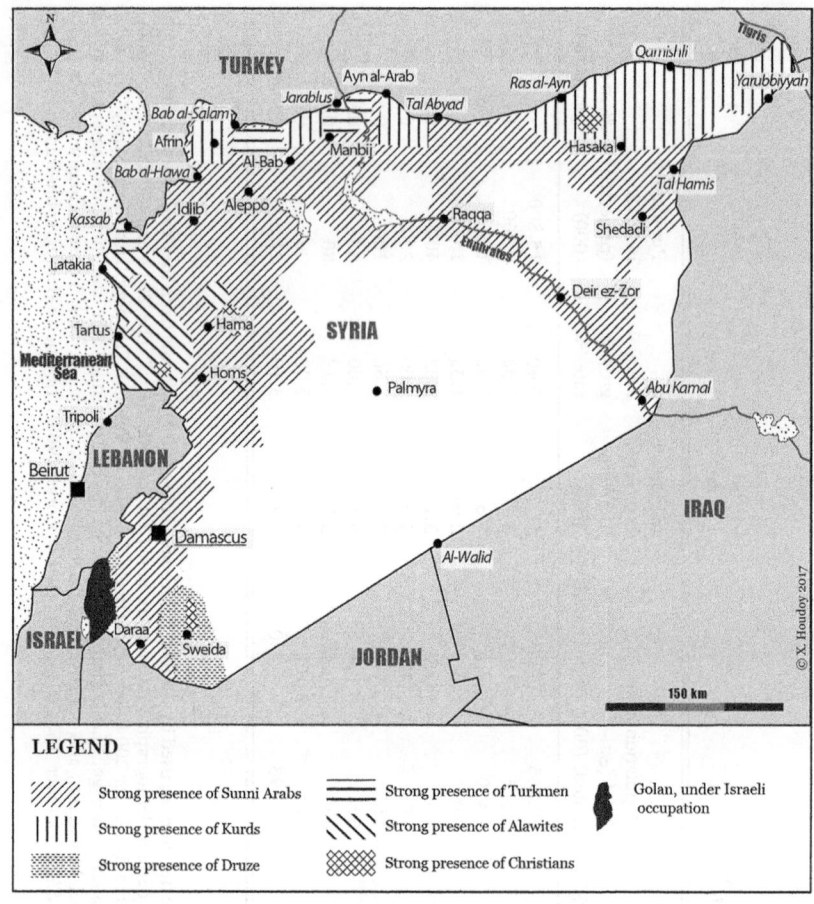

Map 1.1 Ethnic and religious distribution in Syria

social class. Among university networks and internationalized elites, social contact among different communities was fluid.[57] Sunni and Christian entrepreneurs associated freely, sharing complementary networks. However, the informal settlements housing the working classes were more homogeneous. Still, even if some areas had a dominant community, one could not truly point to any regions as belonging to one or another community. Alawites were numerous on the coast, but many Sunnis and Christians also lived there.[58] In such cases,

[57] Ali El Saleh, *op. cit.*, p. 777.
[58] Fabrice Balanche, *La region alaouite et . . .*, *op. cit.*, pp. 13–19 and p. 173.

community membership conditioned professional occupation: In Latakia and in Banias, the Alawites often populated public service functions, while the Sunnis dominated trade and industry – a situation that led to tensions.[59]

For myriad reasons, practices that were ostensibly sectarian proliferated in the decade prior to the 2011 Revolution. This was particularly evident among the Christians, who were deeply troubled by the Sunni revival in Syria and the fate of their Iraqi coreligionists. The Christian resurgence was evident in the Marian devotion of young girls or the increased attendance at church services. Religious festivals in Maaloula, tolerated by the regime, allowed for the reassertion of identity symbols such as crosses and bells as well as the consumption of alcohol.[60] Thomas Pierret highlights the increasing importance of religion among the Sunnis since the 1970s, demonstrated by the growing importance of the influential Sunni ulema.[61] However, while the practice of Ramadan spread among the Alawites, this should not be seen as an assertion of identity (Ramadan not being observed by Alawites) but as an attempt to be acknowledged as Muslim by the Sunni and Shiites. Such alignment with orthodox practices could perhaps also be an indicator of the marginalization of a religious community whose existence was not officially recognized in the schools, where Islam and Christianity are the only recognized religions for instruction.

Worries about identity closely linked to collective communitarian memories, the regional situation, and the policies of the regime translated into increased tensions that escalated into clashes in 2005 between Ismailis and Alawites in Qadmous and Massiaf or the construction of a huge concrete Christ statue to be visible from neighboring Sunni communities. A cleric explained it thus to Caroline Donati: "The Christian fears or despises the Muslim, the Alawite feels rejected by the Sunni who despises the former as still a mountain dweller, and the Ismaili feel besieged by the Alawites."[62]

However, a significant part of the ruling elite inside the Syrian regime did come from the Alawite minority. During the Ottoman period, they had been marginalized, not officially considered Muslim by either Sunnis or Shias. Following the 1963 coup, the new regime, dominated by Alawite officers, upended the hierarchy between communities, with

[59] *Ibid.*, p. 267.
[60] Sylvia Chiffoleau, "Fête et procession de Maaloula: une mise en scène des identités dans l'espace d'un village chrétien," *Revue d'études des mondes musulmans et de la Méditerranée* 115–116, 2006, pp. 176—89.
[61] Thomas Pierret, "Les oulémas: une hégémonie religieuse ébranlée par la revolution," in François Burgat and Bruno Paoli (eds.), *op. cit.*, p. 92.
[62] Caroline Donati, *op. cit.*, p. 295, see also pp. 290–298.

the result – for reasons that were not exclusively sectarian – that the regime was never fully accepted by most Sunnis, including the former Ottoman elites who had dominated post-independence Syria.[63] In addition, decade by decade, demographic changes were shrinking the regime's base: "There is a dilemma here, rarely pointed out. The communities and the regions most securely held by the regime – the Alawite coastal mountains, Jabal Druze, Golan and Damascus – in principle were the most threatened by the explosive demographics of the majority. It would not be long before the loss of demographic heft reached other areas."[64]

The regime therefore adopted a complex power-retaining strategy, based on a rapprochement between the Assad family and orthodox Islam, that saw the Alawite dominance preserved in the security area and representatives from all communities included in the power-holding clique. The Assad family had at first attempted to integrate the Alawites into the Shiite denomination. Under pressure from Syria, the Lebanese Shiite Imam Musa al-Sadr in 1973 had recognized the Alawites as Shiites.[65] Since the Syrian constitution required that the president be a Muslim, it was also a way for Hafez al-Assad to prevent having his legitimacy challenged.[66] During the 2000s, the regime had allowed Shiite proselytizing as part of a rapprochement with Iran. As a resident of Raqqa explained:

The Shia? Previously there were none in Raqqa. They were converted by the Iranians, who came in the 2000s to restore ancient shrines, the tombs of 'Ammar bin Yasser and of Uways Qarni. They lived scattered in the city suburbs. A Syrian who converted received 5,000 pounds a month, paid by Tehran. Many pilgrims from Iran went to Raqqa, they were recognizable because their wives wore an abaya [an Islamic woman's clothing article] that was different from the local one.[67]

Following the conversion of several thousand people, the Sunni religious authorities asked Assad in 2008 to stop the Shiite proselytizing.[68] At the same time, the ruling family was also affirming its religious orthodoxy – by the marriage of Bashar al-Assad to a Sunni, the ruling elite attending

[63] Elizabeth Picard, "Fin de partie en Syrie," *Revue des mondes musulmans et de la Méditerranée* 81–82, 1996, p. 207.

[64] Youssef Courbage, *op. cit.*, 2007, p. 209.

[65] Martin Karmer, "Syria's Alawis and Shi'ism," in Martin Karmer (ed.), *Shi'ism, Resistance and Revolution*, Boulder, Westview Press, 1987, p. 246–249.

[66] In the 1980s, the Muslim Brotherhood demanded that the Constitution specify the Syrian president must be Sunni, Sabrina Mervin, "Des nosayris aux ja'farites: le processus de 'chiitisation' des alaouites," in Baudouin Dupret, Zouhair Ghazzal, Youssef Mujahidin, and Mohammed al-Dbiyat (eds.), *op. cit.*, pp. 359–364.

[67] I-110, in Urfa, September 2013.

[68] Fabrice Balanche, "Le communautarisme en Syrie: lorsque le mythe devient réalité," *Confluences Méditerranée* 89, 2014, p. 38.

public prayers in Sunni mosques, a practice dating to Hafez al-Assad's reign – and by maintaining relationships with Sunni ulema.[69] Far from representing the interests of the Alawite community, the Assad family sought to marginalize Alawite clerics in favor of their own clientele.[70] The community itself, however, remained poor and benefited only marginally from Assad's accession to power. Most Alawites were employed in the lower administrative echelons and were not paid more than the other civil servants.[71]

Nevertheless, the security institutions remained in the hands of the Alawites, a community not able to betray the regime. Entrusting security to a despised minority is a standard technique of imperial or multicommunitarian regimes. To keep up the appearance of openness, Hafez and Bashar al-Assad often made Sunnis Defense Minister and Chief of Staff, the most well-known being Mustafa Tlass, an early Sunni companion of Hafez al-Assad. In the same way, Ali Mamluk saw himself successively entrusted with different leadership positions in the Syrian security services. But even though the army and security services had many Sunnis, the Alawites maintained their dominance.[72] Some Sunnis had command positions (Divisions 7 and 10 in 2011, Companies 554 and 636 of the Airborne Special Forces), but they were rather the exception, while the elite army units that protected the capital – the Special Forces Division, the Republican Guard, and the 4th Division – were in the hands of Alawites.[73] Lower-ranking Alawite officers from the Secret Services or the 4th Division often had more power than a Sunni general. In addition, the regime actively encouraged Alawite populations to settle in certain strategic Damascus suburbs.[74]

However, the regime's functioning – except for the security apparatus – was multisectarian and membership in the ruling classes was based on political solidarity or economic interest more than belonging to the Alawite community.[75] The officers who took power in 1963 came from various communities, with the Baathist ideology serving as a link among

[69] Thomas Pierret, *Religion and the State . . . op. cit.*
[70] Bruno Paoli, "Et maintenant, on va où? Les alaouites à la croisée des destins," in François Burgat and Bruno Paoli (eds.), *op. cit.*, p. 130.
[71] Fabrice Balanche, *La région alaouite . . . op. cit.*, p. 4.
[72] Caroline Donati, *op. cit.*, pp. 145–52.
[73] Through interviews with defected officers in Turkey, Hicham Bou Nassif reconstructed most of the commanding positions during Bashar al-Assad's reign. Hicham Bou Nassif, "'Second-Class': The Grievances of Sunni Officers in the Syrian Armed Forces," *Journal of Strategic Studies* 38 (5), 2015, pp. 626–649.
[74] Fabrice Balanche, "Clientélisme, communautarisme et fragmentation territoriale en Syrie," *A contrario* 11, 2009, p. 129.
[75] Bassam Haddad, "Syria's State Bourgeoisie: An Organic Backbone for the Regime," *Middle East Critique* 21 (3), 2012, pp. 231–257.

officers that transcended religious affiliation.[76] With the liberalization of the 2000s, Syrian politics continued to operate in favor of a multisectarian elite, with common economic interests replacing shared ideological beliefs.[77]

In its dealings with the various communities, the regime reinforced vertical divisions by manipulating the notables. Thus, "Christians are torn between following a clergy close to power that is ready to compromise its principles but can help them in their daily lives, or succumbing instead to a pious, populist movement."[78] As for the Druze, the regime would coopt the clan's elite and in this way establish a form of indirect rule over the predominantly Druze area of Suweida province.[79] Similarly, the Sunni tribal elites, weakened greatly by detribalization policies of the 1970s and 1980s, were either assimilated or marginalized to the profit of the notables close to the regime. North of Aleppo, for example, the most influential members of the tribes and minorities were close to the regime. Near Azaz, the notables of the large tribes (Kenlo, Derbala, Amuri, Ayubi) cooperated with the regime to protect their economic interests and access to positions of power, including the Senate for the most influential among them. "In Aleppo, the government has partnered with two tribal leaders to exercise its control. Thus, the Berris hold the security apparatus of the city, while the Shehadé have a political role that includes a seat in parliament."[80] As a further example, the tribal elites of Raqqa province, especially the Shawi, benefited significantly from the land privatization that accompanied Bashar al-Assad's taking power.[81]

The situation of the Kurds shows clearly the shadowy manipulations of the regime's identity politics.[82] By the late 1950s, the Kurds were suffering from serious discrimination due to Syrian nationalism based on Arabism to the exclusion of other ethnic groups. Thus, land reform, implemented in the rest of Syria, did not apply to Kurdish regions because it would have discriminated against Arab owners and benefited Kurdish peasants. Conversely, the government redistributed land in Kurdish regions to Arab settlers within the framework of the "Arab belt" policy

---

[76] Hanna Batatu, *op. cit.*, p. 326.
[77] Souhail Belhadj, *op. cit.*, pp. 340–343.
[78] Quoted by Caroline Donati, *op. cit.*, p. 293.
[79] Cyril Roussel, "Les grandes familles druzes entre local et national," *Revue des Mondes Musulmans et de la Méditerranée* 115–116, 2006, pp. 135–153.
[80] Caroline Donati, *op. cit.*, p. 299.
[81] Myriam Ababsa, "Contre-réforme agraire et conflits fonciers en Jazîra syrienne (2000-2005)," *Revue d'études des mondes musulmans et de la Méditerranée* 115–116, 2007, pp. 211–230.
[82] Jordi Tejel, *Syria's Kurds, History, Politics and Society*, London, Routledge, 2009.

from 1961 on.[83] The most recent example was the restriction of Kurdish property rights (Decree 49 of September 2008). In addition, political parties and associations were banned from referencing Kurdish culture. Finally, some Syrian Kurds were denied Syrian nationality under the pretext of flushing out the Turkish Kurds who had illegally crossed into the country via the Turkish-Syrian border. In 1962, the government thus lifted Syrian citizenship from over 120,000 people in the Jazeera region.[84] The Kurds had their foreign (*ajnabi*) status formalized via a red identity card. It was transmitted from parent to child, affecting hundreds of thousands of people by the late 2000s.[85] Besides being denied the vote, the stateless Kurds were precluded from owning property, managing a business, owning a passport, or holding office.

These discriminatory measures strengthen the Kurdish sense of identity,[86] but there were still obstacles to its transformation into political mobilization. First, the Kurds did not occupy a homogeneous area. Their claims could not therefore be constructed with reference to a territory.[87] They were found in pockets along the Turkish border, several villages north of Aleppo, and in several districts in the cities of Aleppo and Damascus. The Kurdish character of certain areas, the Jazeera, Ayn al-Arab (Kobane), and Afrin, was unquestionable but they were too small and distant from each other to allow for a separatist strategy. In addition, the overwhelmingly Kurdish districts within Aleppo and Damascus (home to most Syrian Kurds) were contained within a predominantly Arab environment.

Faced with the regime's crackdown, the increasingly isolated Kurdish parties were forced into exile. A party like the Syrian branch of KDP (Kurdistan Democratic Party – Partiya Demokrat a Kurdistane), created in 1957, might operate underground but had little influence inside Syria. "In the 2000s, the political parties have never really supported us," explained a politically unaffiliated Syrian Kurdish protester. "They were not on the ground in Syria, and even from outside, they urged us to show restraint and refused to help us, to keep from antagonizing the regime."[88] The regime would instrumentalize Kurdish figures, notably clerics from religious brotherhoods, such as Ahmed Kuftaro, the Grand Mufti of the Republic (1964–2004), and Muhammed Sa'id Ramadan al-Buti. The regime also recruited certain Kurds into the military, notably into the Presidential Guard, and

---

[83] This policy aimed at settling Arab Syrians in the Northern borderland to control these areas and prevent the formation of a Kurdish homogeneous region.

[84] Jordi Tejel, *Syria's Kurds, History . . . op. cit.*, p. 50.

[85] *Ibid.*, p. 51.

[86] *Ibid.*, p. 59.

[87] Cyril Roussel, "La construction d'un territoire kurde en Syrie: un processus en cours," *Maghreb-Machrek* 213 (3), 2012, pp. 83–98.

[88] I-5, in Erbil, December 2012.

used Kurdish militias against the Muslim Brotherhood in 1980 in Aleppo and in 1982 in Hama.[89]

The regime manipulated the PKK to monitor Syrian Kurds and to destabilize Turkey. After leaving Turkey in 1979, the leadership of the party was based in Syria until the late 1990s. At that time, Syrian Kurdish organizations faced severe repression, but the PKK was free to recruit Syrian Kurds with the proviso that they would not act inside Syria itself.[90] The presence of the PKK and its collaboration with the regime made any significant mobilization of Syrian Kurds difficult. "The PKK was working hand in hand with the regime. Instead of doing your military service for the Syrian state, you could serve within the ranks of the PKK. If someone was opposed to the regime, it was the PKK who denounced him and had him arrested."[91]

In 1998, bowing to pressure from Turkey, Hafez al-Assad expelled Abdullah Öcalan, the leader of the PKK, at the same time as the Syrian security services dismantled the PKK's structures in Syria and arrested hundreds of militants. Despite the creation of a Syrian branch under the name PYD (Partiya Yekitiya Demokrat, Democratic Union Party) by 2003, the PKK was losing influence. This led to a renewed mobilization among the Kurdish population. The protest, which started in Qamishli, is emblematic of the rise of Kurdish protests in 2004. Faced with Kurdish demonstrators demanding civil rights, Damascus could stop the movement only with a brutal crackdown that resulted in dozens of deaths. The regime also relied on recently settled Arabs in Kurdish regions to attack protesters that were accused of holding separatist ambitions backed by the West.[92] In opposing the regime, Kurdish protesters remained isolated with demands that did not resonate with the Arab population.[93] Mobilization was confined to certain Kurdish localities in the Jazeera, in eastern Syria, where security forces were sparser. In Damascus and Aleppo, the regime easily controlled demonstrations that originated in Kurdish neighborhoods. "In 2004 we stood alone against the regime. I was a supporter of the Patriotic Union of Kurdistan (PUK, Yekitiya Nistimani Kurdistane), but the party did not help us. Our mobilization was spontaneous, without organization. With

---

[89] Jordi Tejel, "Les Kurdes de Syrie, de la 'dissimulation' à la 'visibilité'?" *Revue des mondes musulmans et de la Méditerranée* 115–116, 2006, pp.117–133.

[90] It is estimated that between 7,000 and 10,000 Syrian Kurds were killed in the confrontations with the Turkish army, Jordi Tejel, *Syria's Kurds, History . . . op. cit.*, p. 67.

[91] I-6, a Syrian Kurdish militant, in Erbil, January 2012.

[92] Jordi Tejel, *Syria's Kurds, History . . . op. cit.*, p. 126.

[93] Jordi Tejel, "La jeunesse kurde entre rupture et engagement militant," in Baudouin Dupret, Zouhair Ghazzal, Youssef Mujahidin, and Mohammed al-Dbiyat (eds.), *op. cit.*, p. 270.

friends, we went down into the streets to protest."[94] While Kurdish demonstrations failed, they did, however, foreshadow the 2011 movement by their spontaneous nature, the absence of political groupings, and the difficulty the regime had in maintaining control in peripheral areas. Prior to 2011, the regime had created vertical social divisions to avoid widespread protest and had used selected communitarian relays to ensure it remained in control.

A Depoliticized Society

From its inception, the Baathist regime systematically monitored the population, and any form of dissent was brutally and immediately suppressed. Dwindling resources and demographic changes had progressively weakened the system: While the Syria of 2011 was effectively a police state, it was hindered by its own lack of resources. Starting in the 1980s, the state had left certain urban and rural areas under-administered. The Aleppo governorate had less than one police officer per five hundred inhabitants.[95] The situation was worse in the informal neighborhood of Salahaddin (population 100,000) in Aleppo city, which did without a single police station. Similarly, "in our [al-Sukari] neighborhood, there were very few security forces. We had about 40 police officers and 50 to 100 auxiliaries per 300,000 inhabitants."[96] The town of Maraa had roughly fifty police officers for more than 40,000 inhabitants, less than one police officer per thousand.[97]

The security services had two major functions: the control of institutions and the elimination of dissent. On the one hand, the multiplicity of security agencies each monitoring the other was to prevent a *coup d'Etat* by preventing a concentration of power. On the other hand, almost the entire state apparatus was involved in spying on the population to forestall a mobilization, mainly by using *mukhtars* (the representative of the state at the local level).[98] In buildings, the security services invariably enlisted the caretakers for spying on the residents.[99] By working in this fashion, the

---

[94] I-6, in Erbil, January 2012. The PUK, the Patriotic Union of Kurdistan (Yeketiya Nistimani Kurdistane), was founded in 1975 in Syria by Iraqi Kurds.

[95] The governorate had 9,000 police officers for 4.7 to 4.8 million residents in 2011 (our projection of the 2004 census figures, based on the annual growth rate). For the police figures, interview with former regime police officers, in Aleppo, January 2013.

[96] I-7, in Aleppo, December 2012.

[97] I-8, in Maraa, December 2012.

[98] The one in Aleppo's Bab al-Qadim district denounced the protesters; he was condemned to six months in prison by the Free Syrian Army after the district was taken by the FSA in September 2012. I-9, in Aleppo, August 2013.

[99] I-10, in Gaziantep, September 2013.

regime bought repression on the cheap.[100] Similarly, torture and disappearances were used strategically to send a stark warning to anyone contemplating resistance and to dissuade them from taking individual action.[101]

To stifle any kind of opposition, the regime strove to destroy, control, or coopt all key actors – unions, tribes, ulemas, and intellectuals – with any potential for mobilizing the population. This resulted in weakening these and other fields institutionally, leaving them with little independence vis-à-vis the ruling clique. The internal logic in various fields (cultural, economic, religious) was permanently biased by political or security considerations. Proximity to the intelligence services bestowed more influence than could any position within the official institutional hierarchy. For example, the principal of a school in Maraa was obliged to accommodate himself to the school janitor, who was well connected with the party and security services.[102] Even within the Baath party, the support of one of the security institutions was essential to getting promoted. The net effect, even before the crisis of spring 2011, was that Syrians were leading their daily lives in a context of weakened institutions undermined by the security apparatus and patronage networks.

However, starting in the 1990s, the regime's economic weakness significantly undermined its control of the population. Certain fields – religious, cultural, civil society – increased their autonomy, both in daily operations and with respect to their internal organization. During the 2000s, several researchers countered the perception of an all-powerful regime by endeavoring to depict the degree of autonomy enjoyed by the ulama and certain civil society organizations. This same observed condition – functional autonomy coupled with tight control – applied in the cultural field.[103] Cécile Boëx shows how intellectuals, entangled with the regime, could up to a point "criticize the political order through their art"

---

[100] Jordi Tejel, "Les Kurdes de Syrie ..." *op. cit.*
[101] See the numerous prisoner reports: Moustafa Khalifé, *La Coquille. Prisonnier politique en Syrie*, Paris, Actes Sud, 2007; Aram Karabet, *Treize ans dans les prisons syriennes. Voyage vers l'inconnu*, Actes Sud, 2013.
[102] I-11, with a Maraa resident, in Maraa, December 2012. In the same way, Belhadj relates the example of a senior civil servant who feared "his personal secretary or the young courier on his floor or even the colleague he talks with every day," Souhail, Belhadj, *op. cit.*, pp. 318–319.
[103] Thomas Pierret, *Religion and the State ... op. cit.*; Mathieu Le Saux, "Les dynamiques contradictoires du Shamp associatif syrien," *Revue des mondes musulmans et de la Méditerranée* 115–116, 2006, pp. 193–209; and Laura Ruiz de Elvira Carrascal, "State/Charities Relation in Syria: between Reinforcement, Control and Coercion," in Laura Ruiz de Elvira Carrascal and Tina Zintl (eds.), *Civil Society and the State in Syria: The Outsourcing of Social Responsibility*, Boulder, Lynne Rienner, 2012; Cécile Boëx, "The End of the State Monopoly over Culture: Toward the Commodification of Cultural and Artistic Production," *Middle East Critique* 20 (2), 2011, pp. 139–155.

but were "essentially pawns in a strategy that avoided any direct confrontation with the government."[104] To paraphrase Fawwaz Haddad, a
Syrian writer may be freer in his novels than outside them,[105] but, as
Caroline Donati concludes, while "[...] the artists produce original work
of high quality, it is rarely subversive, and they are ultimately controlled
by their paymasters that are invariably from, or related to, the regime."[106]

The religious field had the most autonomy, because the regime could
not interfere in the education of the ulama and, ever since the Islamic
awakening, religious leaders negotiated from a position of strength.[107] As
Thomas Pierret explains, "the religious field is managed by the State for
purely 'negative' reasons. That is, it is focused on neutralizing security
threats which could derive from it."[108] Thus, Sheikh Ibrahim al-Salqini, a
member of a large family of ulama and close to the Muslim Brotherhood
in the 1970s, could be the Mufti of Aleppo in 2011.[109] Furthermore, as
we have seen, Bashar al-Assad sought to project himself as Sunni to the
public. In the 2000s, clerics were gaining influence in education, charitable works, and the media. By exploiting the social capital of the ulama
and financed by private entrepreneurs, the Zayd foundation became the
largest charitable organization in Damascus and managed to negotiate a
certain degree of autonomy.[110] Despite this, after 2008, Bashar al-Assad's
regime would tighten its control over the religious field. Educational institutes directly controlled by the regime were created, and several religious
leaders who had dared criticize the regime were jailed, among them the son
of the former Grand Mufti Salah al-Din Kuftaro.[111] How effective this
strategy was became evident by the time of the protests in 2011: Most of the
important sheikhs and imams from the mosques were now closely collaborating with the security apparatus.

The regime had succeeded in producing a depoliticized society in which
political organizations were disconnected from the rest of society. This
created a gulf between the authorities – designated as they were by an opaque
process – and the population. The elections in Syria were a formality, not a

[104] Cecil Boëx, "Mobilisations d'artistes dans le mouvement de révolte en Syrie: modes
d'action et limites de l'engagement," in Amin Allal and Thomas Pierret, *Au cœur des
révolutions arabes: devenir révolutionnaire*, Paris, Armand Colin, 2013, pp. 87–112.
[105] Max Weiss, "Who Laughs Last: Literary Transformation of Syrian Authoritarianism,"
in Steven Heydemann and Reinoud Leenders (eds.), *op. cit.*, 2013, p. 152.
[106] Caroline Donati, *op. cit.*, p. 346.
[107] Thomas Pierret, *Religion and the State ... op. cit.*
[108] See Thomas Pierret, *Les oulémas syriens aux XXe-XXIe siècles*, Thesis, Sciences Po Paris
– UCL, 2009, p. 78.
[109] Thomas Pierret, "Syrie: l'islam dans la révolution," *Politique étrangère* 4, 2011, p. 886.
[110] Thomas Pierret and Kjetil Selvik, *op. cit.*
[111] Thomas Pierret, "The State Management of Religion in Syria," in Steven Heydemann
and Reinoud Leenders (eds.), *op. cit.*, p. 99-101.

real competition for office, the Baath party allies being mere satellites offering no political alternatives. "In January 2011, just before the revolution," confides a resident of Aleppo, "the mayor of Aleppo was suddenly changed, without anyone knowing why. But this type of event was not unusual; the political system was closed in on itself, and the people had very little information about its leaders."[112]

Moreover, the Baathist regime had in effect eliminated independent political movements. The repression was particularly successful, since, on the eve of the protest movement of 2011, no organized political opposition existed in Syria. After the repression of the 1980s, the Muslim Brotherhood and the left-leaning parties were marginalized.[113] Also, the Kurdish protest in 2004 had served only to reveal the weakness of Syrian Kurdish parties.[114] How ineffective the dissident movements inside Syria were became apparent with the "Damascus Declaration" of 2005, a document worked up by a platform of intellectuals, dissidents, and political parties which, however well-represented it was abroad, merely called for regime opening.

The inability of the institutional actors to lead any form of protest had two consequences: high initial costs for the protesters and the rapid spread of the unrest due to a lack of representatives able to articulate sectorial, negotiable demands.

---

[112] I-12, in Aleppo, January 2013.
[113] Elizabeth Picard, op. cit., 1996, p. 221.
[114] Jordi Tejel, Syria's Kurds, History ... op. cit., p. 85.

2 A Revolution of Anonyms

On March 13, 2011, fifteen teenagers from Daraa, a city in southern Syria, were tortured by intelligence services for having scrawled anti-regime graffiti. Peaceful protests that followed in the city spread quickly across much of the country. These demonstrations raise a series of questions: Why would people take to the streets when the authorities were known to shoot into crowds? How are protests organized given the ubiquitous police surveillance? How to interpret the universalist, inclusive slogans and participation by both ethnic and religious minorities in the marches, despite the supposed sectarian nature of Syrian society?

In Search of a Theory

A first set of tentative explanations for the protests focuses on community tensions and deteriorating economic conditions against a background of uncontrolled population growth. Fabrice Balanche supports the idea that unanswered popular demands set off the demonstrations. The unequal allocation of resources between ethnic and religious groups in a deteriorating economy heightened already prevalent communal tensions. This is how the author of "Geography of the Revolt" reduces the movement in the spring of 2011 to a mobilization of peripheral Arab Sunni areas against the Alawite community: "The territories that revolted are exclusively Sunni, and, more specifically, when cross-referenced with the ethnic criterion: namely Sunni Arabs, comprising the largest community."[1]

Two important misconceptions make this a dubious interpretation: First, the identity of the protesters is derived from the geographical location of the marches, and second, the nature of the claims is deduced from the putative identity of the demonstrators. However, as our interviews made clear, people often protested outside their home areas, making the link between demonstrator identity and the protest rally locations a tenuous one at best. Moreover, neighborhoods are rarely homogeneous,

---

[1] Fabrice Balanche, "Géographie de la révolte ... *op.cit.*, p. 444.

which introduces additional uncertainty. If sectarian dynamics were initially dominant, how was it that Kurdish and Christian youth came to participate in protests in the governorate of Aleppo, and Kurds would rally in the east and Druzes in the south of Syria?[2]

The other part of this interpretation – that protesters belonged essentially to marginalized populations – needs nuancing. The protesters were far from being a throng of poor Sunnis. Children of the bourgeoisie of Aleppo, Damascus, and Homs participated and, in many instances, played a crucial role in organizing the protests. Furthermore, Daraa province, where the protests began, was well represented among the ruling elites and had benefited from considerable investment by the State. Finally, by ignoring the claims of the protesters – termed an "ideological smokescreen" by the author – this analysis strips all subjectivity from the actors in favor of objectivistic explanations, whereby grievances automatically result in ethnic and sectarian mobilization.[3]

This interpretation implicitly refers to Relative Deprivation Theory. This approach has been criticized in the past for lacking criteria for defining the threshold where frustration triggers mobilization.[4] Indeed, it fails to explain why individuals mobilized *at this specific time*. The economico-sectarian hypothesis also fails to analyze the protest itself: the deliberations, the emergence of a new narrative, the creation of specific resources. It thus stymies an understanding of the Syrian revolution's trajectory.

Nor will Resource Mobilization Theory explain the Syrian events.[5] On the eve of the revolution, as it were, no group had the requisite resources for organizing a movement against the government. The few remaining dissidents were either in prison or in exile; institutions were closely surveilled. What Elizabeth Picard found in 2005 retains validity: "Looking into the

---

[2] For the Kurdish mobilizations, see Chapter 8, as well as Arthur Quesnay and Cyril Roussel, "Avec qui se battre ? Le dilemme kurde," in François Burgat and Bruno Paoli (eds.) *op. cit.* Despite the mobilizations being limited in the Druze regions, the Druzes protested in corteges of several hundred individuals, see Cyril Roussel, *Les Druzes du Liban et de Syrie*, Gallimard, Paris, forthcoming.

[3] Fabrice Balanche, "Géographie de la révolte ... *op.cit.*, pp. 437–438.

[4] Ted Gurr, *Why Men Rebel*, Princeton, Princeton University Press, 1970. There are other versions of such socioeconomic explanations. Francesca de Châtel highlights the discontentment caused by the regime's bad management of the 2006–2010 drought without ever explaining why and how this discontentment led to a mobilization, Francesca de Châtel, "The Role of Drought and Climate Change in the Syrian Insurgency: Untangling the Triggers of the Revolution," *Middle Eastern Studies* 50 (4), 2014, pp. 521–535.

[5] Joel Beinin and Frédéric Vairel affirm that Resource Mobilisation Theory is not applicable for all Arab revolutions, "Introduction: The Middle East and North Africa Beyond Classical Social Movement Theory," in Joel Beinin and Frederic Vairel (eds.), *Social movements, Mobilization, and Contestation in the Middle East and North Africa, Second Edition*, Stanford, Stanford University Press, 2013, p. 9.

civil society, secularist intellectual milieux, and the Islamist movement, one must conclude that, even when combined with external pressure and in a context of economic crisis, societal dynamics struggled to bring about democratic change in Syria."[6] The few organizations that did call for protest played only marginal roles and cannot be conceived of as responsible for the initial upsurge of protest. Syrian demonstrations, therefore, fall into a category of mobilizations without mobilizers, like the events in Iran in 1979 and East Germany in 1989.

The two major approaches often used to explain this type of mobilization, Moral Shock and Rational Choice Theory (RCT), cannot be applied here either, as much because of their intrinsic limitations rather than because of the specific Syrian situation. The continual references to the Daraa incident do tempt us to consider James Jasper's Moral Shock theory as an explanation for the protests.[7] However, it also does not explain why the protests occurred at that specific moment. While the Daraa incident sparked outrage and was shared on social media – a novelty in Syria – the torture of fifteen teenagers did not radically alter the way the Syrian people thought about the regime after decades of repression.[8] If so, the Syrian case merely confirms the weakness of a potentially circular argument that makes it difficult to specify at what moment outrage, i.e., "moral shock," rises to such a level that it leads to mobilization.[9] In addition, the role the Daraa events played in triggering protests at a national level needs to be relativized. The Daraa graffiti were part of a series of low-profile protests, ignored by the media, which shows that mobilization was already underway by March 2011. In the context of a repressive regime like this, any public expression of an opinion in fact was an act of protest pointing to an underlying opposition to the regime.

[6] Elizabeth Picard, "Syrie: la coalition autoritaire fait de la résistance," *Politique étrangère* 4, 2005, p. 762.

[7] James Jasper, *The Art of Moral Protest*, Chicago, The University of Chicago Press, 1997, p. 106. Jasper defines Moral Shock as follows: "An unexpected event or piece of information [which] raises such a sense of outrage in a person that she becomes inclined toward political action, with or without the network of personal contacts emphasized in mobilization and process theories."

[8] See Raphaël Lefevre, *Ashes of Hama: The Muslim Brotherhood in Syria*, London, Hurst, 2013.

[9] Ruud Koopmans, Jan W. Duyvendak, "The Political Construction of the Nuclear Energy Issue and its Impact on the Mobilization of Anti-Nuclear Movements in Western Europe," *Social Problems* 42 (2), 1995, pp. 235–251; Francesca Polletta and Edwin Amenta, "Second that Emotion? Lessons from Once-Novel Concepts in Social Movement Research," in Jeff Goodwin, James M. Jasper, and Francesca Polletta (eds.), *Passionate Politics: Emotions and Social Movements*, Chicago, The University of Chicago Press, 2001, pp. 307–308; Christophe Traïni, "From Feelings to Emotions (and Back Again): How Does One Become an Animal Rights Activist?" *Revue française de science politique* 60 (2), 2010, pp. 335–338.

In principle, RCT could also account for the mobilization, but it must contend with a *prima facies* aporia. How is it possible that individuals motivated by the public good take to the streets when the risks they incur (torture, murder) are so high? The individual, as modelled by RCT, has no incentive to protest when suppression presents such risks. In this theoretical framework, the free rider paradox is even more inescapable given the absence of demonstrably selective incentives.[10] In fact, the first individuals to rise in protest were not linked to any institutions that would significantly alter the cost/benefit calculus of the contemplated actions.

To solve the free rider paradox, Mark Granovetter, building on RCT, game theory, and the work of Thomas Schelling,[11] advances Critical Mass Theory (CMT).[12] It holds that the derivative benefits that an individual calculates from his commitment result directly from choices others make. Each person has a predetermined threshold for participating, estimated as the point where the number of demonstrators sufficiently diminishes the cost of his own engagement and makes success likely enough for him to participate. Such successive individual commitments can snowball into massive and unexpected demonstrations. As the thresholds vary from individual to individual, they can make mobilizations susceptible to rapid, unpredictable acceleration.

CMT has been used to explain mobilizations in Iran and East Germany. Timur Kuran builds his analysis of these events on a reduction in the political cost accounted for by the increased number of protesters, each of whom now could express publicly his previously concealed dissatisfaction.[13] Susanne Lohmann generalizes Kuran's assumptions by modelling individual commitment as a signaling game: "The status quo becomes unsustainable when mass protest activities reveal information about its malign nature and lack of public support."[14] By this logic, information regarding the

---

[10] Mancur Olson, *The Logic of Collective Action: Public Goods and The Theory of Groups*, Cambridge, Harvard University Press, 1971. The free rider paradox involves (in absence of individual incitement) acting when the goods called for are public and when an individual's participation does not have a notable influence on the chances of success: A rational individual will therefore refrain from protesting and will in the end benefit from the mobilization's success.

[11] Thomas C. Shelling, "Hockey Helmets, Concealed Weapons, and Daylight Saving: A Study of Binary Choices with Externalities," *The Journal of Conflict Resolution* 17 (3), 1973, pp. 381–428.

[12] Mark Granovetter, "Threshold Models of Collective Behavior," *American Journal of Sociology* 83 (6), 1978, pp. 1420–1443.

[13] Timur Kuran, *Private Truths, Public Lies: The Social Consequences of Preference Falsification*, Cambridge, Harvard University Press, 1997.

[14] Susanne Lohmann, "The Dynamics of Informational Cascade: The Monday Demonstrations in Leipzig, East Germany, 1989–1991," *World Politics* 47 (1), 1994, p. 49.

regime, previously diffuse and imperceptible in a passive population, erupts and triggers a cascade of mobilizations.

CMT appears to be an *ad hoc* theory that is maladapted for the Syrian case and which breaks from RCT postulates at two key junctures. On the one hand, even if the decisive role is given to the first demonstrators, their behavior is this model's *lacuna*. Granovetter and then Lohmann both assume the existence of "extremist" individuals, defined by their propensity to engage regardless of the cost of their actions and the involvement of others. This category has little relevance for our case: The Syrians taking to the streets to demonstrate for the first time, in a country where public protest was extremely rare, would not qualify as "extremists" in Lohmann's definition. They were not members of any political organization. Leaving unexplained the process by which the first demonstrators engaged, CMT does not deal adequately with the genesis of the protests. More generally, it is hard to fathom how the behavior of these so-called extremist individuals could be framed as motivated by self-interest.

On the other hand, additional protesters can join the movement once the perceived risks are lower. However, if such behavior presupposes an individual who evaluates risks and opportunities, it does not require any assumption as to the altruistic nature of his or her objectives. In other words, an individual can commit himself once the risks have diminished but still do so in the name of universalist values and common interests. Eventually, RCT's hypotheses on the self-interest of individuals are an insurmountable obstacle to any explanation of the mobilization.

Finally, CMT assumes that individual motivations remain stable, an idea contradicted by empirical research on the Iranian and East German revolutions, as well as by our own research.[15] In the Iranian revolution, for instance, Kurzman highlights the variance in individual thresholds of engagement between 1977 and 1979, depending on their assessment of the movement's viability.[16] Public engagement does not merely reveal existing preferences; it transforms them and consequently changes the protesters' objectives.

Reinoud Leender's works constitute one of the most thought-provoking analyses by insisting on the role that the density of tribal and criminal networks play in setting off and spreading mobilizations.[17] However, his

---

[15] Charles Kurzman, *op. cit.*; Karl-Dieter Opp, Christiane Gern, Peter Voss, *Origins of a Spontaneous Revolution: East Germany, 1989*, Ann Arbor, University of Michigan Press, 1996.

[16] Charles Kurzman, *op. cit.*, p. 133.

[17] Reinoud Leenders, "Collective Action and Mobilization in Dar'a: An Anatomy of the Onset of Syria's Popular Insurgency," *Mobilization* 17 (4), 2012, pp. 419–434; see also Reinoud Leenders and Steven Heydemann, "Popular Mobilization in Syria: Opportunity and Threat, and the Social Networks of the Early Risers," *Mediterranean Politics* 17 (2), 2011, pp. 139–159.

interpretation, which concatenates RMT and CMT, poses a series of problems. First, the author thinks that Idlib, Deir ez-Zor, Homs, and Daraa, four of the most "tribalized" of Syria's regions, make up the strongest and earliest mobilization areas. He bases these hypotheses on the number of suppressions between March and June 2011: 70 percent of those killed came from 21 percent of the population.[18] However, the regional variations he points to cannot be taken as approximating the level of mobilization, and – besides their unreliability – they are linked to a repression concentrated on Sunni Arabs. Moreover, the social networks the author cites are not clearly defined: The criminal statistics serve to prove the existence of social networks linked to these activities, tribal affiliations would compel individuals to demonstrate, but how the decisions are made is not described. Ultimately, in our opinion, the question of the *early risers* is not decisive. In fact, the idea that without Daraa there would have been no mobilization is tenuous, because the demonstrations started several days apart in different parts of the country and, in the case of Damascus, even before the one in Daraa. Along the same lines, the sharing of the Daraa images in the rest of the country counters the idea of the tribal networks as being key to the mobilizations. The author implicitly recognizes this (p. 142) when he writes that the transformation of the opportunities at Daraa results from the withdrawal of the security forces so they could manage the growing problems in the rest of the country: *a mobilization therefore is already under way.* Still, where social networks were dense, mainly due to the persistence of tribal solidarity, trust-based groups could include a greater number of people, the clan affiliations guaranteeing some degree of loyalty. Per our interviews in the provinces of Raqqa and Deir ez-Zor, the clan networks did indeed facilitate the formation of larger protest groups.[19] Whatever the theoretical framework and the available data, what is striking is the almost universal absence of political parties, associations, major cultural figures, or tribes during the initial stages of the movement.[20]

Thus, it would seem that the Syrian mobilization was highly improbable. Why would individuals, barely politicized, without any mobilizing structure, decide to stand up to such a violent and repressive regime? The mobilization can be explained by what happened outside Syria: The "Arab Spring" led Syrians to believe that they had a window of

---

[18] Reinoud Leenders and Steven Heydemann, *op. cit.*, p. 149

[19] I-27, in Urfa, September 2013.

[20] Donatella Della Porta, *op. cit.* The chapter dealing with Syria (pp. 237–268) in comparison with Libya, Romania, and Albania illustrates the difficulties in talking about the Syrian case. Della Porta overlooks the peaceful phase of the 2011 Syrian protests, inexplicable in the framework of Resource Mobilisation Theory. She focuses, through retrospective bias, on the transition to civil war with the appearance of collective actors.

opportunity. However, these events had an effect only because of deliberations that took place in semi-private spaces. Finally, the repertoire of contention is the product of the constraints imposed by the regime and of the meaning that the protesters themselves attached to their engagement.

The Impact of the Arab Spring

Just like other revolutionary contagions – the Spring of Nations in 1848 and the collapse of the Soviet bloc – the Syrian population saw the "Arab Spring" as a window of opportunity. The events took place in an "Arab public space" that formed a commonality of political regimes and destinies.[21] All the eyewitness accounts we collected show the passion with which the Syrians followed the events: "The revolutions in Tunisia, Egypt and Yemen unfolded like a dream for us! When Tripoli fell, I said to myself that it's possible! That we also had a chance against Bashar in Syria! The impossible became possible!"[22]

The "Arab Spring" category, created jointly by the media and the protesters, helped the Syrians identify the regime with the overthrown Arab regimes. The international media, including France 24, BBC, Al Jazeera,[23] and Al Arabiya, had a key role in this process. Their characterization of the authoritarian regimes as predatory, typified by leader worship and the organized corruption of the ruling clan, made it easy to identify the Syrian regime with those in Egypt and Tunisia. The overthrows one after the other of Zine al-Abedine Ben Ali, Hosni Mubarak, Muammar Gaddafi, and Ali Abdallah Saleh created a perception that the Syrian regime was heading for a fall as well. Even though it minimizes the significant differences between the regimes,[24] this category was performative and played a decisive role in getting individuals to commit: "The more information we received about the events taking place elsewhere, the more our protests seemed realistic."[25]

---

[21] Michel Camau, "L'exception autoritaire ou l'improbable point d'Archimède de la politique dans le monde arabe," in Élisabeth Picard (ed.), *La politique dans le monde arabe*, Paris, Armand Colin, 2006, pp. 29–54.

[22] I-13, in al-Bab, December 2012.

[23] Al Jazeera played a role in triggering the Syrian movement by publishing images of the Tunisian, Egyptian, Yemenite, and Libyan revolutions. But paradoxically, as the Qatari regime was allied with Bashar al-Assad, it did not broadcast images of the first Syrian protests. It was not until Qatar's turnaround, owing especially to the scale of repression, that Al Jazeera was seen to establish itself as the main channel showing images of the protests. In response, the Syrian regime banned its correspondents from travelling; the Internet and mobile phones then made it possible for the channel to obtain news and images from across Syria.

[24] Michel Camau, "Un printemps arabe? L'émulation protestataire et ses limites," *L'année du Maghreb* 8, 2012, pp. 27–47.

[25] I-13, in al-Bab, December 2012.

Here, it behooves us to reflect on Charles Kurzman's analysis of the Iranian revolution: "This appearance of stability was self-fulfilling: if people expected protest to fail, only the courageous or foolhardy would participate. With such small numbers, protests could not fail to fail. So long as revolution remained 'unthinkable', it remained undoable. It could come to pass only when wide numbers of people began to 'think the unthinkable.'"[26]

With the fall of Ben Ali in January 2011, the regime began to anticipate protests by either forestalling incidents or tightening repression. In March, security forces were torturing teenagers in Daraa, while a month earlier, on February 17 in the Hamidiyya Suq of Damascus, the Interior Minister was publicly apologizing for police violence.[27] In addition, Bashar al-Assad actively sought to distance himself from regimes beset by popular protests. As he told the Wall Street Journal on January 31, 2011 "If you want to talk about Tunisia and Egypt, we are outside of this; at the end we are not Tunisians and we are not Egyptians."[28]

From the end of January, the Arab Spring provoked a level of engagement and public expression that would have been unthinkable a few weeks earlier. Some imams from Damascus and Homs, under the guise of preaching against Ben Ali and Mubarak, delivered a veiled criticism of the regime that the public understood perfectly well. The Facebook page "The Syrian Revolution 2011" was created on January 18.[29] In Damascus, on January 31, some hundred Syrian opponents demonstrated in Arnous Square with candles and placards bearing the words "Yes to freedom" (Naʿam lil-hurriyya).[30] On February 17, an altercation between a police officer and a merchant in the Hamidiyya Suq of Damascus triggered a demonstration against police violence.[31] In Aleppo, in February, a man posted on Facebook that he intended to immolate himself like the Tunisian Mohamed Tarek Bouazizi.[32] Another Aleppo man went every Friday to Saadallah al-Jabri Square, hoping to find other protesters there to join in occupying that public space.[33] Simultaneously, calls to protest multiplied across social networks.[34] On March 15 and 16, Syrians demonstrated in

---

[26] Charles Kurzman, *The Unthinkable Revolution in Iran*, Cambridge, Harvard University Press, 2005, p. 172.

[27] For the events in Daraa in detail, see Reinoud Leenders, *op. cit.*, p. 421. For the case of Hamidiyya Suq in Damascus, see Leila Vignal, "Jours tranquilles à Damas. Aperçus de la révolte syrienne," *Esprit* 6, 2011, pp. 94–102.

[28] "Interview with Syrian president Bachar al-Assad," *Wall Street Journal*, January 31, 2011.

[29] www.facebook.com/Syrian.Revolution, viewed December 2014, see appendix 2.

[30] Fabrice Balanche, "La Syrie entre révolution, guerre civile et statu quo," in Linda Gardelle (eds.), *Un "printemps arabe?"* Paris, L'Harmattan, 2013, p. 103.

[31] I-14 and I-15, in Istanbul, September 2013.

[32] I-16, in Aleppo, August 2013.

[33] I-17, in Aleppo, August 2013.

[34] Leila Vignal, *op. cit.*, p. 99.

Damascus despite a crackdown by the security forces.[35] The first protests of any size, on March 18, a Friday, showed that protest was possible or, in the words of another Aleppan, "revolution became thinkable."[36]

The Deliberations

Which analytical approach then best explains both the genesis of the events and their subsequent development? As we see it, the explanation lies in a pattern of "mobilization by deliberation."

The mobilization phase began in early 2011 with informal meetings in which the Arab revolutions were the main topic. The simple act of meeting to discuss current events was considered a crime in Syria and already indicated a degree of political commitment. These discussions were therefore held in semi-private spaces (small groups, Internet chat rooms) that provided a degree of safety. A young female protester from Aleppo explains, "I was overwhelmed by the revolutions, but my mother, who I was close to, told me straight away who I could speak to, which cousin was dangerous or not."[37] A young man from Aleppo, owner of a small web development business, installed a television set on his business premises in order to trigger discussions and get a sense of his employees' views.[38]

The deliberations were of strategic importance because they were simultaneously a venue for exchanging information, to calculate risks and benefits, and to discuss the revolutionary agenda. The constant evaluation of the contexts of action, the emotional intensity, and the definition of a common good fed on each other. This model also helps to understand how informal groups, over months, turned into activist networks.

These nonroutine social contexts affected the probability of engagement in two ways: hypercalculation and group dynamics. Initially, actions proposed created uncertainty, which had the effect of increasing both the time and energy invested in the discussions prior to proceeding. People scrutinized the consequences of their actions because the institutional routines, which would have reduced uncertainty at the individual level, had either weakened or disappeared. The desire to minimize risk did not, however, eliminate blunders, given the extreme uncertainty and inexperience of the activists. Next, the discussions within smaller groups encouraged more risk-taking.[39] This could in part explain the initial decisions,

---

[35] Communication with Felix Legrand, September 2014.
[36] I-18, in Aleppo, January 2013.
[37] I-19, in Aleppo, August 2013.
[38] I-17, in Aleppo, August 2013.
[39] James A. Stoner, *A Comparison of Individual and Group Decisions Involving Risk*, unpublished master's dissertation, Cambridge, MIT, 1961.

when the risks were high and the protesters were not certain if they would have grass roots support.

Moral Grammar and Universal Values

In these semi-private deliberation spaces, the stakeholders would also define the meaning of the conflict, often borrowing themes and arguments from the Tunisian and Egyptian revolutions. These exchanges helped build a collective view on legitimate means and the nature of the demands. First, the demands were national, universalistic, and inclusive, transcending local and community affiliations. The moral and political slogans and symbols, as well as a rejection of socioeconomic concessions by the regime, suggest that the protesters were engaged in a struggle that surpassed, at least temporarily, ethnic, religious, and social divides. Personal or group interests faded before collective, relatively abstract goals. Second, deliberations bearing on the aims of the protest were inextricably linked to the decisions about means. The reference to the "Arab Spring" also implies the choice to demonstrate peacefully, a choice that protestors adhered to despite months of violent repression.

Building on the collective image of the Arab revolutions, the activists defined a shared "moral grammar" of the conflict.[40] Their demands refer to universal values: "we were protesting for our rights as Syrians. At first, I joined the demonstrators in solidarity with the rest of the population, against a regime that had hijacked power."[41] The inclusive character of the protests also fed into the idea of a "struggle for recognition," in which people asserted their rights as moral subjects, demanding dignity and rights independent of their ethnic and religious identity.[42] The moral grammar then defined which arguments were acceptable, which objectives were legitimate, and which methods were permissible for achieving these objectives. Consequently, the movement overall limited itself to a peaceful repertoire of actions.

Like the people of Leipzig in 1989, who marched chanting "We are the people," the Syrian protesters constructed their collective identity around their slogans and demands.[43] Sectarian claims at that time were completely absent from the protests. Later, the activists systematically refused sectarian demands, both as a reaction to the practices of the regime and to avoid undermining their unity. The inclusiveness of the revolt is even

---

[40] Axel, Honneth, op. cit.

[41] I-21, in al-Bab, December 2012.

[42] "Dignity" was the first slogan voted for on the "Syrian Revolution" Facebook page, for the Friday March 18 slogan. For a complete list of the Friday names, see Annex.

[43] Steven Pfaff, "Collective Identity and Informal Groups in Revolutionary Mobilizations: East Germany in 1989," Social Forces 75 (1), 1996, pp. 91–117.

more clearly visible to the protestors since they are young, barely politicized, and strangers to the ideological legacy of the Syrian mobilizations
of the 1980s.

Their slogans were a key part of constructing this inclusiveness. "God is
the greatest" (*Allah Akbar*) was a transgressive watchword for a regime
generally perceived as atheist, where no one, not even God, is above Bashar
al-Assad. This slogan was consensual in a country with an overwhelmingly
Sunni majority and held appeal for the Christian actor Fares al-Helou,
who, in April 2011, chanted it in front of the al-Hasan Mosque in
Damascus.[44] Initially, these slogans did not harbor anti-Alawite connota-
tions, especially since others explicitly referred to the unity of the religious
communities: "Sunnis and Alawites, united, united, united." (*Sunni w
'alawi, wahad, wahad, wahad*) and "United, united, united, the Syrian
people are united" (*Wahad, wahad, wahad, al-cha'ab al-suri wahad*).
Similarly, the weekly slogan on Friday May 20, voted on in Facebook
and chanted by processions throughout the country, was "Azadi," the
Kurdish word for freedom, while that of June 17 refers to Salah al-Ali,
the Alawite leader of the revolt against the French in 1919. While some
slogans related to local issues, others were explicitly national, referring to a
specific problem or city, bringing together protesters chanting them across
Syria, week after week, in solidarity with regions throughout the country. In
this spirit, the protesters adapted nationalist regime slogans by substituting
"freedom" for the names Hafez and Bashar al-Assad in a call for universal
values. "Allah, Syria, Bashar, and that's all" (*Allah, Suriyya, Bashar w bas*) in
processions in Daraa turns into "Allah, Syria, freedom, and that's all"
(*Allah, Suriyya, Hurriyya w bas*).[45] In addition, videos and testimonials
initially contain slogans focusing on the establishment of a political dialogue, but these became progressively radicalized to include the departure of
Bashar: "Our slogans were fairly general to start with. It was only after
several protests that we began to chant slogans against the regime."[46] "The
people want the fall of the regime" (*al-Cha'ab yurid isqat al-Nidham*) and the
vote on Facebook for "Leave!" (*Irhal*) as the weekly slogan for the week of
Friday July 21, 2011 underscores the radicalization of the agenda.

The symbols mobilized in the processions borrowed from a shared
vision of the Syrian nation-state as one explicitly different from that
of the Baathist regime. At first, the protesters used the Baathist flag
(red-white-black with two stars) to signal the national – as opposed to

[44] Communication with Felix Legrand, September 2014.
[45] Reinoud Leenders, "'Oh Buthaina, Oh Sha'ban – The Hawrani is not Hungry, We Want
    Freedom!': Revolutionary Framing and Mobilization at the Onset of the Syrian
    Insurgency," in Joel Beinin and Frederic Vairel (eds.), *op. cit.*, pp. 246–261.
[46] I-12, in Aleppo, January 2013.

the local and the sectarian – nature of the movement.[47] Flags on the front of public buildings become larger and larger, while those carried by demonstrators in processions could be tens or even hundreds of meters long.[48] The pre-Baathist flag (green-white-black with three stars) appeared in the marches starting in the summer of 2011 when protesters began demanding ever more stridently the departure of Bashar al-Assad. That the protestors were interested in the rest of the country is particularly apparent in the weekly slogans voted on Facebook that called for national mobilization.[49] Finally, the constant repetition of "Syria" and "freedom" and, to a lesser extent, "unity" and "nation" in the songs, weekly slogans, names of political groups, websites, and, later, military units, clearly expressed the movement's national and inclusive dimensions.[50]

From Anonymity to Activist Networks

The mobilization caught on because "Arab Spring" was a meaningful category; however, this did not prejudge the choice of means. The Syrians quickly learned that borrowing from the Tunisian and Egyptian protesters' repertoire was not feasible. "After the fall of the Tunisian and Egyptian regimes, we began to discuss the resources available to us. We knew that the Syrian regime was much stronger, and had formidable security forces. And so, we did not do the same as they did in the other countries."[51] The occupation of physical spaces was not a viable strategy due to the violence of the repressive machinery.[52] One such attempt, on Clock Square in Homs, on April 17, ended with dozens dead. Demonstrators quickly abandoned alternative methods, such as flash demonstrations in the wealthy neighborhoods of the large cities.

Initially, the repertoire of actions was limited to meetings and short marches in a public venue (mosque, park, university) to the accompaniment

---

[47] Before the pre-Baathist flag was established among the revolutionaries, soldiers announcing their desertion on film would hang the Baathist flag in the background, following the example of colonel Riyad al-Asaad, future commander of the Free Syrian Army, www.youtube.com/watch?v=M7A5WfIx92Q, viewed August 2014. Communication with Felix Legrand, August 2014.

[48] See for example www.youtube.com/watch?v=EMMt9P_Ouo4 viewed August 2014.

[49] See Facebook, www.facebook.com/Syrian.Revolution, viewed October 2012.

[50] See Cécile Boëx, "La vidéo comme outil de l'action collective et de la lutte armée," in François Burgat and Bruno Paoli (eds.), *op. cit.*, pp. 172–184.

[51] I-22, in Aleppo, December 2012.

[52] A practice that was also found in Egypt (al-Tahrir square), then in Yemen (al-Tahrir encampment), in Libya (in front of the Benghazi courthouse), in Bahrain (Pearl Roundabout), "De la place de la Libération (al-Tahrir) à la place du Changement (al-Taghyir): Recompositions des espaces et expressions du politique au Yémen," in Amin Allal and Thomas Pierret (eds.), *op.cit.*, pp. 31–51.

of anti-regime slogans. There is limited data regarding the participants. Going by videos posted on YouTube and according to our interviews, the processions were mostly made up by young men. Women also took part, however, gathering in the center or at the back of the marches, employing their own repertoire such as throwing rice or ululating. In Aleppo, the protesters were mostly from working class areas but also came from upper middle class neighborhoods in the west. There were Sunnis, but also Christians and Kurds. In the small towns in the Aleppo Governorate, processions were more homogeneous, made up mostly of Sunni men, but they were socially diverse with farmers, notables, merchants, and civil servants marching.

The modalities of protest were born out of the constraints imposed by the Syrian regime that forced the protesters to limit their risk of arrest. Meetings of more than three individuals being prohibited, mosques, regardless of religious function, became the starting point for many events, since adult men could meet in them, particularly during the Friday sermon. "The first event I participated in started from the mosque of a village close to Aleppo – although the imam was pro-regime – after the Friday prayers."[53] The regime was not able to monitor all mosques and souks, and the protesters maintained the tactical upper hand by varying the locations. "Each of our protests took place in a different venue. The protest lasted only a few minutes before we would disperse only to re-group elsewhere."[54]

Similarly, risk assessment by the protesters explains how the demonstrations spread throughout different neighborhoods.[55] Mapping the protests with the protesters' hometowns would not necessarily show a correlation, as they had to take the police presence into account when choosing a venue or, in some cases, to avoid being recognized by someone familiar. In a city like Aleppo, the risk of arrest drove some people, especially the youth from the most heavily policed neighborhoods – the well-off from the west and the Kurds from the north – to show up in the informal, under-policed Sunni neighborhoods. "People in rich neighborhoods, west of Aleppo, supported the protesters, but we quickly gave up on the idea of demonstrating there," explains one protester from the west of the city. "These neighborhoods have wider streets, and are easier for the police to control. They have a heavier presence where they have their barracks, while the suburbs are less patrolled;

[53] I-23, in Aleppo, December 2012.

[54] I-7, in Aleppo, December 2012.

[55] There are exceptions: The Kafr Sousa mosque in Damascus became the main site of protests in the city center despite being in a closely monitored neighborhood. Its Imam, Osama al-Rifai, was one of the rare sheiks to criticize the regime in his preaches, then closely watched, which explains why many Friday protests started from his mosque despite the presence of a post of the Domestic Security intelligence service on the other side of the road. Communication with Felix Legrand, September 2014.

people can gather there more easily. The security forces that come from elsewhere don't know these areas so well." Another protester told us: "Coming to protest in the east of Aleppo was very dangerous for me. I had to pass through several regime roadblocks with the risk of someone recognizing and arresting me. Once in the popular neighborhoods, I had nowhere to live. I needed to stay several weeks in the homes of revolutionary friends before I could risk travelling back home again."[56] Joining the protesters often meant leaving the family to avoid exposing them to retaliation and then settling in working class neighborhoods. In the Kurdish cities (Afrin, Ayn al-Arab) and in the Kurdish areas to the north of Aleppo from September 2011 on, the PYD suppressed any demonstrations held there. Young Kurdish protesters therefore travelled into predominantly Arab neighborhoods to take part in the demonstrations there.[57]

Then there were the informants. So many were working for the regime that it became difficult to coordinate collective action without the security forces learning of it and making preemptive arrests. This accounts for why, at the start, no organizations, such as unions, associations, and clans, were involved or played an important role in the protests. The same was true of well-known personalities. By also monitoring the imams and sheikhs, the regime prevented the religious networks from playing a coordinating role as well.[58] Few imams called for protest, although some demonstrated as individuals.[59] In this context, with the security services monitoring most communications, even the weak ties that can be significant when a protest movement is expanding were rendered useless. The risks of being identified were considerable; protesters were not able to leverage the part of their social capital essentially consisting of these weak ties.[60] For instance, the president

---

[56] I-12, with a former student in the English faculty, in Aleppo, January 2013.

[57] Many interviews in Kurdish revolutionaries from Paris, Erbil (Iraq), and in the regions of Afrin and Ayn al-Arab, in December 2012 and January 2013, mention arrests, detention, and intimidation by the PYD. See also the site Kurd Watch: www.kurdwatch.org/?ai d=2732&z=en&cure=1009, viewed September 10, 2014.

[58] Two imams from Damascus, Osama al-Rifai and Krayyim Rajih, without directly calling for protest, recognized the legitimacy of the protesters' demands in their Friday preaches and criticized the violence of the regime. In Daraa and Banyas, clerics became more directly involved in the protest movement between March and April 2011 but had to withdraw or leave the country in the weeks that followed. See Thomas Pierret, "L'islam dans la révolution syrienne," *Politique étrangère* 4, 2011, pp. 884–888.

[59] An imam from Aleppo explained that he went to protest in a mosque far from his own to remain anonymous (I-112, with a judge at the Court of the United Judicial Council, in Aleppo, January 2013). It was just one month after the first protests that the clergymen from Aleppo, including the Grand Mufti of Aleppo, Sheikh Ibrahim al-Salqini, came out of silence and spoke in favor of the protesters.

[60] We apply here Granovetter's opposition between strong and weak ties, yet in this context weak ties appear useless, Mark Granovetter, "The Strength of Weak Ties," *American Journal of Sociology* 78 (6), 1973, pp. 1360–1380.

of an association who joined the protesters was careful to resign in early April in order to protect the organization, which therefore survived.[61] Likewise, the director of a small business in Aleppo kept his employees in the dark regarding his activism.[62] An employee of the United Nations Development Program resigned from her post and cut herself off from her colleagues once she was involved in the Damascus protests. "I didn't know if my colleagues were for or against the revolution and I was too afraid of being denounced by them. After the first protests, I quit my job and I stopped seeing them."[63] Cécile Boëx reports the case of a film director who participated anonymously, his face covered, after the failure of the intellectuals' protest movement.[64]

The two surest tactics for avoiding arrest were either anonymity or mobilizing strong ties, the latter relying on the solidarity of small groups of friends or family. At the start, as related by a protester, "our first demonstrations were spontaneous and often composed of individuals who did not know each other."[65] The need for anonymity limited the protests, especially early on. Some protesters covered their faces to avoid identification. In this respect, the villages on the urban peripheries played an important role in the initial phase: "Instead of gathering in the inner cities, we started to demonstrate in the villages, with our faces covered."[66] In addition, some protesters would participate with family and close friends. "We were a small group of ten people, friends and cousins. The day of the [first] demonstration, we went out into the street; were we frightened! As we marched on, chanting slogans, others gradually started to join us. There were a lot of regime spies, but they could not follow us all."[67] In this intimate space, in which the transgressive humor that preceded the protests also flourished, people found the courage to begin taking risks. Groups in Aleppo, Volcano, Ahrar al-Sakhur (The Free of Sakhur), Ahrar al-Salahaddin (The Free of Salahaddin), and Ahfad al-Kawakibi (the Grandchildren of ʿAbd al-Rahman al-Kawakibi – an Arab nationalist thinker and native of Aleppo) or the group of youngsters in al-Bab, allowed a prolonged mobilization.[68] At Aleppo University, the groups that emerged were first organized from among students in the same courses, for example, the *Flower* group at the Faculty of Economics and the Kahraba (Electricity)

---

[61] I-7, in Aleppo, August 2013.
[62] I-17, in Aleppo, August 2013.
[63] I-10, in Gaziantep, September 2013.
[64] Cécile Boëx, "Mobilisations d'artistes …," *op. cit.*
[65] I-24, in al-Bab, December 2012.
[66] I-23, in Aleppo, December 2012.
[67] I-25, in al-Bab, December 2012.
[68] I-12, I-13, I-18, I-21, and I-19, with members of various groups in Aleppo and al-Bab, December–January and August 2013.

group at the Sharia department.[69] The fact that the majority of the protesters were young flipped generational hierarchies on their end, with
shabab (youths) taking leadership roles inside families.

The emotional ties between the protest groups were strong, with
constant references to them being like a second family.[70] At a protest
level, once these activist pockets knew the police were after them, they
reached a point of no return, crossing over into clandestinity with some
resorting to violence. Due to the specificities of this engagement, a
revolutionary social capital grew out of the collective action, both as a
necessary condition and as consequence.[71] The anonymity of the protest movement, however, meant that this new social capital was different
from the earlier one. As the protesters emphasized, the ties forged within
small groups of activists and during the demonstrations were novel:
"Before the revolution I didn't know the people with whom I formed a
group," explained one protester from Damascus "It was through our
protests, our discussions, the risks we took together, that we got to know
each other."[72]

The intensity of the discussions and the shared risk-taking caused an
emotional community to coalesce. It enabled the closure of the group, a
process essential for the formation of social capital.[73] The rising number
of killings by the security forces also contributed to forging stronger
intragroup bonds, out of loyalty to the memory of fallen comrades.
Many of our interviewees characterized this feeling of brotherhood as
comparable with family ties: "The group to which I belonged quickly
became a real family. I spent more time with them than with my own
family. It's with them that I feel happiest; everything that happened since
2011, I have shared with them."[74] Adherence to shared moral values also
conditioned group membership. Activism was experienced subjectively as
altruistic as opposed to the instrumentalized sectarian membership in
prerevolutionary Syria. This strong moral dimension was a form of denial
of the utility of social relations akin to one found, for example, among
Western privileged classes.[75]

[69] I-26, in Aleppo, August 2013.

[70] I-17, in Aleppo, August 2013.

[71] Adam Baczko, Gilles Dorronsoro, and Arthur Quesnay, "Le capital révolutionnaire,"
Actes de la recherche en sciences sociales 211–212, 2016.

[72] I-28, in Cairo, January 2014.

[73] Despite a different theoretical approach, we share James Coleman's conclusions on the
importance of the closure of a group, see James Coleman, "Social Capital in the Creation
of Human Capital," *American Journal of Sociology* 94, 1988, p. 99.

[74] I-17, in Aleppo, August 2013.

[75] Bruno Cousin and Sébastien Chauvin, "L'économie symbolique du capital social," *Actes
de la recherche en sciences sociales* 193 (3), 2012, pp. 96–103.

In a context of biographical disruption due to the initial conditions of the protests, the activists' solidarity seemed relatively unpredictable *vis à vis* their pre-2011 social positions. It would be going too far to characterize these unlikely connections as suspending the rigidities of social order, but, subjectively, these new ties appear to obey different rules, hence the nostalgia – or euphoria even – that we noted during many of our interviews. "In 2011, everything began to move, it was fascinating. More than fear, I remember the effervescence and the strength of the links that tied our small group together. During our actions, we met many people from all sorts of backgrounds."[76] This is how a peaceful protest movement against the regime incubated the conditions for a social revolution.

Abu ʿUmar: A Notable of the Revolution

Abu ʿUmar (a pseudonym), in his fifties when we met him, belonged to one of Aleppo's old families. He traded textiles with Turkey. His father, an ex-communist, gave up politics permanently after being jailed for ten days under Hafez al-Assad. Before the revolution, Abu ʿUmar had no political or civil society commitment. In 2011, he participated in the early marches and became a courier carrying messages for different protest groups. This role of trust brought him into contact with many of the protesters engaged in clandestine work. His was a particularly exposed position, because he was one of the few with knowledge of the various networks of protesters in the different parts of the city. He then expanded his contacts within the protest networks of Aleppo. Well-known in revolutionary circles, he stayed in the city when the Free Syrian Army entered. Abu ʿUmar's prestige grew even more when he contributed personal assets to the revolutionary cause.

His role at the nexus of the revolutionary networks meant his home became a natural meeting place for revolutionaries. "When at Abu ʿUmar's place, we all belong to the same family," a revolutionary from Aleppo explained to us there.[77] Every evening, and sometimes even during the day, insurgents would come to his place, unburden themselves and discuss current events. During Ramadan in the summer of 2013, his house was a place for socializing; the revolutionaries would meet there for *iftar* (to break the fast).

These networks allowed him to collect money and coordinate diverse activities in his neighborhood. He set up a canteen for fighters, financed the local bakery, organized food distribution for the needy, and arranged the purchase and distribution of gas cylinders. He also participated in the creation of a district council, which in the summer of 2013 was transformed into the borough's town council.

---

[76] I-28, in Cairo, January 2014.
[77] I-17, in Aleppo, August 2013.

Coordination

Agendas and repertoires were synchronized via mass media and especially the Internet. International news channels helped create a sense of belonging to a national protest movement and fed copycat demonstrations, which, however, remained local in an organizational sense. In the beginning, there were attempts made at coordination, with repeated calls for unity on Facebook. This informal social media campaign failed to produce a unified organization at a national or even local level. However, the uniformity of both the slogans and the repertoires of contention at the national level raise the question of what bottom-up coordination there was.

At first, the protesters learned the modalities of protest by imitation – for instance, a child singing revolutionary refrains through a megaphone. Media coverage, whether recorded by the international media or the protesters themselves, became a blueprint for disseminating protest action. The demonstrators would capture the protests on video, using cameras or mobile phones, and broadcast them via YouTube. As it were, young Syrians were already part of the generation that was streaming its private life. Demonstrating was for Syria's youth an extraordinary development: It was their first anti-regime protest at a historic moment. The Gulf news channels, Al Jazeera and Al Arabiya, made these videos accessible to anyone who had a satellite dish. The demonstrators could therefore watch on television and on the Internet how others went about protesting. The demonstrations hence gradually gained the consistency that came with a shared repertoire, which allowed the participants to see themselves as part of a national movement.

Then, groups aspiring to improve coordination of the protests were careful to compartmentalize their activities.

> We were organized into several small groups of a few people each. These groups had no contact with each other and no one knew the identity of the other individuals. Each group had a leader who was the only one to meet with the leaders of the other groups. As an example, every Thursday, I would meet other group leaders to agree on the location of the next demonstration. If, when the time came, the security services were waiting for us at the venue, it meant that one of the groups was being monitored. We would then exclude them from the network. With this system in place, information and orders could be communicated without putting us all in danger.[78]

Over time, some of the demonstrators took on the role of messengers between the various groups.[79]

---

[78] I-7, in Aleppo, December 2012.
[79] I-9, in Aleppo, August 2013.

Prisons also became meeting places for protesters since, after arrest and torture, the men no longer needed to conceal their identity. Hundreds of thousands of people passed through the regime's prisons, mostly in over-crowded cells. "There were dozens of us in a cell for weeks, and then the regime would transfer us, sometimes to another city. So, I met far more protesters in jail than I could have done outside where our protests lasted only a few minutes. I learned a lot this way about the regime's techniques and about our strength."[80] Prisoners from throughout the country got to know each other this way and could exchange information on cities that were inaccessible, such as Daraa and Jisr al-Shughur. Released activists would often disseminate information and contact the families of their former fellow prisoners.[81]

Ultimately, the repertoires of contention evolved and spread nation-wide via online social networks. In a densely connected society, Skype and Facebook became permanent coordination tools and – with the use of pseudonyms – were relatively safe, apparently being poorly monitored by the regime. Discussion groups and forums sprang up on Facebook and networks grew between individuals using Skype who did not know each other before the protests. Online social networks became a way of circu-lating slogans and information on future demonstrations. They thus allowed a national movement to take shape in the absence of any specia-lized or hierarchical structures. For instance, via Facebook, protesters could participate in weekly nationwide polls for choosing the slogan for the next Friday march (see Annex for a list of slogans). Social networks became platforms of expression without a formal hierarchy, but where cultural capital and technical skills introduced a new bias. To sum up, social media made coordination possible without additional logistical resources, and their use fed a sense of belonging to the revolution.

---

[80] I-17, in Aleppo, August 2013.
[81] Ignace Leverrier, "Communiquer et s'informer dans la Syrie en révolution," 28 August 2011, http://syrie.blog.lemonde.fr/2011/08/28/retour-de-syrie-2-communiquer-et-sin former-dans-la-syrie-en-revolution/, viewed in September 2014.

3   The Path to Civil War

The regime's response to peaceful protest was to refuse all dialogue, try to divide the movement with selective economic concessions, and militarize the repression to radicalize the opposition as had been done in the 1980s. However, the demonstrations grew to the point where they overwhelmed the security apparatus, and the army failed to reassert control. Then the protesters took up arms as the crisis escalated. After an initial phase, during which the opposition forces rapidly gained strength, the situation stalemated and progress for either side ultimately came to depend on foreign support.

Divide, Radicalize, Repress

At the outset of the protests, Assad gave priority to his repressive machinery, which proved to be a winning strategy: The assiduously managed security institutions remained faithful to the regime. In this light, the nomination of Alawis (see Chapter 1) to key positions proved especially decisive. Thus, the situation in Syria differed profoundly from those in Tunisia and Egypt, whose armies played a decisive role in the downfall of their regimes.[1] Unlike in these countries, where Western assistance enabled a degree of independence from the political leadership, Bashar al-Assad controlled where Iranian and Russian support made its impact. In the spring of 2011, at a time when the regime faced increasing pressure by some of its allies, including Qatar and Hezbollah, they were unable to significantly influence policy because of their tenuous contacts inside the regime.[2] Moreover, instead of undermining the regime, the rising violence served in the short run to reinforce the cohesion of the security institutions (intelligence, army, and police). The Syrian regime had built residential communities for officers and their families, which provided

[1] See the special issue, Hillel Frisch (ed.), "The Role of the Military in the Arab Tumult," *Journal of Strategic Studies* 36 (2), 2012.
[2] For Hezbollah, personal communication with Aurélie Daher, November 2014.

them with better living conditions but also made it easier to monitor their families and thus served to cement their loyalty.[3] The numerous war crimes committed by the security organs' cadres probably further tied them to the regime, since they risked indictment in any political transition that did not include Bashar al-Assad. Finally, by turning the conflict into a sectarian one, the regime took the minorities hostage. Alawites played an increasingly central role in it, as they were prevented from joining the opposition after the first few months of repression, a situation that the regime knew how to exploit.

However, this aspect of the Syrian regime did not register with the protesters and so, inspired by the Egyptian and Tunisian revolutions, they gambled on defections from the security forces or on Western intervention. As the repression intensified and the fighting spread, the trickle of individual desertions blinded the Syrian demonstrators to the realities of their situation. Nevertheless, until early 2013, desertions by senior officers created the illusion of an imminent collapse of power, while in fact the central power was restructuring around the security institutions and benefiting from substantial foreign aid.

The regime's strategy of splitting the movement was prosecuted using three tactical approaches. First, it responded to the growing protests by either offering socioeconomic concessions or executing tactical retreats. In Daraa, after negotiations with notables from the province, the fifteen teenagers were released on March 20 and, three days later, the provincial governor resigned. Similarly, in early April 2011, with the protests intensifying in Homs – after Hama, they were the largest in the country – Assad also sacked the governor. Furthermore, in a move to isolate the various regions, the authorities tried to drown the political and moral demands of the protesters in the "icy water of egotistical calculation." However, this socioeconomic response was doomed to failure: when the political adviser Buthaina Shaaban offered higher wages in March 2011, the following Friday in the cities protesters were chanting "Oh Buthaina! Oh Shaaban! The people of Daraa are not hungry!"[4] A revolutionary from Daraa explained how the regime attempted to rally the city's affluent middle classes, "After the first protests in March 2011, the regime made many promises: to free those under arrest, to provide the city of Daraa with

---

[3] Kheder Khaddour, *Assad's Officer Ghetto: Why the Syrian Army Remains Loyal*, Beyrouth, Carnegie Middle East Center, 2015, available at http://carnegie-mec.org/2015/09/30/ass ad-s-officer-ghetto-why-syrian-army-remains-loyal/iigr, viewed January 3, 2016.

[4] For an analysis of the slogans chanted by the protesters, see François Burgat, Jamal Chehayed, Bruno Paoli, and Manuel Sartori, "La puissance politique des slogans de la revolution," in François Burgat and Bruno Paoli (eds.), *op. cit.*, p. 185–200.

more resources, and to help fight unemployment."[5] Similarly, in Azaz (governorate of Aleppo), the regime tried to regain the initiative by responding to old grievances. "During the first demonstrations in Azaz, the regime's security services offered to solve our water piping problems. These problems had existed for years, but suddenly they could be solved in a few days, on condition that parents restrained their children."[6] In addition, measures were approved that were tailored to the Sunni majority: the niqab (full veil) was authorized for teachers a year after it had been banned, a casino was closed, and a religious television channel, Al Nour, was launched.[7] Regime representatives also met with tribal elites and powerful families around the country. That this strategy failed suggests that the regime lacked suitable intermediaries for these negotiations to succeed. The opposition figures in exile had no legitimacy among the protesters, while both the imams and leaders of the grand families were often looked upon as agents of the regime.[8] This was especially the case in Damascus and Aleppo, but the situation was more complex in smaller cities, such as Daraa and Banyas, where some of the most prominent religious figures were directly involved in the protests.[9]

Bashar al-Assad's second tactic was to portray the protests as the work of Sunni Arabs. The line taken by the official media was that the Sunni orchestrated the first clashes in Latakia against their Alawite neighbors with the help of foreign commandos and financed by Sunnis in Lebanon and Saudi Arabia.[10] The regime stigmatized the Sunni population as a breeding ground for Islamic terrorism. "In 2011, the regime's rhetoric changed to propaganda that proclaimed 'the national unity of the Syrians against radical Sunnis.' The security services had begun to treat the population differently, singling out the Sunnis. Everything was done to reject us for being terrorists."[11]

In the same vein, the regime tried to win over the minority populations and to negotiate directly with movements whose ideology was explicitly sectarian. "Very early on the regime sought to isolate us. Openly, their strategy was to avoid alienating the minority communities. For example, to calm tensions, the regime granted citizenship to hundreds of thousands of *bidun* Kurds (Syrian Kurds who had lost their nationality in the 1962 census), something we had been requesting for decades."[12] In the spring

[5] I-29, in Amman, October 2013.
[6] I-30, in Azaz, December 2012.
[7] Carsten Wieland, "Asad's Decade of Lost Chances," in Carsten Wieland, Adam Almqvist, and Helena Nassif (eds.), *op. cit.*, p. 36.
[8] I-31, in Azaz, December 2012.
[9] Thomas Pierret, "L'islam dans la révolution ... " *op. cit.*, pp. 884–885.
[10] François Burgat, "La stratégie al-Assad: diviser pour survivre," in François Burgat and Bruno Paoli (eds.), *op. cit.*, p. 22.
[11] I-31, in Azaz, December 2012.
[12] I-32, in Erbil, February 2012.

of 2011, the regime released Kurdish prisoners and concluded an agreement with the PKK that gave them informal control of Kurdish enclaves – Jazeera, Ayn al-Arab, Afrin, and the Kurdish districts of Aleppo, in exchange for bringing the demonstrators to heel (see Chapter 8).[13]

Furthermore, the regime recruited Alawite village militias while turning a blind eye to the black-market economy there. For example, in northern Latakia province, the government, short of troops, supported the formation of local defensive militias in Alawite villages. However, the militias, paid approximately $75 a month and poorly equipped, as a rule were reluctant to fight and did not attack any Sunni villages.[14]. Damascus trained Druze militias for the same reason. In 2011, the regime began to quell protests in the Druze areas and to imprison the most committed protesters.[15] However, to ensure the community's continued neutrality, it was careful to limit its use of force. The regime also proceeded to spread rumors of massacres by radical Islamists and offered employment to disaffected young Druze in self-defense militias trained by the security services. Again, these militias had an essentially defensive mission, especially since the Druze community was also affected by the crackdowns.[16] As for the Christian populations, they were scattered and divided, unlike the Druze who were concentrated in one area. Christian militias were therefore set up according to the local context, regardless of the politics of the religious elites who frequently worked hand in glove with the regime.[17] The regime exploited Christian fears of the jihadists and made direct payments to create local defense militias. For example, in the mostly Melkite and Greek Orthodox Wadi al-Nasara (Christian Valley), the regime recruited Christians into the militia of the National Defense Forces (Quwat al-Difa'a al-Watani) that were deployed across the country.[18]

---

[13] See Arthur Quesnay and Cyril Roussel, *op. cit.*

[14] Interview in Turkey, September 2013.

[15] Ignace Leverrier, "Les religieux, ultimes garants de la neutralité de la communauté druze de Syrie," April 18, 2014, http://syrie.blog.lemonde.fr/2014/04/18/les-religieux-ultimes-garants-de-la-neutralite-de-la-communaute-druze-de-syrie/, viewed May 10, 2014.

[16] Reports gathered tell of bodies being regularly delivered by local security leaders, I-108, in Amman, October 2013. Some, like the young Tareq Hamed Qumash, refused to join the army and handed themselves over to set things straight. A pacifist protester, Shadi Abu Raslan, was arrested on the Beirut-Damascus road and tortured to death for having stuck the pre-Baathist flag to the back of his mobile telephone, Ignace Leverrier, *op. cit.*, April 18, 2014.

[17] Ignace Leverrier, "Les ressources sécuritaires du régime," in François Burgat and Bruno Paoli (eds.), *op. cit.*, p. 46.

[18] Aymenn al-Tamimi, "Christian Militia and Political Dynamics in Syria," *Syria Comment*, February 23, 2014, www.joshualandis.com/blog/christian-militia-political-dynamics-syria/, viewed May 13, 2014.

However, the Syriac Military Council, created in Hasaka in late 2013, opposed the regime. Its main objective was still to protect the Christian population by combating the jihadi presence.[19]

In a third tactic, the regime encouraged the ideological radicalization of the opposition by having moderates murdered or arrested while it released radicals from prison. It also targeted moderate or respected figures, even if they were not involved with the opposition. On October 7, 2011, Meshaal Tamo, a Syrian Kurd regime opponent but open to dialogue and a member of the CNS, was assassinated.[20] In September 2012, the regime authorized the National Committee for Democratic Change (NCDC) to organize a conference in Damascus.[21] The day of the meeting, NCDC President Abdelaziz al-Khayyer was arrested[22] and has not been seen since. Similarly, in January 2014, the regime imprisoned the parents of opposition negotiators at the Geneva II talks, a few weeks before the meetings.[23]

By late March 2011, even as the arrests kept rising, radical Islamists with ties to the Iraqi insurgency were released from prison.[24] These were to form the core of the future armed Islamist groups that started emerging in early 2012, including Liwa' Suqur al-Sham, Jabhat al-Nusra and Harakat Ahrar Ahrar al-Sham al-Islamiyya. In the ensuing years, rumors flourished concerning links between the Syrian secret services and radical Islamists. Their release did, indeed, give rise to the idea that the regime fostered the Islamist movements in Syria to undermine the peaceful protest. This as-yet unverifiable hypothesis, however, is not needed to understand the regime's strategy. The release of prisoners, some of them veteran fighters from the Iraqi branch of al-Qaida, radicalized the opposition and thus let the regime position itself as a bulwark against the Islamist threat. Besides, the Syrian regime had a long tradition of manipulating violence, supporting, for example, the PKK

---

[19] Syriac Military Council statement, "المجلس العسكري السرياني السوري," www.youtube.com/watch?v=VGbsKFUwuFE, viewed May 13, 2014.

[20] Le Figaro, "Syrie: un opposant kurde assassiné," October 7, 2011, www.lefigaro.fr/flash-actu/2011/10/07/97001-20111007FILWWW00582-syrie-un-opposant-kurde-assassine.php, viewed May 9, 2014.

[21] Composed of left-wing forces and Arab nationalists, from the Communist Action Party (CAP) and from the PYD, it was founded in June 2011 during a conference held in Damascus.

[22] Nicolas Dot-Pouillard, "Les divisions stratégiques des oppositions syriennes: un leadership impossible?" in François Burgat and Bruno Paoli (eds.), op. cit., p.120.

[23] See especially the reports from Amnesty International, www.amnesty.org/fr/region/syria/report-2011, and the Syrian Observatory for Human Rights, www.syriahr.com/.

[24] François Burgat and Romain Caillet, "Une guérilla islamiste? Les composantes idéologiques de la révolte armée," in François Burgat and Bruno Paoli (eds.), op. cit., pp. 73–74.

against Turkey until 1998 and radical Islamists against the United States after the invasion of Iraq.[25]

These attempts to divide the opposition were secondary to the brutal repression that was as much intended to radicalize the opposition as it was to serve as a deterrent.[26] With no figure or organization to target, the regime ratcheted up the risks to individuals associated with the protests[27] Violence became increasingly indiscriminate and its effects less calculable. First, the regime evolved its economy of repression by making torture systematic, a form of individualized violence on an industrial scale. Starting in 2011, it arrested and tortured several hundred thousand people. Based on information provided by a prison employee defector, we have proof that over 11,000 people were tortured to death in less than two years (from Spring 2011 to summer 2013) in Damascus prisons.[28] The total figure is certainly much higher. Despite the regime's determined efforts, the intelligence services, not having a distinct target at which to direct their dissuasive violence, were overwhelmed. As the torture campaign escalated, space in prisons became scarce, leading to severe overcrowding in the cells. While the intelligence services tortured most of their prisoners, interrogation often happened long after their arrest or not at all.[29] Prisoners that were released a few weeks later and their families were threatened to stop them from continuing to protest.[30] While our interviewees recalled seeing informants outside mosques and in the processions, protesters who had been arrested told us that the intelligence agencies were ignorant of considerable areas of their activities. Competition among the eighteen intelligence units did, in fact, limit sharing of information. Several of the most active protesters were released. "The regime stopped me twice, but

---

[25] Bernard Rougier, *L'oumma en fragments*, Paris, Presses Universitaires de France, 2011, pp. 154–160.

[26] This list is common to the authoritarian regimes of the Middle East, confronted with the Arab insurgencies, in Steven Heydemann and Reinoud Leenders (eds.), *op. cit.*

[27] Reinoud Leenders, "Repression Is 'Not a Stupid Thing': The Syrian Regime's Response to the Insurgency," 2012, connexion August 15, 2013, URL: www.kcl.ac.uk/sspp/departments/warstudies/people/pubs/leenders/repression.pdf, viewed April 15, 2014.

[28] See especially the HRW report on the torture centers in Syria "Syria: Torture Centers Revealed," HRW, July 3, 2012, www.hrw.org/news/2012/07/03/syria-torture-centers-revealed, viewed April 11, 2014; "Le régime accusé de torture à grande échelle," Le Monde, January 20, 2014, http://abonnes.lemonde.fr/proche-orient/article/2014/01/20/syrie-le-regime-accuse-de-torture-a-grande-echelle_4351376_3218.htmlrapportconfidentielsurcésarhttp://www.scribd.com/doc/200984823/Syria-Report-Execution-Tort and Adam Entous and Dion Nissenbaum, "10,000 Bodies: Inside Syrian President Bashar al-Assad's Crackdown," Wall Street Journal, July 25, 2014, http://online.wsj.com/articles/10–000-bodies-inside-syrian-president-bashar-al-assads-crackdown-1406315472, viewed November 9, 2014.

[29] I-17, in Aleppo, August 2013.

[30] On the use of torture to demobilize the protestors, Gilles Dorronsoro, "La torture discrète: capital social, radicalisation et désengagement militant dans un régime sécuritaire," *European Journal of Turkish Studies* 8, 2008.

I was always released, even though I was very involved in the organization of events. I wasn't even interrogated. The security services seemed unable to cope."[31]

Unable to control the crowds in the streets, the security forces dispersed the protesters with brutality, even indiscriminately firing on them without warning. The repressive apparatus was now operating beyond all due process and instead relied heavily on the militias (*shabbiha*).[32] "As soon as we came out of the mosque to run away, the police ransacked everything. A militiaman was slashing people with a saber, people right in front of me. One after another, I saw them fall until the crowd pushed me against him. Then, he stopped hitting and started to howl, he had lost his mind."[33] In some cases, the security forces hid in ambulances to catch the demonstrators by surprise; the militia even hunted through hospitals to find the wounded. The repression's reach was significant, too: attacks inside mosques meant that the protesters could not find shelter anywhere. "The use of violence was systematic from the start of the movement, beatings outside the mosques or even inside, knife attacks and sniper fire into the crowd were commonplace."[34] The effect, if not the very objective, of this deregulated violence was to intimidate the protesters by showing them that nothing was off limits to the repression.

Finally, as accounts by high-ranking defectors like the one below inform us, the regime deliberately escalated the violence using shadow committees that mirrored official bodies but were outside the hierarchy, reporting directly to the head of state alone. They orchestrated spectacular attacks that intimidated minorities and discouraged still unengaged individuals from challenging the status quo, going so far as to provoke violence during the demonstrations. Police General Ahmed Tlass, in office at the beginning of the crisis, explained:

Everyone has heard of the Crisis Management Division, established at the beginning of the uprising and placed under the formal authority of the Assistant Regional Secretary of the Baath Party. Everyone also knows that the Syrian Ministry of Defence develops plans regularly to protect the country from aggression. What nobody knows, however, is that there is another instance of decision. It does not officially exist. It does not include the Minister of the Interior, or the Minister of Defence. It never acts in broad daylight but in the shade and this is where the decisions are made. It is here that strategy is defined, not with the Crisis Management Division. It consists of officers from different services, selected one

---

[31] I-31, in Azaz, December 2012.
[32] The term *shabbiha* is used by Syrians to describe, indiscriminately, the regime's support, paid militia and traitors. For clarity, we translate *shabbiha* depending on the context of the interview.
[33] I-33, in Aleppo, December 2012.
[34] I-12, in Aleppo, January 2013.

by one, by name, who are specifically assigned to their tasks and who work at the Presidential Palace. This committee, if one can call it such, since it has no name, is headed by Bashar al-Assad in person. And it is his will that prevails.

He then gave the example of the demonstration on July 1, 2011 in Hama:

The protest happened in front of us without any incident. None of the protesters were armed. But when the crowd reached Orontes Square, about 300 meters from where I was standing, gunfire erupted. According to an investigation by the police to which I had access, it came from twenty people, 22 to be precise from the Military Security, who had been joined by one member of State Security.[35]

The Entry into Civil War

Challenged by events roiling much of the country, the regime responded then by falling back on the military. As in the 1980s, it deployed army troops at the first sign of unrest to back up the police and intelligence services.[36] When the police retreated from a territory, the military moved in. The regime attempted to break the protest movement with militarized suppressive tactics that included bringing in the tanks, making extra-judicial arrests, and setting snipers on demonstrators or on neighborhoods designated as hostile.[37] Over time, the army's expanding operations were responsible for causing massive destruction, especially in the cities.[38]

In the first months, the regime endeavored to replicate the strategic coup scored in Hama in 1982 by luring a large number of the opposition into the open before crushing them with the military. Due to the sheer number of protest hotbeds, however, sweep operations were at best sporadic, with troops often having to move out again after a few days to clean out another area where protests were under way. Daraa, for

---

[35] "Syria. The testimony of General Ahmed Tlass regarding the regime and repression," *Noria Research*, April 2014 www.noria-research.com/2014/04/28/syria-testimony-of-general-ahmed-tlass-on-the-regime-and-the-repression/ viewed September 1, 2015.

[36] Human Rights Watch, "We've Never Seen Such Horror," June 1, 2011, www.hrw.org/node/99345/section/5 viewed September 7, 2014.

[37] Khaled Yacoub Oweis, "Dozens die, thousands flee Syrian tank assault in Hama," *Reuters*, August 4, 2011, www.hrw.org/node/99345/section/5 viewed April 8, 2013; Joseph Holliday, "Syria's Maturing Insurgency," *Middle East Security Report* 5, 2012, p. 15.

[38] Human Right Watch, "Syria: Crimes Against Humanity in Homs," November 2011, www.hrw.org/news/2011/11/11/syria-crimes-against-humanity-homs viewed October 8, 2013; "Syria: Witnesses Describe Idlib Destruction, Killings," March 15, 2012, www.hrw.org/news/2012/03/15/syria-witnesses-describe-idlib-destruction-killings viewed April 15, 2014; "Syria: Government Uses Homs Tactics on Border Town," March 22, 2012, www.hrw.org/news/2012/03/22/syria-government-uses-homs-tactics-border-town viewed May 14, 2014.

example, was occupied by the army, which entered the city on April 25, 2011, indiscriminately killing civilians.[39] The Daraa operation lasted two weeks, and then the army units moved out to attack the Sunni neighborhoods in the city of Banyas, and a few days later they moved again to attack them in Homs. However, in Homs, unlike Banyas and Daraa, the army failed to take control of the city. As desertions accelerated and the first groups of fighters appeared, operations bogged down and the fighting intensified. In the month of September 2011 alone, HRW counted 207 people killed in Homs. As one inhabitant testified, "We lived as if we were at war."[40]

With military operations proliferating, the war zone expanded. On August 13, 2011, the Navy shelled Sunni neighborhoods south of Latakia, signaling to the populace that the regime considered them collectively as the enemy. In July, after a few weeks' respite, the regime bombarded Hama and sent in the tanks. This operation left over two hundred demonstrators dead over the course of three days.[41] After two weeks of wreaking destruction, the troops withdrew from Hama, leaving it alone for three months. Continuing the same pattern, the regime mounted a repeat offensive against Daraa, Banyas, and other centers of resistance. In early 2012, tanks were sent into the countryside north of Aleppo where they stayed a day or two in each town while the troops arrested the men and destroyed homes along the way.

Although extremely violent, the sweep operations met with limited success. Limited resources forced the army to concentrate its operations in strategic zones and along key axes. In the rest of the country, in Rastan (north of Homs) and even in Ghouta (a suburb of Damascus), the army besieged areas held by the rebels with the objective of starving out the protesters, and mounted only brief incursions under the protection of tanks.[42] However, the army, crippled by desertions, lacked reliable troops, especially infantry, that would allow retaking the cities. Shelling, therefore, at first became the regime's preferred method of attack, until February 2012, when aerial bombing became generalized. It punished the

[39] Human Rights Watch, "Syrie: crimes contre l'humanité à Deraa," June 1, 2011, www.hrw.org/fr/news/2011/06/01/syrie-crimes-contre-l-humanit-deraa viewed May 30, 2014.

[40] I-29, with an activist from Daraa, in Amman, October 2013.

[41] Nour Ali, "Syrian Tanks Kill Protestors in Hama," *The Guardian*, July 31, 2011; Nada Bakri, "Civilian Toll Is Mounting in Assault on Syrian City," *New York Times*, August 4, 2011.

[42] Valentina Napolitano, "L'enfer de Yarmouk, camp palestinien en Syrie. La faim ou la soumission," *Orient XXI*, February 20, 2014, http://orientxxi.info/magazine/l-enfer-de-yarmouk-camp, 0518; *Le Monde*, "Syrie: le dernier convoi de rebelles va quitter Homs," May 8, 2014, www.lemonde.fr/proche-orient/article/2014/05/08/l-hotel-carlton-d-alep-detruit-a-l-explosif_4413487_3218.html.

people collectively and kept troops out of harm's way on the battlefield, decreasing desertions. At the same time, the regime lent credence to rumors that the presence of terrorist groups was the reason for the bombing runs. By the end of spring 2011, the government was forced to withdraw from certain marginal neighborhoods and conurbations and redeployed instead to more strategic locations (Alawite neighborhoods, prisons, the infrastructure, the roads, and border posts). The security forces evacuated parts of Daraa and Rastan, as well as neighborhoods in Homs, Hama, and Latakia. The police no longer patrolled the informal neighborhoods of Aleppo and Damascus or the surrounding countryside.

Paradoxically, the multiplying military operations strengthened the rebel movement. While the military tried to suppress the protests in Homs, mobilizations increased in the rest of the country and, by the summer of 2011, any containment scenario on the 1982 Hama model was clearly not going to work. In addition, the protesters hunted by the security services often went underground or took refuge in evacuated areas, depriving the security forces of the ability to identify them. "In the fall of 2011, when I saw my picture on TV and a price on my head, everything changed for me," said an engineer from Daraa. "I sought refuge in the neighborhood of Tariq al-Sad in Daraa, where the police no longer came because of the armed revolutionaries. It was a well-protected place, where the revolutionaries gathered and were organized. I was able to join a group there and continue my activity via the Internet."[43] Once the demonstrators went into hiding they depended that much more on the activist networks to protect, house, and feed them. The number of men going to ground increased in response to the Decree of the 23rd April 2012, which instructed all men fit for military service to present themselves at the local police barracks. "From the first demonstrations, some of us began to change regularly where we stayed. We slept in the countryside, in the villages where the regime had less of a presence. From then on, these villages become assembly points because the regime could not reach us except with major military action."[44] Many of those called up refused to join their assigned regiments and, since this subjected them to the death penalty, had no other option but to go into hiding. Most protesters cut all contact with their relations, family, and friends at least temporarily, and their social life shrank down to fellow activists. The concentration of protesters in various areas of the country had the effect of breaking down barriers between groups of activists. People from the cities and the countryside mingled in Maraa and Tal

---

[43] I-29, in Amman, October 2013.
[44] I-34, in Azaz, December 26, 2012.

Rifaat north of Aleppo, in Rastan north of Homs, in Saluq north of Raqqa, to the east of Latakia, in the Jabal al-Zawiya south of Idlib, or in the Qalamun mountains on the Lebanese border. In the absence of any dialogue between the regime and the revolutionaries, the choice for the latter was simple: armed struggle or exile.

In the summer of 2011, the first armed groups were still marginal. The progressive shift to an armed struggle grew out of local initiatives beginning only in late 2011. The first groups formed spontaneously to protect the marchers and neighborhoods against snipers and regime militias. The first firearms – pistols, rifles, and air guns, rarely Kalashnikovs – started to appear in the summer of 2011. The armed protection gave a new impetus to the protesters. In Homs, in December 2011, the processions swelled with deserters from the army who had come to offer protection. In Hama, too, with gunmen protecting the rallies starting in late June 2011, the regime troops had to evacuate several neighborhoods, letting the protests spread unchecked.[45] Nevertheless, for the first armed groups, just the act of picking up weapons was controversial. "We did not agree on the tactics to use," explained a revolutionary from Daraa. "Some wanted to attack the regime's positions directly, they thought we needed to follow what they had done in Libya. For others, it was a matter only of protecting the demonstrators from the regime militias."[46] Some protesters were dead set against any resort to violence; others were amenable to its limited use if it meant they could continue the protests: "We were against the move to armed resistance in Homs. Our movement was peaceful and we managed to create some flash protests. But if we wanted the movement to survive, we had to have protection when we marched."[47]

In Daraa, the question was in the air from the beginning, given the regime's determination to crush the protest movement by force. In Damascus "after the first protests, the youths would come with a family gun, saying that this way they could intimidate the security service agents not to fire on them. But they were immediately identified by intelligence services and executed even when these young people had dropped their weapons already and were begging for mercy."[48] In Aleppo, "initially most of the armed groups in our neighborhood were created to protect the demonstrators," stated a protester from the Ansari area.[49]

---

[45] Yara Bayoumy, "Syrian Forces Kill 34 in Hama, Crackdown Intensifies," *Reuters*, June 3, 2011; Anthony Shadid, "With Police Absent, Protests Surge in Syrian City," *New York Times*, July 1, 2011.

[46] I-35, a revolutionary from Daraa, in Amman, October 2013.

[47] I-36, in Istanbul, September 2013.

[48] Interview carried out by Matthieu Rey in Damascus in September 2012, in François Burgat and Bruno Paoli (eds.), *op. cit.*, p. 62.

[49] I-37, in Aleppo, January 2013.

At that time, there were opposition groups wanted by the police. We would hide, changing the safe house regularly. Some of us managed to obtain weapons, just simple guns. I remember the first time we used them. The march was surrounded by militiamen who were beating the people on all sides. To get us free, I pulled out my gun and shot in their direction. One of them fell, the others fled, and I could escape with my group of friends. That was the moment we became an armed group. Our goal from then on was to protect the demonstrators.[50]

While the chronology differs from region to region, the pattern was the same: Helped by army deserters, protesters took up arms as a response to the regime's suppressive efforts. The first offensive operations were usually aimed at relatively soft targets, such as isolated military posts, patrols, or police stations, with the aim of releasing political prisoners, capturing weapons, or forcing the regime to withdraw from an area. "Wanted by the police, we laid low outside the city and collectively made the decision to attack the army directly in Azaz," recalls a resident of the town.

We originally tried to protect the rallies with our weapons. The one's held on the 15th and 23rd of February 2012 had been successful, with more than 17,000 people on the streets of Azaz. But the regime then sent large numbers of soldiers with tanks and *dushka* [heavy machine guns]. Demonstrating became suicidal while arrests took place. The population fled the city. That was when we decided to attack. We knew we were wanted and it was only a matter of time before we were caught. But our group was badly organized, with only two pistols, three AK-47s and a few home-made bombs. We needed time to prepare. The first attack against a police station in Azaz failed because we were badly organized and lacked ammunition. Out of 300 people in our group, only 60 were armed. The second attack was also a disaster. We had RPGs but they didn't work and we had to flee from the tanks.[51]

Use of force by the regime left the protesters no other option but to take up arms. In all governorates, activists and defectors formed hundreds of armed groups, as the number of clashes escalated over the winter of 2011–2012.

The Division of the Country

As the crackdown went on, the protest movement turned into an insurrection and it started to defend itself against the army. On June 4, 2011, at Jisr al-Shughur (in Jabal al-Zawiya, near the Turkish border), the Syrian army suffered its first setback. When members of the security forces opened fire on a funeral procession, the protesters looted a police station,

[50] I-38, in Aleppo, January 2013.
[51] I-39, in Azaz, December 2012.

armed themselves and were quickly joined by deserters from a nearby military unit. The army responded with a sweep operation that provoked many more desertions. Soldiers refused to fire on civilians and swelled insurgent groups. By the end of the summer, with Jabal al-Zawiya in rebel hands, the regime military launched a major operation to retake it. Dozens of armored vehicles backed by helicopters moved against the insurgent areas.[52] However, the rebels were able to retreat across the nearby Turkish border and wait out the end of the military's operation. Similarly, the city of Homs became a revolutionary hotbed that the regime, spread too thin on the ground, could not afford to attack before September 2011. Meanwhile, throughout the summer, protesters aided by army deserters were busy organizing the first two major armed groups, namely Katiba Khalid ibn al-Walid and Katibat al-Faruq. When the regime launched the September operation to clean out Homs, it ran into strong resistance that the armed groups had prepared for during the intervening months.[53] However, the insurgents had difficulty holding the city against the more than 250 regime tanks lined up against them. By late September, the last few hundred fighters left in the city withdrew.[54]

That the rebels managed to survive during this period was due in part to the regime's stretched resources, which caused it to abandon entire restive regions. By February 2012, most villages north of Aleppo had therefore passed into the hands of the insurgents. They took and lost Azaz twice before the regime's troops withdrew from the city in June 2012 for the last time. Armed groups that had participated in taking Azaz converged on al-Bab, which fell to them by early July 2012. The regime still controlled the main roads but could only launch incursions into other regions. Within the space of eighteen months, the insurgency had taken control of over half the country.

Thus, the insurgency conquered few territories through frontal assaults. The rebels mostly seized areas that the security forces had withdrawn from. From mid-July 2012, the regime abandoned most towns north of Aleppo. "In the spring of 2012, we had to flee from our village when the regime sent in the tanks," recounted a resident of Maraa. "We waited at the Turkish border. Three days later we returned. The army had left, not before pillaging our houses. From this moment on, we took up arms." "Our village became a gathering place for insurgents in the region," said another. "We were struck by the ease with which we were

[52] Joseph Holliday, "Syria's Maturing Insurgency," *Middle East Security Report* 5, Institute for the Study of War, 2012, p. 22.

[53] Nir Rosen, "Armed Defenders of Syria's Revolution," *Al Jazeera*, September 27, 2011.

[54] Dominic Evans, "Syrian Army Forces Take Back Most of Rastan from Deserters, Activists Say," *Reuters*, October 1, 2011.

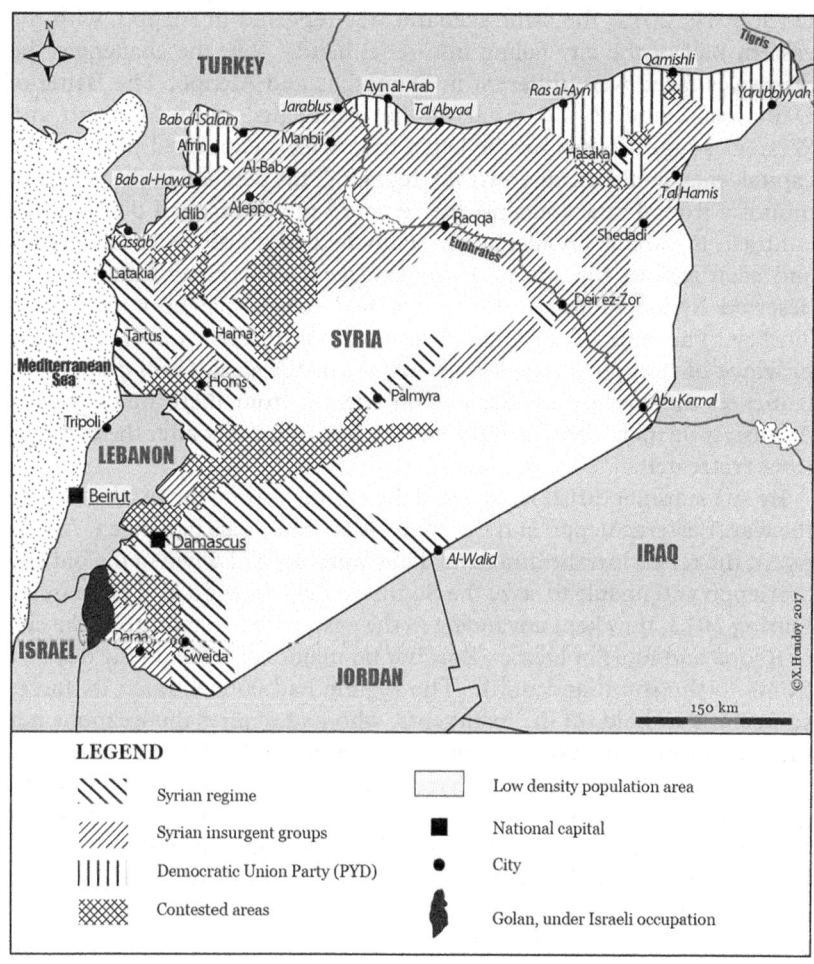

Map 3.1 The military situation (Spring 2013)

able to liberate our city. During the first demonstrations, the police hardly dared to leave the police station. Then they fled the city."[55]

Following the capture of small villages and towns, such as al-Bab and Maraa, the insurrection began large-scale offensive operations to capture the cities. Starting on July 15, 2012, thousands of rebels infiltrated Damascus helped by activists and took control of several neighborhoods.

[55] I-40, in Maraa, December 2012.

On July 19, 2012, the same scenario was repeated in Aleppo, with the eastern half of the city falling into rebel hands. Yet, the challenges the offensives faced were different in Damascus and Aleppo. The Battle of Damascus came as the result of the insurgents' pleas for Arab and Western support based on the belief that, with a concerted push on the capital, they could bring down the regime. This persuaded the rebels to mount a frontal attack against the regime's most seasoned divisions. In contrast, the attack on Aleppo was launched with little external support and even against the advice of the insurgent general staff made up of deserted Syrian military officers that had meanwhile been formed in Turkey. The bulk of the fighters from the northern campaign for the province of Aleppo assembled on July 18 in Liwa' al-Tawhid and then launched the successful offensive on Aleppo from there that, in early August, gave them control of the eastern half of the city after the regime's forces retreated.

By late summer 2012, it appeared the regime was on the brink of losing the war. Eastern Aleppo and the suburbs of Damascus had fallen. At this point, the rebels lost the initiative. They were bogged down in the old city of Aleppo and unable to seize the Southern neighborhoods of Damascus. During 2013, they kept advancing in the east, with the capture of the city of Raqqa and most of Deir ez-Zor, but no major cities fell on the decisive fronts to the south and north. The regime had concentrated its forces sufficiently to hold off the insurgents, who had neither the weapons nor the organization to take the regime's bastions. Indeed, the typical rebel strategy was to encircle the Syrian army bases and starve out the garrisons.[56] If the Damascus regime managed to keep supplies flowing, the garrison force held. The lack of training and organization as well as a lack of ammunition for the frontline fighters explains why the insurgent groups rarely maneuvered far outside their home base area. The units had a few Kalashnikovs, little in the way of heavy weaponry, and no anti-aircraft defense systems. They were incapable of launching a frontal attack against the regime military with its heavy weapons, aircraft, and armor. The revolutionaries might on occasion profit from superior local knowledge of the terrain but, lacking tactical expertise, they regularly suffered significant losses during poorly staged operations. Given these conditions, the rebellion proved incapable of leading coordinated offensives.

[56] In northern Syria, the regime's main military bases fell practically without combat after long sieges. This was the case for the Aleppo infantry school and the Shaala radar station, which fell in December 2012 after being surrounded for several months. The Taftanaz military airports in the region of Idlib and Menegh, north of Aleppo, were taken only after months of siege, in 2013.

From then on, the outcome of the crisis would be determined by success on the battlefield that, in turn, would depend on sustaining internal cohesion and each actor's ability to mobilize resources for the duration of a protracted war. The first outcome of the ongoing fighting was the regionalization of the insurgency. Initially, armed groups, while present throughout the country, did not necessarily control a well-defined territory, which made it difficult to map out the rebel areas during the early months. Differences between regions, however, gradually emerged, especially as the insurgents regrouped in under-administered areas, far from the cities and near international borders. Throughout 2013, the evolution toward more homogeneous territories dominated either by the regime or by the opposition resulted in frontlines being drawn, with the insurgents essentially controlling the areas in the north and south of the country, except for pockets around Damascus in the Qalamun Mountains and north of Homs (for a pointer on the military evolution after 2013, see the end of Chapter 9).

Part II

Revolutionary Institutions

4 The Building of Military Capital

The emergence of armed groups in the summer of 2012 marked the end of the extant economy of violence. In the months that followed, hundreds of armed groups sprang up spontaneously. However, their ability to deliver organized violence, i.e., to build up military capital, depended equally on bureaucratic and management skills. Yet, a lack of resources made it difficult to stabilize the military units, many of which dissolved with time. Initially, the insurgents made do without hierarchical structures and fighters could change affiliation based on the availability of resources.

Far from devolving into a phase of Hobbesian anarchy, the first months of the uprising saw the various military units coexisting peacefully. Until 2013, Syria was spared the competing territorialization of politico-military groups characteristic of the Somali and Congolese civil wars.[1] In line with claims first made in 2011, the fighters saw themselves as belonging to the army of a new Syrian state. In this sense, although organized in small units and in part self-financed, theirs was not a local vision nor did they represent opposing communities. The absence of any political affiliation also limited fragmentation; the preexisting opposition parties were exiled from Syria and played only a marginal role. Finally, many of the fighters, especially those that had deserted from the army, often fought far from their home region, sometimes in groups whose majority did not share either their ethnic or religious affiliation.

In 2012 and 2013, the groups gradually fell into line behind the FSA (Free Syrian Army). Military units that numbered at most a few dozen men expanded to include several hundred or thousand fighters with an emergent hierarchy and increasingly sophisticated organization. Ultimately, however, a lack of support and the ascendency of radical groups marginalized the FSA in the north and east of Syria while it remained dominant elsewhere.

---

[1] Ken Menkhaus, *op. cit.*; Koen Vlassenroot and Timothy Raeymaekers, *op. cit.*

Recruiting

Three issues let us examine the composition of the armed groups: the local recruitment of fighters, the dominance of the rural and working classes, and the increasingly significant sectarian divisions. First, the armed groups recruited largely near where they were based. Their involvement was usually voluntary, grouping a few dozen individuals from networks of activists, friends, or family in defense of their village or neighborhood. Later perhaps came the ambition to join a more distant frontline unit.[2] "In Maraa, the whole town has been involved from the beginning of the revolution. I demonstrated a lot early on in Aleppo, but even more here. When my city was liberated, many armed groups were created. I was initially hesitant to fight, but gradually I came around to the idea. Many of my friends were at the front for several months [. . .], this is how I came to join a group from Maraa fighting in Aleppo."[3] Some of these groups were made up of ex-protesters or were in the opposition primarily as a response to the regime's repression. "I did not participate much in the demonstrations," said a former resident of Damascus. "It was very dangerous to take to the street. But then the regime began bombing our neighborhood. At first no one knew what to do [. . .] We fled our building to take refuge in the suburbs of Damascus. Being in the movement or not made no difference. The repression, the risks, we were all in the same boat. That's how I joined a group in Ghouta [near Damascus]."[4]

Additionally, many of the deserters had done their military service far from home and joined insurgent groups near where they deserted, which nuances the local aspect of recruitment. Indeed, the first armed revolts occurred in garrison towns that had a strong military presence. For example, one of the main insurgent groups in Homs, Katibat al-Faruq, was composed chiefly of deserters who had come from all over Syria. The proliferation of military operations from the summer of 2011 on accelerated the growth in their numbers. In a routine established by Lieutenant ʿAbd al-Razzaq Tlass (commander of the Kataʾib al-Faruq), deserters would show their ID cards to a camera while delivering a morality-toned public statement that included their reasons for joining the insurgency.[5] The first desertions were improvised, opportunistic, or sometimes managed by bribing an officer. Gradually, as the monitoring of especially the Sunni soldiers increased, insurgents took greater initiatives to organize the desertions.

---

[2] I-26, I-41, I-44, I-49, and I-51, carried out with several commanders and combatants in the Aleppo region, December 2012 and January 2013.
[3] I-2, in Maraa, December 2012.
[4] I-68, in Cairo, January 2014.
[5] www.youtube.com/watch?v=POx380poU_8, viewed September 23, 2014.

"I was an artillery man, operating near Idlib up until my desertion in September 2012. At first, to abandon my station seemed a crazy idea. Our officers were watching us very closely and wouldn't hesitate to hit us. We had no contact with the outside world. We were given the coordinates of positions to shell and that was it. But gradually, there were more and more refusals to obey orders. I sabotaged our shells so they didn't explode when they forced us to shell a village. In September, I realized that out of 1,500 men in my brigade, only a thousand were left, the others had deserted. I decided to do the same. I managed to get a phone from which I called my family who put me in touch with a friend, now fighting in the Kata'ib al-Faruq. He told me to join him in Homs. I managed to leave the camp in the car that went into town for provisions. Once in Homs, I discreetly disappeared. My friend was waiting for me in the government zone with some other men. They gave me civilian clothes and paid for the taxi to take me to the liberated part of the city of Aleppo. Everything was planned. I spent a week there at the Revolutionary Security office, which gave me my papers attesting to my desertion and some money so I could pay for the trip back to my family.[6]

The insurgents created networks within each governorate that helped establish phone contact between soldiers and their families so these could encourage their sons to desert. Among other functions, they would also conceal deserters, sometimes hundreds of men, and guide them to local armed groups or help them return home. The Revolutionary Security Center in al-Bab, which we visited in December 2012, specialized in this.

We have two main tasks. The first is to contact the soldiers who have not yet deserted. Families come to us asking us to help their son escape, they give us the soldier's identity and his unit. Alternatively, we contact the soldiers, and then their families as soon as we can. We transmit this information to FSA troops in the area. At the same time, we give the family a phone number to send to future deserters that lets them contact the FSA for help in organizing their escape. Once successful, the FSA sends the deserter to us for debriefing and transfer back to his family.[7]

In the Center, dozens of deserters housed in separate rooms waited to be reunited with their families. "Our second task," says the Center's manager, "is to make sure that the deserters are treated well until they return home. Sometimes it takes time because they live on the other side of the country, in which case they wait here and are fed and housed. If they wish, they can join the ranks of the FSA near where they escaped. They have the choice." Many of the deserters we interviewed told us similar stories.[8]

---

[6] I-43, in Azaz, December 2012.
[7] I-44, a former sergeant, head of the center dealing with deserters, in al-Bab, December 2012.
[8] I-44, I-25, I-48, and I-83, carried out in al-Bab and the surrounding area, December 2012 and January 2013.

The number of deserters, while probably high, is difficult to pin down. The FSA, without specifying its sources, claimed 189,000 soldiers (the equivalent of 61 percent of the 300,000-man army in 2011) were wanted by the military security regime in 2013 for desertion or refusal to enlist.[9] Whatever the numbers, many deserters recounted their fear of reprisals against their families. A former member of the Syrian army general staff, General Mustafa Ahmed al-Sheikh, who deserted on December 16, 2011, believed that the majority of the officers were disgruntled but did not desert out of fear that the authorities would punish their families.[10] Once the insurgents had secured an area, however, this factor diminished. From this angle, desertions were more difficult for the Druze, Alawites, and Christians, who generally came from areas under tighter regime control.[11]

Second, the profile of combatants shows the importance of the rural and working classes. On the one hand, the revolutionaries and deserters were concentrated in rural areas, between Azaz and al-Bab (north of Aleppo), between Saluq and Tabqa (Raqqa province), in Jabal al-Zawiya (Idlib province), in the mountains to the east for Latakia and in the Qalamun Mountains on the Lebanese border. These areas became rallying zones for the revolutionaries, which explains why the first armed groups sprang up there. "I was arrested at the end of the summer of 2011 for protesting," said one Aleppo revolutionary. "When I was released in February 2012, everything had changed. Most of the people I had protested with had taken up arms and gone into hiding in the countryside in Anadan or Maraa. I went to join them. There were training camps sort of, where we were taught how to maneuver in groups, how to make explosives."[12]

---

[9] There were 6,000 officers, 7,500 non-commissioned officers, and 175,000 troops from all groups. Among them, there were said to be 3,000 defected officers taking refuge in special camps in Turkey and Jordan, and 3,700 defected officers remaining in Syria or cooperating with the revolution without having deserted. Ignace Leverrier, "A la veille de Genève 2, le régime syrien en manque de combattants . . .," January 20, 2014, http://syrie.blog.lemonde.fr/2014/01/20/a-la-veille-de-geneve-2-le-regime-syrien-en-manque-de-co mbattants/, report available at https://docs.google.com/document/d/1hp1FmVHsY8TF nfaZOwjJpRXZodZMT9zwc-O_Xd32cF0/edit?pli=1, viewed March 8, 2014.

[10] Ignace Leverrier, "Un général déserteur en faveur d'une zone sûre en Syrie," January 9, 2012, http://syrie.blog.lemonde.fr/2012/01/09/un-general-deserteur-en-faveur-dune-zo ne-sure-en-syrie/, viewed April 8, 2014.

[11] A study with defected officers suggests that ethical and moral motivations played a much greater role than sectarian and economic ones. Dorothy Ohl, Holger Albrecht, and Kevin Koehler, *For Money or Liberty? The Political Economy of Military Desertion and Rebel Recruitment in the Syrian Civil War*, Beirut, Carnegie Middle East Center, available at http://carnegieendowment.org/2015/10/24/for-money-or-liberty-political-economy-of-mil itary-desertion-and-rebel-recruitment-in-syrian-civil-war/ilqf, viewed January 3, 2016.

[12] I-45, in Aleppo, January 2013.

In the cities, on the other hand, the insurgent neighborhoods were generally the poorer ones, because it was easier to protest there than in the more affluent areas where the security forces were in tighter control. The areas where most of the events played out became real battlefields and the massive repression left the inhabitants with only two options: fight or flight. "Believe me, in Latakia, if you were living in a poor neighborhood, you did not really have a choice: we had to take up arms."[13] Without enough troops to control the entire territory, the army made the decision to bomb inaccessible neighborhoods.[14] Initially, the importance of rural areas and poorer neighborhoods did not reflect a specific relationship to violence or greater adherence to the cause by these categories; instead, it reflected the practical considerations of a transition to armed struggle.

Some of the protesters dropped out of the movement because they felt out of step socially and ideologically with the armed groups' resort to violence. Outside Syria, the issue divided the Syrian National Council (SNC – al-Majlis al-Watani al-Suri), while the National Committee for Democratic Change (NCDC), a coalition of left-wing opponents, denounced the use of arms.[15] Similarly, in Homs, the local council disagreed with the insurgents, along lines of an urban-rural split. "We were excluded from the revolution once it became militarized," explained a member of the Homs bourgeoisie. "Most of the fighters came from the surrounding villages, they did not believe in the same methods as we did, they were eager to take up arms. I was against it!"[16] With the end of peaceful demonstrations, the protesters – especially students and the educated – ceased to set the agenda. While the regime brutally suppressed the urban protests, the people revolting in the countryside became the chief protagonists of the armed struggle. To some extent, the militarization of protest marginalized the urban elites, shifting the insurgency's center of gravity toward rural areas. Nevertheless, the contrast between urban and rural was not clear-cut; the liberation of whole neighborhoods in the large cities (Homs, Hama, Aleppo) created military units manned by city dwellers. Because of similar social profiles and experiences of their members, the armed units and the civil institutions born of the insurgency often collaborated. "When Aleppo was liberated, we decided to create

[13] Telephone interview carried out by François Burgat, January 2013, François Burgat and Romain Caillet, *op. cit.* p. 61.
[14] Anthony Shadid, "Syrian Navy Joins Attack on Key Rebellious Port City," *New York Times*, August 14, 2011.
[15] "Syrie: l'opposition en voie de décomposition?" *Le Point*, February 29, 2012, www.lepoint.fr/monde/syrie-l-opposition-en-voie-de-decomposition-29-02-2012-1436196_24.php, viewed December 5, 2014.
[16] I-36, in Istanbul, September 2013.

our own unit with friends from the neighborhood. We also wanted to participate in Bashar's fall and protect our homes. In our unit, most of the fighters were local."[17]

Third, the sectarian rationale came into play later. Druze, Christian, and Alawite Arabs and Kurds often fought in the same units alongside Sunni Arabs. "In 2012, there were several Druze and Alawite deserters in our group," a Daraa revolutionary told us.[18] Similarly, Kurds, Christians, Arabs, and Turks were still fighting in Aleppo in the summer of 2013 under the FSA umbrella.[19] In Tabqa and the east, recruiting for the armed groups reflected tribal affiliations but without causing any noticeable friction.[20] Gradually, however, a sectarian dynamic began to intrude; Alawites were *de facto* excluded from the insurgency, while Christians increasingly organized their own self-defense groups. Furthermore, ethnic differences surfaced between Kurds and Arabs, for example, and started to create a divide between them as the armed groups became politicized (see Chapters 8 and 9).

The Organization of Military Units

The exigencies of combat forced the revolutionaries to improvise their military organization. In early 2012, armed groups began to adopt a military nomenclature: brigade (*liwa'*, *pl. alwiya*), battalion (*katiba*, *pl. kata'ib*), section (*saraya*), and commander (*qa'id*).[21] The insurgents borrowed these terms from the Syrian army where many had served, because, as noted previously, deserters made up a significant proportion of the fighters.[22] "We built our armed group ourselves. To keep things simple, we decided to use the same organization as the regular army."[23] This terminology also tapped into anti-colonialism dating from the time of the Mandate. The use of similar terms in 1925 had allowed the anti-French

---

[17] I-46, with a commander, in Aleppo, January 2013.

[18] I-47, in Amman, October 2013.

[19] Observations in Aleppo, August 2013.

[20] In several interviews carried out in summer 2013, rebels from eastern Syria mentioned that the regime had first tried to manipulate tribal leaders to calm the population, before some important families turned against it. See "Syrian Forces Arrest Top Tribal Leader – Opposition," *Reuters*, July 31, 2011; "Tribesmen Say Deir ez-Zor's Sheikh is Dead; Evidence Indicates He Was Tortured," *Al Arabiya English*, October 6, 2011.

[21] We have broadly translated *katiba* and *liwa'* by "armed group" and "military unit," because their use in the insurrection is ambiguous and sometimes misleading. In fact, certain units keep the name *katiba*, even though they are made up of more men than some *liwa'*.

[22] Here is an explicit case of "vulgarisation of power" with an acute awareness on the part of actors of the state formation process they are taking part in. Bruce Berman and John Lonsdale, *Unhappy Valley: Conflict in Kenya and Africa*, Volume 1: *State and Class*, London, James Currey, 1992, pp. 5 and 13–45.

[23] I-48, in al-Bab, December 2012.

insurgents to regard themselves as nationalists, as opposed to the revolts of 1919, which had been perceived as local and sectarian.[24]

However, behind the formal organizational façade borrowed from the regular army the insurgents were much more informal. The dividing line between civilians and combatants was not always clear: Most did not wear a uniform, and many fought part-time while living at home and joined their affiliated group for specific operations. For example, one Aleppo city councilman divided his time between his frontline unit and his municipal administrative duties.[25] Moreover, there was no clear hierarchy: Volunteers would rally to a group leader for various reasons, such as his bravery in battle or his ability to obtain weapons, but the unit command generally was not conferred based on prewar prominence or position. The two leaders of Liwa' al-Tawhid, the largest military unit within the Aleppo Governorate, 'Abd al-'Aziz Salama and 'Abd al-Qadir Salah, had been teacher and owner of a small business, respectively. Many of the groups would remove their commanding officer if he proved unfit to lead them into battle. Many witness accounts point to a high rate of turnover of unit commanders.

This lack of organization explained that the fighters were free to leave their unit as and when they wished, sometimes to join a different group. "I'm a sniper," we were told by a fighter in Azaz "Few people shoot like me, and as I have friends in different groups, I change units regularly. Besides, I only join units that give me a sniper rifle with which to fight."[26] Gradually, some groups tried to guarantee the fighters' loyalty, but moving from one unit to another remained possible within the FSA. Fighters could even join the Jabhat al-Nusra, the al-Qaida affiliate, and later move on to another armed group. "After several months with al-Nusra Jabhat I was tired of the strict rules they imposed on their fighters. So, I left to join Ahrar al-Sham, one of the biggest units in northern Syria. We are as well armed there, but, above all, free to go home whenever we want."[27]

In frontline areas or in the first weeks after securing a city, the fighters found themselves as the sole authority and as such exercised civil functions. With no legal training, they punished without judging and resolved disputes informally, while enforcement of their decisions generally depended on how strong they were militarily. Subsequently, armed groups sponsoring or exercising civilian functions favored the emergence of new institutions.

---

[24] Nadine Méouchy, "Les mobilisations urbaines et rurales à l'époque mandataire. Remarques préliminaires," in Nadine Méouchy (ed.), *France, Syrie et Liban, 1918–1946: les ambiguïtés et les dynamiques de la relation mandataire*, Damas, IFEAD, 2002, pp. 315–323.

[25] Observations in Aleppo, August 2013.

[26] I-49, in Azaz, December 2012.

[27] I-50, in Aleppo, August 2013.

The Civil Functions of a Military Unit in Aleppo[28]

The Liwa' Ahrar Suriya transformed the local school in the Qadi Askar neighborhood into a police station with jurisdiction over the entire insurgent-controlled area. The unit's commander was a former physiotherapist and bodybuilding champion who had worked in Dubai for several years before returning to Syria to join the revolution. His second-in-command had defected from the regime's security services.

Under their leadership, several dozen fighters patrolled the neighborhood. They monitored traffic and intervened in misdemeanor offenses, often beating and then releasing the perpetrators. The most important offenses were sent to the Court of the United Judicial Council of Aleppo (Mahkamat Majlis al-Qada' al-Muwahhad). In addition, the commander practiced mediation and arbitration in civil disputes (contracts, divorces). The school building also housed the neighborhood's only clinic.

The commander also worked with a notable who lived close to the police station who, with the Liwa''s support, was also responsible for baking and distributing bread in the neighborhood. Leading a surveillance militia, the Katibat al-Mustaqbal (Battalion of the Future), he also led a night patrol with fighters from the police station. He played an important part in establishing a neighborhood council.

Financing the Insurgency

The insurrection lacked the resources for arming, equipping, and feeding its troops. Units regularly disbanded for lack of funding, and individuals, left unarmed, either changed groups or abandoned the fight altogether. As part of their revolutionary commitment, a certain number of Syrians sold their personal assets to finance the struggle. They sold their homes, bought weapons, and funded their own groups. "My store was no longer making money. Rather than carry on that way, I decided to sell everything while I still had the chance. With the money I made, I bought communication equipment, ammunition and vehicles to equip our unit. A small investment, but that got us noticed. From then on money came from outside."[29] Weapons, hard to find and expensive, were trafficked into Syria (from Turkey, Iraq, Lebanon, Jordan) or bought at high prices from Syrian soldiers and police. Handguns cost several hundred dollars, Kalashnikovs between \$1,000 and \$2,000, and ammunition around \$2 a piece.[30] "To

---

[28] Observations and interviews in Aleppo, December 2012–January 2013.
[29] I-41, in Aleppo, December 2012.
[30] For comparison, these prices could be divided by three in Iraq in 2013.

form my group, I had to sell my interior decoration shop," said a fighter originally from Maraa.

Given the situation, I had discounted the goods. In total I raised $ 200,000, just enough to equip about thirty men. A tailor from Maraa made our uniforms. I bought twenty AK-47s and a thousand cartridges for each one, two machine guns and some RPGs. Unfortunately, I only found one sniper rifle. Weapons are scarce and expensive! I bought portable radios and three 4x4s. I had just enough money for petrol and to pay a salary of $50 per fighter for 3 months. The Liwa' al-Tawhid [also from Maraa] gave us more weapons and ammunition whenever they needed us to attack a position. The rest of the time, we would take turns at the front in groups of twenty and the Liwa' al-Tawhid would take care of our supplies. On our side, we'd film our attacks to get help from Syrians abroad.[31]

The weapons taken from the Syrian army and security forces added to whatever the insurgents managed to buy. "We were fighting with one weapon for three," said a fighter from Daraa. "Buying new guns was too expensive, so we used second-hand material taken from our enemies."[32]

The armed groups also managed to secure external resources, notably from the Gulf countries. Syrians in exile also sent money to support them. To be visible to potential donors and at the same time bypass existing channels, armed groups deliberately dramatized their struggles and displayed their ideological credo in videos posted on YouTube and on the group's Facebook page. Each operation was carefully filmed and archived, the unit's logo embedded and images captioned.[33] The videos generally showed military operations so that donors could see what their money was spent for. The insurgents themselves undertook this communication exercise, leading to specialization and the creation of media centers (Maktab I'lami) alongside the logistics and administrative offices. Media coverage was provided by a "journalist" who had a somewhat ambiguous role in the unit that hovered between civilian and combatant. He provided expertise in shooting, processing, and disseminating images of the war. A journalist-activist from the Liwa' 'Asifat al-Shimal explained to us how the propaganda worked: "We are video professionals. Every battle is filmed and then we edit the video adding logos and unity slogans. The goal is to outshine other groups to get more funding."[34] In some cases, the media center was a separate unit directly under the orders of the group's commander. Larger military groups would typically be equipped with cameras, computers, and a satellite link.

---

[31] I-42, in Maraa, December 2012.
[32] I-29, in Amman, October 2013.
[33] A great many videos are available online, see for example Liwa' al-Tawhid laying claim to an attack on Aleppo, www.youtube.com/watch?v=mCxn2VoHxzc, viewed April 10, 2014.
[34] I-102, at the Bab al-Salam Syrian border post, December 2012.

Coordination and Professionalization

As the war ground on, military groups professionalized their operations and improved coordination. The formation of *liwa'* (brigades) is a good starting point for depicting this trend. The formation of a *liwa'* (brigade) can be described from two perspectives: one, as resulting from the internal growth of a *katiba* (battalion), for example 'Asifat al-Shimal in Azaz or Fatah in al-Bab, and the other from the merging of existing *katiba*, with both proceeding in parallel. Most *katiba* that made significant advances, such as taking a city, were strengthened as a result. They were often joined by individual fighters or by other *katiba*.

The generic term *liwa'* (and sometimes that of *kata'ib*, or battalions) covered two organizational models. On the one hand, composite military units, as in Kata'ib al-Faruq or Liwa' al-Tawhid, operated without any *de facto* integration. In such cases, decisions were negotiated between the respective leaders and did not require integration at a tactical level. They appeared on the scene at the same time as the smaller units, and highlighted how fluid things were during the first few months. A *katiba* was free to join one or another *liwa'* with the financial reward or logistical support offered often tipping the balance.

On the other hand, a *liwa'* could be a relatively hierarchical organization, with men affiliated with a *liwa'* but not enlisted in a given *katiba*. The Liwa' Ahrar al-Shahaba, the Liwa' al-Umawiyyin, the Liwa' al-Islam, and the Kata'ib Ahrar al-Sham notably represented this model. "We put in place regulations, a hierarchy between the different offices tasked with administration, logistics, or military operations. Each fighter has a registration card from his liwa'. His weapons are issued to him and he must return them. Everything is recorded, allowing us to know exactly what is available to us."[35] From the fall of 2012, the leaders of certain *liwa'* decided to create new *katiba*, which were thus no longer the product of spontaneous mobilization. With their accumulated resources, *liwa'* absorbed and financed previously independent units, allowing for rapid geographical expansion. The new *katiba* were therefore able to deliver troops to the front line and, in the first months, make rapid advances. For example, the Liwa' Ahrar al-Shahaba and the Liwa' al-Islam had organizational charts, parts of which depicted the responsibilities of a military police force. In addition, while the *katiba* was usually responsible for defining its own area of operations, the *liwa'* could order a *katiba* to redeploy from one area to another. This is an important aspect of professionalizing a fighting force, because once a unit can deploy fighters outside its home territory, it

---

[35] I-48, manager of the administrative office in Liwa' al-Umawiyyin, in al-Bab, December 2012.

gains in cohesion and discipline. To this end, the Liwa' al-Umawiyyin created a system that allowed for the rotation of men between its constituent *katiba*. Finally, the merging of combatants into larger units continued with the creation of divisions (*firqa*) that occurred in two phases: first came the deliberate pooling of resources of various *liwa'* and this was followed by external pressures from national coordinating bodies. By 2013, divisions numbered in the same way as in the regular army were established in the provinces of Idlib, Aleppo, Raqqa, and Damascus.

In March 2012, a coordinating team based in Turkey and backed by the Gulf countries and the West further strengthened the process of centralization that had begun with the formation of *liwa'* at the grassroots level. At a national level, the Supreme Military Council (al-Majlis al-Askari al-A'la) made up of representatives of the main FSA commanders, the General Staff (Hay'at al-Arkan), and five military regions was constituted for better operational coordination.[36] In every governorate, military councils were established to integrate the units vertically, paralleling the appearance of the *firqa* that they were, one day, intended to lead. The Military Councils brought together representatives of the insurgency's main units stationed in a governorate and a minority of career officers who formally managed the structure but had limited weight. In fact, the Military Councils did not have their own staff, their official tasks being limited to advising on military training, preparing operations, and coordinating meetings. For example, to prevent a repeat of the conflicts that arose between armed groups after the taking of the Infantry Military Academy, the Aleppo Military Council in January 2013 called a meeting to coordinate the division of spoils prior to the taking of Menegh military airport (near Azaz). The influence of the Aleppo Military Council increased periodically in line with the distribution of ammunition or fighters' pay. "After the conquest of northern Syria, the Military Council of Aleppo paid salaries of $150 to fighters swearing allegiance to them," noted one commander from Aleppo.[37] By 2013, the head of the Aleppo Military Council, Colonel 'Abd al-Jabbar Muhammad 'Ukeydi, was a well-known figure, appearing regularly on Al Jazeera, but his authority over the day-to-day conduct of the war remained low.[38]

---

[36] "Syrian Rebels Create New Unified Military Command," *Associated Press*, December 8, 2012, www.huffingtonpost.com/2012/12/08/syria-rebels-military-council_n_2263256.html, viewed May 28, 2014.

[37] I-51, in Aleppo, January 2013.

[38] On the tension between Liwa' al-Tawhid and the career officers of the Aleppo Military Council, see Charles Levinson, "Leadership Rifts Hobble Syrian Rebels," *Wall Street Journal*, September 10, 2012, http://online.wsj.com/article/SB10000872396390444082904577608613073062158.html, viewed March 10, 2014.

The Liwa' al-Tawhid

The Liwa' al-Tawhid, set up on July 18, 2012 by a core group of fighters from Maraa, would become a leading military actor in Northern Syrian. It was the first *liwa'* in the province of Aleppo to unify the various *katiba* under a single military leader, 'Abd al-Qadir Salah, and one political leader, 'Abd al-'Aziz Salama. It dominated the north of Aleppo until the autumn of 2013, probably fielding several thousand fighters, although the exact number is uncertain. Liwa' al-Tawhid faced the challenges of rapid growth brought on by an increasing number of combatants coupled with an expanding theater of war. It had to streamline its media centers, their prime tool for bringing the unit to foreign attention and what proved to be considerable funding.[39]

Beyond its military role, the Liwa' al-Tawhid played a key role in setting up insurgent institutions in the north, including the Revolutionary Security (Amn al-Thawra) and the Court of the United Judicial Council. However, from the spring of 2013 when its *katiba* started to engage in economic plundering, the *liwa'* became a drag on the consolidation of institutions. Salah's death in November 2013 also weakened the *liwa'* relative to Islamist groups such as Harakat Ahrar al-Sham al-Islamiyya and ISIL. In January 2014, the opening of a new front against ISIL following their expulsion from Aleppo accelerated the fragmenting of liwa' al-Tawhid to the advantage of other FSA brigades who joined in a new coalition, the Army of the Mujahidin (al-Jaysh al-Mujahidin). Lack of adequate funding kept the *liwa'* from rebuilding a stable leadership and eventually it lost key territories to ISIL again. Salah's death, therefore, knelled the beginning of the end for the *liwa'*, which ultimately disintegrated, with its units joining other armed groups.

Attempts to merge armed groups into larger organizational units highlighted the different approaches used on the southern and northern fronts. In the south, the relatively small size of the territories under insurgent control and their dependence on Saudi funding lent weight to the Military Councils of Daraa and Damascus. The integration here was relatively advanced and tensions between the groups were limited.

In the North, coordination was more complex, particularly because of the fragmented financial donor base, but also exacerbated by the generally spotty control over the Iraqi border. Plundering of certain conquered cities by insurgents undermined their legitimacy. Bringing discipline to the fighters became an imperative that led to the creation of Revolutionary Security (Amn al-Thawra) in August 2012. Their mission was to prevent any one armed group from controlling an entire territory and engaging in

[39] Many of the *liwa''s* propaganda videos are regularly published on the Internet, www.liveleak.com/view?i=627_1389068164, viewed March 25, 2014.

racketeering. Revolutionary Security judges were given jurisdiction over conflicts between most military units within the governorate of Aleppo. Based in al-Ra'i, this new institution ran a prison and a media center. A few hundred meters from the Turkish border, al-Ra'i had the additional advantage of being far removed from combat zones and from being bombed. A second office was created in the Hanano district of Aleppo: This office had jurisdiction over the city, while the one in al-Ra'i adjudicated in the rural areas. During the autumn of 2012, an agreement was concluded among a majority of the governorate's units that expanded the two units' jurisdiction. In addition, a special military unit composed of fighters chosen from the various units was attached to Revolutionary Security and, if necessary, the latter could also count on reinforcements, especially from the Liwa' al-Tawhid. Revolutionary Security was empowered to arrest not just fighters but also *katiba* and *liwa'* leaders. However, the use of force was rare and negotiations commonplace. In general, the Revolutionary Security acted as a deterrent and there were few attempts at interference against the powerful unit.

As its power grew, Revolutionary Security also attracted criticism. Combatants and civilians accused it of being an embryonic security apparatus in the service of the Liwa' al-Tawhid.[40] By the spring of 2013, it had evolved into both a military and civilian police force, as well as a counterespionage service charged with interrogating deserters. The disapproval it garnered allowed Aleppo's Transitional Council to form a new civilian police force (see Chapter 5) to the detriment of Revolutionary Security, which mutated into an internal disciplinary tool of the FSA. However, by the summer of 2013, Revolutionary Security was disbanded for lack of financial resources.

I was responsible for information at the Revolutionary Security until March 2013. The commanders were mostly from Liwa' al-Tawhid, but the fighters were from all different military units north of Aleppo. Our investigations allowed us to stop fighters extorting the population. But we were victims of our own success. The more effective the Revolutionary Security was, the more it irritated the military units. They no longer wanted to fund us, they did not want to be investigated. We were not able to obtain financing from abroad. Without resources, we disbanded.[41]

In the summer of 2013, after the dissolution of Revolutionary Security, several units created their own intelligence functions and the Liwa'

---

[40] I-13, I-12, and I-23, with civilians and combatants from different active units in the Aleppo governorate, December 2012 and January 2013.
[41] I-52, in Aleppo, in August 2013.

al-Tawhid formed a military police unit (al-Shurta al-'Askariyya) responsible for managing relations between combatants and civilians.[42]

Integration met with considerable resistance. Certain *katiba* absorbed into *liwa'* became autonomous later, as shown by the example of the Katiba Abu Bakr, which split from the Liwa' al-Tawhid. Other *katiba* remained de facto independent despite their formal affiliation with the *liwa'*. In addition, certain *liwa'* often were in decline due to a lack of resources and, as the *katiba* regained autonomy, membership in a *liwa'* essentially became a formality, so that, by the summer of 2013, Kata'ib al-Faruq or Liwa' al-Tawhid represented little more than empty labels.

In some cases, a commander, eager to escape supervision, would try to carve out an independent stronghold. North of Aleppo, near the Turkish border in the town of Azaz, the Katibat 'Asifat al-Shimal pursued a territorialization strategy until November 2012 that went directly counter to the prevailing dynamic of integration. Its leader, 'Umar Dadikhi, a former cigarette smuggler working the Turkish border, used cross-border networks to autonomously finance his own group. After taking the town of Azaz, he adopted a predatory economic strategy: Taking control of the border post of Bab al-Salam, he would not only tax vehicles passing through but also resell prisoners captured by his fighters. Concurrently, Dadikhi incorporated other battalions from Azaz and upgraded the *katiba* into a *liwa'*. His men took control of the prison, set up their own police force, and monopolized foreign aid by funneling it through an *ad hoc* organization he set up. He forced the young revolutionaries in the Azaz's media center to stop work when they criticized him (November 2012) and the center's technicians from the center had to work for him at Bab al-Salam, in buildings adjacent to his headquarters.

Practices like this undermined the popular legitimacy of the insurgency and provoked a response from key northern rebel leaders. Several groups, including the Liwa' al-Tawhid, led hundreds of men if not a thousand equipped with heavy weapons against Dadikhi. Under direct threat, he accepted an agreement signed by 'Abd al-'Aziz Salama and 'Abd al-Qadir Salah (the commanders of the Liwa' al-Tawhid), Colonel 'Abd al-Jabbar Muhammad 'Ukeydi (a member of Aleppo's Military Council), and Sheikh Ahmad Feyat (a Revolutionary Security judge). It stipulated that customs tariffs were to be reduced from 300 to 100 Syrian liras per person and from 750 to 500 per vehicle and that these rates were to be posted publicly. Dadikhi's brigade was ordered to withdraw from Azaz, and civil

[42] I-53, I-39, I-60, and I-61, carried out with a commander of the Revolutionary Security, as well as members of various office departments in al-Ra'i and Aleppo, January 2013, and I-64, I-65, and I-66 with the military police in Aleppo, August 2013.

institutions (court, local council, and police force) were to be established and sixty-four prisoners held without trial were to be released. Dadikhi honored these commitments but remained an important figure in the city, by having cronies elected to the city council.

In general, creating a genuine military hierarchy faced two challenges: the low technical competence of the commanders and the lack of pay for fighters. While career officers dominated the Military Councils, the revolutionary groups were led by civilians who had responded to the call to arms. When dealing with the armed groups, the Military Councils, particularly in the North, were handicapped by lack of resources. Before the battle of Aleppo, which began in July 2012, Military Council officers advised against an attack on the city.[43] But, because they lacked control over the insurgent units, including the Liwa' al-Tawhid, they had to acquiesce in an operation they considered dangerous. Promises the Military Councils made concerning pay were never followed through on, further undermining their credibility. On April 1, 2012, the International Conference of the Friends of Syria promised to pay every fighter joining the FSA 150 dollars, the equivalent of a month's salary of an average official.[44] Pay was a crucial issue in ensuring the loyalty of the fighters to their central command. However, a lack of follow-through by the West and the Gulf States on their pledges of funds meant that after the spring of 2013 the pay stopped.

[43] Interview with members of the Aleppo military council, January 2013. See also "Tentative Jihad: Syria's Fundamentalist Opposition," *Middle East Report* 131, International Crisis Group, 2012, p. 26.

[44] I-50, I-51, and I-94 with combatants from various *liwa'* in the Aleppo governorate, see also "Opposition Says Syrian Rebel Fighters to Get Salaries," *BBC*, April 1, 2012, www.bbc.co.uk/news/world-middle-east-17578248, viewed April 20, 2012; "First 'Pay Day' for Syrian Rebels in Aleppo," *Al Arabiya News*, October 23, 2012, http://english.alarabiya.net/articles/2012/10/23/245483.html, viewed November 30, 2012.

5 Administering the Revolution

By the winter of 2012–2013, millions of civilians lived in areas controlled by insurgents that had no public services or administrators (judges, engineers, ranked police officers, mid-level managers) since most had fled the fighting. Supplies of food, electricity, water, gas, and oil were intermittent or nonexistent, schools and hospitals had closed. The insurgents had to respond to a population craving the resumption of public services, not just liberation from the authoritarian ways of the old regime.

Despite the violence of the bombings and lack of resources, by the summer of 2012 alternative civilian institutions were up and running. Gradually resuming police, administrative, and judicial functions, all these institutions faced similar problems: finding qualified personnel, resolving hierarchical relationships among different administrative units, and defining procedures. The ability to monopolize, rationalize, and professionalize the institutions would ultimately determine their efficacy and their legitimacy, but, here too, a lack of resources bedeviled the civil institutions, which, moreover, had to compete with parallel structures set up by political-military groups, a combination of factors that ultimately damaged them.

The Courts

Courts were among the first institutions reestablished by the revolutionaries. Justice had ceased being administered outside regime-controlled areas and many Syrians therefore no longer had access to official tribunals. The new courts dealt with everyday as well as war-related disputes. The courts were more important than ever, since the revolution was a rejection of the arbitrariness of Baathist power, and given the instability and institutional void the war brought with it. "When we took control of the first villages and towns, the issue of justice was raised quickly," explained Sheikh Hossein, one of the first of the insurgency's judges in Aleppo province. "We were fighting against the most terrible dictatorship of the region; our goal was to bring freedom to the region and allow justice to reign once again."[1]

The origins of the new judicial organizations were rooted in the practices of the armed groups. From the first months of the insurgency, these relied on third parties to arbitrate their disputes. The first victories raised questions regarding the division of buildings and weapons seized. Insurgent groups also needed to ensure their own cohesion (e.g., by setting penalties to impose for disobeying orders) and to deal with complaints by civilians against individual fighters. The information we have on the period is incomplete but, north of Aleppo, armed groups would regularly turn to the sheikhs to resolve disputes.[2] "When we liberated the city of Maraa and conquered major military assets, we didn't know how to distribute the spoils among the armed groups. There were also many civilians who came to ask us for justice in their personal business (theft, violence, divorce), in addition to the problems between fighters and civilians. I was the only sheikh around, and so I was chosen to hear these cases."[3]

With the capture of the first major cities, the new judges asserted themselves; justice became a collective endeavor. Courts were established in a madrasa in Azaz, in the municipal service building in Deir ez-Zor, or in a former courthouse in al-Bab. The situation differed from city to city or district to district, each court's composition reflecting the respective balance of power between civilians and the military, the legal profession and the militants, and between the religious and seculars. From this diversity of local situations emerged an embryonic organization that augured the establishment of a judicial system. We describe this emergent organization in four aspects: consensus on a legal code, integration of the courts in a hierarchical structure, the reintroduction of specialist personnel, and, finally, the degree of independence from the military units.

First, the choice of the judicial code to be applied in insurgent zones was as much a response to practical needs as it was an ideological preference. The limited number of judges that had defected meant there were very few available to rebuild the judicial system. The few cases where Syrian civil law was applied in the new courts, such as those in Harem, Salqin (north of Idlib), and Duma (a suburb of Damascus), can be explained simply as a reflection of the availability of judges. Due to pressure from radical Islamists, these courts disappeared by the summer of 2013, beginning in Harem and Salqin. In the rest of the country, north of Latakia, Aleppo,

---

[1] I-54, in al-Bab, December 2012.
[2] A sheikh has religious knowledge without necessarily having followed advanced study. He may be employed in a madrasa or exercise a profession outside the religious field.
[3] I-55, in al-Bab, December 2012.

Raqqa, and Deir ez-Zor, for lack of an alternative Sharia law was established. "I am the only legal practitioner in Azaz," our interviewee explained, "no one here is really trained to dispense justice. The sheikhs were naturally recognized as the established authority. They know Sharia law, which is the source of a large part of Syrian Civil Law. They can therefore help resolve conflicts within the population."[4] Consequently, in the province of Aleppo, the first informal mediation efforts in the spring of 2012 were based on Sharia law, which retained legitimacy in the eyes of most people, especially in rural areas. In addition, the flexible casuistry of the Sharia system was well suited for dealing with uncommon situations not addressed in existing laws.[5]

However, beyond the religious rhetoric, these judgments were pragmatic arbitrations, even more so because their enforcement depended on the insurgent groups. Sharia law was less needed as an actual code than as a way of legitimizing decisions made.[6] "The Judicial Committee struggles to solve intertribal problems in Deir ez-Zor. Recently, three regime soldiers were captured; they belonged to two different tribes. To respect tribal justice, the Sharia court sentenced to death one from each tribe. The third was sent to prison."[7] The reference to Sharia was not only symbolic. Apart from a certain arbitrariness that persisted on the frontlines, commanders relied on judges for rulings on the treatment of prisoners and arrested people, and for the division of the spoils of war.

As the judicial system grew in insurgent areas, revolutionaries adopted the Unified Arab Code. Created in 1996 by a committee of Arab League ulemas funded by Gulf countries, it aimed at providing Arab countries with a Sharia-based civil and criminal law. After its implementation in the fall of 2012, the Court of the United Judicial Council of Aleppo (Mahkamat Majlis al-Qada' al-Muwahhad) was the first to apply the new Code. Most courts throughout northern Syria had adopted it nominally by the following year.[8] "We had a meeting in Turkey to coordinate the courts in Syria," an insurgent judge in the city of Azaz told us. "We decided to regroup the tribunals in the province under the authority of the Court of the United Judicial Council of Aleppo. This initiative applied as much to Islamic courts created by

---

[4] I-56, with an Azaz judge, in Azaz, December 2012.

[5] In Afghanistan and Somalia, we find the same effectiveness of the Sharia system when the State had withdrawn. Adam Baczko, "Judging in the Midst… *Op. Cit.*; André Le Sage, "Stateless Justice in Somalia: Formal and Informal Rule of Law Initiatives," *Centre of Humanitarian Dialogue*, Report, 2005, pp. 38–48.

[6] I-58 and I-59 on punishments and the permanency of negotiation practices, revealing the incapacity of the courts to impose Sharia, in Azaz, December 2012.

[7] I-57, with a revolutionary from Deir ez-Zor, in Gaziantep, August 2013.

[8] Communications Felix Legrand and Patrick Haenni, September and October 2013.

sheikhs as to the courts created by lawyers. The goal was to have a single code of law and one judicial system for all governorates."[9]

Second, in some governorates, a judicial hierarchy was reconstituted. The taking of Eastern Aleppo impelled the military, led by the Liwa' al-Tawhid, to back convening the Court of the United Judicial Council of Aleppo. It implemented a standard court case procedure consisting of a preliminary investigation, assignment of the file to one of the four specialized chambers (criminal, civil, family and military), an investigation, and a hearing. In addition, the Court of the United Judicial Council was, in principle, the Court of Appeal for the governorate.[10] It worked with the other courts of the governorate, urging them to establish a structure consisting of three specialized chambers (criminal, civil, and family), each with two sheikhs and a lawyer, and also to apply the Unified Arab Code. Other actors played a part in this standardization, notably the Governorate Council of Aleppo, whose legal office produced a list of approved courts with whom the Free Police of Aleppo worked exclusively (see below for more on the police).

In August 2013, a conference of approximately forty delegates from courts of the Deir ez-Zor, Raqqa, Aleppo, Idlib, and Latakia governorates was organized in Istanbul to harmonize process. By agreement, it validated the creation of a Supreme Judicial Authority (al-Hay'a al-Qada'iyya al-A'la) and mandated all courts to model themselves on the Court of the United Judicial Council of Aleppo, especially in the use of the Unified Arab Code and the recruiting of legally trained judges, whether Islamic or not.

The standardization of the judicial system met with some resistance. Some courts opposed their absorption into an emerging new judicial system, fearing their own dissolution. In Azaz, the merger of the Sharia court and the legal court made up of lawyers from the City Council was imposed by Aleppo against such resistance. In al-Ra'i, a new court had to be set up when the existing one refused to abide by the new rules. In al-Bab, the court aligned itself with the minority opposition in the City Council and managed to survive with the support of Jabhat al-Nusra fighters. In Daraa and Duma, conflicts arose between the courts created by lawyers and those created by the sheikhs.[11] In the end, most of these conflicts make clear that if integration of the courts into a unified judicial system was to continue, the balance of military forces within the insurgency had to remain stable.

Third, new judicial personnel were recruited from two profiles. One, that of people with knowledge of Sharia, did not necessarily yield competent judges. Most ulemas having supported the regime, judges had to be

---

[9] I-58, with a judge from the Judicial Committee of Azaz, in Azaz, December 2012.

[10] Authors' personal observations and interviews with staff and users of the Aleppo governorate's courts, December 2012–January 2013.

[11] I-29, with a revolutionary from Daraa, in Amman, September 2013.

recruited among the sheikhs that had remained in insurgent-controlled areas. However, most sheikhs were untrained in Islamic law and were often low-level teachers in madrasas. But, starting in May–June 2012, they started to play a key role, among them Sheikh Wada in Tal Rifaat, Sheikh Hossein and Sheikh Zerati in Akhtarin, Sheikh Juma'a and Sheikh Sukar in al-Bab. These Sharia courts let religious personnel redeem themselves with a revolution to which they had generally rallied late.

The other profile for reconstituting a judicial corps competent in legal proceedings were lawyers and judges who were recruited from among members of the committed professional associations, namely the Movement of Free Syrian Lawyers (Harakat al-Muhamin al-Suriyyin al-Ahrar) in Aleppo and the Group of Free Lawyers (Tajammu' al-Muhamin al-Ahrar) based in Turkey. While the profession had often attracted students that had failed their public service exams, the revolutionary upheaval offered lawyers a chance for upward social mobility. To legitimate themselves, they claimed some knowledge of Islamic Law, already the reference for personal status and in family affairs during the Baathist regime.[12] Some relied on certificates issued during the few weeks of training on the Unified Arab Code in Turkey organized by the National Coalition with the help of Western organizations. Nevertheless, the sheikhs who lacked legal training found their authority readily accepted, while lawyers and the (now rare) trained judges had to prove their religious knowledge to be accepted in the new order.

The Court of the United Judicial Council of Aleppo exemplifies the tensions that reigned between the two profiles and the accommodations that had to be made. It operated based on a compromise between lawyers, sheikhs, and the only trained judge to have defected in Aleppo. These individuals had very different priorities and schooling but the creation of a unified system meant that legal training had to become a criterion for selection, even for the sheikhs. The operational organization of the court was decided at a first meeting in Turkey in September 2012 between a lawyer belonging to the Movement of Free Lawyers, a sheikh trained in Islamic law at the al-Azhar University of Cairo, and the sole judge that had defected. The representatives of the three main judicial professions signed off on a complex set of trade-offs: The Presidency was to rotate monthly, alternating between a sheikh and a lawyer. The lawyers were the more numerous, two-thirds of the staff, but the sheikhs, two per chamber, dominated deliberations. The sole judge held a strategic position since he

---

[12] Baudouin Dupret, Souhaïl Belhadj, and Jean-Noël Ferrié, "Démocratie, famille et procédure. Ethnométhodologie d'un débat parlementaire syrien," *Revue européenne des sciences sociales* 65 (139), 2007, pp. 5–44.

assigned cases to the specialized chambers and could call for supplementary investigations.

In the end, this judicial system – not without difficulty – gained some independence. The military units saw that it was in their own interest to hand off the arbitration of conflicts that only undermined their legitimacy. At the same time, they tried to maintain a degree of control and influence over the courts. Thus, during the trial of Abu Talal, the commander of Katibat al-Hajaj (that became Katibat Ansar al-Shari'a upon the creation of the Liwa' al-Umawiyyin in September 2012) illustrated the initial limitations on the judges' authority. In consequence of accusations leveled against Abu Talal, an *ad hoc* tribunal composed of sheikhs was convened in September 2012.[13] Abu Talal was convicted, but sentencing was deferred until the end of the revolution, and he was thus free to resume the leadership of his military unit.[14]

In addition, armed groups and local councils tried to assert their own authority at times when they came into conflict with the courts. Commander Dadikhi, to counterbalance the Judicial Committee (Hay'a Shar'iyya) in Azaz, created his own court in late 2012; in January 2013, when the City Council of al-Bab wanted to challenge the Judicial Committee that supported an attempt to dissolve the Council, the latter set up a prosecutor's office. Thus, the courts were very much part of the local power struggles between various municipalities, some of which had their own judicial police, the support of different military units or city council. Some courts even managed public services, such as the supply of bread and electricity to their towns.

In Aleppo, the Court of the United Judicial Council gained independence, despite initially being a creature of the governorate's major military groups. However, it had to struggle to enforce its decisions on the military groups, which impaired its legitimacy. Certain armed groups (Jabhat al-Nusra, Harakat Ahrar al-Sham al-Islamiyya, the Liwa' Suqur al-Sham, and the Liwa' al-Tawhid) even established their own court, the Judicial Committee, in early 2013 so they would not have to defer to an independent body. Unlike the Court of the United Judicial Council, the Judicial Committee had its own police of 200 men seconded by the armed units that manned checkpoints across the city. The Judicial Committee refused to apply a written code, preferring to rely on Islamic jurisprudence, which included imposing a moral code, mandating the veil for women and

---

[13] Sheikh Yusef Sukar, Sheikh Ahmed Zerati (then judge of a Sharia court in Akhtarin), Sheikh Mustafa Shaabi, Sheikh 'Umar Juma'a. Sheikh Ahmed Nabi had an observatory status because, as imam of the Great mosque of al-Bab, he supported the regime, but remained locally the only cleric to have training in Islamic Law, I-113, with judge in Akhtarin, January 2013.

[14] I-54, I-55, with judges in al-Bab, December 2012, and I-114, in al-Bab, January 2013.

observance of Ramadan. It also had a hand in managing the city, with limited success, and it created competing services for the supply of electricity, education, and health care. By taking charge of administering the Aleppo mosques, which the Municipality had neglected, the Judicial Committee managed here, too, to take control.

The jurisdictional struggle between the two institutions did not lead to violence but, by the summer of 2013, tensions were palpable. The Court of the United Judicial Council of Aleppo, with the support of the FSA units, asked the Judicial Committee to adopt the new procedures and respect the new hierarchy. The Judicial Committee responded that the civil administration and the Court of the United Judicial Council were not staffed by good Muslims. In July 2013, police of the Judicial Committee threw a cordon around the Court of the United Judicial Council several times until forced to withdraw by FSA fighters close to the civil administration. In the meantime, consultations took place seeking a compromise, but, by late 2013, the Court of the United Judicial Council progressively lost importance relative to judges backed by armed groups.

The Police

Starting in late 2012, a police force was established in each city at the instigation of the National Coalition, the Governorate Councils, and the professional association of former police officers. The template for this project was provided by the creation of the Free Police of Aleppo (Shurtat Halab al-Hurra) in October 2012 as the provincial police force. The consolidation of a mixed bag of units looking after public security into a professional police force was designed to break up armed groups that were extorting the population and to send them back to the front. "The creation of the police must release the combatants of the insurgency to fight against the regime. We remove their responsibility toward the civilians, which they willingly accept."[15] From the outset, two dynamics strengthened the policing function: the consolidation of groups already in existence and a gradual professionalization.

The prime objective was to demilitarize conquered territories by setting up a police force several thousand men strong per province and so differentiate fighting from maintaining order. "We are under the command of General Adib Shelaf, who commands the Aleppo police from Sheikh Najjar, and we receive our instructions from the Aleppo Court of Justice. I apprehend suspects and I transfer them to the Court. My second task is to maintain public order. In both cases, I imprison suspects. If there are problems between civilians and FSA combatants, I send the file to the military court

[15] I-66, with a commander of the Aleppo Police, in Aleppo, January 2013.

in the Aleppo Court of Justice. I have no authority to oppose the military."[16] The Court was indeed expected to control military units: "As a law officer for the governorate of Aleppo, my job is to prosecute soldiers who take the law into their own hands," stated a judge from the Court of the United Judicial Council of Aleppo in charge of investigations. "I work closely with the police, with whom I conduct an inquiry. My role is also to ensure that the police receive instructions from the Court of Justice and its military tribunal, rather than the most powerful armed groups in the province."[17]

As it turned out, many military units had already set up their own specialized units with police functions. In Azaz, a few days after the city fell, Sheikh Yusef, one of the leaders of the Liwa' 'Asifat al-Shimal, activated a neighborhood militia and called it Civil Security (al-Amn al-Madani). "Azaz is our town, my men and I could no longer put up with the deteriorating security," Sheikh Yusef explained. "We created the Civil Security of Azaz, reoccupied the old prison and transformed it into a police office."[18] A month later, with the creation of the City Council by the Liwa' 'Asifat al-Shimal, the militia was turned into the city's Security Bureau (Maktab al-Amn) "Now we are an official police unit. We receive wages, 12,000 Syrian pounds for married men, 7,000 for the unmarried. Under the authority of the court, we organize night patrols of the city and check prices."[19] Similarly, in Raqqa, an insurgent unit going by the name Liwa' Umana' al-Raqqa (Brigade of the Trustworthies) formed a police force after taking the city in the spring of 2013. In practice, however, some of these groups acted as vigilantes.[20]

Improvised police forces were also born of local initiatives. In one of Aleppo's districts, a group of young revolutionaries adopted the name of Neighborhood Security (Amn al-Mintaqa).

We are all from the neighborhood of al-Sukari, we demonstrated and formed a resistance group of fighters to defend protesters against the repression by the regime. In July 2012, we fought side by side with the FSA to free our neighborhood. Immediately after its liberation, we decided to organize our own group to patrol the streets and prevent looting. Most of the inhabitants had fled. As soon as the court of Aleppo had been created, we made contact. Now we're waiting to be incorporated into the Aleppo police. We were promised uniforms and salaries provided we agreed to accept orders from the new police force. Our new name, The Free Police of Aleppo, has to be written on our uniforms and on the front of our premises.[21]

---

[16] I-61, with a second commander in the Bustan al-Qasr district police station, in Aleppo, January 2013.
[17] I-62, at the Aleppo Court of Justice, January 2013.
[18] I-63, in Azaz prison, December 2012.
[19] *Idem.*
[20] Observations in northern Syria, winter 2012 and summer 2013.
[21] I-64, with the leader of a security enforcement group in Salahaddin district, in Aleppo, January 2013.

The assimilation policy was driven from above, under a concept of having all police forces fall under a single authority.[22] The establishment of the Free Police, under the authority of the Governorate Council of Aleppo as well as of the Court of the United Judicial Council of Aleppo, proved to be the decisive stage in the process. The Free Police incorporated the self-proclaimed police forces with varying degrees of success, generally by removing their previous leaders. For example, in Azaz, Commander Ahmed replaced Sheikh Yusef after a power struggle lasting several weeks. In Bustan al-Qasr, a former regime police officer replaced the founder of the neighborhood police. In other cases, new police units were recruited and trained to replace unreliable groups. Thus, young protesters in al-Sukari, having turned themselves into a local police unit, hoped to assimilate into the Free Police but were edged out by a more recently trained unit. When some groups refused to give in, the Free Police leadership solicited help from armed groups. To install a police unit in al-Bab, the Free Police leveraged support by the men of the Security Bureau that were linked to the Liwa' al-Tawhid.

The second dynamic, professionalization, came with the establishment of local police forces. Uniforms and internal regulations were adopted: black coats and blue fatigues, pistols, a salute to superiors, respect for the hierarchy. The Free Police recruited and paid its members. The chiefs of staff brought in former police officers to rebuild professional civilian police forces. The commander of the Aleppo police, General Adib Shelaf, was the chief of police in Raqqa prior to 2011. Each commander of a police station was a former officer, reflecting the choice to have revolutionary commitment overridden by professional competence.

I graduated from the Police Academy in Damascus, the class of 1986. I was an inspector in the regime's criminal police. I deserted in June 2012, the work we were asked to do had become inhuman. I paid 400,000 Syrian pounds [2,700 dollars] to my hierarchy to formally leave my post. It was easy, because the police regime is very corrupt. As a civilian, I participated in many events. When Aleppo was liberated, I was naturally appointed by the people to the head of a neighborhood militia to ensure security. Then, with the creation of the Police, I was appointed second-in-command [at the Bustan al-Qasr police station].[23]

Salaries varied from 8,000 Syrian pounds [$55 US] for police officers and 15,000 [$100 US dollars] for officers. A police academy was also founded in a former military base on the outskirts of Aleppo. Here 200 officers received one month of training in 2013 (physical training, investigation

---

[22] I-65, with the head of police administration in Aleppo, January 2013.
[23] I-61, with the second-in-command of the Bustan al-Qasr police station, in Aleppo, January 2013.

techniques, weapons handling, criminal law). "In Bustan al-Qasr, I had 35 men under my command. Each was selected after a background check. Then there was a month's probation before being hired and paid. Except for me and my commander, all other police officers were new to this business. Their recruit training is short, they learn the basics and it's mostly we who are training them."[24] However, police officials had only limited resources and were unable to maintain public order unaided. In January 2013, in the six main areas of Aleppo (al-Sukari, Bustan al-Qasr, al-Ferdus, Azadiyya, Salkhi, Asalkhiyya) and some provincial towns (Tal Rifaat, Hreitan, Anadan, Azaz, and Soran), the police had a total of 1,142 men versus 9,000 fielded by the Baathist regime.[25] Moreover, they did not own enough motor vehicles to be fully autonomous.[26] Whenever possible, the Free Police compensated for these deficiencies by getting support from FSA brigades, especially ones drawn from the Aleppo population.[27]

A professional code based on that of the former regime and on texts found on the Internet, primarily guidelines published by the UN, was issued to new officers.[28] This code ostensibly limited detentions to 24 hours and adopted the presumption of innocence, two provisions that local police forces, however, rarely observed in practice. With former regime officers being reinstated, the traditional investigative and management techniques were revived, such as keeping written records of witness statements and fingerprints. The police oversaw former regime prisons near the Turkish border – in Azaz, al-Ra'i, and Jarablus.

Lack of resources once more soon hampered the process of integrating the police forces attached to armed groups. As a general of Aleppo's Free Police explained to us:

The division of responsibilities between the military police, put in place by the military units, and the civilian police was not free of trouble. In the governorate of Aleppo, under the leadership of the Liwa' al-Tawhid, armed groups in the province had joined forces to establish a military police unit called Amn al-Thawra. This organization allowed the Liwa' al-Tawhid to control the smaller military units. But the leaders of the military police did not want a competing force. We explained that we were not soldiers and that we would not interfere in their affairs. In any event, we

---

[24] *Idem.*

[25] I-66, with an Aleppo police general, January 2013.

[26] *Idem.*

[27] In spring 2013, European and American financial support of 3.5 million dollars was given to the Free Police of Aleppo through the private British security company ARK (Access Research Knowledge). This financing, lasting four months, was to pay for wages, equipment, and training for several hundred police officers. It was designed explicitly as the first stage of a more ambitious plan destined for neighboring governorates, at the time when the National Coalition was pushing the idea of a civilian Police force in all governorates.

[28] I-66, with an Aleppo police general, January 2013.

didn't have the means to challenge the military units, they were better equipped than us.[29]

Still, military units were quick to set up competing institutions. In al-Bab, in a context of tension between the City Council and the Court, the Liwa' al-Tawhid established a Security Bureau (Maktab al-Amn) that competed directly with the Court's police.[30] In the same vein, in Aleppo, the Revolutionary Security, which was also related to the Liwa' al-Tawhid and competed with the Free Police, changed its name in January 2013 to become a military police unit (al-Shurta al-'Askariyya).

The Administration

As soon as the insurgents took a city, their relationship with the population was defined by the insurgency's ability to set up effective civil institutions. The need for armed groups to concentrate on the front forced these to delegate the management of the rear areas. Coordinating committees (tansiqiyyat), often local, spontaneous initiatives, were organized under conditions of extreme insecurity. In fact, everything needed to be reorganized. The fighting had cut water and electricity supply, while the systematically bombed schools and hospitals were closed. A lack of running water and the accumulation of garbage explained the frequency of skin diseases and infections, particularly among children. The people, forced to abandon their neighborhoods while the fighting raged, returned a few weeks later once the fighting had died down.

The core of the civil administrations consisted of informal support groups that had provided medical care clandestinely to demonstrators or that had cared for the displaced. While the repression reduced protests in government-held areas, these revolutionary networks formed the embryonic structures for many local committees. Nevertheless, if the inclusive phase of the revolution suggested that Syrian society was capable of self-organizing, the civil war highlighted the limits to what local initiatives could accomplish. The charities we observed in Aleppo and other northern cities were managed in a highly improvised manner. In fact, they often had to depend on military units to help with distribution of food or clothing.

In cities and towns, the reconstruction of the administrative machinery proceeded relatively quickly. The same structures and the same nomenclature were to be found across the region, without an obvious explanation of their common origin. Under the banner of a Local Council (Majlis

---

[29] Idem.
[30] Authors' observations in al-Bab, December 2012.

Mahali) or a City Council (Majlis al-Madina), they took over existing municipal services, keeping employees (trash collectors, teachers), who were still getting paid by the regime. These local councils operated at the municipal level (sometimes extending into neighboring villages) and, in the case of Aleppo, at the district level. From August 2012, there were similar structures providing similar services, i.e., trash collection, schools, road maintenance, in all the localities.[31] Nevertheless, given their lack of resources, the city councils could not operate independently of the military groups.[32] Reflecting the clan structures (in Maraa and Deir es-Zor), the influence of local military commanders (in Azaz), or that of notables and protesters from 2011 (in al-Bab and Duma), council members were selected for office rather than elected by the population.[33]

At the same time, a process of institutional centralization was underway. With the support of the National Coalition, the Governorate Councils (Majlis al-Muhafadha) started being installed from the second half of 2012. These councils were particularly well developed in Aleppo. From the fall, the Revolutionary Transitional Council of the Governorate (al-Majlis al-Intiqali al-lil-Thawree Muhafadha) was established and given a dual responsibility: As the Municipal Council of Aleppo, it coordinated the District Councils and, as the Governorate Council, it also exercised jurisdiction over the governorate of Aleppo's civil institutions. The two roles were later split and, in March 2013, the Municipality Council of Aleppo set itself up in the Shahr neighborhood, in the city center, while the Governorate Council remained on transitional Council premises in the industrial district of Sheikh Najjar. The neighborhood, removed from the frontlines, was becoming a veritable administrative center running various services, including the Military Council of Aleppo and the headquarters of the Free Police. Similarly, in the governorates of Idlib, Raqqa, Deir ez-Zor, and Daraa, a Governorate Council was established to supervise the local councils. Where the administration was sufficiently centralized to enforce an institutionalized hierarchy, they managed to achieve a certain degree of efficiency.

However, the under-resourced governorates frequently saw their authority challenged. This translated into province-specific problems, depending on the military situation or the local politics. In Aleppo, during

---

[31] The City Councils were divided into departments: health, services, legal bureau, education, media, accounts, police (interviews carried out with different members of the city councils in the Aleppo governorate, December 2012 and January 2013).

[32] Interviews with residents and members of the al-Bab, Maraa and al-Ra'i City Councils, December 2012 and January 2013.

[33] Interviews with residents and members of the Azaz, al-Sukari, Ansari City Councils, December 2012 and January 2013. Since 2013 elections have been organized in other cities, notably Jabal al-Zawiya and Salqin.

the winter of 2013, the Governorate Council met with strong challenges by local councils to its legitimacy, reflecting broader tensions in the opposition between local revolutionaries and appointees of the National Coalition. In Idlib, the provincial capital was still in the hands of the regime, hindering the formation of a new civil administration. In Raqqa, armed groups, including the Harakat Ahrar al-Sham al-Islamiyya, and Jabhat al-Nusra, interfered in Council administration. Finally, in Deir ez-Zor, the Governorate Council, reflecting the political and tribal balance of power, was stalemated. ISIL's conquest of Raqqa and Deir ez-Zor in the summer and winter of 2014, respectively, put an end to the work of the insurgency's administrative institutions there.

From December 2012, two processes, the emergence of local institutions and the attempt to coordinate them from above, converged in elections held in Turkey. The National Coalition instructed consensual personalities to select hundreds of delegates from the insurgent-held parts of the of Idlib governorate. This electoral body then met in Reyhanlı (Turkey) and elected the Governorate Council and then the City Council of Idlib three months later. The same process was repeated in Aleppo with elections at Gaziantep (Turkey) in March 2013: Muhammad Yahya Nanaa, a former official of the municipality, and Ahmed Azuz, one of the first protesters, were elected governor and mayor, respectively. The two led a team of more than a hundred volunteers, selected for both their professional skills and their revolutionary commitment. In the summer of 2013, this push to install a hierarchy and central administration continued with local elections held in sixty-five insurgent neighborhoods of Aleppo. The same process was duplicated in Raqqa in January 2014,[34] in the south in Ghouta in January 2014, and in the rest of the Damascus periphery during the following months.[35]

That these institutions survived in the face of relentless, brutal bombing can be partly explained by the fact that they were financed from the outside. Unable to collect taxes and commercial levies, resources had to come mainly from abroad. Yet, as this external aid remained sparse, the coordination between municipal and national organizations (the Syrian National Council, the National Coalition) was limited. What funds the Western and Gulf countries provided flowed sporadically. Thus, teachers, with salaries, amounting to 25 dollars a month, in Aleppo were rarely paid. Since

[34] "New Local Council Election in Raqqa," The Syrian Observer, February 7, 2014, www.syrianobserver.com/News/News/New+Local+Council+Election+in+Raqqa, viewed September 8, 2014.
[35] Angelova Ilina, "Rebel-Held Suburbs of Damascus: Resilience Mechanisms in the Face of Chemical Attacks," Policy Alternative, Arab Reform Initiative, 2014.

municipal budgets depended entirely on donations from abroad, they were regularly paralyzed. In the absence of a reliable flow of money, city councils continued operating thanks strictly to the volunteer efforts by thousands of employees.

Paradoxically, some of the local councils' resources came from the government in Damascus that continued paying officials even in areas it no longer controlled. Thus, teachers and municipal employees would collect their salary in government-controlled areas (the cities of Idlib and Raqqa, before they were taken, areas held by the regime in Aleppo). This resulted in some of the public services – garbage collection, electricity, schools – functioning more or less normally in areas beyond the control of Damascus even with some officials choosing to stay home out of fear of sanctions against them or their families. Furthermore, salaries being paid created a pool of individuals available for other activities than those they had initially been hired for. So, for example, most of the sheikhs who worked as judges in the insurgency's various courts had been religious teachers and continued to receive their salaries as such. Many members of city councils received their civil service pay from the regime.[36] In December 2012, for the first time, some activists who publicly participated in the opposition were dismissed from the civil service.[37] One possible explanation for this paradox of Damascus funding the insurgency is that the regime wanted to maintain contact with officials in insurgent areas and encourage them not to go over to the opposition, at least publicly.

Despite the lack of resources and the constant bombardments, municipal administrations managed to restore public services within a matter of months.[38] For example, former employees of the regime borrowed trucks to individuals to collect refuse and remove rubble. Trash, collected on each street by the residents, was trucked to an old marble quarry repurposed as a landfill. In Aleppo, a health team visited every neighborhood to spray insecticides along the streets, thereby avoiding a malaria epidemic that threatened the city in the summer of 2013. The municipalities were also engaged in maintaining the infrastructure. They organized technical teams to attend to the electricity and water, but again, due to a lack of resources, were not able to repair the roads that were torn up in regime bombardments.

---

[36] Authors' personal observations in the Aleppo governorate's courts and Civil Councils, December 2012 and January 2013.

[37] Interviews with the regime's civil servants in the Aleppo governorate, December 2012 and January 2013.

[38] Yet to be accounted for, Sheikh Najjar's administrative center, although easy to bomb, remained intact until its fall to the regime in 2014.

Finally, city councils endeavored to keep medical and educational services functioning. Hospitals were set up in secret locations to keep them from being bombed. Depending on an area's accessibility, specialized services could be reestablished, particularly in pediatrics and dermatology. The same problem arose with the schools, which also were targeted by the regime's bombs, and so had to be clandestine and mobile. Regime textbooks or photocopies were used by the students and helped maintain a semblance of normality when baccalaureate exams were held in Aleppo during the summer of 2013. In Idlib, those who wanted to sit for the baccalaureate had to take the exams in regime-held areas. Moreover, in each province, a Civil Defense (al-Difaʿ al-Madani) was established in 2013 to lead readiness efforts, coordinate relief, and clear away rubble.[39] In Ghouta, in the conurbation of Damascus, after the chemical attacks in 2013, the city councils of Duma and Daraya organized the cleanup of rubble and chemical residue as well as the distribution of gas masks and measures to mitigate future bombings.[40]

[39] Observation in Hreitan, August 2013.
[40] Angelova Ilina, *op. cit.*

As the revolution turned into stalemated war, Syrian exiles in the West and the Middle East created insurgency support networks. Encouraged by backing from the United States, France, Saudi Arabia, Qatar, Turkey, and the UK, they formed representative bodies as precursors to a government in exile that would ultimately replace the regime. They reflected various political hues and were to lay the foundations of the future government. Through a set of specialized agencies they would channel international aid flows, coordinate military action, provide humanitarian assistance, and finance local administrations.

Overall, the creation of representative institutions failed. First, tangible support by the West and the Gulf countries was limited with little follow-through on pledges of aid. Then also, these fledgling institutions were riddled by divisions reflective of competition among donors (most blatantly, Saudi Arabia and Qatar), and of ideological differences among Syrian revolutionaries. Finally, the representative bodies failed to carry out their missions, losing credibility with foreign supporters, armed groups, and the insurgency's civil institutions inside Syria.

The Revolution in Exile

From 2011 on, the regime began targeting key opposition figures, most of whom had been forced into exile. "As a former Communist Party member and a signatory to the Damascus Declaration in 2005, I knew I was being watched. I had spent many years in prison under Hafez al-Assad. In 2011, I didn't dare protest, but I participated clandestinely in the organizing of the committee in the city of Suweida. I quickly realized that the regime was monitoring me closely and so I decided to leave Syria for Turkey in the summer of 2011."[1] "We had waited our whole lives for the revolution," explained another former Communist Party member. "But in 2011 we were the first to have to flee or join the insurgents. The regime

---

[1] I-67, with a representative of the National Coalition, in Cairo, January 2014.

knew about us, we had all seen prison. Demonstrating would have been folly for us, we were guaranteed a return to prison within twenty-four hours. Going abroad was our only chance to continue the fight."[2] The demonstrators thought they were going into exile for a limited time and continued to agitate from outside of the country. "In 2011, everything was still possible. When I left Syria for Turkey, then France, I imagined I would be back a few months later after the fall of the regime. I had been in prison before the start of the revolution. In 2011, after having narrowly escaped several arrests, I told myself that I would go abroad, take a break before returning."[3] Departures were often rushed, refugees usually choosing cities where they knew fellow exiled opponents.

For those who managed to obtain the visas, Paris and London were among the top exile destinations. "If I was going to start a new life, I wanted it to be in a country favorable to the Syrian opposition. I came to France with the idea of continuing to advocate, to find support to help the Syrian revolution." [4] Other refugees settled in major cities of the Middle East, either because they could not travel to the West or wanted to stay close to Syria. Amman, Beirut, and Istanbul thus provided many Syrian opponents with refuge. These cities, which offered both a cosmopolitan dimension and proximity to Syria, became important contact points for the opposition. In Turkey, the Erdoğan government, which favored the revolutionaries, provided accommodations for the opposition groups in places like Gaziantep and Antakya near the border with Syria. Many opponents in exile settled in Istanbul, making it a revolutionary hub. In Lebanon, many Damascenes chose Beirut, because it was only a few hours from the Syrian capital and offered intellectuals and activists a full life.[5] Amman was less popular with the Syrian revolutionaries; although it favored the revolution, the Jordanian state more strictly circumscribed the exiles' activities.

For two years, Cairo also became home to many Syrian revolutionaries who were attracted both by the economic opportunities it offered but even more so by the success of the revolution that had begun in Tahrir Square.[6] The new Muslim Brotherhood President, Mohamed Morsi, allowed Syrians to settle without a visa and with the same social rights as Egyptians. "When I had to flee Syria, I had heard that Syrians were welcomed in Egypt. On the revolutionary forums [online], Cairo was described as the place where the revolution continued, having simultaneously the headquarters of the Arab League, a more favorable economic

[2] I-68, with a former communist militant, in Cairo, January 2014.
[3] I-69, in Turkey, April 2013.
[4] I-70, in Paris, September 2012.
[5] I-71, in Beirut, July 2014.
[6] Communication with Maaï Youssef from observations made in January–February 2014.

situation and a regime ready to accommodate Syrian refugees."[7] However, in July 2013, the Egyptian military overthrew the Morsi government and installed Marshal Abdel Fattah el-Sisi. From then on, the exiles, tainted by their association with the Muslim Brotherhood, were vigorously attacked by the media and harassed by the security apparatus. As for the Kurdish political refugees, they gravitated to Iraqi Kurdistan where they had the support of Masud Barzani's Kurdish Regional Government.

Political activism facilitated the integration of refugees. "When I arrived in Cairo, most of my contacts were Syrian protesters in exile. I started working with them. We set up several media centers and organized demonstrations. This got our cultural center known. A few months later, the SNC [Syrian National Council] representative in Cairo offered me a job. That's how I found a part-time job."[8] Another exile had a similar experience in France. "First I was exiled in Paris, where I continued to campaign in small Franco-Syrian associations. Gradually, I met many French sympathizers, I built a network and I made new friends. Carrying on with the activism allowed me to stay active and to find work."[9]

These hubs were of key importance for the Syrian revolution. The proliferating associations raised money and funneled aid to Syria, organized events to highlight the plight of the Syrian people to Arab and Western populations, and lobbied the host countries to support the insurgency. These remained scattered initiatives that never gelled into a coordinated, credible representation for the revolution outside Syria.

From the SNC to a Provisional Government

Despite its weak militant anchoring in Syria, the first steps of the Syrian National Council (SNC) were welcomed both inside and outside Syria's borders. On October 2, 2011, the SNC was established in Istanbul to coordinate opposition to the Bashar al-Assad regime. Composed of 230 members under the chairmanship of Burhan Ghalioun, it brought together over thirty opposition groups, including the Muslim Brotherhood, Liberal, Kurdish, and Assyrian parties. Only seventy-one names were made public; 60 percent of the seats were distributed to the "Syrians on the inside" and 40 percent to those outside. Initially, the SNC's political authority was unchallenged at an international level and within Syria. Thus, on October 10, 2011, France recognized the SNC as the legitimate political authority representing Syria, a move that prompted most Western countries to follow

---

[7] I-72, in Cairo, January 2014.
[8] I-73, in Cairo, December 2013.
[9] I-20, in Paris, September 2012.

suit. The FSA also recognized the SNC on November 29, 2011. In exchange, the SNC proclaimed its desire to "coordinate with the FSA to ensure compliance and harmonization of the actions of the Free Syrian Army on the ground with the political efforts that the Syrian National Council is deploying at regional and international levels."[10]

To secure recognition as Syria's legitimate representative, the SNC established diplomatic representations with the major Western chancelleries and in the Gulf. Anticipating that the Arab League could play a role in the crisis, the SNC moved its headquarters to Cairo, then reversed course because of the coup d'état by Marshal el-Sisi and an ineffectual Arab League. The SNC lobbied Western countries through regular publications detailing the progress of the opposition in Syria or defending the democratic character of the revolution. The work was divided between different departments handling relations with foreign countries, humanitarian affairs, military operations, and the media.

However, the divisions among the parties and political figures in the SNC limited its effectiveness. The Muslim Brotherhood, which held a majority of seats, was accused of imposing their candidates for key positions in the SNC, which caused those in the minority to ally themselves in a counterbalancing move. Thus, the Syrian National Movement and the Damascus Declaration lobbied for an electoral college to replace the SNC's chairman, who they found to be too close to the Muslim Brotherhood. These disagreements led to paralysis in the management of important portfolios. Thus, the SNC was unable to agree on a timeline for transitioning from the current regime, or on the need to ask for Western air strikes against the regime, or the integration of other opposition movements, such as the National Coordination Body for Democratic Change. This inefficiency led to resignations, with the justifications cited including the SNC's opaque inner workings, the reelection of Burhan Ghalioun imposed by Qatar in February 2012, and a lack of coordination with the insurgents in Syria. In May 2012, Ghalioun resigned and was replaced by Abdel Basset Sayda, an independent dissident of Kurdish origin, but who also proved unable to impose his authority. During the battles of Aleppo and Damascus (July 2012), the resignations continued, including that of the spokeswoman Bassma Kodmani, disenchanted by the lack of credibility of an organization plagued with internal rivalry.

A lack of resources was also a limiting factor for the SNC. In April 2012, it announced monthly wages for the FSA fighters but was unable to honor

---

[10] Statement from Dr. Burhan Ghalioun, with Colonel Riyad al-Asaad, November 30, 2011, http://syrie.blog.lemonde.fr/2011/11/30/larmee-syrienne-libre-reconnait-lautor ite-du-conseil-national-syrien/, visited September 8, 2014.

its commitment.[11] Losing credit with its principal donors and facing challenges by local councils in Syria, the SNC was in survival mode. It finally opened its membership to additional opposition parties and amended internal procedures to allow the Assembly to elect a General Secretariat that, in turn, would elect an Executive Committee and a President. Meeting in Doha on November 5, 2012, the SNC incorporated thirteen new opposition groups and some independents that increased its membership to over 400. Three days later, a new General Secretariat of forty members was elected, a large majority of whom belonged to the Muslim Brotherhood. George Sabra, a Christian, was chosen as the new President of the SNC.

Under pressure from the Gulf States and the West, these various attempts by the opposition to consolidate led, on November 11, to the SNC and other Syrian political opposition organizations signing an agreement that formed the National Coalition of Syrian Revolution and Opposition Forces.[12] Moaz al-Khatib headed the National Coalition assisted by three vice-presidents who had all participated in the protests: Riyad Seif, Souheir Atassi, and George Sabra. A fourth, representing the Kurdish National Council, in the end never took office. Mustafa Sabbagh, who was close to Qatar and the Muslim Brotherhood, was appointed Secretary General, a position of special importance to the National Coalition's daily operations. However, the creation of the National Coalition merely increased tensions within the opposition. Paradoxically, the opening of the Coalition to new members reduced the share held by insurgents inside Syria from 35 percent in the SNC's General Secretariat to only 20 percent in the National Coalition's.[13] The Coalition also led to increased competition between two political alliances: on the one hand, Qatar and Turkey supporting the Muslim Brotherhood, and Saudi Arabia and the United States backing the Military Councils led by deserters from the army, the moderates, and the seculars.

On March 18, 2013, an interim government was formed, headed by Ghassan Hito and supported by Qatar and the Muslim Brotherhood. Consisting of technocrats with no political affiliations, this government

[11] "Syrie: le CNS va payer l'Armée libre," *Le Figaro*, April 1, 2012, www.lefigaro.fr/flash-actu/2012/04/01/97001-20120401FILWWW00059-syrie-le-cns-va-payer-l-armee-libr e.php, visited September 8, 2014.
[12] On November 12, 2012, Saudi Arabia, Bahrain, the United Arab Emirates, Kuwait, Oman, and Qatar recognized the National Coalition as the legitimate government in Syria. Turkey, the Vatican, France, Italy, the United Kingdom, the European Union, and the United States followed them.
[13] Yezid Sayigh, *The Syrian Opposition's Leadership Problem*, Washington, Carnegie Endowment for International Peace, 2013, p. 15.

was seen by the National Coalition as a direct competitor, which led to the resignation of the latter's president, Moaz al-Khatib. In response, Saudi Arabia, the Coalition's most important financial backer, cut off funding. Starved for funds at a time when the Syrian regime, supported by Russia, Iran, and Hezbollah, took Qusayr along the Lebanese border and pushed the rebels back from the vicinity of Damascus, the Coalition went through an extremely difficult period. After a three-month standoff, Ahmad Assi Jarba, supported by Saudi Arabia, was elected National Coalition president on July 6, 2013.[14] Saudi funding resumed, but by that time the fall of the regime was no longer in prospect. Yet, internal tensions persisted within the National Coalition, with Ghassan Hito pursuing his political activities using his own organization, the Syrian Business Forum based in Qatar, but making few gains.

With these tensions paralyzing the Syrian representation abroad and its legitimacy dwindling, the National Coalition was kept from serving as the conduit for international aid. Though the grants announced were significant – the Group of Friends of the Syrian People comprising a hundred countries, pledged hundreds of millions of euros in aid – the pledged funds did not always materialize. In addition, the Western as well as Gulf countries bypassed the Coalition, having come to view it as ineffective. Aid from the European Union and the United States was primarily funneled through UN agencies (FAO, HCR) working from Damascus or in the refugee camps outside Syria. Before the July 2014 UN vote on resolution 2165 authorizing cross-border humanitarian aid without agreement by Damascus, the areas in the hands of the insurgents went largely unserved.

Over the ensuing months, the gap between the opposition in exile and insurgents fighting in Syria grew. Within the National Coalition, some members became wary of local councils in insurgent areas, which they perceived as potential competitors partly because they themselves had few connections inside Syria.[15] Despite repeated calls to move the institutions of the National Coalition to insurgent-held territories, members of the Coalition made only sporadic, brief visits to Syria.[16] Many of the most important armed groups refused to acknowledge the Coalition, including the Harakat Ahrar al-Sham al-Islamiyya, the Firqa 19, and

---

[14] "Syrie: le premier ministre de l'opposition démissionne," Le Monde, AFP, July 8, 2013, http://abonnes.lemonde.fr/proche-orient/article/2013/07/08/le-premier-ministre-rebell e-syrien-demissionne_3444359_3218.html, visited September 8, 2014.

[15] Yezid Sayigh, op. cit.

[16] Khaled Kanafani, "The Revolution Between Victories and Stumbling Blocks," Souriyatna, n° 74, February 8, 2013, http://Souriyatna.files.wordpress.com/2013/02/So uriyatna_issue_74_a4.pdf, quoted by Yezid Sayigh, op. cit., p. 29.

the Liwa' al-Tawhid. During meetings held in Syria, members of these groups expressed strong opposition to any external representation that they suspected of trying to appropriate the revolution.[17] In fact, they viewed the National Coalition as resulting from foreign interference, far removed from the population's real needs.

Humanitarian Aid

The institutional deadlock in the National Coalition also had serious consequences for the provision of humanitarian aid. Support from the International Conference of Friends of the Syrian People, particularly from Turkey, gave the Coalition responsibility for centralizing and distributing aid throughout northern Syria. Both the SNC first and then the National Coalition failed to open an office in Syria before the summer of 2013. In addition, instead of directing aid to the nascent civil institutions in Syria, the Coalition let the NGOs operate in an uncoordinated manner.

However, the international actors had initially tried to avoid the scattering of aid and a market for humanitarian aid from developing, the adverse effects of which had been seen in previous crises.[18] Therefore, the National Coalition, with technical help from the European Union, put in place the Assistance Coordination Unit (ACU) in December 2012. Installed in Turkey's Reyhanlı until March 2013 and then in Gaziantep, this organization, directed by a Coalition vice-president, Souheir al-Atassi, coordinated international assistance and monitored the humanitarian situation in Syria and in the camps along the Turkish-Syrian border.

With no interim government and under pressure from the donors, the ACU became involved in the distribution of aid to Syria through local councils and the IDP camps.[19] Its record was mixed; the ACU managed only to spend a small fraction of its budget. The organization did produce new data on the humanitarian situation and even led several vaccination campaigns against polio. However, aid distribution was hampered by a

---

[17] The creation of the National Coalition was in part aimed at weakening Islamist influence within the Syrian National Council, including that of many armed groups fighting inside Syria. Yet the support by Qatar, the main funder of Islamist armed groups, for Mustafa Sabbagh and Ghassan Hito, for a time, facilitated their cooperation. The nomination of Saudi-backed Ahmad Assi Jarba to head the National Coalition triggered a sharp deterioration in its relations with these armed groups. Interviews carried out in the province of Aleppo, August 2013 and communication with Thomas Pierret, November 2016.

[18] Séverine Autesserre, *The Trouble with Congo: Local Violence and the Failure of International Peacebuilding*, Cambridge, Cambridge University Press, 2010.

[19] Official site of the Assistance Coordination Unit (ACU), www.etilaf.org/ الإغاثي-الدعم-و-التنسيق-و-حدة/الإغاثي/الدعم-و-نبذة-عن-حدة-و-الدعم-الإغاثي.html, accessed on May 20, 2014.

lack of experienced staff and the political manoeuvers of Souheir al-Atassi, who excluded local councils she considered close to her rivals within the Coalition – that is, Mustafa Sabbagh and the Muslim Brotherhood. The most important local administrations, specifically those in Aleppo, Raqqa, and Idlib, complained of being excluded from aid programs. In any event, while the ACU received a few million dollars in February 2013 from Qatar, it remained a minor player. As it happened, the $230 million given by the US, the $477 million from the EU, and the $1.5 billion promised in January 2013 at the first international conference in Kuwait flowed through other channels, including UN agencies, directly to the refugee camps or via Damascus.[20]

The bypassing of the ACU was both a reflection of the national strategies of the donors and of the ACU's inability to identify and prioritize needs. The growing gap between the executives of the Coalition and the revolutionaries on the ground made it difficult to construct a workable strategy. Local councils were not considered as reliable interlocutors by the ACU even though it represented them *vis-à-vis* the donors. Consequently, the aid did not reach local councils, while the local data they collected did not find its way back to the ACU. But, without foreign aid, the structures of the insurgency were fragile because they lacked the ability to collect taxes. In each municipality, the attempts toward centralization and provision of public services (hospitals, first aid clinics, education system, garbage collection) barely managed to survive in the absence of support from the National Coalition. Armed groups filled the vacuum and became direct competitors to the local councils.

Despite the strategic nature of Aleppo, the Coalition fumbled its support of the municipality. Hence, after paying partial salaries in July 2013 thanks to a $50,000 donation from a Syrian living in Germany, the Municipality of Aleppo stopped operating in August. With the City Council bordering on bankruptcy, the Aleppo mayor decided, after several fruitless attempts to contact the ACU, to go directly to their offices in Turkey. He was received but left empty handed. The ACU selected projects mainly based on donor priorities and its own contacts inside Syria.

The failure of the ACU left the NGOs free to refuse any coordination with local institutions they labeled "political," while they negotiated directly with the armed groups. Western donors exacerbated the problem by imposing criteria that only the big international NGOs could meet. They also insisted on projects being implemented directly on the ground, thus further encouraging the NGOs to bypass the fledgling municipal

---

[20] Yezid Sayigh, *op. cit.*, p. 11.

authorities. The programs were developed outside Syria, sometimes in the headquarters of NGOs whose expertise frequently did not match up well with the needs. For instance, Telecoms without Borders, a French NGO, distributed iPads in refugee camps on the Turkish-Syrian border in August 2013 and installed satellite Internet connections in hospitals that still had to do without basic medicine, medical instruments, generators, and fuel for producing electricity.[21]

In areas controlled by insurgents, the NGOs worked with Syrians who were often recruited for their knowledge of English, which facilitated access to certain areas. These Syrians sometimes steered the NGO work to their family and social networks. In Aleppo during the summer of 2013, People in Need and Arche Nova thus relied on the same family, which distributed all aid to their neighborhood and refused any contact with the Municipality of Aleppo. Reacting to this situation, the head of the education department at the Municipality of Aleppo said, "They fund seven of our schools in the Ferdusi district and refuse to go through us. They pay $90 for teachers, while we struggle to distribute $10 to $20 in the 200 schools that we run. This creates considerable tension and disorganizes the education system we are trying to rebuild. NGOs don't want to understand that we need a comprehensive response to rebuilding institutions to manage the whole city."[22] Of more relevance to the casualties of war, but unfortunately less typical, Doctors without Borders set up its hospitals in conjunction with the insurgent municipalities. The charity managed to adapt to local needs, promoting maternity care over war surgery, since the seriously injured had already been sent to Turkey, while difficult births, unaided consequent to the collapse of the health system, were responsible for many more deaths.[23]

In the end, most of the NGOs focused on a strip a few dozen kilometers north of Idlib, near the Turkish border, pushing the Syrian population that had remained in insurgent areas to settle there.[24] Most NGOs left Syria in the summer of 2013 due to the risk of abductions by ISIL, which restricted access on the ground even more. As was the case with Peshawar in the 1980s *vis à vis* Afghanistan, the cities of Gaziantep and Antakya attracted Western aid and Syrians living abroad in an international environment disconnected from the realities of life in Syria.

---

[21] Authors' observations in Syria and Turkey, September 2013.

[22] I-74, with a manager in the educational department of the Aleppo city council, in Aleppo, August 2013.

[23] I-114, with a foreign doctor from Doctors without Borders, in al-Bab, January 2013.

[24] I-75, in Antakya, September 2013.

The Military Leadership

On July 29, 2011, a Military Council was created in Rastan by deserting officers who then announced the formation of the Free Syrian Army (al-Jaysh al-Suri al-Hur or FSA). In September 2011, it merged with other insurgent groups, including the Free Officers Movement (Harakat al-Dubat al-Ahrar), and became the opposition's main armed group. The first attempt to establish a national military organization, the FSA, was envisaged as a structure without party affiliation that would cover the entire national territory. However, the rebels inside Syria soon found themselves at odds with the officers issuing orders from abroad. On November 29, 2011, the FSA recognized the authority of the SNC but the latter's president, Burhan Ghalioun, was opposed to the militarization of the insurgency, which opened a gap between him and the fighters. In addition, power struggles erupted in the top ranks of the FSA. Several senior officers, deserters from the Syrian army, left the FSA claiming – unsuccessfully – that they should have the monopoly on the military leadership. For example, General Mustafa al-Sheikh left the FSA in February 2012 to found the Higher Military Council while the SNC created its own military structure.

This multiplying of command centers caused Turkey, Saudi Arabia, and Qatar to push for greater cohesion, particularly regarding the supply of weapons. In the spring of 2012, the officers active inside the country were gaining ascendancy over the defector generals exiled in Turkey. The FSA adopted a joint command with heads of military units established in ten of the fourteen Syrian governorates, while the SNC, previously reluctant to embrace the armed struggle, declared its support of the FSA and announced it would take charge of getting the fighters paid. Following a meeting of 550 former officers and military leaders of the FSA in December 2012, the Supreme Military Council (Majlis al-Askiri al-A'la), the General Staff (Hay'at al-Arkan), and five military regions were created for coordinating operations. Located in Turkey, the Supreme Military Council was dominated by professional officers who had defected to the insurgents.[25]

This organization was intended to bolster the centralization that had begun with the setting up of military units numbering several thousand men. But, from the beginning, the Supreme Military Council was not accepted by the fighters who were desperate for help. "We are sacrificing ourselves in Syria in a heavily unequal struggle, the only thing we ask for is arms and ammunition. With one Kalashnikov for two fighters we have no

[25] "Syrian Rebels Create New Unified Military Command," *Associated Press*, December 8, 2012, www.huffingtonpost.com/2012/12/08/syria-rebels-military-council_n_2263256.html, visited May 20, 2014.

chance."[26] Most fighters we met did not hide their mistrust of the foreign-based command. "For me the National Coalition and the Supreme Military Council are fictions. We see them on television signing alliances and arguing, but here, nothing changes, nothing."[27] Despite the restructuring of the Supreme Military Council, the tensions between those inside and outside the country did not subside. Moreover, the competition between the FSA and the radical Islamist groups, which rejected its authority, increased from the fall of 2012. In September 2012, General Mohamed al-Haj Ali, breaking with the FSA, announced the creation of a Syrian National Army that would address itself to combating the growing influence of Islamist networks. One result was that the FSA moved its Turkish command center to Syria to better control the extremists.

Reacting to what they interpreted as a takeover by outside officers, several large units then joined forces in their own grouping, the Syrian Islamic Liberation Front (Jabhat Tahrir Suriyya al-Islamiyya – SILF), without, however, formally leaving the FSA. The Gulf donors, who feared losing influence if the money was channeled through the military structures directly linked to the National Coalition, supported this move. The split with the FSA came in November 2013, when the SILF military units, except for Kata'ib al-Faruq, declaring that the National Coalition no longer represented them, joined the Syrian Islamic Front (Jabha al-Islamiyya al-Suriyya – SIF) and created the Islamic Front.[28] As a further indication of its decline, in December 2013 the FSA lost control of its headquarters at Bab al-Hawa, on the Turkish border, to the Islamic Front, who plundered it of equipment that the FSA had refused to turn over after they split.[29] In Syria, the legitimacy of the National Coalition and the General Staff had reached its lowest point. Under pressure from its external supporters, the FSA finally agreed to a further restructuring in February 2014 and the Supreme Military Council dismissed Selim Idris as Chief of Staff.[30] From August 2014, the General Staff, renamed the

[26] I-98, with a combatant on the front, in Aleppo, December 2012.

[27] Interviews with combatants in the Aleppo governorate, December 2012 and January 2013.

[28] "Syrie: d'importants groupes rebelles prônent la charia et rejettent la Coalition nationale," *Le Monde*, September 29, 2013, visited May 5, 2014, http://abonnes.lemonde.fr/proche-orient/article/2013/09/25/syrie-d-importants-groupes-rebelles-pronent-la-loi-islamique_3483973_3218.html, visited May 20, 2014.

[29] "Les actions du Front islamique affaiblissent l'Armée syrienne libre," *Le Monde*, December 13, 2013, http://abonnes.lemonde.fr/proche-orient/article/2013/12/13/les-actions-du-front-islamique-affaiblissent-l-armee-syrienne-libre_4333875_3218.html, visited June 13, 2014.

[30] "Syrie: le chef d'état-major de l'ASL limogé pour 'des erreurs'," *Le Monde*, February 17, 2014, http://abonnes.lemonde.fr/proche-orient/article/2014/02/17/syrie-limogeage-du-chef-d-etat-major-de-l-armee-syrienne-libre_4367664_3218.html, visited May 20, 2014.

Syrian Revolutionary Command Council (Majlis Qiyadat al-Thawra al-Suriyya), was operational again. In parallel, many brigades were restructured and centralization continued through the creation of ever-larger combined units totaling more than 10,000 men: the Syrian Revolutionary Front (Jabhat Thuwar Suriyya), the Movement of Steadfastness (Harakat Hazm), the Mujahidin Army (Jaysh al-Mujahidin), and the Islamic Union of the soldiers of the Levant (al-Ittihad al-Islami al-Ajnad al-Sham).

Part III

The Fragmentation of the Insurrection

7 The Crisis Internationalizes

The internationalization of the Syrian crisis stemmed from a two-part process: the exile of millions of Syrians to neighboring countries and intervention by external actors. The effects of international involvement were felt in Syria but also in the adjacent countries. First, foreign actors (states or other entities) imposed their own rationale on the Syrian conflict. It was above all foreign movements and foreign money that led to the insurgency's radicalization. Specifically, the PKK and ISIL each advanced radical agendas, while support by Iran and Lebanese Hezbollah locked the regime into sectarianism. Moreover, the crisis spread into neighboring countries, destabilizing Lebanon's politics and compromising its security, worsening the Iraqi civil war, weakening the Jordanian government, and feeding sectarian tensions in Turkey. With two transnational movements, ISIL and the PKK, straddling Iraq and Syria, the two countries' civil wars became entwined.

The crisis took on a regional and even a global dimension owing to the frequently violent interactions of different types of actors (states, regional institutions, armed groups, tribes, political parties) on varying issues, each of which defined an arena of conflict. 1) The United States (allied with Europe) opposed Russia (allied with Iran and China) on the rules of international order, in particular regarding the overthrow of authoritarian regimes. 2) Iran and Saudi Arabia, supported by their respective allies, competed for regional leadership. 3) The refugee problem spread the crisis into host countries, especially Jordan, Lebanon, Turkey, and Iraq. The internationalization also derives from the implantation of foreign parties in Syria, a topic we will develop in later chapters. In point of fact, the civil war redefined the stakes of the Kurdish question. The PKK broke out of its isolation thanks to its alliance with Damascus, while Turkey reinforced its support of the Kurdish Regional Government (KRG) in Iraq (Chapter 8). Furthermore, the Islamic State's caliphate, while it was opposed by all other regional states, served as a rallying point for jihadist movements everywhere.

Sketching these conflictual transnational arenas leads us to three observations. First, these arenas are not defined by "natural" enmity. In particular, the formation of "Shia" and "Sunni" alliances, implied, regarding the Shia, ignoring differences between Alawites, Seveners, and Twelvers and, regarding the Sunnis, setting aside the often-violent disagreements between the Muslim Brotherhood, Salafists, and followers of popular religiosity. Next, these agonistic arenas did not necessarily involve the same actors and they had their own internal dynamics; thus, allies and opponents could differ from one to the next. Nevertheless, developments in one arena directly affected the others; for instance, the rise of the Islamic State redefined the West's priorities. Finally, certain actors played sometimes critical roles in more than one arena. For example, Turkey supported the insurgents, and was also highly invested in hosting refugees and in the Kurdish issue. An actor's strategy hence emerges from arbitrating various stakes and sometimes contradictory interests, which explains the system's rapid transformations and overall unpredictability.

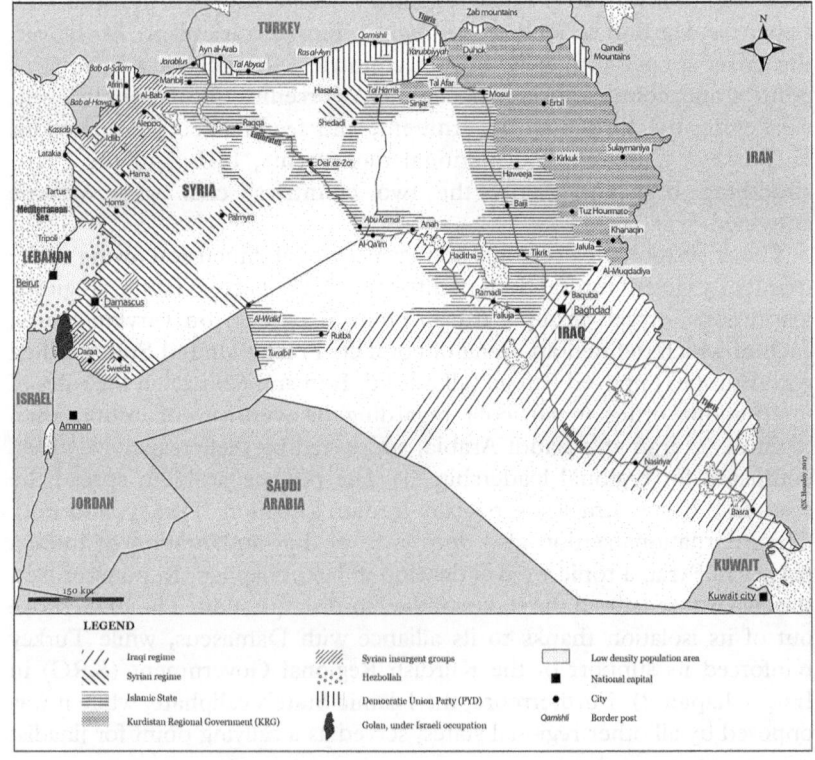

Map 7.1 A regional war (2014)

The Rules of International Order

Beyond the question of Bashar al-Assad remaining in power, the civil war also brought with it a confrontation between Russia and the United States and their respective allies on the rules of international order. In a post-Cold War era, the Syrian conflict should therefore be understood in line with previous crises where the West intervened to overthrow authoritarian regimes.[1] NATO's unilateral intervention in the 1999 Kosovo crisis marked the first one of its kind, followed by those in Iraq in 2003 and Libya in 2011. The intervention in Libya was the result of an imaginative interpretation, to say the least, by NATO countries of UN resolution 1973 aimed to protect civilians and not initiate regime change.

In the West, the Syrian crisis was initially seen as a continuation of the Arab Springs: an endogenous democratization of Arab regimes. To begin with, the United States reacted cautiously to the first demonstrations in Syria, with Secretary of State Hillary Clinton describing Bashar al-Assad in late March 2011 as a "reformer."[2] However, faced by mounting violence in the summer of 2011, President Obama called for Bashar al-Assad's departure and sponsored a UN resolution in October 2011 that condemned the regime's repression and called for sanctions.[3] Convinced of the regime's imminent fall, Western countries began diplomatic maneuvering to delegitimize the government in Damascus. In February 2012, the creation of the International Conference of the Friends of the Syrian People was a first step toward installing the opposition as the legitimate representatives of the Syrian people.[4] However, the West remained reluctant to provide military support and adopted divergent strategies. From 2012 on, the Obama administration refused to support the insurrection militarily in its fight against the regime. Lacking consensus, the European Union limited its action to emergency aid and refugee support. In fact, Germany would stay in contact with

---

[1] Samuel Charap, "Russia, Syria and the Doctrine of Intervention," *Survival* 55 (1), 2013, pp. 35–41.

[2] Khaled Sid Mohand, "Dans les geôles de Bachar Al-Assad," *Le Monde*, May 28, 2011, www.lemonde.fr/proche-orient/article/2011/05/28/dans-les-geoles-de-bachar-al-assa d_1528800_3218.html, visited September 9, 2014.

[3] "La Chine et la Russie opposent leur veto à une résolution de l'ONU condamnant la répression en Syrie," *RFI*, October 5, 2011, www.rfi.fr/ameriques/20111005-chine-russie-opposent-leur-veto-une-resolution-onu-condamnant-repression-syrie/, visited September 9, 2014.

[4] Created in February 2012, the Conference of Friends of Syria is a contact group uniting around one hundred member states of the United Nations. It meets regularly to discuss the support to give the insurrection and sanctions to apply to the Damascus regime.

Damascus, even as France and the United Kingdom openly campaigned on the side of the insurgents.

American engagement, as it were, was limited due to the fiascos of Iraq and Afghanistan. As in Libya, the American authorities wanted to avoid anything that could lead to "boots on the ground." The chemical attacks against civilian populations in Ghouta in August 2013, which caused between 1,000 and 1,500 deaths, later revealed the equivocations of the American government. This attack directly called US credibility into question: President Barack Obama had publicly drawn a "red line" against such attacks in a speech one year earlier.[5] A coordinated bombing campaign with Great Britain and France, limited to some Syrian military bases, thus seemed imminent. However, the "no" vote by the British MPs on September 7 led to the mission being aborted on the eve of the allotted day. President Obama announced he would first get Congress's authorization to carry out the strikes, which spelled doom for any intervention, given that the Republicans controlled the House of Representatives. France, deeply committed to the operation but isolated now, had to stand down its forces.

In the end, the United States' disengagement from the Syrian crisis multiplied an already-divided opposition's difficulties. Liberal currents within the insurgency became ever more marginalized and no longer offset the influence of Saudi Arabia and Qatar. Western countries focused their actions almost exclusively on refugees and the risks inherent in the presence of thousands of foreigners and, especially, of Westerners who had left for Syria to carry out jihad. The military victories of the Islamic State in the summer of 2014 forced the United States to reenter the war with targeted bombing, Special Forces deployment, and military support for the PKK/PYD. While Obama had ruled out the possibility of a no-fly zone in Syria, the United States proceeded to set one up for the Syrian branch of the Kurdish movement that first shielded it from the regime when they clashed over control of the city of Hasaka in August 2016 and, next against the Turks advancing on Manbij in September 2016. Yet the PKK mainly used its weaponry in the service of creating a unified Kurdish territory from Afrin to the Jazeera.

Russia's involvement in the Syrian crisis cannot be explained purely in terms of protecting its own strategic interests. Unlike the Ukrainian crisis

---

[5] James Ball, "Obama issues Syria a 'red line' warning on chemical weapons," *The Washington Post*, August 20, 2012, www.washingtonpost.com/world/national-security/obama-issues-syria-red-line-warning-on-chemical-weapons/2012/08/20/ba5d26ec-eaf7-11e1-b811-09036 bcb182b_story.html?utm_term=.c6b4c3eaa287, viewed September 9, 2014.

in 2014, which affected Russia's self-interest directly, Syria in 2011 was not an important economic or military partner. Syrian arms purchases were not that profitable, and the Russian naval base at Tartus since the end of the Cold War had been of limited importance. In reality, Russia was defending the principle of nonintervention.[6] Thus, Moscow refused when Saudi Arabia in August 2013 offered it arms contracts worth 15 billion US dollars and guarantees of its strategic interests in exchange for an end to Russia's support of the Syrian regime.[7] The Russian government was intent on buying enough time for the Syrian government to stabilize the military situation and to establish itself once more as an indispensable actor on the international stage. Moscow acted on three fronts: It blocked unfavorable resolutions at the UN Security Council, reorganized Bashar al Assad's army, and supported a process of seeking negotiations. Russia shipped arms to the Syrian regime to help its army adapt to fight a counterinsurgency war and modernize its helicopter fleet as well as its anti-aircraft and coastal defenses to defend against potential Western strikes. However, Russia ignored requests from the Syrian government to sell it the most sophisticated anti-aircraft weapons and the latest combat aircraft because Israel and the United States objected.[8]

International bodies, and the UN in particular, became arenas where Russia and the United States confronted each other – and occasionally cooperated – on three issues: the establishment of a peaceful settlement process through negotiation, the chemical disarmament of Syria, and providing humanitarian aid.

First, Russia and China rejected all resolutions condemning the Syrian regime, thus negating any pretext for intervention. A paralyzed Security Council meant the UN was reduced to supplying humanitarian aid and offering its good offices between the parties. However, the negotiations sponsored by the UN would inherently be the product of an ambiguity. On the one hand, Russia wanted to establish a diplomatic process that would have no prospect of success but that would help legitimize its Syrian ally that was on the edge of collapse by 2012.[9] Russia made its diplomatic overtures at a moment when sponsors of the insurgency

---

[6] Roy Allison, "Russia and Syria: Explaining Alignment with a Regime in Crisis," *International Affairs* 89 (4), 2013, pp. 795–823. Moreover, the rise to power of jihadist groups in Syria could affect the north of the Caucase, which remains unstable.

[7] "Moscow 'rejects' Saudi 'offer' to drop Assad for rich arms deal," August 8, 2013, *Russian Times*, http://rt.com/news/saudi-russia-arms-putin-239/, viewed September 9, 2014.

[8] Roy Allison, *op. cit.*, pp. 805–808.

[9] Dimitri Trenin, *The Mythical Alliance: Russia's Syria Policy*, Washington, Carnegie Endowment for International Peace, 2012.

seemed ready to accelerate the provision of military support. Two days after the failure of the Arab League plan (January 2012), which served only to underline the impossibility of a compromise, Russia offered to host informal discussions in Moscow (which ultimately did not take place). On the other hand, Western countries bet on negotiations to facilitate a political transition that, as they saw it, presupposed Bashar al-Assad's departure. After one fruitless attempt,[10] the UN Secretary General appointed Lakhdar Brahimi as international mediator for the Syrian conflict. His threatened resignation after months of impasse triggered the Geneva II negotiations in January–February. Without even a consensus on the meeting's purpose, negotiations never really got off the ground and failed. However, the Syrian regime had been recognized as an interlocutor, while the divisions among the insurgents had visibly widened. Indeed, the National Coalition, pressured by the United States into participating in the Geneva II process, saw its credibility diminish considerably in the eyes of both combatants and refugees. Negotiations were not popular; all the more so since the regime had intensified its bombing and political repression in the weeks preceding Geneva II.

Next, Russia moved adroitly to stymie Western intervention by offering President Obama a way out after he had renounced bombing the Syrian government. President Putin proposed a plan for dismantling Syria's chemical weapons under United Nations supervision. Between September 2013 and October 2014, the OPCW (Organization for the Prohibition of Chemical Weapons) organized the removal and destruction of the most dangerous chemical substances. However, these agreements were not only difficult to enforce; they also failed to prevent a subsequent series of gas attacks.[11]

Finally, the Russians supported a requirement that international humanitarian aid be distributed through the Syrian government to include the insurgent areas, which left them *de facto* excluded, and let the regime instrumentalize the aid. It was not until UN Resolution 2165 in July 2014 that direct aid could pass through Turkey (Bab al-Salam and Bab al-Hawa), Iraq (al-Yarubiyyah), and Jordan (al-Ramtha) without approval by Damascus.

---

[10] From March 2012, onward, Kofi Annan, representative of the Arab League and the United Nations, attempted to establish a ceasefire. On June 20, 2012, the Geneva I conference brought together members of the Security Council, Turkey, and the Gulf States without results.

[11] See the OPCW press release, www.opcw.org/news/article/opcw-fact-finding-mission-co mpelling-confirmation-that-chlorine-gas-used-as-weapon-in-syria/, viewed December 19, 2014.

In September 2015, in response to an official request by the Syrian regime, Russia intervened militarily in Syria. Moscow deployed warships, planes, troops, and heavy weapons (tanks, artillery, and anti-aircraft missiles) and launched a massive bombing campaign against the governorates of Aleppo, Hamas, and Idlib. While Russia justified its intervention as part of the war against terrorism, especially against the Islamic State, it concentrated its strikes on the insurgency, which it deliberately misidentified as Jahbhat al-Nusra. The Russian intervention constituted a turning point in the war favorable to the regime, which retook Aleppo in December 2016, and from then on effectively relegated the United States to playing second fiddle.

Regional Competition

The Middle East is going through a general crisis that is redefining internal political equilibria, the balance of power among countries, and that threatens borders inherited from the colonial era. During the 1990s and 2000s, American interventions in Iraq led to marginalizing the Sunnis to the benefit of Kurds and Shias. Kurdish autonomy, in effect, could presage independence in the longer term, while the historic shift of power toward the Shia majority created the conditions for a Sunni insurgency. Moreover, the Arab revolutions had the effect of threatening the Gulf's authoritarian regimes.

In addition, ever since the Iranian revolution, Saudi Arabia and Iran had been competitors. There were several reasons for this: Saudi opposition to the new Islamic Republic's revolutionary ideology (which initially appealed to Islamists across the region beyond the Sunni-Shia divide), the presence of a Shia population in the Gulf (suspected of being a fifth column), and alliances with or against the United States. This deep-rooted opposition accounts for the emergence over several decades of two regional alliances born of a complex and largely unintended process.[12] The 1975–1990 civil war in Lebanon, the Iran–Iraq war of the 1980s, and the civil war in Iraq from 2003 on revealed the fluidity of alliances that went beyond the opposition between Saudi Arabia and Iran. Syrian politics offered a good example of this variability. In the 1980s, Syria had repeatedly clashed with Hezbollah, the same organization that had now become an essential military ally. The rapprochement between Iran and Syria grew out of their shared support for Hezbollah and, above all, opposition to Israel and

---

[12] Sonoko Sunayama, *Syria and Saudi Arabia: Collaboration and Conflicts in the Oil Era*, London, I. B. Tauris, 2007, pp. 14–48.

Saddam Hussein's Iraq.[13] In the 1980s and the 1990s, the Syrian regime had been close to the Gulf States, even benefiting from their oil revenues in the name of Arab solidarity against Israel and joining the coalition against Iraq alongside Saudi Arabia in 1991.[14] Syria's assassination of Rafic Hariri in 2005 provoked tensions with Saudi Arabia. Yet, on the eve of the revolution, Qatar was still a key ally of the regime in consequence of their rapprochement during the Lebanon war in 2006. The Gulf States finally split with Damascus only after its repression of peaceful demonstrations in 2011 that incensed their own peoples. In the context of the Arab revolutions, the Gulf States were convinced that the regime would follow the same path as its Egyptian, Tunisian, and Libyan counterparts.[15] Even Hezbollah tried to push its Syrian ally onto a more moderate path in 2011. Finally, while Turkey had had numerous disputes with Syria, in particular on Iskenderun's status and Syrian support for the PKK in Turkey, the two countries had drawn closer as the 1990s were ending.[16] It was not until September 2011, six months after the Syrian revolution started, that Turkey finally broke off relations with the Syrian regime.

The civil war in Syria marked the beginning of a period of polarization. For one, Syria, henceforth allied closely with Iran and Hezbollah, radically transformed its foreign policy. In this sense, the Syrian crisis represented a decisive moment in the creation of a "Shia" alliance that was clearly aimed against Saudi Arabia and its allies.

As for Hezbollah, its involvement in the war stemmed from being logistically dependent on Syria (Damascus airport was crucial for ferrying Iranian arms to the party) and from needing to sustain the internal balance of power in Lebanon. However, the civil war in Syria reversed the relationship between Syria and Hezbollah: the regime henceforth depended on the Shiite Lebanese party for its survival and the latter's cadres are now ensconced in the highest levels of the Syrian security apparatus.[17] Thus, Nasrallah, the Hezbollah leader, initially justified the intervention in Syria as part of the fight against Israel, characterizing the demonstrations as an Americano-Israeli conspiracy. But then Hezbollah's rhetoric adjusted to make it part of the fight against Sunni extremists and the defense of holy

---

[13] Bernard Hourcade, "L'Iran contre l'"encerclement sunnite'," in François Burgat and Bruno Paoli (eds.), *op. cit.*

[14] Sonoko Sunayama, *op.cit.*

[15] Claire Beaugrand, "L'engagement des monarchies du Golfe contre le régime de Bachar al-Assad," in François Burgat and Bruno Paoli (eds.), *op. cit.*

[16] Gilles Dorronsoro, *Que veut la Turquie?* Paris, Autrement, 2008.

[17] Aurélie Daher, "Un chiisme combattant face au monde: la politique étrangère du Hezbollah," in Mohamed-Ali Adraoui (ed.), *Les islamistes et le monde. Islam politique et relations internationales*, Paris, L'Harmattan, 2015, pp. 147–164.

places, especially Sayyida Zaynab mosque in Damascus.[18] As for Hamas, previously supported by Iran and Syria, its evolution showed the limits of polarization after 2011.[19] In the face of a civil war that put it in an awkward position, Hamas first edged closer to the Gulf States in 2013, especially to Qatar, but then reconnected with Iran in 2014. By contrast, the Gulf States' policy of supporting the insurgency grew out of their opposition to Iran. The protests of the Shia majority in Bahrain showed that the Gulf's oil monarchies were not immune to the Arab revolutions. Moreover, the Gulf States supported the Sunni insurgents against the Baghdad government.[20]

Finally, Turkish engagement dovetailed with its support of the Arab uprisings in Tunisia and Egypt, but also with a logic of protecting Sunni populations, especially the Turkish-speaking ones, with the added objective of keeping the PKK from returning to Syria. Turkey's policy would progressively shift to the latter objective the more it would find itself isolated in its support for the insurrection. Starting in 2015, Ankara worried over the progress made by the PYD in seeking to unify the Kurdish enclaves in northern Syria. In November 2015, the shooting down of a Russian plane by Turkish jet fighters created a diplomatic furor. Unable to convince the United States to stop supporting the PYD/PKK, Turkey intervened militarily following the conquest of Manbij in the summer of 2016 and took control of the region between Jarablus, Afrin, and al-Bab. From then on, it would gradually move closer to Russia and Iran, notably by acquiescing to Bashar al-Assad remaining in power and, in practice, to the insurgency's marginalization.

The sectarian logic went beyond state strategies. Indeed, the Syrian crisis led to the mobilization of actors (ulama, preachers, associations) who enjoy some degree of autonomy from their respective states. The call to Sunni or Shia solidarity legitimatized but also constrained foreign

---

[18] Vincent Geisser, "Le Liban, au coeur de la crise syrienne, en marge des révolutions arabes ?" in François Burgat and Bruno Paoli (eds.), *op. cit.*, pp. 232–234.

[19] Nicolas Dot-Pouillard, "Le mouvement national palestinien et la crise syrienne: une division contenue," in François Burgat and Bruno Paoli (eds.), *op. cit.*, pp. 268–269.

[20] The Gulf States supported the Iraqi Sunni insurgency by organizing conferences offering the opportunity to distribute funding directly to the leaders of the main rebel groups, generally former Baa'thists. Thus, on June 21, 2014, they met in Erbil and sided with the Islamic State, which had just conquered the city of Mosul. See the statement from one of the leaders of the insurgency, Ali Hatem al-Suleyman, www.youtube.com/watch?v=q B4_6_eKxMA, viewed December 19, 2014. Likewise, on July 17, 2014, a conference in Amman brought together representatives from the Iraqi insurgency in order to organize the fight against Baghdad. "Amman Conference to Save Iraq: Unannounced Calls to Align with ISIS, face the Iranian 'Savadi wave', and agreement to take down the current system," *CNN Arabic*, http://arabic.cnn.com/middleeast/2014/07/17/iraq-jordanconven tion?hpt=continous, viewed July 21, 2014.

policy. Thus, for Riyadh, the protection of holy sites and, for Tehran, the Khomeini doctrine of resistance by the weak against the powerful inspired their state discourses.[21] After Iranians were banned from visiting the sacred sites in Saudi Arabia following the 1987 Mecca incident, Syria had become their main pilgrimage destination – another factor strengthening links between the two countries.[22] For the Sunnis, private donations from the Gulf helped to support the Syrian insurgency, and preachers like Sheikh Adnan al-Aroor and Sheikh Yusef Qaradawi framed the events within a religious narrative. In Saudi Arabia, Islamist circles of influence, especially the sheikhs, justified their support for the revolution by a sectarian reading of the Syrian regime.[23]

Regional power politics therefore aggravated divisions between Sunnis and non-Sunnis in Syria. Regional competition, the effects of which can be seen in Palestine, Iraq, Yemen, and Lebanon, was particularly decisive in Syria. Sectarianism deepened with the growing alignment of regional alliances with local actors.[24] Saudi Arabia's support for the insurgency and Iran's support for the regime accelerated polarization of the political field. On both sides, attempts by actors to present themselves as non-sectarian ceased to be credible. As in Iraq, Yemen, and Lebanon, the Shia-Sunni split became decisive in the Syrian conflict, which it had not been at the start of the revolution. Anticipation of a religious clash accelerated the alignment of actors along sectarian lines, pitting the "Shia crescent" against "Sunni encirclement."[25] This reading of the conflict facilitated the participation by both ISIL and Hezbollah in the Syrian civil war. The increased presence of Shia combatants, Hezbollah militants, Iranian Pasdaran, and Iraqi militiamen from the Liwa' Abu al-Fadhal al-Abbas also affected the functioning of the Syrian regime. Thus, tens of thousands of foreign combatants fought to defend holy sites, some of which had been ransacked by Sunnis. The Damascus regime established militias whose ranks were filled mostly by Alawites and Christians, among them the National Defense Force, the Baath Brigades, Syrian Social Nationalist Party squads, and the Iskandarun Liberation Front. Meanwhile, the rise in desertions by Sunnis from the army reduced the regime's base. Despite its attempts to present itself as secular and as the protector of minorities, the regime was widely

[21] Claire Beaugrand, *op. cit.*, p. 311.
[22] Bernard Hourcade, *op. cit.*
[23] Stéphane Lacroix, "Saudi Islamists and the Arab Spring," Kuwait Programme on Development, Governance and Globalisation in the Gulf States, Kuwait, LSE, 2014.
[24] Likewise, during the Afghan civil war in the 1990s, the alignment of social, political, and ethnic oppositions explains the polarization between the Taliban and the Northern Alliance of Massoud and the intensification of the hostilities.
[25] Salwa Ismail, "The Syrian Insurgency: Imagining and Performing the Nation," *Studies in Ethnicity and Nationalism* 11 (3), 2011, pp. 540–541.

seen as anti-Sunni. Similarly, the involvement by the Gulf States increased the influence of Sunni Islamists (see Chapter 9).

However, Saudi Arabia saw the rise of the Muslim Brotherhood and the Islamic State as an internal threat to its internal stability and therefore found itself on the horns of a dilemma. On the one hand, it opposed the Islamic State, although the latter was fighting against the Shia-dominated regime in Iraq. On the other hand, it supported the Syrian insurgency but rejected the Muslim Brotherhood, which dominated the Syrian National Council and then the National Coalition. Qatar and Saudi Arabia disagreed repeatedly about the insurgency's leadership. Saudi Arabia, fearing domestic upheavals, favored defected officers, conservatives, tribes, and even liberals,[26] while Qatar, politically more open, supported the groups that promoted political Islam, even the most radical ones.[27] The divergence between the two countries was evident in Egypt, where Qatar backed the Morsi government, while Saudi Arabia wholeheartedly approved of General el-Sisi's coup d'état. Egypt's fluctuating Syria policy reflected the same tensions, when President Morsi, a member of the Muslim Brotherhood, officially supported the Syrian insurgency, while his successor, General el-Sisi, repressed the Syrian revolutionaries in Egypt. Indeed, even though Egypt's military junta was on a financial drip from Saudi Arabia, el-Sisi saw Bashar al-Assad's regime confronted by an Islamist threat just as he was in Egypt.[28] Finally, the Islamic State's victories in Iraq in 2014 marginalized the Iraqi Sunni insurgent groups supported by Saudi Arabia. Under revolutionary threat, the latter chose collaboration with the United States and, implicitly, with Iran in order to contain the Islamic State, as it had done against al-Qaida in Iraq.

The Refugees

In just a few years, Syrians have become the largest refugee community in the world, resulting in a crisis comparable to Afghanistan's in the 1980s and the Congo's in the 1990s. Starting in the summer of 2011, the Syrian army's offensives forced tens of thousands to flee. From early 2012 on, with fighting flaring up throughout most of the country and the bombing of cities, displacement of the civilian population accelerated. The relatively unscathed Syrian coast became home to millions. Others fled to

---

[26] Thomas Pierret, "Les salafismes dans l'insurrection syrienne: des réseaux transnationaux à l'épreuve des réalités locales," *Outre-Terre* 44 (3), 2015, pp. 203–204.

[27] David B. Roberts, "Understanding Qatar's Foreign Policy Objectives," *Mediterranean Politics* 17 (2), 2012, pp. 233–239.

[28] Communication with Maaï Youssef, December 2014.

Table 7.1 *Persons of concern registered by UNHCR by country between December 2012 and December 2016*[29]

Date/country	Lebanon	Jordan	Turkey	Iraq	Egypt	Total
Dec. 2012	129,000	117,000	170,000	67,000	13,000	496,000
Dec. 2013	805,000	576,000	560,000	210,000	131,000	2,282,000
Dec. 2014	1,146,000*	620,000	1,165,000*	228,000	137,000	3,296,000
Dec. 2015	1,070,000*	633,000*	2,291 000	244,000	123,000	4,361,000
Dec. 2016	1,017,000*	655 000*	2,815,000	233,000	116,000	4,836,000

*The Lebanese and Turkish governments at the time estimated the number of refugees in their countries at over 1.5 million. By late 2015, a Jordanian national census estimated the Syrians present in the country, including pre-2011 arrivals, at over 1.26 million.

Lebanon, Iraq, Jordan and Turkey. Starting in the winter of 2012–2013, nearly a half million Syrians registered with UNHCR (United Nations High Commissioner for Refugees) in neighboring countries, a figure that rose to 4.8 million by the end of 2015 (see Table 7.1). It is estimated that these official figures undercount the number of refugees by at least one million, not even counting the seven million said to be displaced inside Syria. This means that two out of every three Syrians had been forced to abandon their homes. These numbers also do not take into account the many refugees that did not end up in camps, taking advantage of free movement agreements or dual nationality or simply living without documents.[30] This was especially the case in Lebanon, Egypt, and Turkey. The latter had closed its border crossing points in 2011–2012, yet, when the rebels took control of northern Syria, Turkey opened its border and saw close to a million refugees flood into the country. Those with Syrian passports were free to move around Turkey under existing agreements between the two countries, while others settled in refugee camps. As the numbers kept climbing, Turkey closed its border to anyone without a passport and encouraged the establishment of new camps on Syria's side of the border. However, the border was porous and some Syrians without passports managed to cross it

[29] UNHCR, "Syrian Regional Refugee Response Interagency Information Sharing Portal," http://data.unhcr.org/syrianrefugees/regional.php, viewed February 21, 2016.
[30] In Egypt, especially, hundreds of thousands of Syrians took refuge without registering with the HCR, as they took advantage of the agreements signed in the past between the Syrian and Egyptian governments. They thus had the same rights as Egyptian citizens to healthcare and education. The Muslim Brotherhood government, in solidarity with the Syrian revolutionaries, extended these agreements in 2012–2013 and so saw an influx of Syrians who brought their businesses and resources with them.

anyway.[31] Seeing that the conflict would be of long duration, many refugees left Turkey for Europe in late 2015 to ask for asylum. The European authorities were overwhelmed by nearly a million asylum claims in 2015 and 2016, two-thirds of them lodged in Germany and Serbia.

The refugee factor in spreading conflict – "refugee warriors" – has been analyzed for several civil wars, notably those in Afghanistan and the Central African Republic-Chad-Sudan triangle.[32] Several studies have established a strong correlation between refugee presence and the expansion of armed conflict in both time and space. They suggest that refugees play varying roles in conflict dynamics. First, stable borders allow safe havens to be established.[33] Humanitarian assistance provides resources and legitimacy to armed groups that redistribute the aid in their own name.[34] As a result, the state targeted in the attacks may decide to intervene in the neighboring territory. In addition, refugees transform the host country's demographics and economic situation and are sometimes instrumentalized to benefit local causes.[35] These models can be applied to the Syrian case, but we put the stress on the state's role in the host country.[36] The Syrian crisis spread differently by host country, which raises three issues: the insertion of refugees in cross-border networks, their instrumentalization in internal conflicts, and, finally, the role of states.

First, multifarious economic, familial, and tribal connections facilitate conflict expansion by fostering exchanges across poorly controlled borders. After Massey on the United States and Harpviken on Afghanistan, the political effects of the refugee presence are a function of how integrated they are into the host country's social

---

[31] Observations in Syria, December 2012.

[32] Aristide R. Zolberg, Suhrke Astri, and Sergio Aguayo, *Escape from Violence, Conflict and the Refugee Crisis in the Developing World*, Oxford, Oxford University Press, 1989; Elke Grawert, "Cross-Border Dynamics of Violent Conflict: The Case of Sudan and Chad," *Journal of Asian and African Studies* 43 (6), 2008, pp. 595–614; Jennifer Giroux, David Lanz, and Damiano Sguaitamatti, "The Tormented Triangle: The Regionalisation of Conflict in Sudan, Chad and the Central African Republic," *Crisis State Research Center*, working paper no. 49, 2009.

[33] Boaz Atzili, "When Good Fences Make Bad Neighbors: Fixed Borders, State Weakness, and International Conflict," *International Security* 31 (3), 2006/2007, pp. 139–173; Idean Salehyan, "Transnational Rebels: Neighboring States as Sanctuary for Rebel Groups," *World Politics* 59 (2), 2007, pp. 217–242.

[34] Sarah Lischer, "Collateral Damage: Humanitarian Assistance as a Cause of Conflict," *International Security* 28 (1), 2003, pp. 79–109.

[35] Idean Salehyan and Kristian Skrede Gleditsch, "Refugees and the Spread of Civil War," *International Organization* 60 (2), 2006, pp. 335–366.

[36] Howard Adelman, "Why Refugee Warriors Are Threats," *Journal of Conflict Studies* 18 (1), 1989.

networks.[37] In Lebanon, the town of Ersal in the Bekaa saw its population increase from 40,000 to more than 100,000 inhabitants between the spring of 2011 and the summer of 2013. Thanks to family ties, economic links, and religious solidarity, the town's Sunni population and, especially, the municipal authorities, actively supported the refugees. In the absence of a national policy, local authorities took over direct coordination of refugee arrivals, with financial help from the Gulf States. Kuwaiti funds, for instance, made it possible to open a clinic in February 2014. Numerous rebels passed through the town, which served them as a rallying point. Cross-border networks funneled arms and supplies to the Syrian rebels and to Ersal residents who had left home to fight in Syria, just as others had gone off to fight in Iraq after the American invasion, although in smaller numbers.[38] When the Lebanese army detained Syrian fighters in the summer of 2014, Jahbat al-Nusra retaliated by killing several Lebanese soldiers in the town.

Next, reciprocal identification between refugees and a community inside the host country is a critical element in diffusing the crisis. In Iraq, where relations between Sunnis and Shias played a key role in the civil war, the Syrian crisis was read as an extension of the Iraqi situation. In Lebanon, both the Shia Hezbollah and Michel Aoun's Free Patriotic Movement regarded the arrival of refugees, most of them Sunni, as a threat, especially with the rise in Syria of internationalist Jihadi groups such as Jabhat al-Nusra and ISIL.[39] The influx of refugees disrupted demographic balances, which have historically conditioned the political calculations of Lebanese actors. Hence, from 2012 on, Vincent Geisser could speak of "the Lebanese actors capturing the 'Syria question' for purposes of internal legitimization, and even political hegemony" but the phenomenon's dimensions increasingly constrained them.[40] Shiite Hezbollah and Amal supported the Syrian government, while the Future Movement and the Sunni Islamist movements supported the insurgency. Moreover, fighting in Tripoli and attacks against Hezbollah hinted at the possibility of clashes in Lebanon along the same divisive lines as in Syria. The capture of Qusayr, Homs, and the Qalamun mountains by the Syrian

[37] See Douglas Massey and Felipe Espana, "The Social Process of International Migration," *Science* 237, 1987, pp. 733–738; Kristian Berg Harpviken, *Social Networks and Migration in Wartime Afghanistan*, London, Palgrave Macmillan, 2009.

[38] See Laure Stephan, "Ersal, base arrière de la rebellion syrienne dans la vallée libanaise de la Bekaa," *Le Monde*, published online on April 21, 2014, http://abonnes.lemonde.fr/in ternational/article/2014/04/21/ersal-base-arriere-de-la-rebellion-syrienne-dans-la-val lee-libanaise-de-la-bekaa_4404689_3210.html, viewed September 9, 2014.

[39] Aurélie Daher, "In the Wake of the Islamic State Threat: Repercussions on Sunni-Shi'i Competition in Lebanon," *Journal of Shi'a Islamic Studies* 8 (2), 2015, pp. 209–235.

[40] Vincent Geisser, *op. cit.*, p. 222.

army considerably increased the number of Syrian fighters taking refuge in Lebanon. However, the Lebanese Druze leader Walid Joumblatt's opposition to the Syrian government when the Druze in Syria remained pro-government, as well as the divergent positions of the Christian movements showed that actors refusing to conform to the sectarian divide still enjoyed maneuvering room.

The situation in Turkey was just as problematic. Some Turkish Alevis felt a sense of solidarity with the Alawites and identified with them despite deep religious differences and the absence of close ties in the past. The Turkish government and the majority of Turks supported the Sunni rebels, while the Alevis were overrepresented in the opposition to the AKP (Justice and Development Party) government. The Syrian crisis became a factor in domestic confrontations. Tensions were particularly high in Antakya, where Alevis and Alawites saw an influx of Syrian refugees of all religions.[41] Yet the main problem from the Turkish government's perspective remains how Turkish Kurds identify with their Syrian counterparts. The PKK instrumentalized the Syrian crisis, especially the battle of Kobane (Ayn al-Arab), to mobilize support in a context of deep polarization between the Turkish State and the Kurdish social movement.

Finally, contagion varied with how much neighboring states were in control of their own territories. The more a state took charge of refugees and controlled the border, the more it could instrumentalize the armed groups; the less capable a state was of managing the refugees, the more it had to be neutral, even hostile, toward them. In particular, one of the challenges for states was how to control the NGOs dealing with refugees. In Lebanon, NGOs were relatively independent, while in Turkey and Jordan they were closely monitored. Iraq, owing to its instability, did not host a significant number.

Although it cost Turkey nearly a billion dollars for the year of 2012 alone, the country thus managed to control the flow of refugees, the majority of which were concentrated in the border regions of Antakya, Gaziantep, and Urfa. Similarly, Jordan provided a safe haven for rebels who fought in southern Syria, while also keeping a close eye on their movements. Jordan tried to concentrate its refugees in the cities and camps in the country's northern region. In August 2013, the Zaatari camp with a population of more than 120,000 ranked as the fourth largest city in Jordan.[42] One year later, in the summer of 2014, this policy had sufficed to limit the impact of the more than one million refugees equaling

---

[41] Cengiz Candar, "Is Syria War an Additional Spark to Alevi Protests in Turkey?" *Al Monitor*, September 2013, www.al-monitor.com/pulse/originals/2013/09/turkish-alevis-protest-syria-war.html#, viewed September 9, 2014.
[42] UNHCR website, www.unhcr.fr/pages/4aae621d5c5.html, viewed May 4, 2014.

a fifth of the Jordanian population. However, Jordan was already sheltering hundreds of thousands of Iraqi refugees who had fled during the American occupation, and Palestinians made up a third of the population. The Hashemite kingdom had, in fact, banned Palestinians living in Syria from taking refuge in the country. Jordan still bore the scars from the Black September episode (1970), when Palestinian refugees had attempted to overthrow the Hashemite monarchy.

Unlike Turkey and Jordan, where the state managed the refugee problem directly, in Iraq and Lebanon community support was the more significant factor. Both countries resisted letting their territories be used as safe havens by insurgents for fear of the conflict spilling over their borders. Lebanon, for one, had never had the resources to control its border with Syria to begin with. The more than one million Syrian refugees registered by the end of 2014, plus several hundred thousand that were not registered, made up a fourth of the Lebanese population. The war's economic impact on Lebanon alone was enormous: According to the World Bank, it had cost the country an estimated 7.5 billion dollars by the end of 2014. Unemployment had doubled and public services were strained, especially the schools and hospitals.[43] While Sunni cities near the Syrian border were most affected by the massive influx of refugees, their impact was felt throughout the country. Sunni neighborhoods in Lebanese cities, such as Bab al-Tabbaneh in Tripoli, saw their populations explode with the arrival of refugees, some of them fighters that clashed repeatedly with Jabal Mohsen's Alawite militiamen. Similarly, in Iraq, the Syrian crisis had heightened tensions between the Shia-dominated government, Kurdish forces and the Sunni insurgency, each seeking allies in Syria on the basis of ethnic or religious solidarity. Consequent to the Kurdish rebellions, there had been ongoing movements of refugees and fighters back and forth between the two countries since the 1980s. In the 2000s, with Syrian support for the anti-American insurgency in Iraq, the frequency increased. From 2011 on, Baghdad had struggled to keep control of its border, especially in the Sunni zones where tens of thousands of Syrians had found refuge, particularly in al-Anbar province. In 2013, certain Sunni cities became places where the Syrian and Iraqi oppositions interacted. Prior to ISIL's summer of success in 2014, however, Iraq was used less as a safe haven, being relatively insulated by distance from the combat zones in northern and southern Syria

[43] "Syria War, Refugees to Cost Lebanon $7.5 billion – World Bank," *Reuters*, September 19, 2013, www.reuters.com/article/2013/09/19/syria-crisis-lebanon-idUSL5N0HF3 I220130919, viewed September 9, 2014; Omar S. Dahi, "Breaking Point: The Crisis of Syrian Refugees in Lebanon," *Middle East Report Online*, September 25, 2013, www .merip.org/mero/mero092513, viewed September 9, 2013.

and because Syrian and Iraqi security forces were cooperating against Sunni movements in both countries.[44] The KRG (Kurdistan Regional Government) took in nearly 200,000 Kurdish refugees, mainly in the camp at Domiz. Despite the changed situation on the ground resulting from ISIL's offensives against Erbil and Sinjar in 2014, the Iraqi Kurd authorities maintained close control of the border in a context of continuing rivalry between the KDP and the PKK. In the end, the Syrian crisis contributed to the sectarianizing of the regional political scene and to the building of transnational alliances based on ethnic or religious identity.

[44] "Iraqi Helicopters Hit Convoy in Syria," *Al Jazeera*, April 27, 2014, www.aljazeera.com/news/middleeast/2014/04/iraq-security-forces-ambush-syria-fuel-convoy-201442711304 9340239.html, viewed September 9, 2014.

8 The Kurds and the PKK

In 2011, Kurds that took to the streets did so both as Syrian citizens and to protest the discrimination against their community. To block this movement, the regime in Damascus permitted the PKK, under the name of the PYD (Partiya Yekitiya Democrat – Democratic Union Party), to return to Syria in exchange for putting down the protests.[1] Then, in the summer of 2012, when the regime withdrew from the Kurdish enclaves in Afrin, Ayn al-Arab (Kobane), and Qamishli, it handed them over to the PYD, thereby creating autonomous territories and dividing the insurgency. By the end of 2014, the PYD became the Western coalition's main ally on the ground against the Islamic State. This support enabled it to conquer large Arab territories in northern Syria, where it established its own institutions, collectively known as the Autonomous Administration (Idara Zatiyya).

The Kurds and the Revolution

Interviews we conducted with Syrian Kurds in Iraqi Kurdistan between 2011 and 2014, and in Afrin and Ayn al-Arab between December 2012 and January 2013 witness to the significant mobilization of the Kurdish population following the Daraa incident.[2] The first Kurdish demonstration in solidarity with the victims took place on March 18, 2011 in the town of Amuda.[3] "I was always against the regime," a Kurd from Ayn al-Arab

---

[1] The PYD is the Syrian branch of the PKK. After Abdullah Öcalan's arrest in 1999, its new leader, Mourat Karayılan, decided to set up local branches: in Iraq in 2002, it was the PÇDK (Parti Çareseri Dimukrati Kurdistan – Party for a Democratic Solution in Kurdistan), in Iran in 2004, the PJAK (Partiya Jiyana Azad a Kurdistane – Party for a Free Life in Kurdistan), and, the same year, the PYD in Syria. Harriet Allsopp, *The Kurds of Syria: Political Parties and Identities in the Middle East*, New York, I.B. Tauris, 2014, p. 41.

[2] Arthur Quesnay and Cyril Roussel, "Avec qui se battre ? Le dilemme kurde," in F. Burgat and B. Paoli (eds.), *op. cit.*; "Syria's Kurds: A Struggle within a Struggle," *Middle East Report* 136, International Crisis Group, 2013.

[3] Interview with Syrian Kurdish revolutionaries in Erbil, March 2013.

told us. "My friends and I did not pass up the opportunity to show our opposition. During the Nowruz festival [Iranian New Year, celebrated on March 21], for example, we went out with Kurdish flags shouting pro-Kurdish slogans. After the revolts in Egypt and Tunisia, we were waiting for our turn in Syria. By the time things started happening in Daraa, we were already active."[4] The Kurds regarded the 2011 movement against the Bashar al-Assad regime as a continuation of previous civil rights-focused protests.[5] Unlike those demonstrations, however, the Kurds were now also part of a national movement. They joined it even more readily because many were convinced, after several decades of repression, that there was little chance of their demands being met with an authoritarian government in power. Cognizant of their minority status, Kurds nevertheless considered themselves part of Syrian society, especially the younger generation spearheading the movement. "I am a Kurd from Afrin, but I have always lived in Aleppo, with Arabs," one young Kurd explained.[6] "At school, my friends were Arabs, we went out to cafés together ... there were no differences between us." Ethnic issues could all the more easily be ignored since the main Kurdish parties remained inactive.

Unlike 2004, this time the regime responded by trying to reconcile with the Kurds by restoring the Syrian citizenship of 150,000 stateless Kurds (*bidun*) on April 7. It was a tactic by Damascus to limit the 2011 uprising to the Sunni Arabs. What mattered more for the Kurds, however, was the inclusive tone of the Syrian Revolution: "We were greatly shocked to have our citizenship reinstated. We were protesting for our political rights as Syrians and once again the regime treated us as if we belonged to a separate group."[7] The lack of trustworthy intermediaries further hindered setting up any formal negotiations between Kurds and the regime.

In Aleppo and Damascus, Kurds generally mobilized within the same networks as the Arab revolutionaries. "I went to my first demonstrations with my university friends, including several Kurds," an Arab resident from Aleppo explained. "We got together the day before to finalize our itinerary and choose our slogans. We were united."[8] Kurdish demonstrators saw themselves as an intrinsic part of the opposition, campaigning for the creation of a democratic state. "During the first months of the insurrection, we

---

[4] I-76, in Ayn al-Arab, December 2012.
[5] Picking up where they had left off during the 2004 insurgency, the Kurds called for recognition of their language, for the right to establish cultural bodies, for access to land, and for the *bidun* to be given citizenship.
[6] I-77, in Erbil, May 2013.
[7] I-78, with a Syrian Kurdish militant, in Erbil, January 2012.
[8] I-12, in Aleppo, December 2012.

chanted the same slogans as the rest of Syria: 'Down with the regime.' We protested on Fridays about the same issues as the other protesters."[9]

When the regime launched attacks against rebel districts in Homs and Hama, protests erupted in the Kurdish regions. As elsewhere, coordinating groups were set up to organize marches, post videos online, and contact other groups throughout the country. "In Aleppo and Damascus, Kurds mingled with the Arab population daily. The demonstrations were mixed. There were many Arabs in the group of friends I demonstrated with. Sometimes, cousins from Jazeera came to visit us in Damascus. They gave us advice on how to deal with the police, how to disband after a demonstration."[10] Kurdish protesters reactivated the skills they had acquired during the 2000s. "We had learned how to counter the regime when Kurdish political parties were expelled [the PKK in 1998, and also fifteen other Kurdish parties that had been banned since the 1970s]. We knew how to assemble, how to take to the streets without being arrested, which parts of town it was more or less easy to demonstrate in. We had already acquired all that, while the Arabs took a few months to learn."[11] Kurdish protestors were also setting up federations of local committees and forming youth movements, the most significant of which was the Kurdish Youth Movement (Avahi) to foster a Kurdish agenda within the revolutionary movement.[12]

Still, the geographical dispersion of the Kurds and the scale of repression by the regime made it impossible to develop effective coordination between the various resistance hubs. Protesters had difficulties communicating from one town to another. "We wanted to create a nationwide coordination in the north straight away," a Kurdish revolutionary reported, "but it was practically impossible. The repression left us little chance to bring together delegates from different regions. Forming a coordinating structure was impossible. We could only use the Internet, but that did not allow us to build an effective movement. Moreover, the situations in Kurdish and Arab territories quickly became different."[13]

---

[9] I-79, with a Syrian Kurdish refugee, in Erbil, December 2012.

[10] I-80, with a Syrian Kurdish activist, in Erbil, December 2012.

[11] I-81, with a Syrian Kurdish activist from Amuda, in Erbil, December 2012

[12] Including the Movement of Revolutionary Youth, Union of Cooperation of Kurdish Youth and the Kurdish Youth Union, the Youth of the Birth of Freedom, the Alliance of Sewa Youth. For more information, read the interview with Abdussalam Uthman, founding member of the Union of Cooperation of Kurdish Youth, and close to the Kurdish Future Movement in Syria. www.kurdwatch.org/syria_article.php?aid=2719& z=en&cure=240, visited May 20, 2014.

[13] I-82, with a militant of the Avahi movement, in Erbil, January 2012.

During the transition to armed combat, Kurds from mixed Kurd-Arab zones joined predominantly Arab groups. A revolutionary from Aleppo reported:

The regime suppressed our movement in Aleppo's Kurdish districts very quickly. We went to protest in the working-class Arab districts a lot so as not to be noticed. Then it became impossible to do so without many being killed. I left for one of the liberated villages near Turkey. There armed groups made up of Arabs, Kurds and Christians were starting to form . . . I joined them.[14]

However, Kurdish involvement in the insurgency became increasingly problematic owing to the Arab opposition's refusal to open a dialogue on the status of the Kurdish minority. In addition, the regime used different tactics to repress demonstrations depending on the local ethnic and religious composition. The army bombed Arab rebel districts, but only intervened by deploying police in the mainly Kurdish territories. In 2012, the regime's alliance with an external actor, the PKK, meant that Kurdish enclaves were definitively separated from the rest of the insurrection.

The PKK Returns

From the summer of 2011, the PKK succeeded in negotiating with Damascus a gradual return to the three Kurdish pockets on the Turkish border (Afrin, Ayn al-Arab, and Jazeera). In exchange, it would subdue the Kurdish protesters[15] and refrain from aligning with the FSA.[16] The PKK revived a strategy from the 1990s of aligning with Syria in order to gain a sanctuary for its operations in Turkey. This strategic turning point resulted in Murat Karayılan's replacement by Camil Bayık as head of the party organization.[17] In Syria, PYD militants, who had been arrested in

---

[14] I-83, with a Kurdish combatant from the FSA, in al-Bab, January 2013.

[15] Many interviews with Kurdish militants in Paris, Iraqi Kurdistan, and in the Afrin and Ayn al-Arab regions (December 2012 and January 2013) telling of arrests, detention, and intimidation by the PYD; see also the Kurd Watch site: www.kurdwatch.org/?aid=2732&z=en&cure=1009, visited April 20, 2014.

[16] Various interviews date the return of the PKK to spring 2011. In April 2011, Salih Muslim Muhammad, leader of the PYD, returned to Syria with several militants from the party who had been pardoned by the regime. According to International Crisis Group, the PKK at this time sent nearly 1,000 combatants to reinforce the PYD in Syria, "Syria's Kurds: A Struggle within a Struggle," *Middle East Report* 136, International Crisis Group, 2013.

[17] Officially enacted on July 9, 2013 by the Congress of the Kurdish People (Kongra Gele Kurdistan), the PKK's legislative assembly, the appointment of Camil Bayık to replace Murat Karayılan to head the organization formalized a reality apparent since 2011. This year constitutes a pivotal moment for the PKK, which tried to return to the regional game by allying itself once more with Iran. In charge of operations against Iran at the time, Murat Karayılan ceded his place to a successor inclined to resume the dialogue. The PKK's clandestinity prevents grasping the relationships of the internal forces that led to this reversal.

the 2000s, were released, and the party formed a militia to bring the Kurdish regions under control. It marginalized other Kurdish parties – highly fragmented and lacking any military organization – through targeted violence, including assassinations.[18]

Our group of young people was formed in April 2011. We were able to protest for several months without any repression by the regime. Doubtless, it had the means. Then everything changed when the PYD arrived. Our funding was cut off. Almost all of us were arrested and interrogated by the PYD. Some of us were tortured. They told us to stop protesting.[19]

In the Kurdish territories, protesters were disbanded, forced into silence and the protest movement stopped dead in its tracks.[20]

Under the deal, Syrian security forces no longer intervened in the three Kurdish enclaves. The army remained in its barracks until July 19, 2012, when the FSA's seizure of a large part of the north caused the regime to withdraw from the Kurdish zones. The regime's place was immediately taken by the PYD. "PKK militia were in Ayn al-Arab for several months," reported a city resident.

You could not go out and protest without the risk of being arrested. From May on, the regime's security forces were no longer to be seen. The PKK enforced the law on the streets. On July 19, we saw army convoys leaving the town, just like that, without gunfire. When I went out, all the official buildings were occupied by the PKK. They had even taken possession of the police cars. The police had handed over the keys before taking off.[21]

This carefully planned transition was carried out in a day. PYD militants took control of administrative buildings and positioned themselves as the official authorities in the Kurdish enclave.[22]

The bureau of Asayish [security services] was formed in May,"

explained their leader in Ayn al-Arab.

Interviews carried out in Iraqi Kurdistan in April 2011 and Syrian Kurdistan in October 2016.

[18] The most prominent assassination, carried out on October 7, 2011, was that of Mashaal Tammo, one of the founders of the Kurdish Future Movement, an opposition organization that maintained links with Kurdish committees.

[19] I-91, in Erbil, April 2013.

[20] "Syria's Kurds: A Struggle within a Struggle," *Middle East Report* 136, International Crisis Group, 2013, p. 15. For further details, see www.kurdwatch.org/index.php?cid=, visited September 8, 2014.

[21] I-84, in Ayn al-Arab, December 2012.

[22] The PYD immediately took over from the regime. This transition, doubtlessly arranged ahead of time, was carried out without violence and the Kurdish towns did not suffer any destruction. In the districts of Ashrafiya and Sheikh Maqsood in Aleppo, the situation was different, with incursions by the regime, partial control by the PYD, and occasional clashes.

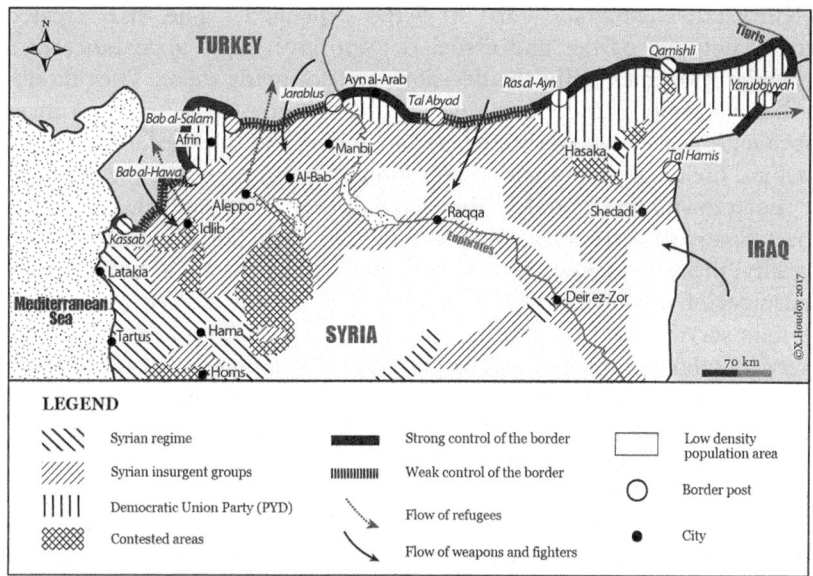

Map 8.1 PYD controlled territory (October 2013)

"From then on, we began setting up recruitment and training for the new Kurdish police. At that time, the regime's police had stopped working in the town; they were no longer leaving their bases. When they evacuated on July 19th, we took control of their bases without any gunfire.[23]

Once in command of the Kurdish enclaves, the PYD made Kurdish identity the touchstone for belonging to its politically distinct society with its own territory and institutions. PYD, as the local branch of the PKK, is part of a transnational party, working to form an independent Kurdistan. The PYD thus openly positioned itself against the thrust of the national protest with the aim of pulling Kurds and Arabs apart.[24]

In the Kurdish territories, the setting up of a coalition, the TEV-DEM (Tevgera Kurden Demokrat – Democratic Kurdish Movement) allowed projecting a pluralistic image for the benefit of external observers and the Syrian population. In theory, the TEV-DEM was to be run by a committee representing its various constituent associations and parties. In reality, the PKK remained the true authority behind the diverse activities of the individual TEV-DEM bodies. "No one really knows who holds power in the TEV-DEM," a notable from Ayn al-Arab and cadre of the KDPS

[23] I-85 in Ayn al-Arab, December 2012.
[24] Interviews with members of the People's House, city councils, schools, hospitals, and courts in Ayn al-Arab (December 2012) and Afrin (January 2013).

(Kurdistan Democratic Party of Syria) explained. "The PKK created many fictional parties and associations to give it the appearance of a popular movement. But the decisions are not made there. They do not ask our opinion. In the same way, the PYD in Ayn al-Arab is a mere facade. It has a few, poorly educated members and they certainly weren't behind the creation of such organizations."[25]

Each town had a People's House (Mala Gel), ostensibly designed as a participative institution to implement the TEV-DEM's authority. In reality, these were powerless fronts controlled by the PKK.[26] Under the auspices of this civil assembly, a local council was elected to organize public services and manage the town. It took charge of the municipal services whose employees were still paid by Damascus in 2014. "We have around one hundred employees in Afrin," the new mayor explained, "only the people who had been elected [under the Baathist regime] were changed. I was appointed mayor after elections organized on February 13th, 2012. The city council is made up of 25 elected members, all from Afrin."[27] In alignment with the official PYD ideology, the new leaders described these institutions as being the "expression of the people."[28]

The new organization of the Kurdish zones is born out of the thought of Abdullah Öcalan's [the historical leader of PKK]. It is a deep and thoughtful ideology, designed to protect the population by the formation of local councils. It is the first step towards self-determination for Syrian Kurds. The goal is for people to govern themselves, without any bureaucracy and elites. Power comes from the base.[29]

To implement a justice system, tribunals were set up in the three enclaves and in the Kurdish districts of Aleppo (until the PYD's partial expulsion in early 2013). "In accordance with TEV-DEM ideology, we have a set quota for women members of the tribunal. Our directive is to deliver justice to the people and coordinate mediation between conflicting parties."[30] The judicial staff comprised lawyers and legal practitioners who based their rulings on a combination of Syrian and customary law. "We administer justice according to Syrian law, but certain cases require

---

[25] I-115, in Ayn al-Arab, December 2012.
[26] I-84, in Ayn al-Arab, December 2012. Many examples are available on the *Kurd Watch* blog, "Ayn al-'Arab: Asayis Beat up Village Mayor," *Kurd Watch*, September 9, 2014, www.kurdwatch.org/index.php?aid=3209&z=en&cure=1016; visited September 22, 2014.
[27] I-107, in Afrin, January 2013.
[28] Interviews with members of TEV-DEM, the PYD, and various civil institutions linked to the PYD in Erbil, Ayn al-Arab, and Afrin between December 2012 and January 2013.
[29] I-140, with a PYD militant, in Ayn al-Arab, December 2012.
[30] I-53, with a tribunal judge, in Afrin, January 2013.

us to refer to traditional law."[31] A commission based in Qamishli was empowered to create a new legal corpus modelled on Western legal codes. "For Kurds, self-governance by the Kurds of our territory makes it is necessary to create our own legal code," a female PKK cadre explained. "A special commission has been established to study this matter and create a composite between the jurisprudence delivered in our courts of law and the western legal codes that we are using to inspire our modernization of Syrian law."[32] The legal system was highly centralized, with a High Court whose nine judges were appointed directly by the PYD to oversee all other tribunals. "As lawyers, we do not have a great deal of power," a member of the Ayn al-Arab tribunal confided, "we don't really follow the cases, we just record proceedings. If a trial is too contentious, one of the nine judges from the High Court steps in to judge."[33] At the tribunal in Afrin, judges seemed poorly trained and their principal activity appeared to consist of recording complaints.

Security forces played a key role, especially the Asayish whose job was to monitor the population, and the YPG (Yekineyen Parastina Gel – People's Protection Units) military units. YPG combatants were mentored by PKK cadres that came from Turkey and Iraq, including many Syrians who had trained at the guerrilla bases in Iraq's Qandil Mountains. The entire male population and a part of the female population were drafted for military service per instructions from this core group.[34] All draftees were rotated through guard duty at the enclaves' borders and the many checkpoints. "I do not support the PKK, but they forced us to join the YPG. The only way to be let off from serving was to pay for the right to stay at home."[35] Starting in 2013, some Kurds enlisted with the YPG after being repeatedly attacked by the most radical insurgency elements, including ISIL. "Everyone has to fight here, it is a question of life or death," reported an Ayn al-Arab resident, "whether you are for or against the PKK, you have no choice. ISIL attacks don't differentiate."[36]

---

[31] I-104, with a lawyer, in Ayn al-Arab, December 2012. This persistence of Syrian law in areas controlled by the PYD caused some residents in surrounding regions to register administrative documents, especially marriage certificates, so they might be recognized by the regime.

[32] I-105, with a female PKK cadre, in Ayn al-Arab, December 2012.

[33] I-84, in Ayn al-Arab, December 2012.

[34] Since 2012, the PYD effected several waves of conscription to defend the Kurdish enclaves, "Amuda: PYD Compiles Lists of Names for Recruitment," *Kurd Watch*, September 6, 2014, www.kurdwatch.org/index.php?aid=3208&z=en&cure=1016, visited September 22, 2014.

[35] I-116, in Ayn al-Arab, December 2012.

[36] I-87, with an individual from Ayn al-Arab, in Beirut, July 2014.

The PYD financed itself by levying mandatory contributions on the population. Businessmen had to pay a tax to ply their trade. "I transport grain by truck between the city of Raqqa and Ayn al-Arab," explained a businessman in Ayn al-Arab, "when the YPG was set up, I immediately agreed to pay for the right to pass the checkpoints because I was very scared of losing my trucks. But I regularly have problems with them. Suddenly, the price will go up for no reason. If I refuse to pay, the YPG seizes my goods, which then disappear."[37] The movement also controlled the enclaves' resources. "In Jazeera, oil wells have passed under PKK control," reported a Qamishli resident, "by agreement with the regime, they are paid to export the oil."[38] In Afrin, the PYD organized a troop of forest rangers to control logging in the state forest.[39]

The People's Houses had the additional responsibility for distributing fuel and food to the population. "The PKK had been gone from Kurdish territory for over ten years. The only way for it to win back a following was by controlling the access to resources," explained a PDKS militant.[40] "The PKK delegates gave control of the least profitable economic networks to the People's Houses. It managed the supply of flour, oil and raw materials itself, however. These are extremely lucrative sectors."[41] Even access to hospital services established by the PYD in Kurdish territories was strictly controlled.

The Fragmenting of the Kurdish Opposition

On October 26, 2011, in Erbil (Iraqi Kurdistan), a number of the other Kurdish parties formed the KNCS (Kurdish National Council in Syria) *ad-hoc* coalition to counter domination by the PKK. By May 2012, it had grown to include fifteen movements that coordinated among themselves instead of forming a coherent political organization.[42] Lacking proprietary

---

[37] I-86, in Ayn al-Arab, December 2012.
[38] I-88, in Gaziantep, September 2013.
[39] I-117, with a PYD forest guard, in Afrin, January 2013.
[40] I-118, in Ayn al-Arab, December 2012.
[41] I-86, in Ayn al-Arab, December 2012.
[42] KNCS member Kurdish movements (May 2012) with their leaders/founders: Kurdish Democratic National Party in Syria (Tahir Sfook), Kurdish Democratic Equality Party in Syria (Aziz Dawe), Kurdish Democratic Progressive Party in Syria (Hamid Darwish), Syrian Democratic Kurdish Party (Sheikh Jamal), Kurdish Left Party in Syria (Muhammad Musa), Kurdish Yekiti Party in Syria (Ismail Hamo), Yekiti Kurdistani (Abdul Basit Hamo), Kurdish Democratic Party in Syria (Abdul Rahman Alouji), Kurdish Democratic Party in Syria (Feysel Yusuf), Kurdish Democratic Wifaq Party (Nash'at Muhammad), Kurdistan Democratic Party of Syria (Dr. Abdul Hakim Bachar),

funding sources, the KNCS member movements depended entirely on support by Masud Barzani, president of the Kurdistan Regional Government (KRG) and head of the KDP (Kurdistan Democratic Party). Also, the KNCS was composed of parties in exile that had few militants on the ground in Syria. "The KNCS does not represent us," a Kurdish revolutionary who had taken part in the first demonstrations in Syria explained, "these parties have no presence in Syria and people do not really know them. They are incapable of sending aid."[43]

In its first few months, what legitimacy KNCS did enjoy it acquired thanks to Masud Barzani's support. He provided the financial and logistical backing that let the KNCS display a certain degree of cohesion. However, his patronage also had the effect of locking the Syrian Kurdish parties into the Iraqi PDK's pan-Kurdish strategy. Anxious to find international support and lessen their dependence on Masud Barzani, the KNCS's principal Kurdish parties sought to join the Syrian National Council while simultaneously reaffirming their desire for territorial autonomy within a hypothetical federal Syrian state. To no one's surprise, these negotiations failed.

Unable to fight the PYD head-on, the Kurdish parties attempted to join local committees inside Syria. The PDK, for example, courted one of the most active committees, the TCK (Tevgera Ciwanen Kurd – Kurdish Youth Movement).

Our movement was very well-known and reputed for having coordinated several demonstrations. So, political parties contacted several of us. They wanted us to take on their slogans and would represent us abroad in exchange. We were against it, but the PKK's return forced some of us to accept. Faced with the PKK and the regime, we could no longer remain isolated. We were paralyzed by this competition between parties.[44]

The Kurdish parties were further discredited by their inaction. "We never understood why the Kurdish parties did not come to help us fight against the regime," a female Kurdish revolutionary from Afrin reported. "We were isolated and no one could understand their inaction."[45]

In the summer of 2012, Barzani tried to mediate between the KNCS and the PYD in an attempt to rein in the PYD's growing influence. The Erbil agreements were concluded on July 11, 2012 and renewed in September 2012. They provided the framework for sharing power in

Kurdish Democratic Unity Party in Syria (Sheikh Ali), Azadi Kurdish Party in Syria (Mustafa Oso), and Azadi Kurdish Party in Syria (Mustafa Jumaa).
[43] I-89, with a Kurd from Aleppo, in Erbil, May 2013.
[44] I-90, in Erbil, September 2012.
[45] I-91, in Erbil, April 2013.

Kurdish zones by setting up the Kurdistan Supreme Committee and joint security forces. However, enforcing these agreements met with resistance from the militarily superior, Damascus-supported PYD, which rejected any KNCS presence in Syria.[46] The latter's constituents fell to quarrelling among themselves, with the result that four of the principal parties broke away in December 2012 to negotiate directly with the insurgency, a strategy that quickly failed.[47] "We have been incapable of adapting to the Syrian revolution," reported a Kurdish militant we met in Erbil, "the KNCS has to comply with rules imposed by the Iraqi Kurdistan government. We don't have the means for an independent policy or any new alliances with which to return to Syria." The KNCS had reached an impasse: It was not only banned by the PYD from operating in Kurdish zones but also marginalized simultaneously within the insurrection because of its federalist policy. "Our mistake was not supporting militarization of the uprising when it started. The PKK returned to Syria at that moment. Without weaponry, we could no longer campaign. We were beaten."[48] The Kurdish parties consequently hid behind a sort of neutrality: not with Bashar, not of the opposition. "We have no choice," a PDKS representative explained. "It is impossible for us to confront the PKK, the only possible route is compromise."[49] Faced with ISIL advances, the PKK signed a new power-sharing agreement with the KNCS in Dohuk on October 10, 2014. In exchange for sending Iraqi Kurdish troops to defend Ayn al-Arab, the KNCS received permission to reopen its offices in Syria.

Faced with these divisions, the Syrian Kurds confronted a dilemma. Joining the insurgents to fight the regime gave them little assurance of gaining recognition, due to the espousal of Arab nationalism by a large contingent of the rebels and the rising strength of Islamism. However, Kurdish political organizations were criticized both for being inefficient (KNCS) and for authoritarianism and accommodation with the regime (the PYD). A significant number of Kurds, especially those who had participated in the first demonstrations, disapproved of the Kurds withdrawing from the rest of the insurrection into the enclaves. "The protests started as a national movement. We continue to support the revolution even if it has changed form."[50] In areas with mixed populations, the

---

[46] I-120, in Paris, September 2012; I-91, I-93, I-82, and I-81, in Erbil, February, September, and December 2012; I-86, in Ayn al-Arab, December 2012.

[47] In December 2012, the presidents of the four parties in the KNCS (Dr. Abdul Hakim Bashar, Ismail Hamo, Mustafa Jumaa, and Mustafa Oso) announced the formation of a new coalition, the Kurdish Syrian Democratic Union.

[48] I-92, in Erbil, May 2013.

[49] I-93, in Erbil, April 2013.

[50] I-94, with a commander from a Kurdish FSA unit, in Gaziantep, September 2013.

already fragmented Kurdish opposition was weakened, with many Kurds joining the insurgent groups and rejecting PYD policy. In the end, Kurdish opposition to the PYD fragmented. On one side, independent Kurdish movements and insurgent groups coordinated their fight against the regime, and on the other, FSA units and the PYD allied to fight ISIL.

The PKK Expansion into Syria's North

By 2014, the PKK's strategy of going its separate way had reached its limits. The Kurdish enclaves did not constitute a unified territory (see Map 8.1) and, as late as 2012, more than half the Kurdish population was living in Aleppo and Damascus, in districts beyond PKK control. Crucially, the Kurds living in the enclaves depended in part on their Arab neighbors for food and energy. "The situation in Qamishli is more and more difficult," explained a city resident, "the PYD closely controls all food supplies from Iraqi Kurdistan. That controls the population to whom it redistributes aid. But it, too, depends on these resources, and cannot go too far in opposing the FSA and the Iraqi Kurdish government. The risk of ending up isolated would become too great."[51] To prevent an embargo, the PYD therefore had to negotiate with the Syrian insurgents. However, in areas where the PYD positions were close to the regime's, there were recurring clashes with insurgent groups, especially in the Kurdish districts of Aleppo and the Jazeera region. Finally, the rise of ISIL put growing military pressure on Kurdish regions from 2013 onward. ISIL offensives during the summer of 2014 pushed the PYD to form alliances with certain insurgent groups, even to the point of letting them use the Kurdish enclaves for bases.[52] In Ayn al-Arab, many rebel fighters whose units had been scattered by ISIL enlisted in the YPG or affiliated with it in reconstituted armed groups. To fight ISIL, many rebels from the Shammar tribe (members of the FSA's Liwa' Ahrar al-Jazeera) joined the ranks of the YPG.[53] The Islamic State's offensive against Ayn al-Arab (Kobane) initially strengthened cooperation between the Syrian insurgents and the PYD in August 2014, but the latter continued nevertheless to collaborate with the regime in Qamishli and Afrin. To block an Islamic State offensive in Iraqi Kurdistan, the PKK intervened in Iraq in August 2014. It engaged with ISIL especially in Sinjar to cover the evacuation of the Yazidis, a sect from which the PKK would later recruit additional fighting units.

[51] I-119, in Erbil, April 2013.
[52] YPG internal documents confirm certain agreements between insurgency groups in Aleppo (Ahl al-Sham) and the YPG. See the document April 25, 2014, http://the-arab-chronicle.com/dialogue-collaboration-syria-kurds-rebels/, viewed July 15, 2014.
[53] Felix Legrand's communication, September 2014.

The battles against the Islamic State in Syria and Iraq confirmed the PKK as one of the principal allies of the United States. Following the battle of Kobane, the Americans sent significant amounts of military aid to the PYD and deployed Special Forces to train its fighters. They set up a de facto no-fly zone, keeping the air forces of the Syrian and Turkish regimes from bombing the PYD. American support allowed the Kurdish movement to wrest large stretches of northern Syria from the Islamic State and other insurgent forces. In late 2016, the PYD succeeded in linking two of the three Kurdish enclaves (Qamishli and Kobane) and to double its territory by taking areas inhabited by Sunni Arabs in the governorates of Hasaka, Raqqa, and Aleppo. However, Turkey intervening in September 2016 prevented connecting all three enclaves because it would have let the Kurds effectively control the border with Turkey.

The territorial expansion led the PYD to reform its administrative structures. Until 2014, the Kurdish party had associated minorities, including Christians and certain armed FSA groups, with its activities. However, having conquered Arab Sunni populations, the Kurdish movement confronted a dual political and logistical challenge. The YPG lacked both the manpower to control these areas and legitimacy because of its ethnonationalist political agenda. In October 2015, the Syrian Democratic Forces (Hezen Suriya Demokratik, SDF) were set up, incorporating Christians, Yazidis, and Sunni Arabs in its ranks. The YPG was integrated into the SDF, but its units remained Kurdish in make-up and were led by PKK militants. The FSA's armed groups allied with the PYD were forced to integrate into this new structure. The creation of the SDF was effective in increasing the number of fighters and making progress against the Islamic State, but it forced the armed wing to integrate more and more Sunni Arabs led by a limited number of Kurdish cadres who, frequently, did not speak Arabic. This organization's conflicted character manifested itself when the PKK's cadres, with their Marxist-Leninist background, ordered the Sunni Arab combatants to fight in the name of Öcalan and of Allah *at the same time*.[54] As a Sunni Arab fighter in the SDF put it: "I joined for two reasons. One, because our group of friends had no other alternative for countering the Islamic State, and, second, fighting on the side of the PKK meant fighting on the side of the Americans from then on."[55]

Under the Autonomous Administration name (Idara Zatiyya), the PYD set up local committees in the three enclaves, but in parallel centralized the decisions. A first reform was announced in January 2014, coinciding with the Geneva II negotiations that the PKK had not been

---

[54] Observations in Qamishli, October 2016.
[55] E-161, with a SDF fighter, Hasaka, October 2016.

invited to join despite its repeated demands. Three "cantons," Jazeera, Kobane, and Afrin, were provided with twenty "ministries" staffed by PYD followers. In the ensuing months, these new institutions decreed limits on the right of assembly and free speech and prohibited all unregistered parties, associations, and institutions. Thus, a pyramidal institutional organization was progressively put in place at every level from village to district, with Peoples' Committees elected by the PYD and centralized at the level of the three canton's councils.[56]. The latter organize public services, and individuals not listed with the committees cannot obtain aid. This system lets the party control the population and ensures the proper functioning of the draft.[57] In December 2015, paralleling the establishment of the SDF, the Syrian Democratic Council (Meclisa Demokratika Suriya) was created to integrate the representatives of the conquered territories where the PYD installed its system of autonomous administration. Finally, in March 2016, the Kurdish entity announced – in Arabic – that it was installing a federal system at Rojava, highlighting the move as marking the birth of a Federal Syria. The rejection of the declaration by the Assad regime, by the National Coalition, and by Turkey suggests that, despite support by the United States, the PKK's presence in northern Syria remains precarious.[58]

---

[56] Jordi Tejel, "Au delà de la Bataille de 'Kobané': la société civile kurde en sursis," *Moyen-Orient* 25, 2015, p. 59.
[57] E-162, with an inhabitant from Qamishli, Qamishli, October 2016.
[58] "Final Declaration of the Federal System Constituent Assembly Announced," *ANFNEWS*, 2016, https://anfenglish.com/kurdistan/final-declaration-of-the-federal-system-constituent-assembly-announced, viewed December 20, 2016.

For many commentators, the Arab Spring was the death knell for a political Islam that was already in decline, especially for the radical version represented by al-Qaida.[1] The younger generation mobilizing against authoritarian regimes meant that the Arab countries would be opening to political normalization. This interpretation was wrong, and the resilience of the declinist thesis illustrates the difficulty in thinking of Islamism beyond the duality of decline and growth. In fact, this perspective obscures the diversity and the mutations of this political current. As the election results in Egypt and Tunisia have shown, the Arab Spring did not provoke a shift by the popular classes toward post-Islamism. Moreover, the incumbent regimes in Algeria, Egypt, Morocco, or Pakistan used the language of Islam to gain legitimacy by laying claim to morality, waging the fight against corruption, and critiquing of Western countries. The general failure of the Arab transitions marginalized supporters of an open society. With liberals forced to support authoritarianism or else face repression, as in Egypt, political Islam once again became the language of dissent on the Arab political scene. Not surprisingly, this political shutdown favored the most radical currents as they moved to hijack the social movement born in 2011.

In an apparent paradox, in Syria, Islam was used to both justify revolutionary inclusiveness and the exclusionary, even excommunicatory rhetoric that tore the insurgency apart starting in 2013. Contradictory projects, from political pluralism to Salafist-inspired theocracy, were able to coexist initially because of the polysemy intrinsic to a religious discourse reduced to a few symbols. The emergence of parties and political currents within the revolution did not contribute to the creation of a pluralistic and open

---

[1] Olivier Roy and Gilles Kepel repeat this idea in almost identical terms. The first wrote that "Arab Springs meant the political death of Al-Qaida," Olivier Roy "La mort d'Oussama Ben Laden, son dernier grand role," *Le Monde*, May 5, 2011, http://abonnes.lemonde.fr/idees/article/2011/05/05/la-mort-d-oussama-ben-laden-son-dernier-grand-role_1517404_3232.html; and the second penned "The political death of the leader of Al-Qaida, liquidated by the Arab democratic revolutions," Gilles Kepel "La mort de Ben Laden clôt une 'sombre décennie'," *Le Monde*, May 2, 2011, http://abonnes.lemonde.fr/idees/article/2011/05/02/la-mort-de-ben-laden-clot-une-sombre-decennie_1515870_3232.html.

society. Instead, the inclusive slogans of 2011 that affirmed the unity of the Syrian people were progressively replaced by violent sectarian rhetoric. The insurgency's unity fragmented largely due to an influx of foreign funding and the rise of transnational politico-military organizations. After 2014, the civil war pitted a plurality of territorialized actors against each other, with the Islamic State taking on a growing significance.

The Meanings of Islam

How did Islam become the consensual language first of the protests and then of the insurrection? Generally speaking, it supplied the rebels with a shared universe of meaning, an aesthetic, and a resource with which to attract external sponsors.

First, since the 1970s, Islam had become the language of protest in the Muslim world.[2] The Iranian revolution of 1979 played a pivotal role, in shifting the revolutionary reference from Marxism to Islam even for the Sunnis, with its complexity highlighted in discourses and individual trajectories. The discrediting of Marxism after the fall of the Berlin Wall (1989) and the resurgence of neoliberal ideology in Western countries gave Islam a near-monopoly as the language of protest. Islam's revolutionary dimension was asserted successively with the crises of Afghanistan, Egypt, the Caucasus, Yugoslavia, and Algeria.[3] In a context of intensifying religiosity, a repertoire of contention developed through the charity work of various Islamic organizations and through the emergence of international jihadist networks.[4]

The common language in the Syrian demonstrations was Islam, and its meta-political nature let Islamist, secular, and leftist discourses coexist. During the peaceful stage, the historically transgressive nature of Sunnism – the denomination of an overwhelming majority of the population – against the Bashar al-Assad regime made Islam a legitimate and effective language of protest. In the first demonstrations (regardless of political agenda), references to Islam included slogans (*Allah Akbar*), places (mosques), and days of protest (Fridays). "I am not a practicing Muslim, but Islam became a unifying element," a revolutionary told us.[5] Meanwhile, the narratives of secular protesters, notably from the

---

[2] François Burgat, *Face to Face with Political Islam*, New York, I.B. Tauris, 2002.
[3] This dimension has been particularly well studied in the Algerian case. See Luis Martinez, *The Algerian Civil War 1990–1998*, New York, Columbia University Press, 2000.
[4] Quintan Wiktorowicz (ed.), *Islamic Activism: A Social Movement Theory Approach*, Bloomington, Indiana University Press, 2003 and Janine Clark, *Islam, Charity and Activism: Middle-class Networks and Social Welfare in Egypt, Jordan, and Yemen*, Bloomington, Indiana University Press, 2004.
[5] I-12, in Aleppo, January 2013.

Marxist left and liberals, failed to take root and, consequently, so did their political agenda.

War added the jihadist register to the moral grammar of protest, where pacifism had previously played a central role. Jihad was initially national and inclusive, in the sense that it did not exclude any community.[6] Many military units were named after the Prophet's companions (Katiba Uthman, Liwa' Abu Bakr) and certain Koranic terms concatenated with the words 'freedom' and 'revolution'. Such references (e.g., Katibat al-Faruq in Homs, from the sobriquet for the second caliph, 'Umar ibn al-Khattab and Liwa' al-Tawhid in Aleppo, "the indivisible oneness of God," a term from the Koran) did not indicate any political program or degree of radicalism nor were they derived from consistent ideological considerations. Conversely, some Salafist groups took non-religious names, for example, Katiba Ahrar al-Sham (the Battalion of the Free Men of Syria, later Harakat Ahrar al-Sham al-Islamiyya). The rise in importance of jihadist symbolism was signaled when the black flag with the *shahada* (Islamic creed) in white letters on it came into use. But this banner, interpreted by the West as the distinctive symbol of Islamic radicalism, was also used by armed groups that were not radical.

In addition, jihad was linked to an imagery of martyrdom that gave meaning to death, the fate likely to befall the majority of fighters in Syria. Religious references multiplied as the risks incurred mounted and the casualty numbers rose. Invoking God became a source of comfort for the insurgents who fought in an environment where violence was endlessly replayed via video recordings.[7] As Pierre Centlivres had observed in 1980s Afghanistan, martyrdom offered an eschatological meaning when faced with the risk of dying.[8] As they helped combatants in Afghanistan and Iran in the 1980s or soldiers in France during the First World War, religious references helped the Syrian fighters face the terrors and hardships of a prolonged war.[9] Between 2011 and 2013, Syrian insurgents redefined their relationship to religion. A former communist militant,

---

[6] For instance, in a historical perspective, the declaration of jihad in 1909 by the Sultan Abdülhamit did not prevent minorities, notably Christians, from willingly supporting the Ottoman army. See François Georgeon, *Abdülhamit le Sultan calife (1976–1909)*, Paris, Fayard, 2003.

[7] We observed it regularly during our stays, especially during the mourning ceremonies. The documentary "Homs – Chronique d'une révolte" by Talal Derki and the web documentary "Syrie: Journaux intimes de la revolution" by Caroline Donati and Caroline Lefebvre-Quennell show this evolution in all the people filmed during those years. For the second, http://syria.arte.tv/, viewed October 2, 2014.

[8] Pierre Centlivres, "Violence légitime et ... *op. cit.*

[9] See Annette Becker, *La guerre et la foi: de la mort à la mémoire, 1914–1930*, Paris, Armand Colin, 1994.

newly appointed to head the revolutionary municipality in al-Bab, took up prayer: "I am a Communist but, in Syria, only God is with us."[10]

Second, the aesthetic world of the fighters drew on religious signs. The presentation of self-combined Islamic and revolutionary symbols, such as a beard, 'traditional' attire, a *sura* (Koranic verse) on clothing, amulets, bracelets, and headbands reflected the revolutionary Syrian flag inscribed with the *shahada*. These codes were partly borrowed from the esthetic of combatants from Afghanistan or the Caucasus but also from American action films. Given this context, it would be impossible to interpret these signs unequivocally. Markers like the wearing of black and white or khol on the eyes associated with an unambiguous adherence to a radical Islamist program in other situations (Afghanistan, Caucasus, Iraq, Somalia), here often reflected personal taste or fashion. Some individuals who were deeply conservative on the moral and political level went clean-shaven, while young fighters without particularly strong religious convictions affected long beards and a clean-shaven upper lip in the fundamentalist manner. In Aleppo, some fighters adopted the external appearance of international jihadism but were hardly religious, neglecting to pray, for example, when they were apart.[11] It was not until after 2013 and the rise of the radical groups that clothing or hair became an unambiguous marker of political affiliation.

Third, the armed groups adopted Islamic rhetoric to help attract funding. With Western countries providing little support, the Gulf States and their wealthiest citizens became the main supplier of military aid to the armed units.[12] To obtain financial support, armed groups highlighted the jihad theme in videos and on social networks. One-upmanship crept in among groups keen to make themselves known to Saudis, Qataris, and Kuwaitis by resorting to anti-Shia discourses.[13] Such rhetoric became performative as armed groups found themselves constrained in their recruiting (due to excluding non-Sunnis), alliances, and relationships with the population. The need for matching words to deeds transformed the rationale for engagement. Islam, in the beginning a meta-political and moral language, now became the cornerstone of any ideological discourse and circumscribed the legitimate political field.

---

[10] I-95, in al-Bab, December 2012.

[11] Observations in Aleppo, December 2012 and August 2013.

[12] For cases of funding strategies by wealthy Gulf citizens and their combined effects on the insurgency, see Thomas Pierret, "La révolution syrienne: un 'moment islamiste'?" in Michel Camau and Frédéric Vairel (eds.), *Soulèvements et recompositions politiques dans le monde arabe*, Montréal, Presses universitaires de Montréal, 2014, pp. 405–412.

[13] The same phenomenon occurred in Afghanistan in the 1990s. Saudi Arabia's funding of Ittehad-e islami led to various anti-Shia operations, including against civilians.

This inclusive use of Islam was in phase with another feature of the Syrian revolution's initial stage: the rejection of political parties. Not only did parties represent a threat to the unity of the revolutionary movement, they also risked precipitating *fitna* (rifts in the community of believers). Invisible in the protest movement, they also did not participate in the armed struggle, in part because they had relatively few militants inside the country.[14] Thus, the insurgents could chant "Syria is united and the Syrian people are one." "We are a united movement, we put our political differences aside," as the mayor of Aleppo explained to us.[15] In this context, political parties for the most part competed only for control of representative bodies based outside Syria. The few parties that sprang up counted few members (several dozen for the Umma party in 2013) and, most importantly, lacked military wings.[16] Left-leaning parties in exile refrained from opening offices in Syria. While some of their members returned on their own initiative, they did not flaunt their party membership. Members of various exiled political parties refused to divulge specific affiliations when in Syria, "In Syria, I'm protesting as a citizen. We are all united against the regime," as one reported.[17] In reality, the Communist People's Party and the Nasserist Socialist Party did contribute to the funding of some brigades but did so discreetly and minimally.

The Muslim Brotherhood's Syrian branch, driven out in the 1980s, did not recruit new members and initially made it official that it would hold off on any involvement in Syria until Bashar al-Assad had been overthrown. The party would instead concentrate its efforts on representing the insurgency outside the country. "Our members who go to Syria do so on their own initiative. The party has no strategy to return to Syria, as the revolution is a single unified movement that must not be divided."[18] Still, the Syrian Muslim Brotherhood had a longer-term strategy, seeing itself as well-positioned to benefit from political upheaval. The electoral victories in 2011 and 2012 of parties close to the Muslim Brotherhood (Ennahda in Tunisia and Freedom and Justice in Egypt) showed that these parties enjoyed popular support and electoral credibility in the Arab world. The Muslim Brotherhood's ideology, in fact, probably corresponded to the leanings of a large portion of Sunni Arab insurgents. On March 25, 2012 it adopted a charter espousing a "pluralist democracy [. . .] in which all citizens would be equal, regardless of their race, religion, community or [political] orientation." Read out by their

[14] I-96, with a militant of the Syrian Muslim Brotherhood, in Istanbul, April 2014.
[15] I-97, with the mayor of insurgent Aleppo, in Aleppo, August 2013.
[16] I-121, with members of the Umma party, in Azaz, December 2012.
[17] I-122, in Antakya, September 2013.
[18] I-96, in Istanbul, September 2013.

leader, Sadreddine Bayanouni, during a press conference in Istanbul, it set out "the principles the Brothers commit to working for in Syria after the fall of Bashar al-Assad."[19] In fact, the Muslim Brotherhood did try to open local branches in Syria in late 2011 but, "their recruiting efforts seemed to meet with qualified success, notably because of the social and cultural chasm separating the young Brothers, who came from the upper middle classes and graduated from foreign universities, from the activists in the field who frequently came from the rural or urban working class."[20] Absent an organization in place, their influence was mostly of a financial nature. Thus, the Muslim Brotherhood supported certain armed groups via Hay'at Himayat al-Madaniyyin (Committee of Civilian Defense), responsible for coordinating military aid and funding in Syria, and then via Hay'at Duru al-Thawra (The Committee of the Revolutionary Shields) from the summer of 2012 on. The Liwa' al-Tawhid, Liwa' Suqur al-Sham, and Harakat Ahrar al-Sham al-Islamiyya also received money from the Muslim Brotherhood, but turned down any political ties and, in general, ended these relationships during the course of 2013.[21] While talk of certain brigades being close to the Muslim Brotherhood (Liwa' al-Tawhid, for example) was not uncommon, members of the former rejected the innuendo, revealing the extent to which displays of party affiliation were still not acceptable in revolutionary circles.

In the end, armed groups were not formed along ideological lines and many political shades coexisted within them. They were poorly organized, possessed little hierarchy and individuals switched fluidly between groups. The ranks of the larger military units established starting in the fall of 2012 (al-Tawhid in Aleppo, al-Faruq in Homs, Idlib and Raqqa, Suqur al-Sham in Idlib) were generally filled with nonpoliticized combatants with diverse, mostly undefined leanings. Similarly, the various national alliances of rebel groups that were created successively in 2013 (Syrian Islamic Front, Syrian Islamic Liberation Front, Islamic Front) brought heteroclite ideologies together. The political spectrum of these groups comprising several thousand fighters ranged from secularism to international Islamist militancy. Toppling Bashar al-Assad was their priority; the rest could wait. Secularist liberals were particularly well-represented in the insurrection's civil institutions and in the armed units of the Idlib and Daraa governorates. But these activists did not

---

[19] The declaration was then published in *L'Orient le jour* on March 27, 2012.

[20] Thomas Pierret, "La révolution syrienne ... *op. cit.*, p. 397.

[21] The Muslim Brotherhood attempted to attract Salafists, despite being in ideological disagreement with the movement. Competition with Jabhat al-Nusra accounts for this openness, Aron Lund, *Struggling to Adapt: The Muslim Brotherhood in a New Syria*, Washington, Carnegie Endowment for International Peace, 2013, pp. 17–22.

coalesce into a party, despite frequent discussions on the topic, because they lacked external resources and popular support.[22] As they became progressively marginalized, political Islam became the insurgency's ideological center of gravity.

The Formation of Islamist Groups

The splintering of the insurgency was provoked by the creation of politico-military groups in the transnational jihadist margins. There were militants who had in fact seen action prior to the Syrian revolution. Most of the leaders of Islamist politico-military groups had fought in the war that ensued with the 2003 invasion of Iraq by the United States. Damascus supported these groups in their fight against the United States, which had openly envisioned the overthrow of the Syrian regime. These transnational networks, in coordination with the Syrian secret services, had trained many Islamist fighters. In 2009, the Assad regime's *rapprochement* with the United States in the context of the American withdrawal from Iraq led to a paradigm shift in Syrian politics. Jihadist networks were dismantled and militants arrested and imprisoned. As in Algeria in the 1990s, the prison experience was a key element in reorganizing and strengthening jihadist networks. In the spring of 2011, while peaceful, moderate demonstrators bore the full brunt of repression, the regime released hundreds of radical militants, notably from the Sednaya prison. They were to form the hard core of the first Islamist groups created in late 2011 – early 2012. Ahmed Abu Isa al-Sheikh (who would command Liwa' Suqur al-Sham in Idlib), Zahran Aluch (who would direct Jaysh al-Islam near Damascus), Abdul Rahman Suweis (of Liwa' al-Haqq), Hassan Abud (the founder of Harakat Ahrar al-Sham al-Islamiyya), and probably Abu Mohammad al-Julani (a Syrian al-Qaida in Iraq leader who took command of Jabhat al-Nusra, al-Qaida's Syria branch) were among those released.[23]

Until 2013, these groups were poorly established and made the strategic choice to coexist alongside other fighting units. Two groups, however, were different: Ahrar al-Sham and Jabhat al-Nusra began to oppose the insurgency's institutions in order to develop their own. The split with Jabhat al-Nusra then allowed ISIL to pursue an aggressive strategy against all the other groups.

Ahrar al-Sham, a Syrian Islamist Project   In January 2013, Harakat Ahrar

---

[22] Interviews in Aleppo, January and August 2013.

[23] Rania Abouzeid, "The Jihad Next Door," *Politico*, June 23, 2014, www.politico.com/maga zine/story/2014/06/al-qaeda-iraq-syria-108214.html#.VCA0mRbxfDs, viewed September 22, 2014.

al-Sham al-Islamiyya was born of the fusion of various small Islamist groups that had formed by early 2012.[24] Very active in the fighting, it extended its national presence by absorbing other armed groups throughout the country. It gained footholds especially in the Homs, Damascus, Latakia, and Raqqa governorates and played a key role in seizing the city of Raqqa (March 2013).

Although Salafist, the movement's organization closely resembled the rest of the insurgency. It meant that its fighters were free to come and go and, although foreign fighters did join the group, its ranks were predominantly Syrian. Early in its existence, the movement had imposed uniforms and collective practices, such as prayer before combat (a practice that was not unique to this group). The peculiarity of Harakat Ahrar al-Sham al-Islamiyya lay more in its political dimension. In this sense, the choice of the name *harakat* (movement), rather than *liwa'* (brigade) or *jaysh* (army) was significant, since it served to emphasize the political dimension while avoiding the more structured-sounding word for party (*hizb*), which was unpalatable to Syrian revolutionaries.[25] The political and armed wings were separate and when a fighter left a military unit, he nevertheless remained politically affiliated with the group, part of its longer term strategy for building up its strength. "Fighting is not everything, you also have to get ready for what comes after the war. Commitment to Ahrar al-Sham is made for the long term," explained one member.[26] The group depended on funding from the Gulf and its political program was to establish an Islamic state under Sharia law.[27] In the summer of 2013, the movement was only partly involved in the insurgency's civil institutions but distributed aid through its networks. Finally, Harakat Ahrar al-Sham al-Islamiyya sought control of economic channels, especially via a presence at the border posts of Bab al-Hawa in the Idlib governorate and Tal Abyad, respectively located in the Idlib and Raqqa governorates.

Harakat Ahrar al-Sham al-Islamiyya did not break with the armed groups that grew out of the peaceful demonstrations and fought

---

[24] The first video dates from April 2012, see Aron Lund, "Syria's Salafi Insurgents: The rise of the Syrian Islamic Front," March 2013, p. 29, www.euromesco.net/index.php?option= com_content&view=article&id=1941%3Asyrias-salafi-insurgents-the-rise-of-the-syrian-isla mic-front&catid=88%3Amembers-publications&Itemid=79&lang=en, viewed March 9, 2014.

[25] The construction of Harakat Ahrar al-Sham al-Islamiyya as a "movement" occurred in multiple stages according to alliances. The group first appeared as a *katiba*, then as the combination of several *kata'ib* before appearing in January 2013 as a "movement," www.youtube.com/watch?v=D64QLg-F9_Q, viewed September 22, 2014.

[26] I-123, in Gaziantep, September 2013.

[27] "Charter of the Syrian Islamic Front," *Carnegie Endowment for International Peace*, February 4, 2013, http://carnegieendowment.org/2013/02/04/charter-of-syrian-islamic-front, viewed September 22, 2014.

alongside these fellow insurgents. The movement agreed that defeating Bashar al-Assad had priority before determining the nature of the regime that would follow. Despite its rejection of the National Coalition's authority, it let the civil institutions do their work and attended public meetings organized by Salim Idriss, the head of the FSA.[28] Increased US pressure on the Gulf States to stop funding radical Islamist groups led Harakat Ahrar al-Sham al-Islamiyya to sign a covenant with other armed groups on May 17, 2014. Its stated objectives were "the fall of the regime," "territorial integrity," "revolutionary work," and "the rejection of fundamentalism and radicalism."[29] In the following weeks, some of the movement's most radical leaders stepped aside as a token gesture to placate the West and potential backers from the Gulf. The group then explicitly positioned itself as a "moderate" actor, between Jabhat al-Nusra on the one hand and the rest of the Syrian insurgency in the north on the other. In September 2014, a bomb wiped out the movement's leadership during a meeting in Idlib province, yet with little impact on the group's political trajectory. In March 2015, Ahrar al-Sham absorbed Liwa' Suqur al-Sham[30] and then forced Jabhat al-Nusra to accept a civilian administration in Idlib when it was taken. In July 2015, it mounted a public relations campaign in the *Washington Post* and the UK's *Telegraph* in a bid to gain support for fighting the Islamic State.[31]

Jabhat al-Nusra, Jihadist Internationalism   From its creation on January 24, 2012 to the split in March 2013, Jabhat al-Nusra li-Ahl al-Sham (The Support Front for the People of Syria) exemplified the first strategic attempt to implant the Islamic State in Iraq (ISI) in Syria.[32] In late

---

[28] Thomas Pierret, "Crise et déradicalisation: les rebelles syriens d'Ahrar al-Sham," *Confluences Méditerranée* 94 (3), 2015, p. 47.

[29] Pieter van Ostaeyen, "Islamic Front Revolutionary Covenant," May 17, 2014, http://piet ervanostaeyen.wordpress.com/2014/05/17/islamic-front-revolutionary-covenant/, viewed September 22, 2014.

[30] Aron Lund, "Islamist Mergers in Syria: Ahrar al-Sham Swallows Suqour al-Sham," Syria in Crisis, March 23, 2015, available at http://carnegieendowment.org/syriaincrisis/?f a=59471, viewed January 3, 2016.

[31] Thomas Pierret, "Crise et déradicalisation ... *op. cit.*, pp. 43–49. Labib Al Nahhas, "The Deadly Consequences of Mislabeling Syria's Revolutionaries," *Washington Post*, 10 juillet 2015, www.washingtonpost.com/opinions/the-deadly-consequences-of-mislabeling-syrias-r evolutionaries/2015/07/10/6dec139e-266e-11e5-aae2-6c4f59b050aa_story.html, viewed January 2, 2016; Labib Al Nahhas, "I'm a Syrian and I Fight Isil Every Day," *Telegraph*, July 21, 2015, www.telegraph.co.uk/news/worldnews/islamic-state/11752714/Im-a-Syrian-and-I-fight-Isil-every-day.-We-need-more-than-bombs-from-the-West-to-win-this-battle.h tml, viewed January 2, 2016.

[32] A video announced its formation on January 24, 2012, www.youtube.com/watch?v=Fu h1cI9vlR0, viewed in December 2014.

2011, Abu Bakr al-Baghdadi, the emir of the Islamic State in Iraq (then aligned with al-Qaida),[33] sent a group of several hundred fighters, veterans of the Iraq war, to Syria, some of whom had been imprisoned in Sednaya. Despite fielding only a small number of combatants and having limited support, the group did have funding networks, seasoned fighters and cadres who were used to operating clandestinely. These resources enlisted in the service of a regional strategy gave Jabhat al-Nusra a clear advantage over the rest of the insurgency. Jabhat al-Nusra's superiority further lay in its internal cohesion and centralized chain of command. The movement had two types of fighters. With a first oath (bay'a), a fighter committed himself to fight in Syria and to adhere to a strict moral code (no smoking, praying five times a day, no swearing, etc.). Then, if the combatant so wished and his conduct was exemplary, he could take a second oath to commit to serve international jihad with missions outside Syria.[34] A fighter could leave the organization but was sworn to keep the inner workings secret. "Since I left Jabhat al-Nusra, several fighters and some emirs I knew continue to come see me to talk. Officially, I am no longer a member of the group but they consider me to be so, and I can depend on them if I need to."[35] Moral and physical control of fighters played a key role in the organization's internal cohesion. They were segregated from the populace, lived among themselves and only rarely were able to see their families. An emir at the head of each unit organized daily politico-religious discussions and fighters were regularly moved around to maintain discipline under the hierarchy.

Jabhat al-Nusra built its reputation on its military exploits, on fair treatment meted out to the (Sunni) civilian populations and on their fight against crime. The movement served on the frontlines in all the major offensives and attracted the most spirited fighters. Numerous witness accounts testified to this. "The Jabha men's courage is unparalleled," related one fighter, "one time the front line was pierced and, faced with the regime's men, everyone fled. I was stuck with two other fighters in a building. We were about to be killed when two Jabha 4x4s counter-attacked, alone, and managed to extract us under fire."[36] Another combatant explained why he had chosen the group: "I have fought with a great many different groups. But the only

---

[33] Owing to the culture of secrecy within Jabhat al-Nusra, it is difficult to obtain precise information on the movement, starting with its origin. Press articles and reports on the movement are based on few sources and very few direct observations.

[34] I-49, with a former member of Jabhat al-Nusra, in Aleppo, December 2012.

[35] I-50, in Aleppo, August 2013.

[36] I-98, in Aleppo, January 2013.

really powerful one is Jabha. When you fight with them, you are well armed, you can count on your brothers, no one runs away. The attacks are well prepared and often victorious."[37] Indeed, funding and logistics from Iraq allowed Jabhat al-Nusra to equip its fighters properly. Military operations were recorded on video and posted on social networks. Each video with the balaclava-covered faces, black flags, military discipline, omnipresent religious symbols, and evident courage under enemy fire contributed to building the movement's image. Thanks to the widespread media coverage, Jabhat al-Nusra, until its separation from ISIL, recruited many of the foreigners who came to fight in Syria. Still, Jabhat al-Nusra did not have a monopoly on recruiting foreign fighters; they also joined many other brigades. In addition, the group was capable of carrying out suicide missions in government zones and on the front lines. Despite the insurrection's general military inferiority, the Jabhat al-Nusra tactic of launching suicide attacks prior to an assault created a breach in the regime's forces and could give it a decisive element of surprise. "Only the Jabha plans suicide missions. Its combatants have no fear. They are all ready for martyrdom and they fight to the death."[38] Thus, when the US State Department listed Jabhat al-Nusra as a terrorist organization on December 11, 2012, most other armed groups and part of the population in the insurgent areas pledged their solidarity to Jabhat al-Nusra.[39] Indeed, so as to not cut themselves off from the population, Jabhat al-Nusra proceeded cautiously in certain matters. Although Salafist, and therefore ideologically opposed to the cult of saints and in favor of *hudud* (serious fixed punishments in line with Sharia law), Jabhat al-Nusra deferred the application of these measures pending the creation of an Islamic regime. Depending on the local context, this allowed it to ignore, at least for the time being, practices it considered unorthodox.[40] A Jabhat al-Nusra emir thus explained in January 2013 that Syrians were not ready to vandalize the tombs of saints, these being pilgrimage sites.[41]

Another Jabhat al-Nusra's hallmark was that it systematically circumvented the insurgency's institutions. From the winter of 2012–2013 on,

[37] I-99, in Azaz, December 2012.
[38] I-41, with a commander of the FSA, in Aleppo, December 2012.
[39] Joshua Landis reported that several Syrian coordination groups affirmed their solidarity with Jabhat al-Nusra, "Syrian Militias Establish New Command – Pro-Jabhat al-Nusra Alliance Emerges," *Syria Comment*, December 10, 2012, www.joshualandis.com/blog/?p=16924&cp=all, viewed May 10, 2013; "Syrian Protesters Slam U.S. Blacklisting of Jihadist Group," *AFP*, December 14, 2012.
[40] I-31, with a judge from the Azaz court, January 2013.
[41] I-58, in Azaz, December 2012.

Jabhat al-Nusra set up a competing administration that paralleled the one recognized by the Coalition, giving priority to its own activities to enhance its reputation for integrity among the population. Advancing an anti-corruption platform, it meddled in the administration of rebel-controlled areas. In the autumn of 2012, Jabhat al-Nusra refused to recognize the judicial system set up by the National Coalition and joined with other Islamist groups to set up their own courts and prisons.[42] In addition, Jabhat al-Nusra manipulated local power struggles to make inroads. "There is not always consensus for creating tribunals and deciding who could police a town," explained a member of the Revolutionary Security of Aleppo. "The Jabha combatants take advantage of this to open a base and organize patrols. If they manage to get control of the tribunal, they use its rulings to make arrests, starting with their opponents."[43] Events that took place at the court in the city of al-Bab fit this pattern[44]: in December 2012, when a conflict arose between the new executives of the municipality, one faction called on the court that dealt primarily with civil disputes to annul the appointment of certain city council members. In this unsettled situation, Jabhat al-Nusra set up a Judicial Committee (Hay'a al-Shari'yya). Two judges backed up by about thirty armed men took over an office in the court, then took on the role of a moral police (veils for women, Ramadan observance). These men, all strangers to al-Bab, some wearing balaclavas, had no ties to the local population. Despite the limited numbers of the intruders, the deeply divided local elite expressed no opposition. In fact, some of the local justices called on Jabhat al-Nusra to reinforce their own authority, while certain armed groups looked to benefit from its military support.[45] It took just a few months for Jabhat al-Nusra to control al-Bab's court and the municipal police. Similarly, in Aleppo, the insurrection's judicial apparatus was in direct competition with the Jabhat al-Nusra's Judicial Committee created late in 2012 with the support of Harakat Ahrar al-Sham al-Islamiyya, Liwa' Suqur al-Sham, and Liwa' al-Tawhid. From the outset, it made secret arrests. "Since the Jabhat tribunal was created, its morality police have arrested revolutionaries. The trials take place behind closed doors, no one hears about them. At the beginning, there were rumors. Then some released prisoners have talked about their incarceration. According to them, Jabhat is detaining dozens of

---

[42] I-124, with a revolutionary activist, ex-prisoner of Jabhat al-Nusra, in Aleppo and with members of the Court of the United Judicial Council of Aleppo, January 2013.
[43] I-18, in Aleppo, January 2013.
[44] Observations in al-Bab, December 2012 and January 2013.
[45] Interviews with members of the Azaz and al-Bab courts, December 2012 and January 2013.

people in its prisons, often revolutionaries."[46] The Aleppo Judicial Committee also attacked the National Coalition's institutions by accusing its members of being "secular," or "unbelieving" and took a hand in providing public services. In towns and villages, Jabhat al-Nusra very early on concentrated on reopening mosques abandoned by the official imams. Jabhat al-Nusra could now diffuse its political vision through the preaching of imams it appointed, once again strengthening its hold on the communities. In addition, the movement used its limited resources to focus on politically advantageous services while it eschewed less visible administrative tasks. "Several times Jabhat attempted to create its own food distribution network, a garbage collection service and several other services of this kind in Aleppo," an employee at the Aleppo city council explained, "but it didn't work because these activities require long term resources and know-how that only the city council possesses. Jabhat only looks for visible activities from which it gains prominence."[47]

In addition, until it was driven out by ISIL in the spring of 2013, Jabhat al-Nusra maneuvered itself into a key role in transport of energy and other essential supplies in the north. Between 2012 and 2013, making the most of its links with the Islamic State in Iraq, Jabhat al-Nusra took control of gas and oil transportation. It controlled flour transport in the province of Aleppo and sat on most of the councils controlling the flourmills. The organization did not so much seek to make a profit as to gain popularity by reducing prices and providing reliable supplies.[48] To this end, it also distributed aid and organized care for the sick and injured.

After the split with ISIL in March 2013 (see below), Jabhat al-Nusra kept hedging its strategic bets by either building coalitions with the rest of the Syrian insurgency or going all out for a takeover. In November 2013, it announced a change of name – al-Qaida in the Levant (al-Qaida fi Bilad al-Sham) – to assert its legitimacy in the face of ISIL. In August 2014, it withdrew from the Judicial Committee to set up its own courts, the Dar al-Qada' (Houses of Justice). Though they were much less widespread than the Judicial Committee courts, they rapidly gained visibility by applying *hudud*, such as death by stoning, and then publicizing the punishments to compete with the Islamic State.[49] The same month, a video

---

[46] I-100, in Aleppo, January 2013.
[47] I-97, in Aleppo, August 2013.
[48] Interviews with leaders of the Aleppo's Revolutionary Transitional Council of the Governorate, in Aleppo, January 2013.
[49] Maxwell Martin, "Al-Qaeda's Syrian Judiciary – Is It Really What al-Jolani Makes It Out to Be?" *Syria Comment*, November 9, 2014, www.joshualandis.com/blog/al-qaedas-syrian-j udiciary-really-al-jolani-makes/; "Dar al-Qada in its own words," *Goha's Nail*, October 27, 2014, https://gohasnail.wordpress.com/2014/10/27/dar-al-qada-in-its-own-words/.

leaked of Abu Muhammad al-Julani describing to its followers his project to set up an Islamic Emirate in Northern Syria.[50] In October 2014, in Jabal al-Zawiya, it also attacked FSA-related groups (the Syrian Revolutionary Front and the Movement of Steadfastness).[51] Yet, under pressure from Turkey and the Gulf Countries, and with the Islamic State advancing in northern Syria, in the spring of 2015 Jabhat al-Nusra changed its strategy. In March, it entered into a new coalition with Ahrar al-Sham and former FSA units, the Army of Conquest (Jaysh al-Fatah), and compromised on sharing the administration of Idlib City. Though at first it refused to disavow its link to al-Qaida,[52] Jabhat al-Nusra shifted to insisting on the entirely Syrian nature of its objectives. In an interview in May 2015 with *Al Jazeera*, Abu Muhammad al-Julani declared, "Nusra Front doesn't have any plans or directives to target the West. We received clear orders not to use Syria as a launching pad to attack the US or Europe in order to not sabotage the true mission against the regime. Maybe al-Qaida does that, but not here in Syria."[53] In the same interview, the leader of Jabhat al-Nusra denied the existence of the "Khorasan" network, which, according to US intelligence, was targeting Western countries. Finally, in July 2016, faced with military pressure by the regime and its allies, by the PYD and the Islamic State in northern Syria, the group officially broke off all ties with al-Qaida. It changed its name and became the Front for Victory in the Levant, which facilitated staging joint operations with other groups of the insurrection.

The Islamic State and the Breaking of the Insurgency In April 2013, the Islamic State in Iraq (ISI) and fighters that had quit Jabhat al-Nusra fused and called themselves the Islamic State in Iraq and Levant (ISIL). The fighters who stayed with Jabhat al-Nusra aligned themselves with the historic al-Qaida led by Ayman al-Zawahiri and made fighting the Syrian regime alongside the remaining armed groups its priority. Meanwhile, ISIL broke with al-Qaida and claimed Iraq and the Levant (Syria, Lebanon, and Palestine), and then, in June 2014, under the name of the Islamic State, proclaimed a global caliphate

---

[50] Thomas Pierret, "Les salafismes dans l'insurrection ... *op. cit.*, p. 211.

[51] Abdallah Suleiman Ali, "Idlib Prepares for War between Factions and Jabhat al-Nusra," *Al-Monitor*, August 20, 2014, www.al-monitor.com/pulse/security/2014/08/syria-idlib-war-jabhat-al-nusra-factions.html#.

[52] Aron Lund "The Nusra Front's Internal Purges," *Syria in Crisis*, August 7, 2015, http://carnegieendowment.org/syriaincrisis/?fa=60967.

[53] "Nusra Leader: Our Mission Is to Defeat the Syrian Regime," May 28, 2015, *Al Jazeera*, www.aljazeera.com/news/2015/05/nusra-front-golani-assad-syria-hezbollah-isil-150528 044857528.html, viewed December 15, 2015.

with the mission of unifying all Muslims. We can distinguish two phases in ISIL's strategy: the first, lasting until 2014, was to establish control over economic and logistical flows, and the second was one of generalized confrontation.

Before 2014, ISIL strategy was not directed against the Damascus regime. The objective of the armed operations ISIL took part in (the seizure of Menagh airport, of the al-Safira arms factory, and the headquarters of Base 17 in the Raqqa governorate) was to clear out the remaining government positions in northern Syria. Widely covered by the media, they were politically significant, but did not have a large military impact and did not require troop deployments of long duration. The sole front north of Latakia that ISIL fought on was distinguished by the presence of Alawites, which gave the fighting a sectarian tinge. In similar fashion, ISIL carried out a raid on the Ismaeli city of Salamiyah in April 2014.

What ISIL was really after was gaining control over resources in the northern rebel areas. While ISIL was dependent on supplies of fighters and weapons that moved east to west from the Iraqi safe haven into Syria, the rest of the insurgency depended principally on a north-south supply route, relying on the Turkish sanctuary to supply the fronts in Aleppo, Hama, and Homs, and relying on Jordan for supplying Daraa. The two routes intersected in northern Syria and controlling them was therefore vital. The need to secure the flow of men, arms, and money was one of the causes of the conflict with the other insurgent groups that broke out in January 2014.

Initially, ISIL did not bother with administering territories, since that would have required a significant investment of men and resources; instead, they targeted strategic spots. It focused especially on controlling the roads leading to Turkey. Rather than seizing the border posts, it seized towns near them to avoid Turkish retaliation and direct conflict with the FSA. In this way, the movement conquered al-Dana, near the border post of Bab al-Hawa; Azaz, near Bab al-Salam; Saluq, located about 10 kilometers from Tal Abyad, and Jarablus. Within a few months, ISIL was capable of choking off FSA supplies from Turkey. The 2013 clashes with PYD in the Aleppo and Hasaka governorates were primarily over control of border regions, especially the posts of Tal Abyad on the Turkish border and Tal Hamis and Yarubiyyah on the Iraqi border. The Kurdish organization had established bases in the Kurdish enclaves bordering Turkey. Late in 2013, ISIL laid siege to the Kurdish villages on the Turkish border close to Afrin (notably Duweidan) and Ayn al-Arab. In 2013, ISIL, supported by Jabhat al-Nusra and certain FSA brigades, led ferocious offensives in Jazeera, Ras al-Ayn, and in the countryside around Qamishli.

ISIL also took over factories, warehouses, grain silos, and distribution outlets for gas and bread. In a fundraising technique learned in Iraq, it extorted the South African MTN telecom company in return for letting it continue operating its cellular network in Aleppo's Hanano district.[54] More generally, by monopolizing transportation of key supplies and installing checkpoints at strategic locations, ISIL could exert pressure on the other groups by controlling their supply lines.

Finally, in order to gain control over information and humanitarian aid, ISIL proceeded to ban Westerners from northern Syria.[55] From the spring of 2013 onward, targeted kidnappings of activists, of fixers working for the Western press, and of Syrian journalists multiplied. ISIL was directly responsible for roughly thirty disappearances in the summer of 2013 in Raqqa and Aleppo. The movement also held several Westerners prisoner who had been working for NGOs in the Aleppo and Latakia governorates, and it confiscated goods from a Western NGO in the Raqqa governorate. While intent on expelling all Westerners, until January 2014 ISIL still tolerated the presence of Syrians doing NGO work. Then, when it tightened its grip on eastern Syria, ISIL banned Western NGOs altogether. However, it arranged for a Vice News journalist to stay and shoot a documentary about the movement's governance.[56] It later published a set of rules for journalists wanting to work in the areas under ISIL control, starting with the requirement to pledge allegiance to the caliphate.[57]

Throughout 2013, ISIL's strategy led to regular clashes with FSA brigades, combat between rebel groups heretofore having been rare and highly localized. ISIL strove to implement a global strategy of gaining the upper hand over the fragmented insurgency, whose various components each had a parochial view of each violent encounter. It therefore directly attacked FSA groups but in such a way as to keep them from forming a common front. ISIL then went on the offensive in the town of al-Dana on July 6, 2013 to take control of the route leading

[54] I-126 in Kirkuk and I-127 in Hawija, April 2013.
[55] See especially RWB (Reporters Without Borders), http://fr.rsf.org/syrie-syrie-12-03-20 12,42016.html, viewed September 9, 2014.
[56] www.vice.com/fr/vice-news/l-etat-islamique-version-integrale-125, viewed September 30, 2014.
[57] See the 11 rules on the site *Syria Deeply* www.syriadeeply.org/articles/2014/10/6200/isis-issues-11-rules-journalists-deir-ezzor/.

to the border at Bab al-Hawa. Killing some thirty FSA fighters, ISIL captured the town after having joined forces with local armed groups. In September and October 2013, it also took over most of the town of Azaz. Also, that October, it took control of Atmeh, the border town that Bab al-Hawa depended on. Likewise, ISIL tightened its hold on Raqqa by challenging FSA units one by one (see text box). It did not even refrain from attacking Liwa' al-Tawhid in its home base, the town of Maraa. And finally, it liquidated anyone who publicly opposed it: for example, the imam of the Great Mosque of Mambij and a judge in Azaz were assassinated in August 2013.

After 2014, ISIL's break with the insurrection was unmistakable. The movement only fielded a few thousand hardened fighters, but its strategy had forced all groups to choose sides. In January 2014, the necessity of the FSA groups securing their supplies of men, arms, and money from Turkey led to open conflict. Jabhat al-Nusra and the Islamic Front were forced to take sides and took up the fight against ISIL. After a month of fighting in northeastern Syria, the fronts stabilized. ISIL withdrew from Idlib province and the surrounding areas of Aleppo, but tightened its control over the east, including in the provinces of Raqqa and Hasaka, where it had mostly driven out other armed groups. During the summer of 2014, ISIL's very rapid advances in Iraq enabled it again to go on the offensive against other armed groups in Syria but also, for the first time, against the regime. Using arms captured in Iraq, it eliminated FSA pockets in the east and advanced into the Aleppo governorate. Signaling its new ambitions, ISIL engaged for the first time in a head-to-head conflict with Syrian regime forces at al-Shaer and took control of bases around Raqqa.

ISIL's Rise to Power in Raqqa

The conflict in Raqqa offers a case study in ISIL strategy. The city of Raqqa, capital of the governorate of the same name and taken by the insurgency in March 2013, is located on the Aleppo-Deir ez-Zor road. The city was held by FSA brigades (including ones affiliated with Kata'ib al-Faruq and Alwiyat Ahfad al-Rasul) and Harakat Ahrar al-Sham al-Islamiyya, with Jabhat al-Nusra playing a minor role. With support from Kata'ib al-Faruq, Harakat Ahrar al-Sham al-Islamiyya, and Alwiyat Ahfad al-Rasul, a functioning administration was established, including the municipal council and the Judicial Committee. The Liwa' Umana' al-Raqqa also organized a police force to keep other military units out of the city.

Lack of coordination among the insurgents explains ISIL's rapid progress in a matter of a few months starting in April 2013. One after the other, it took on Jabhat al-Nusra, Kata'ib al-Faruq, Liwa' Umana' al-Raqqa, and Alwiyat Ahfad al-Rasul. Harakat Ahrar al-Sham al-Islamiyya, the largest armed group in Raqqa, did not come to the aid of any of the units that ISIL attacked and even joined the fight against Kata'ib al-Faruq on ISIL's side. In each case, ISIL relied on a familiar strategy of assassinating the unit's leader and a few of its commanders, causing the fighters to disband. Moreover, when ISIL and Jabhat al-Nusra split, most of the latter's fighters went over to ISIL while the remnants withdrew to Tabqa, in the governorate's west.[58] As a result, Kata'ib al-Faruq combatants fled to Turkey; Liwa' Umana' al-Raqqa was marginalized, after its leader Abu Taif was kidnapped, and so was Alwiyat Ahfad al-Rasul when its leader was killed in a suicide attack.

Even so, by the fall of 2013, ISIL still had not established control sufficient to let it govern the city. For instance, women rarely wore the niqab. The movement did not have many fighters inside Raqqa, but it held the city's main entry points, and it did implement its own system of aid distribution inside the town. Adopting another tactic employed in Iraq, ISIL also formed alliances with local tribes, notably with some Afadlah clans. However, its influence was still far less than that of Ahrar al-Sham, which remained the most powerful group in the governorate until late 2013. In January 2014, the FSA launched a huge military operation meant to drive ISIL out of Syria. On January 8, 2014, it briefly took Raqqa, then lost it again a few days later when ISIL reinforcements arrived from Iraq. Raqqa now became ISIL's primary base, with the city definitively cleared of all other groups.

The Territorialization of Politico-Military Actors

Contrary to a commonly-held belief, the frontlines in Syria were never static. Each side would eliminate enemy positions in piecemeal fashion in the areas it dominated. Despite some setbacks, the opposition kept growing in 2014 and 2015 and continued to rely on Turkish and Jordanian sanctuaries. Over time, as regime, insurgent, PYD, and Islamic State areas each homogenized, the military map became increasingly simplified. Then, with the Russian intervention in September 2015 and the increased Iranian and Hezbollah presence, came a strategic turn in the war as the regime took back cities from the insurgents, most importantly Aleppo in late 2016.

---

[58] This accounts in part for ISIL's more rapid takeover of Raqqa, unlike Deir ez-Zor, where most Jabhat al-Nusra combatants refused to pledge allegiance to the movement.

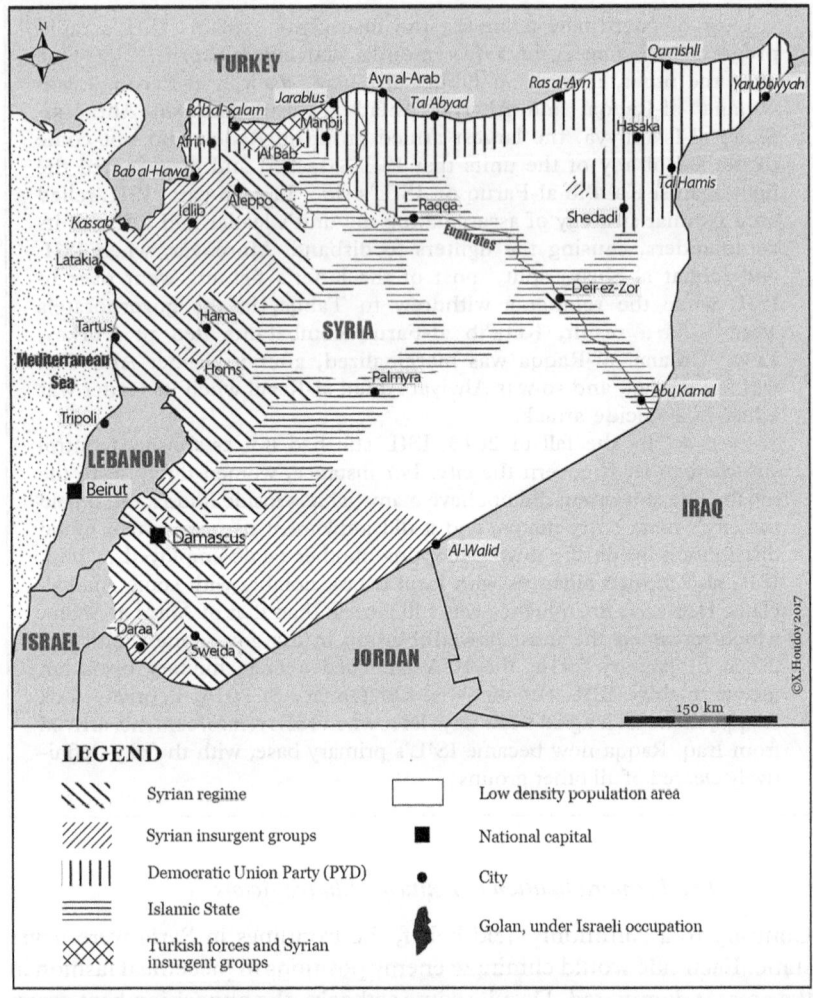

Map 9.1 The military situation (December 2016)

First, from late 2013 on, the FSA's internal crisis (see Chapter 6), regime pressure, and the threat of ISIL led to a complex reconfiguration of the insurgency both within and beyond the FSA, which, however, still did not yield a coalition capable of stabilizing the political landscape. In the context of the fight against ISIL, isolated actors disappeared, as the hundreds of independent groups, created in the first months of fighting, formed large coalitions. Thus, with the Syrian Revolutionary Command Council (Majlis Qiyadat al-Thawra al-Suriyya) failing to recreate a unitary command, former FSA units joined new national organizations such as Jabhat Thuwar Suriyya (Syrian Revolutionary Front) and Harakat Hazm (Movement of Steadfastness). Three regional coalitions of former FSA fighters emerged: Jaysh al-Mujahidin (Mujahidin Army) in Aleppo, al-Ittihad al-Islami li-Ajnad al-Sham (Islamic Union of the Soldiers of Levant) in Damascus, and Jaysh al-Yarmuk (Yarmuk Army) in Daraa.[59]

Yet, due to their lack of resources, such military structures remained unappealing. Military coalitions were attempted outside of the FSA, especially by other Islamist groups. In September 2012, Jabhat Tahrir Suriyya al-Islamiyya (SILF, Syrian Islamic Liberation Front) brought together the Liwa' Suqur al-Sham, Jaysh al-Islam, and Liwa' al-Tawhid. In December 2012, Harakat Ahrar al-Sham al-Islamiyya announced the formation of Jabha al-Islamiyya al-Suriyya (SIF, Syrian Islamic Front), which united several additional groups.[60] In the wake of FSA's failure, the disastrous Geneva II negotiations, and ISIL's rise to power, in November 2013 the environment became more favorable for negotiation between the groups affiliated with SIF and SILF. Supported by the Gulf States and Turkey, they formed Jabha al-Islamiyya (the Islamic Front), making it the insurrection's largest alliance. In summer 2014, confronted with ISIL's continued advances in the north, some FSA groups joined forces with two of the largest Islamic Front brigades (Suqur al-Sham and Jaysh al-Islam) in the Syrian Revolutionary Command Council.[61] This group was founded on a "charter of honor" signed in May 2014, which proclaimed it to be resolutely moderate and affirmed the Syrian nature of its fight to counter the growing involvement by

---

[59] Thomas Pierret, "Fragmentation et consolidation de l'opposition armée," *Confluences méditerranéennes* 89 (2), 2014, pp. 45-51.

[60] "We, who are the widest spectrum of Islamic brigades working on the soil of beloved Syria, hereby announce the creation of the Syrian Islamic Front. It is a comprehensive Islamic front, representing Islam as a religion, a creed, a path, and a conduct. Its beliefs spring from the path of Ahl al-Sunna wal-Jamaa, understood as that of the pious ancestors, without extremism or negligence. It aims to overthrow the Assad regime, and to build a civilized Islamic society ruled by God's law [sharia], in which Muslim and non-Muslim alike will enjoy the justice of Islam. To realize its goals, the Front relies on many different means. The military movement aims to overthrow the regime and establish security. The civil movement follows various paths – political, missionary, educational, relief, and humanitarian – within the confines of sharia rulings. In addition to this, the Front is considered one of the [many] Islamic forces working in the Syrian society, and therefore it works to preserve a unified discourse and a coalition, and to avoid division and differences, while striving for understanding with everyone who works for Islam, with whom it is possible to cooperate based on a common understanding of devoutness, piety, and a righteous vision." www.youtube.com/watch?v=qPzWVz4Pqbo, viewed September 9, 2014.

[61] "Translation: The formation of the Syrian Revolutionary Command Council," *Goha's Nail*, August 3, 2014, http://gohasnail.wordpress.com/2014/08/03/translation-the-formation-of-the-syrian-revolutionary-command-council/, viewed September 7, 2014.

foreign combatants and the Syrian revolution's transformation into a global jihad.[62] These coalitions remained fluid until late 2016, with new ones emerging, for instance, Fatah Halab (Aleppo Victory) in Aleppo and Jaysh al-Fatah (the Army of Conquest) in Idlib, Hama, and Latakia. Also, groups kept moving in and out of them and internal strife continued to break out, pitting Jabhat al-Nusra against Jabhat Thuwar Suriyya in the north in the fall of 2015, and Jaysh al-Islam against FSA units in Eastern Ghouta in spring 2016.

In addition, ISIL, flush with its success in Iraq, launched a series of offensives in the summer of 2014. It advanced in northern Syria, threatening Maraa and Azaz and attacked the PYD strongpoint at Ayn al-Arab (Kobane). At that point, the United States decided to intervene on the side of the Kurds and its aerial support proved decisive in helping YPG repulse the ISIL offensive. With US support, the PYD then reconquered all Kurdish territory from the Islamic State and moved into the Arab territories of the governorates of Hasaka, Raqqa, and Aleppo. ISIL, under attack in both Iraq and northern Syria, made no more progress except in the east, where it took Tadmur and the Palmyra site in May 2015.

The regime at last saw the situation tilt in its favor. Supported by Hezbollah and Iran, it was able to take Qusayr and score victories around Hama and Homs, raising the odds for its survival. Yet, when the Islamic State captured Palmyra in 2015 and the insurgency took Kessab, Idlib, and Jisr al-Shughur in the north and the Quneitra corridor, these setbacks laid bare the Syrian army's steady disintegration. The regime survived thanks to its militias and the increased presence of Hezbollah and the Iranian Pasdaran, who relied on a strategy of massive, indiscriminate shelling of areas held by the insurgency. Russia's intervention in September 2015 marked a turning point in the war. The Russian air force concentrated its bombing campaign on the insurgents, allowing the regime to retake Homs in December 2015, to launch an offensive against Aleppo in January 2016, and to retake Palmyra in March 2016. In coordination with the Kurdish PYD, the regime cut the road between Aleppo and Turkey in July 2016 and besieged Aleppo's eastern neighborhoods. Turkey, the insurgency's major supporter, gave up on Aleppo and pulled part of its defenders back to use in its own offensive in August 2016 against the PYD and the Islamic State. The insurgency's offensive in the summer and fall of 2016 failed to break the siege of Aleppo whose defenses crumbled in late November. The fall of Aleppo constitutes a major victory for the regime, and in essence reflects the swing of international support in its favor.

---

[62] Thomas Pierret, "Fragmentation et consolidation ...," *op. cit.*

10 The Caliphate

> "The creation of the caliphate was announced in each mosque by an Islamic State fighter who was taking the place of the usual imam. The members of Daesh were mad! We saw military parades with tanks, Scuds missiles, and even fighters on horseback ... Before the caliphate, we had the feeling that the Islamic State still did not dare to carry out their ideas. But after the proclamation, they considered that they had all the rights. And the population started being really afraid."[1]

On June 29, 2014, the Islamic State proclaimed a caliphate, asserting the right to govern all believers (*Umma*) and announcing that Abu Bakr al-Baghdadi henceforth would be the caliph, with the title of Commander of Believers (*Amir al-Mu'minin*). Variously described as "mad," "fanatical," or "medieval," the Islamic State's rationality remains a political enigma on three levels: the behavior of its militants, its relationships with society and with the outside world. Does the propensity of its militants to carry out suicide attacks on such a scale signal a peculiar irrationality? Why resort to such extreme brutality to impose a social order that undermines the economic and demographic bases of their intended caliphate? What is the logic of a movement that, in a situation of strategic emergency, alienates potentially supportive or neutral actors by lashing out in all directions and broadcasting dramatic videos of its extreme violence?

Typically, most interpretations struggle to describe the specific logic of the Islamic State. First, the prevailing analyses in the literature on terrorism are unable to explain how the Islamic State administers bureaucratically a population numbering several million people, while its use of violence is only marginally directed against Westerners.[2] Furthermore, explanations in terms of deviance, brainwashing, cult-like phenomenon, or fanaticism clash with the known aporias of the psychological explanation

---

[1] I-149, with a Syrian activist from Raqqa, Skype, February 2015.
[2] Thomas Hegghammer and Petter Nesser, "Assessing the Islamic State's Commitment to Attacking the West," *Perspectives on Terrorism* 9 (4), 2015, pp. 14–30.

of political behavior. The literature finds various and often contradictory variables in the psychological profiles of suicide bombers.[3] More generally, the focus on individual behavior misses the organizational dynamic, a necessary element in any explanation of the Islamic State. Second, analogies drawn with other Islamist movements and their relationships with society are only partially enlightening. The moral order imposed on the population and the destruction of archaeological sites invite comparison with other movements, such as the Afghan Taliban, the Malian Ansar Dine, or the Somali Shabab.[4] Yet the Islamic State is not simply a more extreme version of existing Islamist movements, but follows a distinct logic. For example, the generalized use of *takfir* (excommunication) and the systematic massacres of non-Sunnis are traits specific to the Islamic State. Moreover, where the Taliban movement sought to integrate the Islamic Emirates of Afghanistan in the international state system,[5] the Islamic State rejects its underlying principles. Finally, far from constituting a resurgence of a traditional form of domination, the rational-legal functioning of the Islamic State, its affinity for technologies, its discourses and stated objectives witness to its being a modern, globalized movement.[6] Still, its eschatological nature is too decisive to be overlooked: By choosing to exclusively focus on the constitutional and judicial aspects of the caliphate, Andrew March and Mara Revkin left our questions about the movement's logic unanswered.[7]

To solve this riddle, we articulate the question of rationality through a regime of truth. According to Michel Foucault,

each society has its regime of truth, its 'general politics' of truth: that is, the types of discourse which it accepts and makes function as true; the mechanisms and instances which enable one to distinguish true and false statements, the means by which each is sanctioned; the techniques and procedures accorded value in the acquisition of truth; the status of those who are charged with saying what counts as true.[8]

---

[3] Amélie Blom, "Do Jihadist 'Martyrs' Really Want to Die? An Emic Approach to Self-Sacrificial Radicalization in Pakistan," *Revue française de science politique* 61 (5), 2011, pp. 867–891.

[4] Pierre Centlivres, "The Controversy over the Buddhas of Bamiyan," *South Asia Multidisciplinary Academic Journal* 2, 2008, URL: http://samaj.revues.org/992 viewed January 6, 2016; Emily J. O'Dell, "Waging War on the Dead: The Necropolitics of Sufi Shrine Destruction in Mali," *Archaeologies* 9 (3), 2013, pp. 506–525.

[5] Gilles Dorronsoro, *Revolution Unending . . . op. cit.*

[6] Graeme Wood, "What ISIS Really Wants," *The Atlantic*, March 2015, www.theatlantic .com/magazine/archive/2015/03/what-isis-really-wants/384980/, viewed January 2, 2016.

[7] Andrew March and Mara Revkin, "The Caliphate of Law: ISIS' Ground Rules," *Foreign Affairs*, 2015, www.foreignaffairs.com/articles/syria/2015-04-15/caliphate-law.

[8] Michel Foucault, "The Political Function of the Intellectual," *Radical Philosophy* 17, 1977, pp. 12–15.

The regime of truth conditions the validity of arguments about ends and means or legitimate objectives. The perceived irrationality of the Islamic State results from the formation of a new regime of truth, based on an eschatological reading of Islam, which subordinates alternative modes of veridiction, whether judicial, scientific, or ethical.[9] This *"general politics of truth"* sets it apart from the Iraqi and Syrian societies and the rest of the world.

The Islamic State's apocalyptical *Weltanschauung* constitutes the backbone of its ideology. In a charismatic rationale, the victories of the movement are further proof of divine favor, as the return of the caliphate signals the end of historical time and Islam's impending victory.[10] Add to this that the Islamic State expresses the main concepts and categories of the most rigorous version of Salafism.[11] Its distinctive characteristic is a very peculiar practice of *takfir*.[12] In a logic inspired by Sayyid Qutb, and more distantly by Ibn Taymiyya, *takfir* is interpreted as a refusal to swear allegiance to the Islamic State and its caliph.[13] This refusal justifies excommunicating individuals or groups, hence killing them, on a political basis independent of their individual religious practices.

The extreme closure of the Islamic State lets it actualize its ideology, which, in turn, makes this regime of truth crucial for the movement's internal functioning. First, an eschatological interpretation of the world reduces the cognitive dissonance created by military defeats and the lack of popular support, thus preserving the charismatic nature of the movement.[14] Diminished cognitive dissonance then

---

[9] Michel Foucault, *The Courage of the Truth (The Government of Self and Others II): Lectures at the Collège de France, 1983–1984*, Basingstoke, Palgrave Macmillan, 2011. In totally different ideological contexts, one can remember the Soviet Lysenkoism and the Nazi attacks against Einstein's theory of relativity.

[10] This vision pervades all videos and publications of the Islamic State. For example, see "Al Qaeda of Waziristan," *Dabiq* 6, http://media.clarionproject.org/files/islamic-state/isis-isil-islamic-state-magazine-issue-6-al-qaeda-of-waziristan.pdf, viewed January 2, 2016.

[11] Cole Bunzel, *From Paper State to Caliphate: The Ideology of the Islamic State*, Washington, The Brookings Institution, 2015, www.brookings.edu/~/media/research/files/papers/2015/03/ideology-of-islamic-state-bunzel/the-ideology-of-the-islamic-state.pdf, viewed January 2, 2016.

[12] Camilla Adang, Hassan Ansari, Maribel Fierro, and Sabine Schmidtke (eds.), *Accusations of Unbelief in Islam: A Diachronic Perspective on Takfir*, Leiden, Brill, 2015.

[13] Eli Alshesh, "The Doctrinal Crisis within the Salafi-Jihadi Ranks and the Emergence of Neo-Takfirism: A Historical and Doctrinal Analysis," *Islamic Law and Society* 21, 2014, pp. 419–452.

[14] Leon Festinger, Henry Riecken, and Stanley Schachter, *When Prophecy Fails: A Social and Psychological Study of a Modern Group That Predicted the Destruction of the World*, New York, Harper-Torchbooks, 1964.

induces a threat-driven misperception of the strategic situation.[15] Next, the compartmentalization fueled by *takfiri* discourse creates the conditions conducive to mass atrocities and enslavement.[16] Finally, this regime of truth limits the tensions inside the organization in two ways: for one, charisma is depersonalized because it stems more from the movement than from its leader, but the legal-rational organization, necessary to its survival in a context of extremely heavy military pressure, is reinforced.[17] For another, this regime of truth facilitates the aligning of individual behavior with organizational interests. Islamic State militants fight to fulfil the objectives of the movement, subsumed in a "Promise of Allah," which is the realization of the Islamic reign on earth. Therefore, while its worldly success is proof of the movement's divine election, the militants will reap their reward in the afterlife. Individual behaviors unambiguously follow an ethic of conviction, which also explains the total sense of sacrifice of fighters prepared to carry out suicide attacks.[18] Overall, the Islamic State's regime of truth allows rational-legal procedures, an ethic of conviction, and a charismatic legitimacy to coexist within the same organization.

The Closure of the Islamic State

The Islamic State's closure makes imposing an eschatological discourse possible, which, in turn, serves to further alienate the militants from the world outside. Under the name of al-Qaida in Mesopotamia (AQM – Tandhim Qaʻidat al-Jihad fi-Bilad al-Rafidayn), the Islamic State emerged during the American occupation of Iraq as a small group of militants isolated from the rest of society. It developed a specific organizational culture of pervasive violence. The militarized, centralized functioning precluded all debate on the ends to be achieved by its members. This closure derived from a three-part legacy: the authoritarian practices inherited from the Baathist party, the shared experience of imprisonment during the American intervention after 2003, and the absolute clandestinity required to escape international surveillance and targeted killings. The presence of foreign fighters reinforced the closed nature of the group. The abrupt change from the clandestine oppositional phase to seizing power in parts of Iraq and Syria resulted in a particularly brutal revolutionary moment.

[15] Robert Jervis, *Perception and Misperception in International Politics*, Princeton, Princeton University Press, 1978.

[16] Abram De Swaan, *The Killing Compartments: The Mentality of Mass Murder*, New Haven, Yale University Press, 2015.

[17] Max Weber, *Economy and Society: An Outline to Interpretative Sociology*, vol.1, Berkeley, University of California Press, 1978, pp. 1111–1158.

[18] Max Weber, *Weber's Rationalism and Modern Society*, New York: Palgrave Macmillan, 2015.

The extreme closure of the Islamic State stems from its clandestine character, which partly explains its extraordinary distance from the population and conspiratorial view of politics. First, the movement was born out of a shared experience of the American prisons of Iraq, where the leaders could build their networks (paradoxically it was safer to network inside the prisons than outside), and where al-Baghdadi and the movement's leadership successfully imposed their authority.[19] A resident of Tikrit (Iraq) described how prison turned a friend of his into a fighter for al-Qaida and then the Islamic State:

From Tikrit originally, he was mistakenly arrested during a raid by the American army in 2006. He was held prisoner for 5 years in the Buka prison in Southern Iraq. The prisoners were piled up in collective cells, regardless of their offense, which enabled the Islamic State to recruit and train new fighters. My friend was a graduate of the University of Economics of Tikrit and was unemployed since 2003; he was a perfect target for their recruitment. During his five years in prison, he went through a full ideological indoctrination. When he was freed in 2011, he came back to settle in Tikrit, and then disappeared without trace.[20]

Second, again often stemming from being thrown together in prison, some Baathist elements joined the nascent Islamic State, reinforcing further a culture of violence and secrecy. According to an individual from Tal Afar (Iraq):

Abu Muslim al-Turkmani, also known as Saud, is a former resident of Tal Afar whom my family knew well before 2003. He was a colonel in the Iraqi army under Saddam. At the fall of the [Iraqi] regime, he started working normally and tried to open several businesses that failed. Unemployed and threatened by the policies of de-Baathification, he joined the insurgency in Mosul and then entered al-Qaida. His military experience rapidly made him someone important in the organization. He in fact managed to convince many of Saddam's former officers to join him, which enabled him to build a network of trusted experts in clandestine actions, military operations, and espionage ... His trajectory is not clear, but when Mosul fell, he appeared in the organizational charter of the Islamic State as one of Baghdadi's seven lieutenants in charge of special operations.[21]

The presence of former Iraqi military personnel in the Islamic State underlines the important role played by the transfer of skills from the former regime to the organization. A former Islamist opponent of Saddam Hussein's regime notes that

the current practices of the Islamic State were brought by the officers of the former regime. Without them, it would have been impossible for the Islamic State to

---

[19] I-141, with a tribal notable from Hawija, in Kirkuk, May 2013.
[20] I-155, with an inhabitant of Tikrit, in Erbil, March 2015.
[21] I-156, with a former inhabitant of Tal Afar, in Kirkuk, February 2015.

transform so rapidly into such a well-organized armed movement with a security apparatus as opaque as it is efficient. These are the same methods as those employed under Saddam's dictatorship.[22]

Third, American covert operations required maintaining a high level of secrecy and made the entire organization paranoid. The American military's surveillance and communication interception capabilities made the strictest security rules paramount for survival. "The members of the Islamic State live in fear and are constantly under surveillance," explains a resident of Hawija (Iraq). "Everyone spies on everyone in an environment of generalized paranoia."[23] Between 2003 and 2009, any security lapse systematically led to the arrest or elimination of most members of a network by the American Special Forces. This led to a brutal selection of fighters: those who survived have internalized exceptionally rigorous clandestine practices. In addition, the Islamic State learned a great deal from the counter-insurgency techniques used by the American army in Iraq, including the use of local intermediaries such as the *sahwa* militias (Harakat al-Sahwa al-Suniyya – Sunni Awakening Movement) in 2007 to fight the insurgency. This caused the movement to set up an intelligence apparatus responsible for controlling the militants and neutralizing the counter-insurgency operations. In Syria, a fighter from Raqqa and former member of the Free Syrian Army told us:

Before its takeover in January 2014, Daesh took an interest in tribal society and social divides. The idea for Daesh was to go slowly so as not to repeat the mistakes that had been made in Iraq. It included infiltrating the poor neighborhoods and spotting which groups and individuals were feeling humiliated or frustrated and thus could be susceptible to working with them. There was quite obviously an element of class revenge that Daesh exploited successfully and that was ignored by the rest of the opposition. The Islamic State grew on the outcasts of the revolution. The FSA was thus caught off guard.[24]

Furthermore, the presence of tens of thousands of foreign fighters (up to 30,000 according to some sources[25]) reinforces the organization's closure since they have no ties to the population and are totally dependent on the hierarchy. In fact, several groups composed exclusively of foreign

---

[22] I-157, with the leader of the Iraqi Islamic Party, in Kirkuk, March 2015.
[23] I-158, with a tribal notable of Hawija, in Kirkuk, March 2015.
[24] I-151, with an inhabitant from Raqqa, Skype, February 2015.
[25] By June 2014, about 12,000 foreign fighters had joined rebel groups in Syria since 2011, including the Islamic State; see Soufan report: http://soufangroup.com/foreign-fighters-in-syria/. By December 2015, this figure has risen to approximately 30,000, http://soufangroup.com/foreign-fighters/.

combatants fighting in Syria pledged allegiance to the caliph: Jaysh al-Muhajirin wal Ansar (Army of Emigrants and Companions of the Prophet), which included many Caucasians; Jund al-Sham fi-Bilad al-Sham (Soldiers of the Levant in Syria), mainly made up of Lebanese ex-Fatah al-Islam fighters; and the Egyptian fighters manning the Katibat Usud al-Khilafa (Lions of the Caliphate Battalion). Many fighters come with their families and live in the same neighborhoods, notably in Raqqa and Mosul. "In Raqqa, ISIL fighters are sometimes Syrians, but the large majority of emirs are foreigners. It is very difficult to negotiate with them and we fear them a lot," a resident explained to us in September 2013.[26] *De facto*, the organization limits its interactions with the population as much as possible.

In general, Daesh avoids all relationships between its members and society. When I was arrested for the first time, I managed to negotiate my liberation with an emir from Raqqa of the Bariaj clan (Afadla tribe) thanks to common acquaintances. But this was at the start of Daesh's presence; now I doubt it would still be possible. This amir was transferred just after my liberation, because he would do favors for people he knew from Raqqa. Daesh has always tried to avoid that its emirs establish bonds with society. Often, they place local personalities in important roles when they need to control a territory and a population. Once they feel certain of their control, they name an outsider for the job and remove the local personality. The ties between the organization and the population are only useful during the first phase of control. And, generally, the cadres are changed regularly.[27]

Another element of this closure is an impersonal brotherhood, which includes being addressed in specific terms. The fighters generally call one another *hajj* or *akh* (brother), and practice a revolutionary brotherhood that is reminiscent of Communist terms of address like "comrade." In addition, as confirmed by all of our observations, interviews, and the available videos, the movement has developed a peculiar esthetic. The insistence on external appearance, for example, reflects a desire to create a shared identity between militants. The members of the Islamic State dress in either black fatigues or the "Afghan" way, or more precisely the "Kandahari" way: mid-calf length pants and long shirts. The colors vary; white, black, brown are the most common; flashy colors are avoided. They wear their hair long and grow beards and often use kohl eyeliner and thus conform to the global image of Jihadism.

---

[26] In the Islamic State, the term emir refers to a high-ranking civil and military cadre. I-125 with a militant from Raqqa, in Urfa, September 2013.
[27] I-151, with an inhabitant of Raqqa, Skype, February 2015.

A Security-Centered Apparatus

Although the movement manipulates symbols of Islamic culture, the state-like organization takes on classic bureaucratic forms.[28] The Baathist vision of the state plays a central role in explaining the caliphate's organization. Even before its territorial conquests, the Islamic State had developed a functioning archive system, including annual reports (al-Naba').[29] An executive "Shura" council, a military council, and deputies assist the caliph in making decisions. For the most part, these are companions from the American occupation that are used to the organization's discipline. The efficiency of this inner circle of battle-seasoned fighters helps the Islamic State ensure the cohesion of the tens of thousands of militants that carry out the movement's daily functions and fight on the frontlines. Though as a consequence of the organization's clandestine culture very little information trickles out about this inner circle of militants, there appear to be stable institutional leadership mechanisms, including one for choosing the caliph.[30]

However, because of the speed of its expansion and military constraints, the administration of the Islamic State varies by locality and not all the institutions are uniform. The difference between urban and rural areas is significant. In addition, the frontline sectors, mostly in rural areas, are not stable enough to set up a proper administration, and, in a few places, the Islamic State is forced to adapt its governance to the balance of power among the tribes in the area.

Public services are not a priority for the movement and they generally function erratically. The Islamic State attempts to exercise control without having the means to deeply transform existing institutions.

There are certain services in Raqqa, but generally speaking Daesh does not want to spend money and settles for the minimum when it does not cost them too much. For example, Daesh has taken over the electricity infrastructures in Raqqa and Tabqa. Daesh provides electricity to the population and sells some to [the Syrian] regime. In reality, it is the employees of the regime that do all the work and

---

[28] The caliphate is divided into eighteen Provinces (*wilaya*) in Iraq and Syria: Anbar, Baghdad, Diyala, Fallujah, al-Janub (the South), Kirkuk, Nineveh, Salahuddin (Iraq), Aleppo, al-Badiah (Homs), al-Baraka (Hasaka), Damascus, Hama, Idlib, al-Khair (Deir ez-Zor), al-Raqqa, al-Sahel (Latakia) in Syria, and al-Furat between Syria and Iraq.

[29] For 2012–2013, "Military Operation Islamic State Periodical Bulletin in Iraq and Syria," available at https://azelin.files.wordpress.com/2013/08/islamic-state-of-iraq-and-al-sh c481m-22harvest-of-operations-for-the-year-1433-h-in-iraq22.pdf; for the 2013–2014 ISIS operation see Al-Binc, available at https://azelin.files.wordpress.com/2014/04/al-bi nc481-magazine-1.pdf. The Institute for the Study of War analyzed both files and deemed them accurate, see "ISIS Annual Reports Reveal a Metrics-Driven Military Command," Institute for the Study of War, May 22, 2014, available at hwww.under standingwar.org/sites/default/files/ISWBackgrounder_ISIS_Annual_Reports_0.pdf.

[30] Andrew March and Mara Revkin, *op. cit.*

who continue to get their salaries (those who can travel to the regime zones). Daesh does nothing; all they do is produce invoices through the Administration of Islamic Services (Hay'a al-Islamiyya lil-Khadamat).[31]

Once again based on the centralized Baathist regime model, the security institutions are at the core of the system. The Security Office (Maktab al-Amn) is the equivalent of the intelligence services of the former Iraqi regime, and erstwhile members of Saddam Hussein's security apparatus are said to play an important role here. Its operatives stay anonymous as they monitor the organization's members. An interviewee from Raqqa explains it like this:

They take care of anything serious. We do not know much about them. They have a branch that specializes in house searches and arrests. For example, those who came to search my house were from the Security Office. They are the most powerful. It seems that they work in secrecy and apparently independently from any other Islamic State institution. Even the members of the Islamic State fear them. My family tried to find out about the search at my place, they went to the Complaints Office and to the Islamic Court and no one was able to inform them on the reasons behind the search. Even worse, they said that no one had done a search and that they had no record of such an event. The people from the Security Office are a bit different from the other members. They are often Iraqis, former officers and war veterans. There also are people from Raqqa, and some Tunisians. Those are the most feared ones, they are the most radical and bloodthirsty.[32]

To control the population, in the most important cities, the Islamic State has implemented a judicial system with courts (al-Mahakim al-Shar'iyya) and a police force (al-Shurta al-Islamiyya). For the Islamic State, Islamic law is a core element of its governance, and its divine nature legitimizes the lack of the consultation of the population. Omnipresent in the discourses, it informs all aspects of militant behavior. The tribunals impose severe sentences based on their interpretation of Islamic law: amputation of a hand for theft, stoning for adultery, execution of homosexuals, beheading, hanging and crucifixion of cadavers, etc. The sentences are carried out in public. "The new rules are posted in the mosques and announced in the bazaars by a car with speakers travelling around the city. The executions, amputations for theft and whippings are carried out publicly, people are invited to witness them and the bodies remain exposed in the middle of the bazar. It is even allowed to take pictures."[33]

However, the punishments for the same offense often vary.[34]

[31] I-152, with an inhabitant of Raqqa, Skype, February 2015.
[32] I-149, with an activist from Raqqa, Skype, March 2015.
[33] I-143, with an IDP from Nineveh province, in Kirkuk, January 2015.
[34] According to Andrew March and Mara Revkin, this could be due to the application of the doctrine of siyasa shar'iyya, which "sets up a kind a dualistic model of law and governance.

I don't think that the sentences are codified anywhere. I never saw it written down that it is 20 lashes for a cigarette, even if that is what we get in general. Sometimes they force people to learn some verses of the Koran, or to undergo Islamic training. These kinds of punishment are more frequent for felonies related to praying, for example, if someone walks in the streets during the prayer or, for a shop owner, if they haven't closed their business. But we don't always go to the judge. Sometimes the members of the Hisba (Diwan al-Hisba, Regulation Bureau) punish us on the spot. Once they saw me smoking a cigarette and took my packet and forced me to eat the remaining cigarettes. Another time, they simply randomly stopped me and smelt my fingers, of course they smelled of cigarette so they hit my fingers with their gun handle. Some friends were arrested by the Hisba, which decided on their own the number of lashes to give without going through the Islamic court. I do not understand their logic, I don't think that they bother much about procedures, when they feel like it they do not go to the judge.[35]

The Islamic justice courts essentially take care of the punishment of deviations from the moral code, but in contrast to a movement like the Taliban, which uses justice as a tool to penetrate society,[36] the Islamic State mainly uses judges to enforce its rule. Although the Islamic State has called for people to file complaints against its fighters,[37] our interviews suggest that going to the court is difficult, even risky, for the people. An Iraqi from Baji told us:

It is not easy to go to the Islamic Court to file a complaint. To have access to the Islamic Court, you need an authorization from the chief of the neighborhood (Mudir al-Nariyya) or the village chief (Mudir al-Balda) who send the request to the tribunal. In general, the only ones to go are those who were arrested by the Islamic State. They are brought there by force by fighters without having the possibility to provide for their defense before the judge.[38]

Furthermore, most of the repression of moral or political deviance takes place outside the courts, through the repressive structures of the

On the one hand, the system requires sharia courts for the application of Islamic legal rules in routine matters for which specific rules exist. But it recognizes that rules do not exist for every conceivable matter. And so, the 'siyasa shar'iyya' theory posits that there are legitimate authorities – from market inspectors to military commanders and governors up to the caliph himself – that have the right to make lawlike decisions as long as those decisions are issued solely with the welfare (*maslaha*) of the Muslim community in mind and do not violate known laws." Andrew March and Mara Revkin, *op. cit.*

[35] I-152, with an inhabitant of Raqqa, Skype, February 2015.

[36] Adam Baczko, *Judging in the Midst. . . op. cit.*

[37] "Caliphate of Islamic State Call for Subjects to Appear Before the Board of Grievances for any Complaint Against its Soldiers or its Emirs," document printed by ISIS and published on the Internet by Islamic News Agency, December 2014, www.dawaalhaq .com/?p=21065, quoted by Mara Revkin, "The Legal Foundations of the Islamic State," *Syria Comment*, www.joshualandis.com/blog/legal-foundations-islamic-state -mara-revkin/.

[38] I-146, with IDPs from Baji, in Khanaqin, January 2015.

Security Office and the Bureau of Regulation. An inhabitant of the Mosul region explains:

The Bureau of Regulation is the local executive. Five people work there, they are responsible for surveillance of the population and the respect of religious rules. These five people are from the village. They live in their own houses, they are the same people as before the arrival of the Islamic State except now they wear a beard. They know everyone in the village and were chosen for that reason.[39]

More generally, fear plays a central role in Islamic State governance.

The Islamic State does not want to control the city council and creates a security apparatus just to control the population. The people are held through fear in a context where many videos of executions circulate on mobile phones. Even if there are no public executions, there is a real fear of reprisal. In general, when the Islamic State arrests someone, no one ever gets any news.[40]

Spying and denunciations are pervasive; children are used as informants. Rumors circulate about the prowess of the Islamic State intelligence, most likely exaggerating its actual capabilities but raising the level of fear. The public and publicized executions are part of a terror strategy aimed at the local population. Multiple accounts witness to the Bureau of Regulation gathering passers-by (men, women, and children) to make them watch capital punishments. Thus, in Mosul, twenty-two persons accused of homosexuality were thrown from the top of a public building in front of hundreds of people that had been herded together by the Islamic State for the event. The many execution videos circulating on mobile phones diffuse and amplify the effects of the executions. Furthermore, it is impossible for the families of individuals arrested by the Islamic State to obtain information on them, which adds to the spreading rumors about disappeared people being executed and their cadavers burned.

Politicization of Society

The organizational closure of the Islamic State enables it to impose its rule on millions of Iraqis and Syrians at the cost of destroying both societies. The reworking of the body politic is accomplished by annihilating suspect categories and the elimination of intermediary bodies and local notables. To begin with, the Islamic State redefines the political community through the oath of allegiance to the caliph Abu Bakr al-Baghdadi: anyone, independent of nationality and residence, can become a member of the Islamic

---

[39] I-145, with IDPs from villages near Mosul, in Debaga, January 2015.
[40] I-144, with IDPs from Nineveh province, in Debaga, January 2015.

State as long as they adhere to the Sunni denomination. However, even within the Sunni population, certain "enemies within," are surveilled, expelled, or killed. Moreover, the Islamic State refuses political intermediaries as a way of individualizing the relationship with its subjects.

The political community is constituted by the oath (bay'a) of allegiance to the caliph Abu Bakr al-Baghdadi, which presupposes belonging or converting to Sunnism, independent of ethnicity or nationality. Thus, one of Baghdadi's deputies is a Turkmen, and some fighters are Kurds, Caucasians, Europeans, etc. The call to Muslims to perform the *hijra* (emigrate to Muslim lands), presented as a religious duty, is a constant theme in Islamic State propaganda. The Islamic State aims to increase its population by preventing Sunnis from emigrating and encouraging them to immigrate. In *Dabiq*, Abu Bakr al-Baghdadi thus declares, "The State is a State for all Muslims. The land is for the Muslims, all the Muslims. Muslims everywhere, whoever is capable of performing hijra to the Islamic State, then let him do so, because hijra to the land of Islam is obligatory."[41] Beyond the theological aspect, the Islamic State aims at filling the shortfall in cadres by appealing to qualified foreigners.[42] Moreover, the Islamic State forbids emigration, and temporarily leaving the caliphate is subject to particularly stringent rules. A person wishing to do so must provide a guarantor (*kafil*), furnish the Islamic State with a document stating where he lives and listing his family members by name. If the individual fails to return, the family is at risk of arrest, the house may be leveled and the guarantor executed. Thus, in Alam (Iraq), "people are not allowed to leave the town. To leave, people must have a guarantor, and if people are absent more than fifteen days, they execute him."[43]

Being Sunni is not enough for the Islamic State, whose goal is to purify the community of believers. Unaffiliated or suspect Sunnis are fought against as if they were infidels (*kuffar*). As is often the case in revolutionary situations, the Islamic State casts a very tight surveillance net over the population, especially certain suspect categories. In this respect, it recalls the Terror during the French Revolution or even certain practices of the Soviet Union and the Khmer Rouge in Cambodia. Thus, in Iraq, members of the army, the police, and the militias are specially targeted as

---

[41] "The Return of Khilafah," Dabiq 1, http://media.clarionproject.org/files/09-2014/isis-is il-islamic-state-magazine-Issue-1-the-return-of-khilafah.pdf, p. 6.

[42] "A Message to the Mujahidin and the Muslim Umma in the Month of Ramadan" was released on July 1, 2014 by the Islamic State' al-Furqan Media Foundation. The Islamic State's al-Hay'at Media Center then issued additional translations of the transcript in English, Russian, French, German, and Albanian. https://news.siteintelgroup.com/Jiha dist-News/islamic-statI-leader-abu-bakr-al-baghdadi-encourages-emigration-worldwid I-action.html.

[43] I-143, in Kirkuk, January 2015.

suspects accused of forming a "fifth column." When Mosul fell to the
Islamic State, it seized the city's official records, giving the militants files
on police officers and members of the military that they can access on
laptops when manning checkpoints. Officers are generally killed, but the
movement has a more ambiguous attitude toward the enlisted ranks.
The Islamic State also occupies or dynamites the houses of members of
security forces that have fled. Those who have stayed must renounce
their former opposition to the Islamic State. Within a stipulated period,
usually lasting about twenty days, they must sign the document of
formal repentance (al-Tawba), pay a fine ranging from US $2,000 to
$3,000, and surrender their weapons. A former soldier from al-Qayara
(Iraq) explained:

I discovered the functioning of the repentance at my return. You have to register
at a special office of the Islamic State. You have to give your identity and give back
your weapon. You do not have to swear the oath of allegiance. The Islamic State
does not register us as Muslims but as people who have left the faith because of our
collaboration with the Iraqi government.[44]

Thereafter, special restrictions apply to their movements; they must
always name a guarantor and cannot leave for more than a few days. In
addition, the *mukhtar*, individuals responsible for administrative tasks at a
village or neighborhood level, are suspected because they used to spy for
the government. Their situation varies between the towns and the countryside. In Tikrit, most of the *mukhtar* have left, as they worked for the
regime. In the countryside, they often held a more ambiguous position
and have generally not been bothered by the Islamic State, which uses
them to obtain information on the populace. In Syria, former fighters of
the Free Syrian Army and other insurgent groups are priority targets for
the Islamic State. Thus, in Tal Abyad,

during the takeover of the city by Daesh, they made an announcement stating that
during one month, they had their door open for repentance. Those that repented
had to go through some kind of Islamic reformatory course. In order to return to
the territories held by Daesh, someone local, known and recognized by Daesh,
must act as the guarantor. If the repentant betrays again, the guarantor is held to
account. Then also, the repentant must check in every week, in what they call
"repentant meetings" (Ijtima' al-Ta'ibin). This is for surveillance purposes, but
also to indoctrinate them. For approximately one year, they are not allowed to
leave the town.[45]

Finally, non-Sunnis are condemned to death, exiled, or brutally marginalized. Even though the Islam of the first centuries constitutes a recurring

[44] I-144, in Debaga, January 2015.
[45] I-150 with an IDP from Aleppo, resettled in Tal Abyad, Skype, March 2015.

reference, the Islamic State rejects any multiconfessional coexistence and pursues the expulsion or elimination of non-Sunnis. This process increases sectarian tensions and the territorialization of communities, strengthening at the same time the Islamic State's control over the Sunnis (see Chapter 13).

To foster a revolutionary dynamic, the Islamic State creates a direct relationship between individuals and the political authorities to the detriment of existing intermediary bodies. Individualism, more generally, is part of the Islamic State's ideological and doctrinal discourse, emphasizing the direct relation of each person with God and, more to the point, with his representatives on earth. It holds appeal for some people in the Muslim world and in the West who can also find an opportunity for self-fulfillment in their involvement with the Islamic State, as revealed, for example, by the account analyzed by Thomas Pierret and Mériam Cheikh of a Syrian woman who joined the Islamic State and then shared her sense of accomplishment on social networks.[46] From a political perspective, elections are considered non-Islamic and the people cannot put up any other candidates (notables, imams, tribal leaders) to speak for their concerns. For example in Alam, "the notables of the city have all left, the Islamic State takes over their land and their property and employs agricultural workers to farm the fields."[47] Similarly, all of our interviewees hailing from tribal and rural regions have underlined the fact that the Islamic State does not recognize the tribes – which were already weakened by the Baathist regimes – as interlocutors.[48] The movement thus only recognizes individuals as personally responsible to the caliphate's authorities. "You have to go to the Islamic State as an individual," explains a young man from the vicinity of Muqdadiyah (Iraq).[49] Similarly, a Sunni Arab from near Mosul told us that: "The contacts with the Islamic State happen in an individual way. It is impossible to negotiate collectively. At the most, an older member of the family can represent a person, but this is generally not accepted by the Islamic State."[50]

In the governorates of Raqqa, Deir ez-Zor, and Hasaka in Syria, and Anbar in Iraq, the tribes have mounted sporadic opposition to the Islamic State. It notably led to the massacre of hundreds of members

---

[46] Thomas Pierret and Mériam Cheikh, "'I Am Very Happy Here': Female Jihad in Syria as Self-Accomplishment," *Journal of Women of the Middle East and the Islamic World* 13, 2015, pp. 241–269.

[47] I-143, with an IDP from Alam, in Kirkuk, January 2015.

[48] I-141, with a tribal notable of in Hawija, in Hawija, May 2013; I-142, with a tribal notable of Kirkuk, in Kirkuk, April 2012.

[49] I-147 with an IDP from Muqdadiyah, in Khanaqin, January 2015.

[50] I-145 with an IDP from Nineveh Province, in Debaga, January 2015.

of the Al-Sh'itat tribe in Mohassan (Deir ez-Zor) in August 2014 that was precipitated by a dispute over the seizure of local oil. However, the Islamic State is careful not to become enmeshed in a generalized tribal conflict. For example, it delegates repression to Islamic State fighters belonging to the targeted tribe to further its strategy of sowing discord to divide tribal members. As long as its grip on Syria before January 2014 and on Iraq prior to August 2014 remained precarious, the Islamic State had to compromise with tribes that were strong locally. The fact that there is also a Ministry for Tribal Affairs in Raqqa, with a department for each governorate, evidences a concern for the tribal factor, but the logic remains one of avoiding or of weakening the tribes, especially since Sharia strongly condemns many tribal practices. A resident of Raqqa testified on this strategy of tribal dissolution.

At first, Daesh created ties with each tribe; they would take a member of each tribe that had joined the organization and would give him a lot of power (money, weapons, car, string-pulling) so that he could impose himself within his tribe and serve as the link with the organization by guaranteeing the tribe's support or at least its docility. At that time, the Islamic State invited the sheikhs of the tribes, the militants would send gifts when an elder died, they would organize large meals. But this was before they seized Raqqa. Since then, the fighters of the Islamic State do not care anymore and feel invincible. Thus, between April 2013 and the takeover by Daesh in January 2014, the most important office was the Bureau of Communication with the Tribes (Maktab al-Ittisal lil-'Acha'ir). The person in charge of that bureau was an Iraqi who knew the conflicts and the histories between the clans very well. And because he is not from here, he was not perceived as being in favor of this or that clan. Now, this Bureau has no purpose apart from gathering intelligence to prevent the tribes from organizing against the Islamic State.[51]

The Islamic State manipulates the imams. Since mosques are one of the few places where the population is allowed to assemble, they become a central element of Islamic State governance that makes possible homogenizing their discourse. Especially during Friday prayers, control of the mosques allows the Islamic State to communicate its orders or recommendations through placards and through the Friday prayers. The Islamic State requires full obedience from the imams, under penalty of death, but does not fully integrate them into its administration, which makes it different from the Taliban case. "In my village [around Gwer (Iraq)], 15 imams have accepted the Islamic State as the legitimate authority, 5 refused and were executed. In another village, the Islamic State murdered one of the imams and the inhabitants had to get the body from the hospital, he had been executed with a bullet to his head."[52]

---

[51] I-151, with an inhabitant of Raqqa, Skype, February 2015.
[52] I-148 with IDPs from Nineveh Province, in Debaga, February 2015.

The Moral Order

Contrary to the Afghan Taliban and the Somali al-Shabab movement, the Islamic State is not only interested in enforcing a moral order but also requires individuals to actively support the revolutionary process. The "authentic" believer is morally regenerated by fulfilling his scriptural obligations (prayers, respect of Koranic rules), but also by committing to Jihad, which becomes *de facto* an obligatory duty. Thus, military conscription, Islamic education, and moral order reinforce each other in building a new society. The body of the fighter is produced, as is the Sunni who has pledged allegiance, by imposing a style of dress and behavioral modes that install a bodily hexis.

By imposing a moral code, the Islamic State redefines individual behavior, private and public space, and gender relations. Accounts by Sunnis who escaped life under the caliphate and written sources available elsewhere provide a coherent picture. A religious police, the Regulation Bureau, enforces respect for the law and Islamic mores similar to the Taliban's mohtaseb or the Mutawwa'i al-Shurta al Diniyya in the Saudi Kingdom. The name is a reference to the moral police first created by the caliph 'Umar Ibn al-Khattab (634–644) to ensure respect for his prerogatives in accordance with the Koran: "He who commands the good and forbids the evil." The Katibat al-Khansa' is the female police counterpart of the Regulation Bureau.[53] Patrolling on foot or in cars bearing their insignias, the Regulation Bureau is often the only Islamic State presence in the villages.

The men of the Hisba patrol the streets and say 'you are not well dressed, it's ok for this time, but be careful the next time' or 'you should take this poster down from your shop, or you will risk this or that punishment'. Once we know that something is forbidden, we tell our friend and neighbors, 'be careful, now they forbid to do this'. There always are things considered as contrary to religion, but sometimes we do not know if it is only advisable not to do something or if it is really forbidden. But when they start the repression, word gets around very quickly.[54]

A first set of rules standardizes physical appearance, with special strictness for women. The men must not shave their beards, although we came across a few exceptions. Short beards, which recall the Muslim Brotherhood, are also banned. Only electric razors are allowed; razors with blades are

---

[53] "Women of the Islamic State, A Manifesto on Women by the Al-Khansaa Brigade," translated by the Quilliam Foundation, February 2015, www.quilliamfoundation.org/wp/wp-content/uploads/publications/free/women-of-the-islamic-state3.pdf, viewed January 2, 2016.

[54] I-150 with an IDP from Aleppo, resettled in Tal Abyad, Skype, March 2015.

prohibited. Styled cuts for beards and hair, very popular in Iraq and Syria, are prohibited. People are flogged in public and the strokes are applied with the full arm: twenty lashes if they do not respect the rules and forty for a styled cut. Barbers are held responsible for the haircuts they give their customers and some have been beaten publicly. Their opening hours are regulated and closely monitored by the Regulation Bureau. Jeans and sneakers are often banned, as well as clothes with Western writing or images, but sweat pants are tolerated in lieu of a traditional dress. A man cannot wear any makeup other than kohl and the only approved perfume is musk (mentioned in the Koran).

Women must wear the integral headscarf, leaving only the eyes uncovered. Furthermore, in Raqqa, the Diwan al-Hisba demands the wearing of a "shield," a thick piece of fabric which hides the body from head to toe, under penalty of 100 lashes and a $150 fine for non-compliance.[55] Women may only leave the house accompanied by a *mahram*, a brother, their father, their husband, or a son. Wearing pants, makeup, or any other form of ornament is banned. Women found guilty of infractions are not punished, since they are not subject of the law; their husbands are.

Smoking is also forbidden, which is particularly problematic in Syria and Iraq where it is common practice. The penalty for the first infraction often takes the form of a warning and sometimes a fine or a few slaps in the face are meted out. A second infraction can lead to a $300 fine and the breaking, even the amputation, of two fingers. Television and music are banned, but still people have them in their homes despite the danger of getting caught. At roadblocks, the Islamic State fighters check if phones contain music or photos, notably of women. If this is the case, the phone is taken away, a fine is levied or a flogging administered. Even musical ringtones are banned on mobile phones. In cities, the Islamic State closes down all cafes, shops, and other places where people might socialize.

Attendance at Friday prayers is compulsory for all, but certain groups are the focus of Islamic State surveillance. Shopkeepers must close down during the prayer (as in several Gulf countries and under the Taliban regime). They are subject to special scrutiny and the Regulation Bureau checks whether they indeed close their shops the required fifteen minutes before prayer starts. However, residents told us that it is possible to walk past a mosque during prayers without entering and not be bothered. Finally, the destruction of tombs and other places where the cult of saints is practiced is emblematic of the distance separating the transnational organization from the majority of the population.

---

[55] Abu Ibrahim Raqqawi, "Prisoners in Their Own City: ISIS Bans Women under 45 from Leaving Raqqa," *Raqqa News*, January 20, 2015, www.raqqa-sl.com/en/?p=332.

A priority for the movement is to raise up a new generation brought up in an "authentically" Muslim society. The school programs have been modified,[56] with certain subjects, including English, history, geography, and the natural sciences, banned outright. The University of Tikrit has closed down; the one in Mosul continued to function for a while, although the humanities, social and natural sciences were banned, but eventually it also closed down. Also, adults and children are invited to preaching centers to study Islam.

The ultimate logic of the Islamic moral order and its system of education is to mobilize for jihad. Until December 2014, recruitment took place through persuasion or pressuring families. After that, the Islamic State occasionally executed young people who refused to join and the movement was accused of kidnapping teenagers or children. In addition, the Islamic State recruits some children, teaches them how to fight, and, in certain cases, transforms them into militants.

Daesh recruits the children off the streets and in the orphanages and sends them to training camps. Many teenagers in conflict with their parents have joined Daesh. I even met a father who would supply drugs to his son as the latter threatened to join Daesh if he didn't get some.[57]

Confronted with Western bombings and pressure from the Iraqi Shiite militias in the south and the Kurdish Peshmergas in the north, the Islamic State has implemented mandatory conscription. Since December 2014, each family with more than three sons has to send the excess ones to fight, though the practice seems to vary from place to place.

The Islamic State project has run into isolated instances of resistance in the territories under its control, as the unstable military situation and the Islamic State's limited resources make systematic monitoring of the population impossible. Some witness reports testify that it is possible to negotiate with the low-ranking militants of the Islamic State: "We negotiate with them through personal connections, of more or less influential people. If we know someone we can negotiate, but very few people know people from the Security Office, so we try to negotiate at the lowest level of the hierarchy."[58] Furthermore, the instability of the political situation and the impossibility of sealing the Islamic State's border impede the normalization of their regime, its resigned acceptance by the population. It would thus be incorrect to consider the population as entirely passive.

---

[56] Ali Mamuri, "Islamic State Imposes New Rules on Education in Syria," *Al Monitor*, Iraq, October 21, 2014, www.al-monitor.com/pulse/originals/2014/10/islamic-state-impose-education-program-iraq-syria.html#.
[57] I-151, with an inhabitant of Raqqa, Skype, February 2015.
[58] I-150, with an inhabitant of Tal Abyad, Skype, March 2015.

For most individuals, resistance is often limited to compromises, escapism, and multiple avoidance strategies. "In people's houses, life has not changed. We continue to smoke [at home] and those who do not pray stay at home during the prayer and continue not praying. There are even still drugs and alcohol."[59] However, isolated clandestine movements have organized sporadic attacks (terrorist attacks, assassinations), for example in Raqqa and in Mosul.[60] The situation in Syria differs from the one in Iraq. In the latter, fear of the regime (regarded as Shia) deters defections, while, in Syria, other Sunni armed movements exist besides the Islamic State.

Rejection of the International Order

The Islamic State's international strategy derives from two elements. For one, the movement perceives the international environment as ontologically hostile; hence it mounts preemptive attacks in anticipation of the inevitable aggressions to come. This perspective causes the Islamic State to reject international norms on two key points: citizenship and territory. By denying the principles of border and citizenship, the Islamic State rejects all form of inclusion in the international order as it was constituted in the nineteenth and twentieth centuries. By doing so, it establishes a perpetual war against all states, in particular the Western and Muslim states, including the Sunni ones. On the other hand, the Islamic State also aims at reunifying under its exclusive authority all jihadist movements, hence its attacks – rhetorical or military – on other movements, such as the Taliban or al-Qaida.

Ignoring even the nature of its regime, the Islamic State applies a conception of sovereignty that forbids its integration into the international system. Although the stability of international borders has been an essential foundation of interstate relations since 1945, the Islamic State denies all legitimacy of existing states and therefore of the international order. In point of fact, the borders of the caliphate are only temporarily stabilized depending on the military balance of power. Thus, the current conquests represent no more than a step in the expansion of the caliphate. In his proclamation, Abu Bakr al-Baghdadi declared that,

"The legality of all emirates, groups, states and organisations becomes null by the expansion of the caliph's authority and the arrival of its troops to their areas." [...]

[59] I-149, with an inhabitant of Raqqa, Skype, Febuary 2015.
[60] I-153, with a KDP-affiliated commander of the Kurdish security forces in Mosul, in Dohuk, May 2015; I-154, with a fighter of Katiba Thuwar al-Raqqa, Skype, June 2015.

So rush O Muslims and gather around your Khalifah, so that you may return as you once were for ages, kings of the earth and knights of war. Come so that you may be honoured and esteemed, living as masters with dignity. Know that we fight over a religion that Allah promised to support. We fight for an Umma to which Allah has given honour, esteem, and leadership, promising it with empowerment and strength on the earth. Come O Muslims to your honour, to your victory. By Allah, if you disbelieve in democracy, secularism, nationalism, as well as all the other garbage and ideas from the west, and rush to your religion and creed, then by Allah, you will own the earth, and the east and west will submit to you. This is the promise of Allah to you. This is the promise of Allah to you.[61]

This perspective recalls the classical distinction between the *Dar al-Islam* (Land of Islam), where Islamic Law applies, and the *Dar al-Harb* (Land of War), which is open to conquest and proselytizing. Notably, the Islamic State rejects the legitimacy of international institutions and of international laws (International Humanitarian Law, for example). The contrast with the Taliban is blatant here, the latter having been intent on gaining recognition as a legitimate state by claiming a seat at the UN and by sometimes cooperating with the ICRC, UN agencies, and certain NGOs, both while it held power in Kabul (1996–2001) and as an insurgency (post-2001).

The Islamic State's hostility toward all states in the region carries an enormous strategic cost. Its policy of all-out attack has not only deprived it of any support, but has also led some of these states to undertake military operations against it. The Islamic State, *de facto* the only Sunni movement to have confronted both the governments in Baghdad and Damascus – and thus Iran – could potentially have benefited from support, or at least tolerance, by the Sunni states in the region and even the Kurdistan Regional Government (KRG). Before the fall of Mosul, the KRG had indeed supported several Sunni insurgent movements to counter-balance the Shiitization of power in Baghdad. "Between June and August 2015, there were many exchanges, notably economic, between the Islamic State and certain Kurds from the KDP (Kurdish Democratic Party)," explains a Sunni Arab former official from Mosul (Iraq). "At that moment, the KDP thought it could coexist with the Islamic State, which would have allowed it to weaken Baghdad. But the Islamic State decided to attack Erbil (capital city of Iraqi Kurdistan) and came so close to succeeding that it led to an immediate response from the International Coalition."[62] Similarly, the

---

[61] The speech has been transcribed in a document titled *The Promise of Allah* and diffused on the Internet via social networks, Abu Muhammad al-'Adnani al-Shami, "This Is the Promise of Allah," *Al-Hay'at Media Center*, June 19, 2014, https://ia902505.us.archive .org/28/items/poa_25984/EN.pdf, viewed January 2, 2016.

[62] I-153, with a KDP-affiliated commander of the Kurdish security forces in Mosul, in Erbil, March 2015.

Gulf States, led by Saudi Arabia, have never accepted Iran's influence in Iraq and fear of the formation of a Shiite crescent is at the core of their policies. However, the Islamic State has not endeavored to capitalize on these oppositions, which might have provided it with enough support to challenge Baghdad and Damascus.

The Islamic State's international jihadism marks a break from previous movements. The terrorist attack is just one of the techniques employed by the organization, not the principal one as in the case of al-Qaida. The use of suicide attacks thus does not preclude standing up a regular army with conscription starting in the winter of 2015. This valuing of territory goes hand in hand with a hegemonic claim over the jihadist movement as a whole.

The genealogy of the Islamic State explains its competition with al-Qaida. As it happens, during the war in Iraq in the mid-2000s, the Islamic State was originally a local branch of the latter, called al-Qaida in Mesopotamia (AQM). To fight the American army, the movement, initially led by Abu Musab al-Zarqawi, ended up developing a guerrilla strategy that involved a certain degree of territorial control and made the Shiites the principal enemy. These two innovations then triggered a significant transformation of the jihadist project. First, as early as the 1990s, the question of territorial control became a source of tension between Osama Bin Laden and his Sudanese and, later, Afghan supporters.[63] Some local branches had already started consolidating their territorial control, notably in Yemen and Somalia, but none had yet pushed this logic to its conclusion.[64] As it fought against the American occupation, AQM pursued a strategy of territorial control based on radicalizing the sectarian divide. Second, in 2004–2005, AQM made the Shiites its main target, whereas al-Qaida until then had given the West priority. Al-Qaida's main branch rejected this evolution and Ayman al-Zawahiri reminded Abu Musab al-Zarqawi in a 2005 letter that the main enemy was the West and that anti-Shiite attacks could be misunderstood by Muslims and therefore be counter-productive.[65] In 2011, the debate ended for a few years with the defeat of AQM brought

---

[63] In 2004, a book was published by an al-Qaida militant promoting a strategy similar to that of the Islamic State, see Abu Bakr Naji, *The Management of Savagery: The Most Critical Stage through Which the Umma Will Pass*, 2004, https://azelin.files.wordpress.com/2010/08/abu-bakr-naji-the-management-of-savagery-the-most-critical-stage-through-which-t he-umma-will-pass.pdf, viewed January 2, 2016.

[64] Will McCants, "Al Qaeda Is Doing Nation-Building: Should We Worry?" *Foreign Policy*, April 30, 2012, http://foreignpolicy.com/2012/04/30/al-qaeda-is-doing-nation-building -should-we-worry/, viewed January 2, 2016.

[65] "Zawahiri's Letter to Zarqawi," *Combating Terrorism Center*, 2005, www.ctc.usma.edu/posts/zawahiris-letter-to-zarqawi-original-language-2, viewed January 2, 2016.

about by its indiscriminate violence and its refusal to take into account social demands. After the American withdrawal from Iraq in 2011, the anti-Sunni policy of Iraqi Prime Minister Noor al-Maliki weakened his political opposition and facilitated the resurrection of the al-Qaida branch as the Islamic State in Iraq (ISI).

In Syria, ISI saw the insurgency's conquest of large territories in 2012 as an unanticipated chance to rebuild itself sheltered from Baghdad's repression. For this reason, it deployed under the name of Jabhat al-Nusra in Syria. Funded and armed by its Iraqi sponsor, it recruited Syrian combatants and took its place alongside the other rebel groups in the fight against Damascus. In April 2013, however, conflict broke out between Jabhat al-Nusra and ISI over the global jihadist strategy. Despite mediation attempts by al-Qaida's top leader, installed on the border between Afghanistan and Pakistan, the two movements split definitively. The al-Qaida leader publicly condemned ISIL's acts and made Jabhat al-Nusra its sole representative in Syria. The latter has come to be composed primarily of Syrian recruits and takes an active part in the struggle against Damascus in cooperation with the rest of the insurgency. Conversely, since January 2014, the Islamic State has waged open war on the Syrian insurgency and through mid-2015 avoided confrontation with the forces of Damascus as the more difficult of the two to defeat.

This factional division mirrored a fundamental strategic divergence. In Syria in 2013, al-Qaida still followed a strategy of collaboration with the rest of the insurgency while the Islamic State sought to build a Sunni caliphate at the expense of the neighboring regimes and armed groups. In January 2014, after long maneuvering to weaken the Syrian insurgents in northern and eastern Syria, the Islamic State took over most of the provinces of Raqqa, Deir ez-Zor, and Hasaka. Then, in August 2014, it used the fall of Mosul to eliminate all other groups, Islamist or not (Jaysh Rijal al-Tariqa al-Naqshbandiyya, Jaysh al-Mujahidin, Ansar al-Sunna/Islam) to gain a monopoly on representing Iraq's Sunnis. In Syria, the Islamic State still competes with the Free Syrian Army, Jabhat al-Nusra, and other groups in Aleppo, Hama, and southern Syria. In its *Dabiq* magazine, the Islamic State has also been very critical of the Taliban. The reason is that Mullah Omar also claims the title of Commander of the Believers (*Amir al-Mu'minin*), thus pitting him against Abu Bakr al-Baghdadi. However, the heart of the disagreement here is the conflict between a national jihad embedded in internationally recognized borders and a transnational, global jihad. While the Taliban seeks to negotiate with the Kabul government and the United States, the Islamic State's opposition is absolute.

The allegiance to the Islamic State of movements outside the region came from multiple directions. The Islamic State proclaimed governorates (*wilaya*) in November 2014 in Libya (Tripolitania, Cyrenaica, the Fezzan desert), in Algeria, in Egypt (Sinai), in Yemen, and in Saudi Arabia.[66] Three months later, another governorate was announced in Afghanistan and Pakistan under the name of Wilayat Khorasan.[67] The rallying of Boko Haram to the Islamic State in March 2015 shows the reality of a dynamic that relies heavily on the organization's media presence. In Saudi Arabia, the movement has established a limited presence; in Yemen it remains weak because of competition from al-Qaida in the Arabian Peninsula (AQAP, which proclaimed an emirate in Abya in 2011–2012) and in Afghanistan and Pakistan because of competition from the Taliban. Finally, the rallying to the cause by individuals in Western countries does not seem to announce the building up of locally significant movements because there the social base is lacking.

How useful is this transnational network to the Islamic State? The arrival of fighters from other countries benefits it on two levels. First, the educated ones among them can serve as cadres in a movement that is always short of expertise.

So, this is more than just fighting, this means more than just fighting. We need engineers, we need doctors, we need professionals, we need volunteers, we need fundraising. We need everything. There is a role for everybody ... Your family will live here in safety, just like how it is back home. We have wide expanses of territory here in Syria, and we can easily find accommodation for you and your families

exhorted a Canadian fighter in a video aimed at attracting foreign combatants.[68] Second, by definition these foreign militants are from outside the local society, which helps to reinforce the movement's separation from the population. However, these allegiances ultimately prove to be counterproductive for the movement. Indeed, the terrorist attacks do

---

[66] Rita Katz, "Interactive Map: The Islamic State's Global Network of Pledged and Supporting Groups," *Insite Blog*, February 17, 2015, http://news.siteintelgroup.com/bl og/index.php/entry/360-interactive-map-the-islamic-state%E2%80%99s-global-net work-of-pledged-and-supporting-groups, viewed January 2, 2016.

[67] Adam Withnall, "Syria, Iraq ... and Now Afghanistan: Isis Advance Enters Helmand Province for the First Time, Afghan officials Confirm," *The Independent*, January 13, 2015, www.independent.co.uk/news/world/middle-east/syria-iraq-and-now-afghani stan-isis-advance-enters-helmand-Province-for-the-first-time-afghan-officials-confirm-9974304.html, viewed December 10, 2015.

[68] "ISIS Video Features a Canadian Fighter Urges Muslims to Join Jihad," *YouTube*, July 11, 2014, www.youtube.com/watch?v=n8-PYZxSLgU, viewed September 9, 2014.

not shift the international balance of power in their favor. The Western reaction to these attacks has invariably been to intensify the fight against the Islamic State, which presents a crucial impediment to the movement's military operations. Moreover, the movements that have sworn allegiance to the Islamic State are incapable of offering significant support to it on either the military or political levels.

Part IV

A Society at War

11   The Variations of Social Capital

This chapter aims to explain how social capital, defined as "the aggregate of the actual or potential resources which are linked to possession of a durable network of more or less institutionalized relationships of mutual acquaintance and recognition,"[1] was transformed in Syria. Most Syrians' social capital decreased during the civil war, chiefly due to impoverishment, insecurity, and migration. However, despite the context of growing individual isolation, a minority of Syrians experienced the reverse, thanks to their participation in the protest networks. This specific form of social capital emerged from ties formed during demonstrations, ties that would endure long after the events. This "revolutionary social capital" was simultaneously a resource for the individual agent and an integral part of the mobilization process during which it was formed and which it, in turn, helped to produce.

The hypothesized formation of revolutionary social capital calls for several observations. First, this revolutionary social capital does not result from the continued accumulation of already existing social capital or the conversion of a different type of capital (economic, cultural, religious, etc.). Next, the revolutionary institutions are in part born from the institutionalization of the protesters networks. In other words, it is mobilization that creates institutions. However, the prior capital of the actors significantly determines the distribution of positions of power within the new institutions. While rural populations and the working classes played a dominant role in military institutions, the middle classes established themselves in the re-emerging civil administration, and the elites in representative institutions outside Syria. These social divides often intersected with ideological positions, as armed combat increasingly fell within the sphere of radical jihad. Finally, insertion into revolutionary networks led to biographical disruption, especially for the rare female activists.

---

[1] Pierre Bourdieu, "The Forms of Capital," in John Richardson (ed.), *Handbook of Theory and Research for the Sociology of Education*, New York, Greenwood, 1986, p. 51.

The Loss of Social Capital

A loss of social capital was one of the effects of civil war in insurgent areas, but its severity varied by social strata.[2] Indeed, social capital differed among social groups: It had strong territorial moorings for the middle class and even more so for the working classes,[3] while for the elite, it was a more complex, more diversified playing of a double game of the autochthonous and the international.[4]

In working class circles, social capital was generally linked to neighborhood sociability (a street, an apartment block), even though urban and seasonal migrations oblige us to nuance this observation.[5] In certain cases, social capital was partly built on tribal ties.[6] Also, these social networks were linked to professional activity and specific spaces such as cafés or the mosque.[7] However, as urban areas became strategic targets for the belligerents, many public venues closed. The regime's bombing campaigns most often targeted institutions such as schools, hospitals, and administrative buildings and working class districts, which were hotbeds of the first demonstrations. Anyone in the open in a public space – elderly people in front of their buildings, children playing in the street, queues outside a shop – were exposed to risk.

The destruction of economic capital and insecurity also affected the middle class. Thus, the total or partial destruction of people's housing, rising food costs, and the lack of heating in winter paralyzed everyday socializing. Added to this were the electricity shortages and the regime's

---

[2] The tripartite split in Syrian society – elites, middle classes, working classes – appears, implicitly at least, in the literature, see in particular Baudouin Dupret, Zouhair Ghazzal, Youssef Mujahidin, and Mohammed al-Dbiyat (eds.), *op. cit.* For our purpose, these categories are more ideal types than organized groups.

[3] Sylvia Chiffoleau, "La Syrie au quotidien: cultures et pratiques du changement," *Revue des mondes musulmans et de la Méditerranée* 115–116, 2006, pp. 9–18.

[4] Bruno Cousin and Sébastien Chauvin, "L'économie symbolique du capital social," *Actes de la recherche en sciences sociales* 193 (3), 2012, p. 102.

[5] Marc Lavergne, "L'urbanisation contemporaine de la Syrie du Nord," *Revue des mondes musulmans et de la Méditerranée* 62, 1991, pp. 195–208.

[6] Thus, the town of Raqqa is divided into districts, each occupied predominantly by one clan; see Myriam Ababsa, "La recomposition des allégeances tribales dans le Moyen-Euphrate syrien (1958–2007)," *Etudes rurales* 184, 2009, pp. 65–78. Likewise, in the town of Maraa (Aleppo governorate), five clans occupy distinct districts, observations in Maraa, December 2012.

[7] See, for example, the sociability of traders in the Aleppo Suk, Annika Rabo, "Affective, Parochial or Innovative? Aleppo Traders on the Margin of Global Capitalism," *Revue des mondes musulmans et de la Méditerranée*, 115–116, 2006, pp. 43–58. This type of sociability is also found in other Muslim countries, for example in Morocco, Raffaele Cattedra and M'hammed Idrissi-Janati, "Espace sacré, espace de citadinité, espace de mouvement. Les territoires des mosquées au Maroc," in Mounia Bennani-Chraïbi and Olivier Fillieule (eds.), *Résistances et protestations dans les sociétés musulmanes*, Presses de Sciences Po, Paris, 2003, pp. 127–175.

destruction of microwave towers that hindered communication, especially among the young for whom cell phones are key to sociability.[8] Only the few people who had a generator and satellite antenna could still access the Internet.[9] Security concerns complicated movement, especially where the front lines were fluid. Many of our interviewees spoke of having lost contact with their friends and sometimes their family.

However, the chief cause of the disruption of social networks was the forced displacement of the population. In December 2014, more than half of the Syrian population no longer lived in their homes, a proportion that was even higher in insurgent areas. People are cut off to varying degrees from social, professional, and family networks and their social capital diminishes as a result.[10] The majority of the refugees in the camps (especially in Turkey and Jordan), fenced spaces where families were isolated, came from the working classes.[11] Forging new ties even under normal circumstances takes time but is especially difficult when complicated by being uprooted by a change of camp, clandestine migration, or a return to Syria to a place far from the original home.

Middle class passport holders, in contrast, could stay out of the refugee camps and assimilate more easily in other exiled groups. Finally, for the well-off, established networks outside Syria's borders facilitated their resettlement in the Arab world and in the West, in places like Paris, for example, where there were established, decades-old Syrian communities.

A Teacher's Loss of Social Capital

Our interview with an English teacher in the town of Azaz, in northern Syria, illustrates what a loss of social capital entails.[12] He welcomed us to his apartment in January 2013. The electricity was down, the place was unheated, and the relatively new building had suffered serious bombing damage. The apartment reflected the taste of the Syrian middle class that had thrived economically in the 2000s. The living room sofas faced a television; the kitchen was equipped in a European style. We were not received in a separate room as would have been the case in a traditional house. His wife participated actively in the conversation with us (three

---

[8] See Leila Hudson, *op. cit.*

[9] For an analysis of the use of communication tools in Idlib province, see Enrico De Angelis and Yazan Badran, "Interacting in a Context of War: Communication Spaces in Idlib," *Confluence Méditerranée* 99, 2016–2017, pp. 149–160.

[10] Interviews with Syrian refugees in Iraq, Turkey, Jordan, and Egypt between September 2012 and January 2014.

[11] Pierre Centlivres tackled this question in 1987 during fieldwork in the Afghan refugee camps in Pakistan, Pierre Centlivres, "Les trois pôles de l'identité afghane au Pakistan," *L'Homme* 28 (108), 1988, pp. 134–146.

[12] I-30, in Azaz, December 2012.

foreign men), something that would have been inconceivable in a more conservative household.

Before the war, our host had taught in a secondary school in the town center but derived most of his income from giving private lessons. He had owned an apartment in Aleppo and a country home in the Azaz area, which he often visited with friends in his free time. He now no longer left the town because of the security situation. This had caused him to lose contact with his friends in Aleppo and in the countryside, many of his friends having left Azaz to seek refuge in Turkey. His school had closed; there was no longer any demand for private lessons, which further diminished the professional component of his social network (colleagues, parents of private students). Being a teacher no longer brought him the same social recognition; some of his former students, involved in the revolution and promoted to leadership positions, now held higher social rank than he did. We had first met him by chance on the street in front of his building where he was talking with some of his unemployed neighbors.

The Benefits of Revolutionary Capital

Revolutionary capital afforded activists positions in administrative, religious, media, and judicial fields. It did so, however, only when combined with other forms of capital, especially educational. Our data indicates that being part of a revolutionary network conditioned access to elective or administrative positions within insurgent areas starting from 2012. Most local council members had participated in the 2011 demonstrations and were also members of activist networks. The approximately one hundred volunteers working for the Aleppo city council came from this background.[13] In other words, these new institutions emerged from the objectivization of the revolutionary networks formed during the 2011 protests.

However, access to institutional positions also depended on certain technical and interpersonal skills. Unlike the young demonstrators that, on the whole, made up the first coordinating committees (*tansiqiyyat*), the Aleppo city council's managers often were older and had professional experience (as primary school teachers, engineers, computer engineers) that predisposed them to office work. "A committee is responsible for choosing the volunteers who work in the various municipality offices," explained a former management student at the University of Aleppo with responsibility for the municipality's human resources. "For me, afterwards, it is a question of checking the work carried out, so as to be sure

---

[13] Observations and interviews in the City Council of Aleppo, August 2013.

that the volunteer has the required skills."[14] In the Idlib governorate, a degree was required for elective office, formalizing the *de facto* monopoly of political representation by the middle and upper classes.

The religious field was also transformed by the departure of clerics linked to the regime. When insurgents took over towns or villages, most imams fled and new ones were appointed by the armed groups (Harakat al-Fajr, for example) or by neighborhood committees, as in al-Sukari in Aleppo. Competition for these positions was exacerbated by the religious field's weak institutionalization before 2011, especially with regard to training and appointments. Additionally, most Sunni movements were present in insurgent areas. The appointment of religious figures that were marginalized under the former regime reveals the politicization of the field, something the government had sought to avoid. "Before the revolution, I was studying Islamic studies in Damascus and taught at a religious school. I was not interested in politics. For me, it was an inaccessible world, corrupt and contrary to religious morals. Since the start of the revolution, everything has changed. As a judge, I have to get involved in political and economic debates and find solutions for the residents," explained a judge in the Islamic court in al-Bab.[15] Many examples support this hypothesis: "Before 2011, I was about to stop my Islamic law studies," explained Sheikh Yusef, police commander in Azaz between 2012 and the summer of 2013. "After the town was captured, it was difficult to find cadres. Because I had been involved from the start in the demonstrations and knew Islamic law, I became the police chief."[16] Similarly, in al-Bab, Sheikh Juma'a, an inconsequential imam in the prerevolutionary religious establishment, became an important figure thanks to his political involvement.[17]

For the media in insurgent areas, being part of the revolutionary networks eased their access to military units, civil institutions, and representative bodies outside Syria. Journalists, photographers, documentary makers, fixers, and other media activists were generally under thirty and conversant with social networks and new technologies. Moreover, the revolutionary media field in Syria was replete with publications in Arabic, in English, and, to a lesser extent, in French. Knowledge of English was crucial for communicating with Western journalists, bloggers, and humanitarian workers. Speaking a foreign language was also a necessity for working as a fixer, which, besides the considerable salary (US $100–200 per day), brought with it access to useful contacts. Most media activists engaged in a range of

[14] I-128, in Aleppo, August 2013.
[15] I-106, in al-Bab, December 2012.
[16] I-63, in Azaz, December 2012.
[17] Observations and interviews in al-Bab, December 2012.

activities and, depending on the context, might refer to themselves as journalists or revolutionaries. Given their involvement on the insurgent side, their status was ambiguous, but Amnesty International and Reporters Without Borders classified them as journalists. These media activists connected via social networks (Facebook, Twitter, and Skype), publications (newspapers, websites, media offices of armed groups, and civil institutions) and seminars organized by international NGOs. They had thousands of contacts on Facebook and large numbers of followers on Twitter, platforms with larger audiences than the Syrian publications they worked for. "In the beginning, we were all using our mobile phones to shoot videos of the demonstrations. Then with friends, we organized a media center. We spoke English, which meant we could get in touch with foreign media, host journalists and work as fixers to earn money and buy better materials. Some of us even went to Turkey to train in journalism."[18] Based on our interviews, individuals with this profile often came from well to do backgrounds and had opted to stay in Syria out of political engagement. In contrast, most media activists covering the fighting and demonstrations seemed to belong to the middle or working classes. They often learned how to take photos or videos during the protests, generally using their mobile phones. With the transition to civil war, while their friends and family took up arms, they committed to the revolution by joining media centers (Maktab I'lami) connected to military groups or civil institutions.

In the legal field, converting revolutionary capital into institutional positions (as judge, prosecutor, or lawyer) was impeded by the issue of real or ostensible legal competence. The greater autonomy of the judicial field *vis-a-vis* the insurgent movement was complemented by a new porosity with the religious field. In fact, legal practitioners and clerics achieved dominant positions independent of whether they participated in the 2011 demonstrations or not. For instance, a judge who defected after the fall of Aleppo was working at the Court of the United Judicial Council.[19] His responsibilities covered the legal classification of offenses, requiring an in-depth knowledge of the procedures. Similarly, religious legitimacy meant that it was possible to obtain a position in the court without having taken part in the protests. In December 2012, the revolutionary court judges in al-Bab were mostly former imams. Even if they had limited training or did not finish university, they derived authority from being a judge, highlighting the disconnection between being legitimate interpreters of the law and knowing Islamic law.[20]

---

[18] I-18, in al-Bab, January 2013.
[19] Interviews at the Court of the United Judicial Council, in Aleppo, January 2013.
[20] Interviews with sheikhs working in courts in al-Bab and Aleppo, December 2012–January 2013.

The need for education or technical skills favored the middle classes in gaining access to positions of power. Conversely, the working classes were relegated to menial positions (as chauffeurs, cooks). The Aleppo municipality, owing to recruitment difficulties, reinstated police officers, garbage collectors, and technicians in their previous municipal roles. In the fighting units, things proceeded differently. Our interviews suggest that military leaders often came from more modest backgrounds, in part because these armed groups often formed in rural areas and impoverished suburbs.[21]

The Unlikely Trajectory of the Mayor of Aleppo

Ahmad Azuz, mayor of insurgent Aleppo from March to September 2013, personifies how revolutionary capital gets converted to institutional positions.[22] He welcomed us into his apartment in Hanano, a district populated by civil servants, where he had lived since 1989. By outward appearances, Ahmad Azuz was thoroughly middle class (contemporary furnishings, household appliances). He came from a line of shopkeepers; his father exported Islamic women's clothes (abaya) to Saudi Arabia. Both his father and grandfather had held low-level posts in the Baath party. His three brothers worked in interior design. Our host Ahmad had studied economics at the University of Aleppo for a time but was expelled for refusing to join the Baath party. He then worked as an accountant in a steel works. In 1998, he founded his own business, an IT shop that was still open in 2013 despite the war and the subsequent exodus of many local residents.

He joined his first demonstration on March 18, 2011 at the Great Mosque of Aleppo. He and a group of about twenty people shouted "Allah Akbar" at the exit of the mosque before melting into the crowd to avoid arrest. He only knew the other demonstrators by their pseudonyms. Gradually, they started to organize via Skype or Facebook. Each public event brought a chance to connect with new demonstrators. In November 2011, he was arrested and spent five months in prison, where he came into contact with more activists. He rejoined the demonstration as soon as he was released, but the movement had changed scale. Most of his activist friends had left for the village of Maraa in the governorate of Aleppo, where they were preparing for armed struggle. He hid weapons for the FSA in his apartment in Aleppo. When the insurgency took over his district, he reconnected with former demonstrators turned fighters. In the autumn of 2011, aided by his networks he helped form his district's local council and later that year took part in reconstituting the technical department of the Aleppo governorate's Revolutionary Transitional Council. He ran his business to provide for his family while continuing his revolutionary activities. In

---

[21] The groups of combatants from the University of Aleppo are an exception.
[22] Interviews in Aleppo, August 2013.

> March 2013, he and other well-known insurgents were chosen to travel to Gaziantep, where elections were being organized. There he was elected mayor of Aleppo, a post that he held until he lost his reelection bid in September 2013. In the spring of 2014, his building was flattened by bombs and he sent his family Turkey, but he remained behind in the practically deserted district of Hanano.

That the middle class played a key role also stemmed from the disappearance of the old elites. Most of the ground taken by the insurgents from the summer of 2012 on was in rural or working class districts; the wealthier areas were for the most part still under regime control. The political aspirations and, above all, the habitus of revolutionaries from rural and working class origins differed from those of the middle and upper classes. "From the beginning of the revolution, I was very involved. With my friends, we organized demonstrations and clandestine clinics," described a revolutionary from an important family in Homs, "but, little by little, we were marginalized by people from the villages and poor neighborhoods who were better organized. The transition to armed struggle led to our failure. We disagreed about using arms and we were totally left behind. [...] In the end, I came to Turkey to carry on with my political activities."[23] For the elite, being part of the revolutionary networks did not offset a feeling of having been downgraded socially.

However, the revolution did make it possible for powerful families marginalized by the Baathist government of the 1960s to return to center stage. While they played a limited role inside Syria, their younger generation was highly represented in the insurgency's delegations outside the country, in nongovernmental and international organizations, and in the fundraising networks abroad. The Assistance Coordination Unit, which operated from Turkey in the insurgent cause, for example, mainly recruited the offspring of the more prominent Syrian families because they were the only ones with the necessary qualifications, including language skills. They are less heavily represented in the Syrian National Council and the National Coalition, where several figures (Haytham al-Malih, Imad al-Din al-Rashid, Abd al-Rahman al-Hajj, and Radwan Ziyade) from humbler backgrounds gained positions thanks to skills and network contacts acquired in pre-2011 human rights campaigns and political activism.[24] In

---

[23] I-15, with the former manager of a large company in Homs who took part in the city's first protests, in Istanbul, September 2013.

[24] For more background on these four actors, see Thomas Pierret, "Religion and the State ..." *op. cit.*, pp. 139–141.

fact, with regard to the insurgency's political representation, the political parties and the sponsorship by foreign powers acted as a counterweight to social determinism.

The elite's social and educational capital explains their positions in the insurgency's representation abroad. Some enjoyed dual nationality and, having been educated abroad, knew Western languages and cultural codes. They were thus well positioned to be employed by international aid networks (NGOs, international organizations) and handle relations with the media. Having been socialized in international environments, they were able to use their social capital decisively when new institutions were being formed. Here, our 2013 interview of a member of the Assistance Coordination Unit is instructive.[25] The then 28-year old scion of a wealthy Damascene family, he had left Syria in 1980 to settle in California. After completing management studies in Washington DC, he traveled to Turkey in 2013 to protest against the regime. His connections and resume gave him ready access to positions of responsibility, despite his youth and remoteness from Syria. In similar fashion, members of the Syrian elite could take advantage of professional or family connections in the Gulf States, whose governments were financing the insurgency. Adib al-Shishakly, for example, became a key opposition figure abroad thanks to his connections in the Gulf. Also from a prominent Damascene family, he had lived for ten years in the United States and later had moved to Saudi Arabia to work in aviation. When the demonstrations erupted in 2011, he helped found the Syrian National Council and the Assistance Coordination Unit, whose vice-president he became. In 2013, he was appointed the insurgency's ambassador to the Gulf States.

An Heiress Heads up the Assistance Coordination Unit

The president of the Assistance Coordination Unit, Souheir al-Atassi, belonged to the Syrian elite.[26] She was the daughter of Jamal al-Atassi, a well-known Homs politician, who created an eponymous forum in 2000 at a time when Bashar al-Assad's ascent seemed to augur a more liberal era.[27] She had studied literature in Damascus and in France. She then went to work for her father's forum and took over its leadership in 2009 upon his death. She moved in liberal, educated circles (architects, students, cinematographers) that campaigned for human rights and took part in the spring 2011 demonstrations. Arrested on March 16, 2011 for her activism, her family intervened to obtain her quick release. She left Syria in late 2011, joined the Syrian National Council's general commission, and in

---

[25] I-129, in Gaziantep, September 2013.
[26] Interviews with members of the ACU, in Gaziantep, September 2013.
[27] Elizabeth Picard, *op. cit.*

November 2012 became vice-president of the National Coalition and head of the newly formed Assistance Coordination Unit. In December 2013, she stepped down from her role as vice-president. At the same time, challenges to her authority within the Assistance Coordination Unit resulted in her *de facto* discharge. An executive director, Osama Kadi, took over and wielded the real power while she continued in office as a mere figurehead.

The diverging trajectories of revolutionaries inside and outside the country sharpened their social differences. Domestically, the focus was on a war that paralyzed everyday life, while the international elite moved daily in diplomatic and humanitarian circles. Revolutionaries inside the country generally regarded the return of prominent families to the political scene as illegitimate. Their actions were often misconstrued. The National Coalition felt compelled to take a stand in international debates, but to militants confronting daily violence in-country, they seemed abstract at best. Conversely, a number of actors outside Syria, especially in the West, rejected all references to political Islam.

Female Activism and Biographical Disruption

Participating in demonstrations and getting involved in the revolution brought biographical disruption to the lives of all activists, but it took on a particular dimension for women. Some had to take on new roles, which gave them unprecedented access to positions in the public arena and transformed gender relations in complex ways in their private lives. The biographies of three female activists, each extraordinary in her own way, offer valuable insights into these changes, similar to the trajectory analyzed by Thomas Pierret and Mériam Cheikh.[28]

Three Women of the Revolution

The profiles of these three women involved in the uprising reflect heterogeneous social backgrounds and modalities of engagement.

Before Daraa, Fatma,[29] from a middle class family she described as non-politicized, did not oppose the regime. She liked Bashar al-Assad during the early years of his presidency, but his speeches during the Tunisian and Egyptian revolutions shocked her and she became active on Skype and Facebook. She ended up sharing information and becoming a contact for Reuters and Al Jazeera. She became well known on Facebook by creating the Freedom Idlib (Hurriyya Idlib) group on the popular social media platform. A

---

[28] Thomas Pierret and Mériam Cheikh, *op. cit.*
[29] The three names are pseudonyms.

skilled dressmaker, she sewed masks for the demonstrators to wear during protests. Her family also became involved: Her brother helped fugitives wanted by the regime escape their town. As a woman, she was able to circulate easily, gather eyewitness accounts, and correspond with Al Jazeera. Wanted by the army, she eventually left Idlib in March 2012, leaving her husband and sister behind. Locally prominent, she was elected in December 2012 to a seat on Idlib's Governorate Council, which she still held when we met her in Antakya in September 2013. Although her commitments and political activities meant she considered herself more liberated, she missed prerevolutionary family life and regretted the loss of personal ties that resulted from her exile.

Our second interviewee, Adiba was from a prominent family in Ansari, a wealthy district in Aleppo. In September 2011, with her family on the verge of taking refuge in the city's regime-controlled west side, she refused to leave the insurgent areas when her husband and family moved. Setting up a clinic, a school, and a center for aid distribution made her popular. In March 2012, she divorced her then husband and married a childhood friend who was equally engaged in the revolution. On account of his humble background, she explained to us, before the war their families would never have let them marry. Shortly after the insurgents took control of eastern Aleppo, Adiba ran against some notables in the Amariyya district council elections. Facing down the pressure and with strong local support, she was elected in April 2013. Her opponents challenged the vote, but in August 2013 the Aleppo municipality ruled in her favor and she was appointed head of the District Council. When we interviewed her, she expressed feelings of isolation and loneliness in a revolution made up of working class and middle class men she had relatively little in common with. This change of *milieu* was for her the most difficult aspect of her new life, even though she described her revolutionary companions as "her new family."

Our third interviewee, Samia, a licensed pediatrician, came from an old Aleppo family. Long before 2011, she had mobilized on behalf of Hamas in support of the Palestinian cause. When the revolution came, she was living with her family in west Aleppo. She took part in the first demonstrations with five of her female friends. They demonstrated outside their own neighborhood and met other protesters, both men and women. Most of her friends were arrested in 2011, and she left abruptly for Turkey. In September 2012, she returned to Aleppo, but, for security reasons, stayed in the insurgent districts and did not return to see her family, which still lived in the regime area in West Aleppo. She described the revolution as personally liberating for her: She left the bourgeois neighborhoods and discovered a world beyond her medical milieu. She lived alone in an apartment, was engaged to a lawyer from the countryside, drove a car (rare for a woman in Aleppo), and met with revolutionaries and journalists, some of them foreigners. She was responsible for coordinating hospitals operated by the municipality of Aleppo. Her reputation, built on her revolutionary activity and her medical profession, protected her and allowed her to pass untrammeled through checkpoints manned by armed groups.

Prior to the revolution, not only the regime discouraged women from entering politics outside the Baath party, but so did families. Samia had to deal with opposition from her parents, especially her mother, when she helped raise funds for Hamas in 2010. "As a woman, it was difficult for me to become involved in a humanitarian or charitable organization. My parents tried to stop me on the grounds that it was wrong for my future."[30]

As we have seen, during the early peaceful demonstrations, women did participate in marches and revolutionary groups. Social media presence was less gender-driven. Fatma started posting messages of support for Tunisian and Egyptian revolutionaries on Facebook, which, in the Syrian context, meant both taking a risk and a position. Samia took part surreptitiously in the first demonstrations in March 2011, "For me, taking to the street was very important, but I could not demonstrate. On one hand, there was the repression by the regime, but also because my family would have forbidden me to go there."[31] The conflict's militarization curbed participation by women in the public sphere, because women were barred from taking dominant roles, especially fighting ones, in an increasingly radical ideological context.[32] Still, the absence of men (casualties of war, away fighting on the frontlines, or living abroad) transformed many women's lives. For some women from conservative families, it was their first time working outside the home. Others who fled Syria were able to continue their political work and venture into new spheres of action.[33]

Though it cost these women significant biographical disruption, their activism helped them overcome the growing marginalization of women in the public space. The radical break their engagement represented is clearly on display in how their choices placed them at odds with their families and social circles. When Adiba decided to stay behind to provide shelter to FSA fighters on the eve of the battle of Aleppo in July 2012, instead of moving with her husband and her family to west Aleppo, she went against their wishes. "I believed in the revolution and I did not want to leave. My family threatened me, but I did not give in. This decision to stay changed my life."[34] In March 2013, she broke with her prominent family when she remarried. Similarly, when Fatma left Idlib ahead of the army that was looking for her, she cut herself off from her taxi driver husband and her sister. "In our household, many things were my responsibility. After I left, my husband must have had to learn to live alone, and I

---

[30] I-19, in Aleppo, August 2013.
[31] *Idem.*
[32] There are exceptions, https://news.vice.com/video/syria-al-qaeda-39-s-new-home, see min 11 to 13.
[33] I-4, in Gaziantep, September 2013.
[34] I-130, in Aleppo, August 2013.

had to learn to contend daily with a man's world that had not been mine before."[35] Finally, Samia, who had lived all her life in the bourgeois district of west Aleppo, moved to the eastern districts and for the first time lived in that working class environment.

The cost of these disruptions, isolation and a loss of social status, explains the rarity of such stories. Our three interviewees found themselves cut off from their families owing not only to territorial divisions between the regime and the insurgents, but also because of being arrested, going into exile, and taking opposing political positions. The revolution became a "new family" in the metaphorical sense, with strong friendships, but also literally, through marriages that would otherwise have been inconceivable. Adiba divorced and remarried a protester she met during the revolution. "What is hard is this feeling of loneliness and solitude," she confided,

I have not seen my family for more than seven months. Although I am very busy with my work for the revolution, I sometimes feel disconnected from the others. We do not share the same things, we have not experienced the same things until now. Everything has changed for me, I no longer live the same way, I belonged to a very rich family, I never needed to work. Now I am poor, with no real friends apart from the revolutionaries, my new family.[36]

These profound biographical disruptions had two-fold consequences. On the one hand, they let women escape from traditional assigned roles within their families and communities. They belonged to mixed groups of revolutionaries. Samia took part in the first deliberations that led to the demonstrations in Aleppo. Fatma used her status as a woman to gather witness accounts for the foreign media. Adiba sheltered combatants, later setting up schools to compensate for the disappearance of the public ones. By participating in revolutionary activities, by sharing the risks, they gained legitimacy. Every evening, they would be in meetings where activists talked, sang, and danced. This accumulating revolutionary capital was convertible into institutional positions. Thus, Fatma in December 2012 was elected to the Aleppo Governorate Council by indirect ballot, Samia was appointed coordinator of health services in Aleppo, and Adiba was elected mayor of Amariyya District following a turbulent election. "Having official status is important, it allows me to be recognized as a revolutionary and not just a woman," explained Samia. They also saw their personal lives transformed by a whole range of possibilities opening before them. In our interviews, these revolutionaries expressed a feeling of liberation from social norms.

[35] I-4, in Antakya, September 2013.
[36] I-130, in Aleppo, August 2013.

"Being engaged in the revolution means so much more. It means mixing with tens of new people every day, travelling all over the place. People are no longer prejudiced because they see I am taking risks; I am like them now."[37] For these women, the revolution multiplied social ties and brought opportunities never before available in either the public or private spheres.

[37] I-4, in Antakya, September 2013.

12　The Economy for War

The withdrawal of a state from large parts of its territory allows accumulating military capital whose formation and maintenance call for expending significant economic resources. Violence or threats of it become the principal mechanism for accumulating resources, specifically through taxation, extortion, and control of economic flows. At first glance, this would correspond to the theory of Georg Elwert, a German sociologist who introduced the concept of a "market of violence": a space where actors compete to accumulate the means of violence and employ them in order to gain economic benefits.

Markets of violence generally originate in conflicts of a non-economic nature. The continuation of the violence is, however, based on economic motives or unconscious economic behaviour. From the perspective of the warlords, violence can be used to maximise profit to such an extent that it is on a par with other economic methods. The fact that the balance sheet is far from positive in its effect on the overall system is irrelevant. This inherently rational economic behaviour can continue as long as the warlords are able to exercise their power without the support of the majority.[1]

His concept was subsequently taken up again in various forms, for example in David Keen's *Economic Functions of Civil Wars* or, more recently, with Alex de Waal's "political marketplace," and it underpins current studies in the economics of civil wars.[2]

However, while it highlights the economic rationality inherent in these conflicts, the concept of a "market of violence" is misleading. In fact, the formation of military groups and the conversion of coercion into an economic resource do not follow market logic, largely due to the lack of a competitive equilibrium. The quest to accumulate military capital leads to the pursuit of political supremacy, since any intermediate situation of divided control between armed groups is inherently unstable. Indeed,

---

[1] Elwert Georg, *op. cit.*, pp. 85–102.
[2] Keen David, *op. cit.*; Alex de Waal, "Mission Without End: Peacekeeping in the African Political Marketplace," *International Affairs* 85 (1), 2009, pp. 99–113.

there are no (or few) mechanisms that guarantee the security of actors on a shared territory. In the case of Syria, the consequences of this theory (creation of fiefs, centrality of economic stakes) are not empirically validated: Military actors did not reinvest the capital they accumulated based on an economic rationality, which would have led to resource-sharing agreements. On the contrary, the actors used their resources to wage war, except in very specific and generally temporary situations that we will describe. The accumulation of economic resources led to an intensification of violence in a drive toward monopoly.

The Destruction of Economic Capital and the End of a National Market

The war had three consequences: the destruction of economic capital, the emergence of regional markets, and the reorganization of economic and human flows. First, the Syrian economy was severely impacted by the collapse of manufacturing and destruction of the capital stock. International aid and cross-border traffic did not compensate for the massive increase in poverty since these limited resources often benefited groups outside Syria (refugees, traffickers). Impoverishment impacted regions and social groups differently, heightening inequalities within Syria. The working classes and small entrepreneurs, insofar as they held capital inside Syria, were the most severely affected: civil servants and those living in regime-controlled zones were relatively untouched. Second, the national market had disintegrated and been replaced by economic regions, which were controlled by actors or coalitions of actors. Third, the flows of goods and people were restructured in line with political risk and the degree of closure of new regional markets. The labor market thus became segmented and certain international borders were no longer controlled, leading to an intensification of international exchanges. Contrary to a widely held view, the borders did not "disappear," since cross-border regions did not constitute unified markets, and the higher returns that resulted from crossing a border remained the rationale for doing business.[3]

The war destroyed a significant portion of Syria's economic capital, a loss whose magnitude the Syrian Center for Policy Research (SCPR) has

---

[3] In this respect, the Afghan-Pakistani border is comparable, Gilles Dorronsoro, "The Transformation of the Afghanistan-Pakistan Border," in Shahzad Bashir and Robert Crews (eds.), *Under the Drones: Modern Lives in the Afghanistan-Pakistan Borderlands*, Cambridge, Harvard University Press, pp. 30–44.

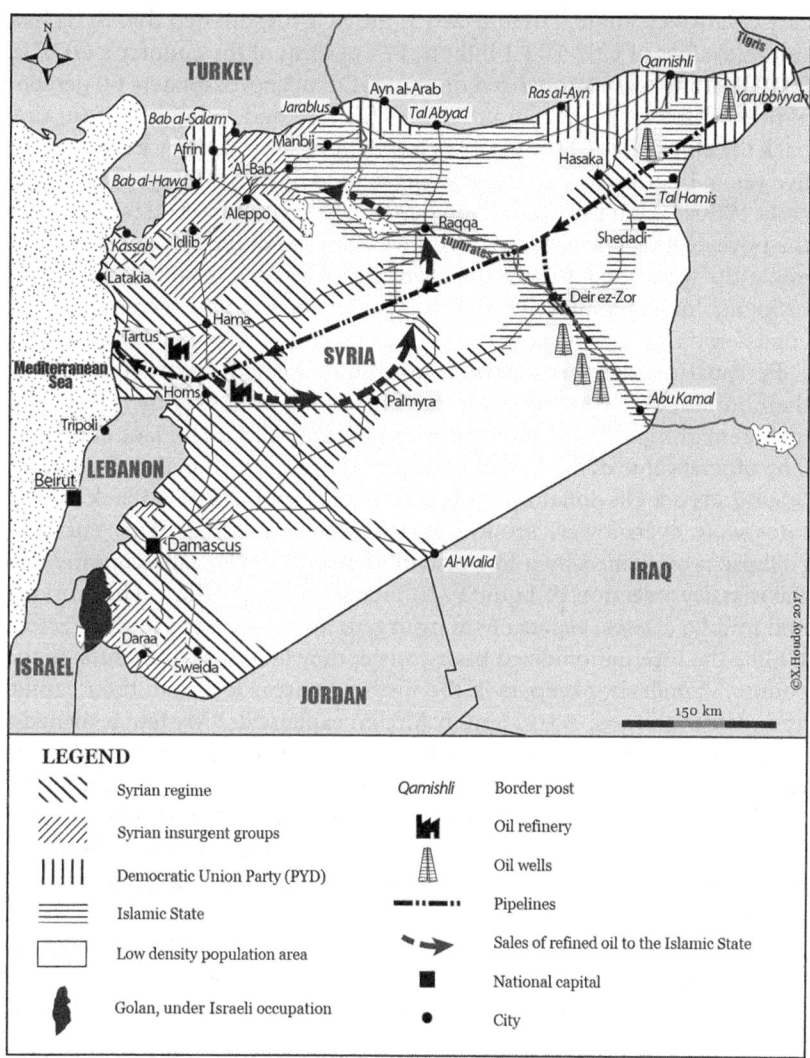

Map 12.1 War economy in Syria (2014)

tried to assess in collaboration with the United Nations.[4] Owing to the
difficulty of data collection, the most that can be achieved will be a

---

[4] Rabie Nasser, Zaki Mehchy, and Khaled Abou Ismail, "Root and Impact of Syria Crisis,"
Syrian Center for Policy Research, 2013, http://scpr-syria.org/en/S33/Roots-and-Impact-of-
the-Syrian-Crisis, viewed September 9, 2014.

conservative estimate.[5] In mid-2013, the SCPR estimated that Syria had suffered a loss of US\$ 103.1 billion, 174 percent of the country's GDP in 2010, leading to an annualized drop in GDP of approximately 60 percent between June 2011 and June 2013. This loss had the effect of turning back the clock on the Human Development Index (HDI) by nearly thirty-five years. In other words, it was equivalent to Syria's HDI quotient of the early 1980s.[6] Half the population living in Syria in 2010 had fallen below the poverty line, and a further third was close to doing so. "Here, people make do with what they have been able to save," testified an al-Bab resident, "most families live on charity. Even people who were previously considered rich have to join the poor to go and find food and aid."[7]

Personal savings were often completely depleted. Many Syrians lost their homes, destroyed by bombings or pillaged by the regime's troops or insurgent groups.[8] Even intact property became illiquid for lack of buyers. The official value of the Syrian pound dropped more than threefold, from 50 pounds per US dollar in 2011 to 180 in December 2014. Black market rates were even lower, around 300 pounds per dollar. This currency collapse is explained by a loss of confidence in the Syrian economy and the massive injection of liquidity to finance the war effort. The working and middle classes, especially in insurgent areas, were the most affected: Unlike the internationalized bourgeoisie, they lacked savings outside the country. Small shopkeepers in the insurgent areas lost both their capital and their livelihood. A resident in Aleppo explained: "My father owned a white goods store in Aleppo. He had to close when the battle of Aleppo started [July 2012] and has not been able to reopen. Since then, the family is ruined. Of my six brothers and sisters, none of us have found work."[9] Moreover, the currency devaluation produced high inflation. Nominal prices often doubled and, for lack of proportional salary rises, Syrians saw their buying power plummet.[10]

Industrial manufacturing also declined dramatically with the pillaging, dismantling, and destruction of most manufacturing sites in insurgent areas. Entire factories were taken apart in Sheikh Najjar, an industrial

[5] The report substantially underestimates the number of refugees, because it is based on United Nations data that only take into account requests made to the HCR.

[6] The HDI is a composite index created by the United Nations Development Programme (UNDP) in 1990, which rests mainly on three criteria: life expectancy at birth, education and per capita income.

[7] I-131, in al-Bab, December 2012.

[8] Leyla Vignal, "Destruction-in-Progress: Revolution, Repression and War Planning in Syria (2011 Onwards)," *Built Environment* 40 (3), 2014, pp. 326–341.

[9] I-132, in Aleppo, January 2013.

[10] "The Syrian Catastrophe: Socioeconomic Monitoring Report First Quarterly Report (January-March 2013)," *Syrian Center for Policy Research*, 2013, p. 15, http://scpr-syria .org/att/1374248216_kQVrL.pdf, viewed September 11, 2014.

zone in the north of Aleppo, and were moved either to areas that were spared the bombing, for instance Afrin or Latakia, or abroad, including Egypt, Turkey, and Lebanon. The son of a manufacturer from Aleppo explained: "By the end of 2011, the situation around Aleppo was increasingly unstable. Most manufacturers started to relocate their factories to the coast or abroad."[11] In Egypt, the Morsi government helped Syrian entrepreneurs set up their businesses anew. A Syrian manufacturer who had moved to Cairo confided: "My shop and furniture-production workshops were located near Damascus. When the crisis started, I immediately tried to find somewhere to move them. I had a contact in Cairo and I relocated everything there."[12]

Beyond destroying economic capital, the war broke up what had been a unified national market. In its place emerged regional markets that were congruent with a political actor's territorial control. Respect for property rights varied widely in them, from relative stability in regime-controlled areas to insecurity in the insurgent regions. The value of economic capital varied by territory. The withdrawal of the state also reduced control of international borders and restructured economic and human flows. A first effect was for trade to sometimes be taxed more heavily between different regions than across international borders. For example, it became more difficult to transport goods from East Aleppo to West Aleppo than to ship them from Aleppo to Gaziantep (Turkey). Then also, the labor market was no longer national in scope. It was often easier to go work abroad than to cross political borders within Syria. "Before the war I earned $200 to $250 a month," explained an electrician from Aleppo,

I have a wife and five children and we just about managed. Right now, there is almost no work left in Aleppo. You have to go to the zones held by the government like Tartus or Latakia, but even there it is very difficult to find work. Plus, the risk of being arrested is great. The only answer is to go to Lebanon with a contact and find work on a building site. The work is under miserable conditions, but it's the only way to bring home something to live on.[13]

A final effect was to make international trade essential in the non-regime areas. The Islamic State controlled large sections of Iraq and, while some PYD enclaves were relatively isolated, Jazeera's border with Iraq's independent Kurdish region played a critical economic role. At the same time, Jordan and Lebanon represented both safe havens and transnational markets for the insurgent-controlled zones in Daraa and Damascus, respectively.

[11] I-1, in Antakya, September 2013.
[12] I-133, in Cairo, January 2014.
[13] I-134, in Aleppo, January 2013.

Four economic zones can be distinguished: the regime's, the PYD's, ISIL's, and the insurgency's. These four markets were structurally different, especially with regard to the level of control exerted over their economies by the respective political actors. In the context of a war economy, the regime, ISIL, and the PYD established tight control over the markets and supply chains in their respective zones. In contrast, the economy in the areas controlled by the insurgency functioned in a decentralized manner. Indeed, the development of city councils, which assumed growing importance in 2012 and 2013, differed by region and by the level of aid they managed to obtain. No one armed group had the means of controlling the channels of trade and no taxation system had been put in place by 2014. Everything depended on the ability of economic actors to negotiate with the armed groups.

These four economic territories were not self-sufficient entities. Trade could continue between areas specifically in three situations: when an area was encircled, when indivisible goods required cooperation, or when resources were sufficiently lucrative for the actors to share in the benefits. In the first scenario, once front lines had stabilized, a neighborhood, group of villages, or region was sometimes left surrounded, which favored a special organization of trade. The crossing between East and West Aleppo in the Bustan al-Qasr district, which remained open in 2013, is a good example. During the first half of 2013, the regime held only one route to Aleppo and bread began to run short. In contrast, after a hard winter marked by shortages and cold, the insurgents managed to regularly supply the town. The crossing therefore became a place where food was bought and sold and a profit could be made because the price of bread differed in the two halves of the city, but also solidarity could be expressed by Aleppans getting food to their families caught in the Western part of Aleppo. Business was also conducted between Turkey and regime-held areas:

Businessmen, often settled in Turkey, trade between the regime-held part of the town of Aleppo and the part held by the insurgency, especially in food, petrol, fuel oil [used for heating and electrical generators]. In northern Syria, everything comes from Turkey and a little from Iraq: goods leave Turkey, pass into the free zone, then are resold in the government zone. No one checks this trade, even on the regime's side where intelligence services have become the main authority, especially the al-Mukhabarat al-Jawwiyya [Air Force Intelligence Services]. The army and militia look out for their own interests; each commander has his own agreements and tries to make money.[14]

[14] I-1, in Antakya, September 2013.

Similarly, before seizing Idlib the insurgents were never able to blockade it. Many FSA combatants' families lived in the city and many civil servants went there to collect their salaries. As in other places, economic interests and family ties were inseparable. "In Binnish [a town just outside Idlib held by the FSA], when the insurgent units shut down the movement of goods to Idlib, the population protested right away. Besieging the city also meant a loss in income for the armed groups holding the roadblocks around the city. All that made it easier to resume negotiations for food supplies."[15] The Kurdish enclaves were not self-sufficient either and Turkish authorities allowed nothing to pass through the border posts held by the PYD. The Afrin and Ayn al-Arab enclaves therefore had to negotiate constantly with the insurgents for provisions. The head of the Afrin local authority explained: "Supplying bakeries is a real business. The FSA takes a 20% cut on flour sales and we need 30 tonnes of flour a day in Afrin! A gas cylinder has gone for as much as 4,000 pounds,"[16] double the price in Azaz, only a few kilometers away. In 2013, tensions with insurgents led to regular cuts in the supply of water and electricity.

In the second situation – cooperating on indivisible goods – the splitting of a town or region could create problems in managing indivisible goods like water and electricity. In Aleppo, when the regime wanted to cut off the electricity supply to the rebel zones in 2012, the insurgent groups retaliated by shutting down the transformers under their control, causing a blackout in west Aleppo. This led to negotiations between the insurgent municipal authorities with the regime administration to preserve vital infrastructures. Water distribution presented a similar problem in principle but did not lead to cooperation. A number of water towers sat on the frontlines and access was essential to secure a sufficient water supply for both sides of the city. However, the Syrian army on the frontline generally refused to negotiate with the insurgents. The water supply was therefore restricted and intermittent even though repairs to pipes and water towers in the east of the city had made it possible to flow to taps for several hours each day. In Damascus, where the insurrection was based on the outskirts of the city, there were no arrangements of this sort, perhaps owing to the intensity of combat and the capital's special status. The same problem arose with the Tabqa dam reservoir that ISIL diverted water from around the clock, causing the level of Lake Assad to fall by six meters and producing water shortages in Aleppo and Raqqa.[17]

---

[15] I-4, with an activist from Idlib, in Antakya, September 2013.
[16] I-107, with the mayor of Afrin, in Afrin, January 2013.
[17] Danya Chudacoff, "'Water War' Threatens Syria Lifeline," *Al Jazeera*, July 7, 2014, http://www.aljazeera.com/news/middleeast/2014/07/water-war-syria-euphrates-201475 7640320663.html, viewed September 10, 2014.

In the third situation, agreements proliferated between armed actors around resources such as oil and gas in the provinces of Hasaka and Deir ez-Zor.[18] In 2013, the PYD and the insurgency (including ISIL) took control of hydrocarbon wells. Yet the refineries on the coast and in Homs belonged to the regime, while various armed groups controlled the oil pipelines and roads. In some cases, these resources could be supplied via alternative routes. A portion of the demand for oil in Aleppo and Idlib was met by Turkish gas stations near the border, which charged over two euros a litre during the winter of 2012–2013, double the normal price in Turkey. However, most of the time, the actors were forced to compromise. Oil, after being sold, was transported by tanker trucks or pipeline to the regime's refineries. Referring to the oil extraction sites east of Deir ez-Zor, a revolutionary explained: "Oil and gas wells are controlled by the regime but surrounded by the FSA. Oil is brought to Homs directly from the east of Syria by pipeline. The FSA have cut off the supply several times, but each time the regime would retaliate by cutting off electricity. This is the deal they made: gas and oil in exchange for electricity for all of the east."[19] To benefit the radical jihadists, in 2013 the government chose to sell refined oil to ISIL rather than to the insurgents. In the summer of 2013,

ISIL contented itself with manning roadblocks and taxing tankers that passed through, without trying to control the oil wells directly. One litre of refined petrol cost 75 Syrian pounds in the governmental zone. When a truck passes through the ISIL-held checkpoint on the road between Palmyra and Raqqa, the price per litre rises to 250–300 pounds, owing to the tax taken by ISIL. The oil is then distributed in the north of Syria held by the FSA. To keep prices from rising too high, ISIL makes sure it is the only group that siphons off a tax.[20]

The Local Resources of Armed Groups

With combatant numbers rising and distances to the front increasing, armed groups that in the beginning had survived thanks to their local networks needed to find other resources. In nongovernmental areas, the economy ran on more or less institutionalized levies – taxes, transport taxes, border levies – but also on exploiting of resources (oil and gas, flour mills, forests). A portion of the sums raised by levies went to paying for public services (water, electricity) and for subsidizing essential supplies.

---

[18] Wheat posed a specific problem. The grain silos and flour mills belonged to different groups. Moreover, we saw evidence that the sacks of flour supplied by the United Nations to the Syrian regime were resold on the black market in rebel zones. Insurgents sold flour to the Afrin enclave, held by the PYD.

[19] I-135, with an activist from Raqqa, in Gaziantep, September 2013.

[20] Ibid.

However, where establishing a taxation system was difficult, fighters lived off the land but at the risk of alienating the local populations.

First, the ability to establish a taxation system depended directly on an armed group's level of organization. The PKK and ISIL displayed an unequalled capacity for systematically raising funds. In 2012, the PKK's uncontested return to the Kurdish enclaves let it exploit the territories of Afrin, Ayn al-Arab, and Jazeera. Businessmen, entrepreneurs, and taxi drivers had to pay a monthly tax. "All shopkeepers in the town of Afrin have to give a percentage of their income to the PYD. Taxi drivers no longer have the right to work if they do not present an authorization from the new authorities at checkpoints. Likewise, a businessman cannot access the town market without having paid this tax."[21] Taxation of olive oil factories in Afrin represented an added, substantial revenue source for the movement. The populace also had to pay user fees for public goods. "In Afrin, cutting down a tree to stay warm in winter costs 1,000 pounds [15 dollars]," a member of the PYD explained.[22] The movement also taxed the networks that supplied food, water, and electricity. These levies exceeded the local administration's needs, in large part because Damascus was still paying salaries. The PYD also controlled infrastructure, such as the well-equipped Afrin hospital, which treated PYD/PKK fighters at no cost but that charged for treating others.

Along with its territorial expansion in 2014, ISIL started to impose levies on income. Income tax brackets ranged from 5 percent to 50 percent, but Christians paid an additional tax proportional to their income and tied to their "protected" (*dhimmi*) status. The movement also imposed a customs tax of 30 percent on goods entering its territory. ISIL funds were first and foremost used to finance the war, but also to reestablish social services (courts, health, education) and infrastructure (water, electricity, roads).[23] It also charged for these services: "I'm paying electricity, water and telephone bills every month to ISIL men, while the regime has started deducting telephone and electricity bills from my salary," a teacher from Raqqa lamented to the journalist Hala Kodmani.[24] At the same time, the Islamic State, following the regime's model, set up subsidized shops.[25] ISIL also continued to employ civil servants whose salaries were paid by the regime.

[21] I-109, in Afrin, January 2013.
[22] I-117, in Afrin, January 2014.
[23] ISIS report on the Aleppo governorate, June 26, 2014, http://justpaste.it/HalabReport, viewed September 10, 2014.
[24] Hala Kodmani, "Le système totalitaire de l'Etat islamique," *Libération*, August 8, 2014, www.liberation.fr/monde/2014/08/08/le-systeme-totalitaire-de-l-etat-islamique_1077864, viewed September 10, 2014.
[25] "Islamic State Works to Win Hearts, Minds with Bread," *Al Monitor*, March 29, 2014, http://www.al-monitor.com/pulse/originals/2014/07/islamic-state-bread-subsidies-syria-iraq-terrorism.html, viewed September 10, 2014.

Second, the wheat silos in northern Syria were a significant source of profit and hence of tension between armed groups. In Aleppo, the wheat supply fed clashes between Liwa' al-Tawhid, which monopolized 43,000 tons of wheat stocked in the al-Bab silos, and the other armed groups of the city. Early in 2013, with people protesting bread prices rising from 10 to 100 pounds, Aleppo's Municipality and Governorate Council, with the help of the Military Council, tried to negotiate a lower price with Liwa' al-Tawhid. However, it took the intervention of Jabhat al-Nusra and a judge from the Judicial Committee in the summer of 2013 to force Liwa' al-Tahwid to let Jabhat al-Nusra ship wheat and flour to Aleppo. "Before the war, a kilo of bread cost 10 pounds. During the war, the price has risen considerably. The Districts Councils had to restructure the supply chain of flour to bakers. A real improvement resulted when Jabhat al-Nusra regained distribution and put an end to corruption. The price of bread then fell back to 50 pounds."[26] In al-Bab, the creation of a Bread Committee in December 2012 helped resolve similar conflicts; its members included the mayor, a judge, and leaders of two groups, including Liwa' al-Tawhid.

Controlling oil and gas resources also became a key issue for the armed groups in Deir ez-Zor. "Insurgent units regularly attack oil wells, but fail to coordinate. This lack of unity has made it possible for independent groups to take control of oil fields and seize the income."[27] Until 2014, most oil and gas wells were controlled by local entrepreneurs who used their oil revenues to stockpile enough weapons to keep the FSA units at bay. In the summer of 2014, ISIL seized Deir ez-Zor's oil wells and artisanal refineries and also took control of the oil and industrial refineries in the Iraqi Sunni triangle (Bagdad-Ramadi-Tikrit). To gain momentum, ISIL negotiated alliances with clans previously dependent on the regime.[28] By pledging allegiance to ISIL, some managed to retain control of the oil wells they had seized. Similarly, in Iraq certain Sunni tribes regained the income streams from oil that they had lost after the fall of Saddam Hussein. Even though oil exploitation and export was a complex business, the significant sums at its disposal brought ISIL meaningful financial independence. For its part, the PYD controlled a number of Jazeera's oil and gas wells and sold their production to the regime.

Finally, armed groups sought to control economic flows, especially cross-border. Following the capture of Azaz in July 2012, Katibat 'Asifat al-Shimal boosted its influence by taking over the Bab al-Salam

---

[26] I-136, with the manager of a bread factory, in Aleppo, January 2013.

[27] I-57, with a Deir ez-Zor resident, in Gaziantep, September 2013.

[28] Felix Legrand, "The Colonial Strategy of ISIS in Syria," *Policy Alternative*, Arab Reform Initiative, 2014.

border post. Controlling the border let it tax vehicular traffic and goods and seize international aid shipments, all highly profitable activities. Transporting cash or aid necessitated negotiation with all actors stationed along the route they would take. The Syrian director of an NGO based in Turkey described his difficulties in getting aid shipments to northern Syria in the summer of 2013. "To get an aid truck into Syria and do a few kilometers, I need at least two weeks of negotiation with the various groups controlling the road. It is impossible to trust the Free Syrian Army leadership."[29] Furthermore, the PYD had control of the border with Iraqi Kurdistan, with a high volume of men, goods, and taxed vehicles crossing the border. However, tensions between the PKK and Barzani's Iraqi PDK led to repeated closure of the border. Controlling border posts was also central to ISIL's strategy. In 2013 and 2014, ISIL progressively took possession of border posts, first at Tal Abyad, where it initially shared revenues with Harakat Ahrar al-Sham al-Islamiyya, then at Jarablus and, briefly, at Bab al-Salam. Similarly, food sent by the Assistance Coordination Unit to the province of Raqqa in the summer of 2013 was confiscated by ISIL, which then distributed it in its own name. A few weeks later, ISIL closed down the town's last foreign exchange office, cutting off residents' access to remittances from abroad.[30] This strategy of depriving the insurrection of resources increased the resolve of most armed groups to confront ISIL in January 2014.

While these various levies were relatively organized, there were also more brutal forms of taking, namely looting, hostage taking and theft. Practices varied greatly from one group to another, as a businessman from Aleppo explained to us:

Armed groups' turnover is very quick, which makes it difficult to find people to speak with. The honest military units are mainly on the front, and concern themselves little over what happens behind the lines. So, to do business, a businessman must deal with the corrupt units that stay behind. You have to negotiate at every stage. For example, this is the situation in the north of Aleppo: Jabhat al-Nusra is said to not steal, but may confiscate merchandise if an emir wants to punish a shopkeeper for any fault, ISIL issues fatwas to confiscate goods; the units created after Aleppo was seized, like Liwa' Ahrar al-Suriyya, often steal and are particularly opportunistic, those created before the fall of Aleppo, like al-Tawhid, were honest at the start of the revolution and then became dishonest, notably due to the fact that the central leadership did not manage to control the armed groups under their command. For example, a

[29] I-75, in Antakya, September 2013.
[30] Alison Tahmizian Meuse, "Raqqa's FSA Brigades Join Jabhat al-Nusra," *Syria Deeply*, September 20, 2013, http://www.syriadeeply.org/articles/2013/09/2493/raqqas-fsa-brigades-join-jabhat-al-nusra/, seen September 10.

group may initially protect a factory in the name of the revolution, then suddenly decide, for one reason or another, to sell off the material for a tenth of its value.[31]

Some commanders drew substantial incomes from the war economy.

Being the leader of an armed group has many advantages. The commanders have nearly all become entrepreneurs and accumulated a lot of money. In general, the money does not make it down to the basic fighter, who has no idea about the funding networks of his bosses. This is why many of them do additional jobs and try to manage by on their own.[32]

In insurgent areas, designating an individual as *shabbiha* (a pro-regime militiaman) allowed his possessions to be confiscated or a ransom to be extorted from his family. Selling prisoners to the opposing camp occurred frequently. There are numerous accounts of flying checkpoints where vehicles were requisitioned and people were kidnapped for ransom. International aid was occasionally misappropriated, even stolen: "Most of the time NGOs have no contacts in Syria and no understanding," explained the head of an NGO based in Turkey, "they deliver aid without really knowing what happens next. Yet, sometimes, military groups seize it for their own ends."[33] Certain commanders systematically exploited a territory. One of the most well-known examples north of Aleppo is that of 'Umar Dadikhi, commander of the Liwa' 'Asifat al-Shimal.

Dadikhi is from the town of Azaz, which his armed group partly controls. It is a powerful position since this town provides access to the border post of Bab al-Salam with Turkey. Dadikhi took advantage of this to levy a tax of 300 pounds on vehicles passing through. He also managed to insert his men at the head of the city council. He thus controls the bulk of economic activity and aid coming from Turkey. In passing, he takes advantage of this to extort money, arrest people who criticise him and release them against ransoms paid by their family.[34]

Most insurgent groups resold weapons seized from the regular army among themselves, with supply networks extending into Iraq and Lebanon.

Outright looting was relatively rare and then mostly linked to the capture of new territories. When it seized Raqqa, Harakat Ahrar al-Sham al-Islamiyya plundered the gold stored in the local branch of the Central Bank of Syria. In zones nearer the front line, some districts were pillaged when armed groups moved in once the populace had already fled from the regime's bombings.

[31] I-1, in Antakya, September 2013.
[32] I-12, in Aleppo, January 2013.
[33] I-137, in Gaziantep, September 2013.
[34] I-52, in al-Ra'i, January 2013.

Plunder or Protection? The Tale of Two Aleppo Districts[35]

The question of looting by the FSA is complex. How armed groups conducted themselves varied significantly depending on the military context and the presence of local fighters. Comparing two districts in Aleppo, Bab al-Nasser and Salahaddin, both conquered in July 2012 and from then on part of the frontline, brings to light the factors that determined whether looting took place or not.

The district of Bab al-Nasser (the east entrance to the Old Town) was not looted. Even though the vast majority of the civilian population had fled, the shops remained undamaged and the padlocks on the metal shutters were not tampered with. The district was closely patrolled by military units and the remaining residents, some of whom belonged to the FSA. The efficacy of the control and the local origin of the military units accounts for the absence of looting.

Conversely, the newer Salahaddin district was systematically looted after the residents fled from the regime's bombing. From the very start, successive units on the front pillaged the neighborhood. Unlike in Bab al-Nasser, the front was not stable and the combatants only loosely controlled. In this context of impunity, entire apartment blocks were looted, with some commanders receiving bribes to turn a blind eye.

However, these predatory practices were relatively rare. The fighters came and went regularly to see their families and were in touch with other activists. The existence of these networks limited acts of looting and encouraged the fighters to protect public institutions (electrical generators, wheat silos, factories). The population was free to openly criticize these practices, was not brutalized, and, indeed, the most committed fighters attempted to restore order.[36]

On the regime side, the continual expansion of the security apparatus led to increased predatory practices. Recruitment into the militia or the security services ensured, in theory, a salary, but the regime often lacked the funds to pay its men. "On the regime's side, salaries are low and are not the principal motivation. The military is very poorly paid: militiamen earn $75 a month, policemen $70 to 75, a bodyguard for a politician earns about $100. It is very little. On the other hand, when you work for the regime, you can do anything you want ... "[37] Membership in the security apparatus made it possible to prey on the population with impunity. In an economy controlled by the

---

[35] Authors' personal observations, December 2012 and January 2013.
[36] Interviews carried out with militants and traders in various districts in Aleppo and in the towns/cities of al-Bab, al-Ra'i and Azaz, December 2012-January 2013.
[37] I-75, in Gaziantep, September 2013.

regime, members of the security services had access to numerous illegalities. "Normally, with the help of government subsidies, a kilo of bread costs 25 pounds, but in reality it rises to 120 to 130 pounds because militiamen control the bakeries in some districts and see to it that bread is sold at a higher price."[38] Another resident added: "The militiamen from the al-Baath brigade of Aleppo are some of the most corrupt, they hold all the rights and control supplies in several districts."[39] In the end, the sources of revenue inside Syria were insufficient to meet the needs of the armed groups, which therefore depended once again on outside support.

The Dependency of Syrian Actors

The constant need for resources created a momentum toward dependency that freed Syrian actors from local political constraints and encouraged radicalization of discourses and practices. The dependency came in two forms: the transfer of resources within transnational organizations and support by external actors. The two transnational actors, the PKK and ISIL, both created economic models based on self-reliance. The PKK's resources essentially came from the Kurdish diaspora in Europe and various smuggling activities, but the ambition was to make the three enclaves of Afrin, Ayn al-Arab, and Jazeera self-sufficient. ISIL initially received support from donors in the Gulf, but became financially independent via extortion of the Iraqi Sunni population and by taking control of the oil wells. Two other major actors, the FSA and the regime, were much more reliant on outside help.

The war had reduced the regime to a state of international economic dependency. While in 2010 Syrian debt had amounted to only 23 percent of GDP, by the end of 2013 it had risen to 126 percent and continued to grow.[40] Without aid from Russia and Iran, the regime would have faced collapse. The Syrian state lost all revenues derived from hydrocarbon exports, customs duties, and taxation. And, while revenues were reduced by three-quarters, spending had doubled. The regime imported nearly 500 million US dollars' worth of oil each month and increasing spending on the military added another 8 billion US dollars to its deficit between 2011 and the end of 2013.[41] To avoid a total currency collapse, the Central Bank of Syria depended largely on Russian subsidies.[42] Iran also lent the regime

---

[38] I-12, in Aleppo, January 2013.
[39] I-159, in Aleppo, August 2013.
[40] "Squandering Humanity," *Syrian Center for Policy Research*, May 2014, p. 24, http://scpr-syria.org/att/SCPR_Squandering_Humanity_En.pdf, viewed January 11, 2015.
[41] *Ibid.* p.23.
[42] Marek Menkiszak, *Responsibility to Protect . . . Itself? Russia's Strategy Towards the Crisis in Syria*, Helsinki, The Finnish Institute of International Affairs, 2013, www.fiia.fi/en/pub lication/341/responsibility_to_protect..._itself/, viewed September 11, 2014.

Table 12.1 *Revenues, expenditures, and budget deficit of the Syrian government (as % of GDP), 2010–2013*[43]

	Actual			Projected			
	2010	2011	2012	2013 Q1	2013 Q2	2013 Q3	2013 Q4
Revenue	22.7	17.4	9.8	10.4	4.8	8.4	10.9
Oil-related proceeds	7.0	5.0	2.9	2.6	1.4	1.4	1.3
Non-oil tax revenue	9.4	8.4	5.1	6.4	2.7	5.4	7.9
Non-oil non-tax revenue	6.3	4.0	1.8	1.4	0.7	0.8	0.6
Expenditure	24.9	26.3	30.0	41.7	28.4	39.4	40.3
Current expenditure	16.2	19.4	25.7	40.3	26.3	35.3	35.1
Wages and salaries	10.7	13.5	16.3	24.0	15.5	23.5	23.5
Goods and services	1.3	1.4	1.6	2.2	0.7	0.9	0.7
Interest payments	0.8	0.9	1.3	2.1	2.9	3.8	3.8
Subsidies and transfers	3.5	3.7	6.6	12.0	7.2	7.2	7.2
Development expenditure	8.7	6.9	4.3	1.4	2.2	4.1	5.2
Budget balance	−2.2	−8.9	−20.2	−31.3	−23.6	−31.9	−30.7
Budget balance with off budget subsidies	−2.2	−12.1	−33.7	−59.1	−40.1	−54.2	−53.7

* GDP in 2013 are seasonally adjusted

money: In 2013, it provided 3.6 billion US dollars for the purchase of petroleum products and subsequently disbursed a second loan of one billion US dollars to the regime.[44] Between 2011 and January 2014, Iran reportedly sent aid worth more than 15 billion US dollars to Syria.[45] Iran, Hezbollah, and Iraq also sent in-kind aid in the form of combatants and weapons. In addition, the UN – and, therefore, Western donors – indirectly subsidized the regime. Humanitarian aid to Syria had to pass through Damascus until July 2014 because the Russians vetoed any resolutions allowing aid to reach insurgent areas from neighboring countries.[46] The regime thus controlled

[43] "Squandering Humanity," *Syrian Center for Policy Research*, May 2014, p. 23, http://scpr-syria.org/att/SCPR_Squandering_Humanity_En.pdf, viewed January 11, 2015.

[44] Will Fulton, Joseph Holliday, Sam Wyer, *op. cit.*

[45] "The Interim Finance Minister: 15 Billion Dollars Iranian Support to Assad," *Syria Economic Forum*, January 24 2014, www.syrianef.org/En/?p=3029, viewed September 11, 2014.

[46] "Chine, Russie: le double veto qui protège la Syrie," *RFI*, May 22, 2014, www.rfi.fr/m oyen-orient/20140522-chine-russie-le-double-veto-protege-syrie-tchourkine-onu-cpi-j ustice-internati/, viewed September 19, 2014.

the bulk of the humanitarian aid and distributed it according to a political calculus, with Kurdish enclaves and insurgent-held areas on the whole excluded.

To help it stay in control, the regime kept to its policy of public sector employment. While more than 2.67 million jobs had disappeared since the start of the war,[47] the salaries of millions of remaining civil servants became the sole income for many extended families. Although the regime raised salaries regularly, it was not enough to offset inflation. For example, on March 24, 2011, a decree provided for a 30 percent raise for civil servants and military monthly pay under 10,000 pounds (200 US dollars), and a 20 percent increase for higher salaries.[48] A similar decree in June 2013 provided an increase of 40 percent in civil servant monthly salaries under 10,000 Syrian pounds (60 US dollars) and of 20 percent for higher salaries.[49] Pensions payments also increased, easing the fall in purchasing power. The regime continued paying salaries even in insurgent areas at least until 2013 as a token of sovereignty over these regions. From the beginning of 2013, however, individuals who occupied an official position in insurgent institutions were automatically cut from the regime payroll. The regime also subsidized basic products. In public bakeries in the regions held by Damascus, a kilo of bread officially cost 25 pounds in 2013, while prices varied between 80 and 300 pounds in the rest of the country. Likewise, gas cylinders cost 500 to 600 pounds, five to ten times less than in the rest of the country. Water, electricity, and petrol were similarly subsidized.

Unlike Damascus, which enjoyed the constant support of its allies, the insurrection was always on a quest for outside funding. Western countries sent little aid, despite supporting the insurrection diplomatically, and the Gulf States lacked a coherent aid strategy. Unlike in other civil wars (Afghanistan and Democratic Republic of Congo), the states financing the insurrection did not encourage the creation of organized political movements. In this, the Syrian situation differed from the Afghan war, where Pakistan determined which political parties received Western and Arab aid, and also from the war in the Democratic Republic of Congo, where Rwanda and Uganda controlled closely which groups received support. As for support from the Gulf, it was a combination of state and

[47] *Ibid.* p. 28.

[48] "Syrie/fonctionnaires: hausses de salaires," *Le Figaro*, March 24, 2011, www.lefigaro.fr/flash-actu/2011/03/24/97001-20110324FILWWW00688-syriefonctionnaires-hausse-de-salaires.php?cmtpage=0#comments-20110324FILWWW00688, viewed September 11, 2014.

[49] "Syrie: coup de pouce aux salaires des militaires et fonctionnaires, piliers du regime," *RFI*, June 22, 2013, www.rfi.fr/moyen-orient/20130622-syrie-hausse-salaires-militaires-fonctionnaires-piliers-regime/, viewed July 20, 2014.

private aid. Private donations came from Syrians connected with the Gulf States either because they had lived there or because of family ties. A multitude of donors and intermediaries opened their wallets to any group that made a name for itself on the Internet or exhibited fighting prowess. This dynamic contributed to a fragmentation of the insurgency since it meant that various armed groups could obtain resources through affiliating with large military coalitions.

13 New Identity Regimes

Although religion and ethnicity played only marginal roles in the 2011 protests, with time they became key factors in determining most political involvement. In a new context of the ever-growing centrality of identity politics, the divide between Sunni and non-Sunni emerged as the principal rift. While still prevalent in the north, the Kurd-Arab division at first was less significant, since Kurds were generally Sunni and tolerated Arab refugees in Kurdish regions. The formation of several distinct political territories (the regime's, PYD's, the Islamic State's, and the insurgency's) led to the parallel existence of competing identity regimes. Indeed, being Kurdish, Arab, Alawite, Christian, or Sunni had different implications depending on the location: in Latakia in the regime zone, in Raqqa dominated by the Islamic State, in Ayn al-Arab, a Kurdish town controlled by the PYD, or in the part of Aleppo held by various insurgent groups.

Notwithstanding the obvious emotional aspect, the sectarianization and ethnicization of politics may *also* be interpreted as a cynical strategy of mobilization. For the most radical movements, the hardening of sectarian or ethnic boundaries often left people with no choice but to support them. Thus, while few Syrian Kurds identified with Abdullah Öcalan, the historical leader of the PKK, and few Sunni Arabs adhered to the Islamic State's ideology, these two movements nevertheless managed, at least in part, to become the champions, respectively, of the Kurds and the Sunnis. The support of Iraqi Baath officials for the Islamic State gives an idea of the transgressions made possible when identity supplies the rationale for political alignments.

New Identity Hierarchies

From 2013 on, the regime, ISIL, and the PYD accelerated the sectarianization and ethnicization of the civil war. In their respective zones, this political polarization of identity was the result of their strategies, while, for the decentralized FSA, the process was much more confused and reactive. Regardless of their degree of internal cohesion, these policies triggered a feedback effect. The regime refocusing on non-Sunnis, the Kurdish ethnic nationalism of the PKK, and the Sunnitization of the insurgency resulted in exclusions that reverberated throughout the country. For the PKK and ISIL, the principle of belonging to the political community negated the Syrian borders, for the former in the name of Kurdish nationalism and the community of believers (*Umma*) for the latter, while the regime and the insurgents maintained a primarily national perspective. The establishment of an identity regime therefore was a redefinition, and at times an attempt at transcendence, of the nation-state framework. In Syria, these four political territories each developed their own identity regime: the Damascus regime, the PYD, ISIL, and the insurgents.

First, the territorial fragmentation of Syria meant the end of ethnic and sectarian balances previously maintained by the regime, which had coopted allies by applying political and economic rather than identity criteria. From this point on, the regime relied openly on minorities, starting with those it assimilated into the Shia fold. Consistent with a repressive strategy targeting Sunnis, the regime sought to militarize the minorities and use them as auxiliary forces. After 2011, the regime selectively deployed majority Alawite army units and security services to repress the uprising and fight the insurgency. The regime also established Alawite militias, which leant a sectarian edge to the battles. "From 2011, Alawite militia were placed in Latakia," a city resident testified, "the regime helped and armed them with a sole objective: to set them loose on the Sunnis, whoever they were. The aim was to ignite fear."[1] In a feedback effect, the policy made the Alawites increasingly dependent on the regime, despite the fact that many had frequently been critical of Bashar al-Assad, some ultimately castigating him as being the community's gravedigger. Likewise, the regime's strategy of preventing the Druze from taking part in the revolution gave them significant autonomy and cut them off from Sunni neighbors in Daraa province. The instrumentalization of ethnic and sectarian tensions was effected by manipulating incidents:

When the FSA kidnapped the son of a Druze general from Suweida near the city in April 2012, the regime immediately turned him into a national hero. But, instead of responding militarily, it delegated the repression to the Druze militia. They went to Daraa to take revenge and kidnapped Sunni students. Then, the regime asked the Druze sheikhs from Suweida to negotiate the hostage release. So, independent of this affair, they attempted to peacefully resolve the tensions

---

[1] I-101, with a sheikh from Latakia, in Antakya, September 2013.

and ensure there would be no further attacks between Druzes and Sunnis. But this conciliation only lasted a few months. Another armed group carried out kidnappings, most likely to extort money, and violence broke out once again.[2]

Likewise, the regime's sectarianization strategy reinforced the divides between Christians and Sunnis. Christians, faced with the rise of political Islam and the generalization of violence, protected themselves by forming their own militias. In parallel, Sunni populations were marginalized or forced into exile, especially by the security forces that suspected them of insurgency leanings.

Beyond the military aspect, the regime's strategy led to a restructuring of the political system by changing sectarian and ethnic balances. For Damascus, forming alliances with minorities (Christians, Druzes, Alawites) and marginalizing the Sunni Arabs on the political and economic level was its best bet for survival. With Sunnis making up the largest proportion of internally displaced people, economic power tilted to favor the relatively protected minorities and disadvantage the Sunni Arab majority. In addition, because the main combat zones were inhabited mostly by Sunnis, they also made up a large majority of the refugees. Despite the huge number of refugees, however, the demographic balance between Sunnis and non-Sunnis had not fundamentally shifted, since there was also a massive Christian exodus. It can be estimated that the proportion of the Sunni Arab population at 72.8 percent of the 21.6 million Syrians[3] did not change enough to strengthen the regime.

Second, the PYD in the territories under its control acted on an ideology that based political community on ethnicity.[4] The party cultivated Kurdish nationalism through cultural and military action. It established a conscription system that obligated Kurds to serve for a few days every two months or pay 5,000 Syrian pounds (approximately 40 US dollars in 2013). After July 2014, pressed by the Islamic State offensives in Ayn al-Arab and Jazeera, the PYD required all able-bodied men between the ages of 18 and 30 to enlist in the YPG (Yekineyen Parastina Gel – People's Protection Force) for six months. In schools, the language of instruction was in part Kurdish (it was Arabic during the Baath regime) and many cultural activities (festivals, writing and drawing workshops) promoted Kurdish identity. The cult of martyrs also affirmed a historical Kurdish destiny rather than a Syrian one. In every "People's House" (Mala Gel), a room was dedicated to memorializing PKK martyrs. Hundreds of portraits with mountainous

---

[2] I-108, in Amman, October 2013.

[3] See Table 1.1, Chapter 1.

[4] In theory, all residents, regardless of ethnicity or religion, were represented by the bodies controlled by the PYD. In reality, one must be affiliated with the PYD, hence Kurd, to have access to positions.

backgrounds and a Kalashnikov planted in the ground, symbolizing armed struggle and martyrdom, were displayed in them. The party colors (yellow, red, and green), photographs, and Öcalan sayings adorned the walls and the portraits. Behind this display of Kurdish popular commitment to the PKK, the political propaganda promoted a political model that excluded non-Kurds. Although this meant that Arabs were marginalized, it did not prevent the Kurds from collaborating with them, especially on the military level. Faced with the rise of ISIL in the summer of 2014, Kurds and Arabs thus fought side by side. Arab villages surrounding the Ayn al-Arab enclave in the north put themselves under PYD protection against the Islamic State and hosted Kurdish institutions. FSA fighters sheltering in the Kurdish zones were commanded by the YPG in battling the Islamic State, with some Arabs actually enlisting in the YPG.

Third, in areas that it seized, the Islamic State installed a very strict sectarian hierarchy. To be Sunni was a prerequisite for having a place in the religious and political communities, the two being indistinguishable. The new caliphate had the ambition of uniting all Sunnis regardless of nationality. Minorities were persecuted, killed, or forced to flee. When the Islamic State seized the city of Raqqa, in the autumn of 2013, it pillaged the two churches and organized a bonfire of Christian books. Pursuant to an agreement with the city's bishop, the Greek Orthodox Our Lady of the Annunciation church was still operating in mid-2015, while the al-Shuhada Armenian Church was transformed into a center of Islamic preaching.[5] In Deir ez-Zor, the Armenian Church was destroyed in September 2014. The Christians who chose to stay were declared *dhimmi* (protected persons) and had to pay the head tax (*jiziyya*). They were also subject to significant restrictions on their religious practices. Most Christians left the city as a result and had their possessions confiscated by the Islamic State.[6] The Islamic State came down especially hard on Shias, denying them any religious status and thereby depriving them of any rights. Alawites were declared heretics (*murtad*) and driven out or killed. The Islamic State's conquests in Iraqi territory drove out millions of people.[7] The Christians of Mosul and the Yazidis of Sinjar for the most part fled to the Kurdish regions or even overseas. Mixed areas disappeared and the Shiites abandoned Tal Afar, Tikrit, and Mosul to resettle south of Ramadi

---

[5] Aymenn Al-Tamimi, "The Islamic State of Iraq and ash-Sham's Dhimmi Pact for the Christians of Raqqa Province," *Syria Comment*, February 26, 2014, www.joshua landis.com/blog/islamic-state-iraq-ash-shams-dhimmi-pact-christians-raqqaprovince/, viewed September 9, 2014.

[6] Chris Looney, "Al-Qaeda's Governance Strategy in Raqqa," *Syria Comment*, December 8, 2013, www.joshualandis.com/blog/al-qaedas-governance-strategy-raqqa-chris-looney, viewed September 11, 2014.

[7] See the UNHCR Iraq data, www.unhcr.org/pages/49e486426.html#.

and north of Baghdad, areas cleansed of Sunnis. During the summer of 2014, the Islamic State slaughtered hundreds of Shiite soldiers, retouching the videos of the execution to heighten the brutality of the images. The Yazidis, since they did not qualify as People of the Book (*Ahl al-Kitab*) were classified as polytheists. Consequently, the men were told to convert and executed if they refused. They were slaughtered by the hundreds in Kocho, Qiniya, and Jdali. Some 5,000 were forced to convert in the villages near Tal Afar. Moreover, the Islamic State enslaved and sold some 3,000 Yazidi women between the ages of 10 to 35. Considered as "spoils of war" (*al-Ghana'im al-Harbiyya*, a Koranic term), four-fifths were shared among the fighters and the remainder given to the Islamic State. Some of them were publicly sold in the markets of Raqqa and Mosul; others were detained, raped, and resold by the fighters.[8]

Finally, in the insurgent-controlled territories, political participation was contingent on being Sunni. While the protests were inclusive in 2011, from 2013 on the insurgent discourses rarely included Alawites in the envisioned political system. The most radical Islamists reduced Christians to "protected" (*dhimmi*) status. Certain groups were therefore beyond the pale: Christians, Druzes, Alawites, Shias, and Ismaelis. These minorities had their possessions pillaged on the pretext that they were regime collaborators. Living in perpetual insecurity, they fled to regime-controlled areas. Protesters and fighters belonging to minorities, despite their revolutionary credentials, were also affected. An Alawite was urged to leave Damascus and stated she could no longer enter rebel zones notwithstanding her engagement from the start of the protests.[9] A Druze commander in the Idlib region, having led a unit of several hundred men, left Syria at the beginning of 2014 after receiving death threats.[10] Similarly, in April 2014, the supply convoy of an insurgent Trotskyist group, the People's Liberation Faction, was stopped by Jabhat al-Nusra at a checkpoint. An attempt to disarm Christian and Ismaeli fighters resulted in several deaths on both sides.[11] Until 2013, Christians were able to participate in the protests and other political activities in insurgent areas,

---

[8] Interview with Viyan Dakheel, Yazidi deputy at Iraqi Parliament, Erbil, March 5, 2015; see also Amnesty international, "Escape from Hell: Torture and Sexual Slavery in Islamic State Captivity in Iraq," December 2014, www.es.amnesty.org/uploads/media/Escape_from_hel l_-_Torture_and_sexual_slavery_in_Islamic_State_captivity_in_Iraq_-_English.pdf; United Nation, "Report of the Independent International Commission of Inquiry on the Syrian Arab Republic," November 14, 2014, www.ohchr.org/Documents/HRBodies/HRCouncil/CoISyria/HRC_CRP_ISIS_14Nov2014.pdf; the Islamic State boast about these events in his monthly Magazine, "The Failed Crusade," *Dabiq* 4, http://media.clarionproject.org/files/isl amic-state/islamic-state-isis-magazine-Issue-4-the-failed-crusade.pdf.

[9] I-103, in Gaziantep, September 2013.

[10] Communication with Felix Legrand, September 2014.

[11] *Ibid.*

but their situation became increasingly fraught. By 2013, Alawite exclusion was largely normalized. A sheikh from Latakia, who took part in the first demonstrations and in 2012 supported the formation of Alawite units within the Free Syrian Army, a year later wrote poems calling for their corpses to be urinated on.[12] Such outrages were encouraged by the arrival of foreign combatants, notably from Iraq. "Combatants from Jabhat al-Nusra were the first ones to introduce slogans to form a caliphate and exclude Alawites and Christians. And it was the same in some of the mosques."[13] An Alawite risked his life, or at least his freedom and possessions, by remaining in insurgent zones, while Christians were routinely harassed and extorted. Though Kurds were subject to abuse, they were treated much better in comparison. Some brigades continued to be mixed, for example the Liwa' Fajr al-Hurriyya (Brigade of the Dawn of Freedom), Liwa' Shams al-Shimal (Brigade of the Northern Front), and especially Jabhat al-Akrad (The Front of the Kurds), which was made up mainly of Kurds, some of whom lived in the Kurdish districts of Aleppo, Ashrafiyya, and Sheikh Maqsood.

Christian, Alawite, and Kurd participation in the insurgency therefore continued to shrink and, in essence, was restricted to representative bodies in Turkey and Europe. Still, even exile circles were affected by the ethnicization and sectarianization of the conflict, with competitive victimhood generating rival hierarchies of suffering. Still, while the close relations between the insurgency's representative institutions and the Muslim Brotherhood contributed to sectarianization, the opposition in exile remained vastly more inclusive.

Discrimination

Three mutually reinforcing practices sustained the new identity hierarchies: discrimination, violence, and discourse. They also had the indirect effect of legitimizing reprisals.

First, discrimination, whether written into the law or informal, played a decisive role in relations between groups. Where each community had its own family law before the 2011 revolution, the application of Sharia law in insurgent-held areas led to discrimination against non-Muslims, all the more systematically by being more rigorously enforced. The issue of the legal status of Alawites – are they Muslims or heretics? – and of Christians was a recurring topic of discussion in insurgent areas. When tribunals were established, the Free Syrian Lawyers (al-Muhamin al-Suriyyin al-Ahrar)

[12] I-101, in Antakya, September 2013.
[13] I-138, in Aleppo, January 2013.

opposed the sheikhs that supported the application of discriminatory measures. In the regions under Islamic State control, the application of Sharia law was a key tool for enslaving non-Sunnis. Beyond the confines of the law, all groups faced discriminatory practices. Arab refugees, for example, often had to pay double, if not more, for living quarters in the Kurdish enclave of Afrin. "If you are Kurdish, you stand a much better chance of getting by in Afrin," a refugee Arab doctor, who worked in one of the PYD hospitals, explained,[14] "despite being a qualified doctor, which stands me in good stead, I had a great deal of trouble finding decent accommodations." What is more, Sunni refugees fleeing the Syrian army bombings were housed in tents or abandoned houses and received UN aid distributed by the regime. The Alawites on the coast, fearing an influx of Sunnis, met them with hostility. At the same time, Alawites fleeing rebel zones were given shelter in homes vacated by Sunnis who had fled. In insurgent-held zones, Christians were subjected to systematic extortion. A Christian could be forced to give money or medicines to an FSA commander in exchange for the release of fellow Christians.[15] Christians we met in Aleppo avoided the rebels or relied on personal contacts in the insurgency to protect their possessions. Finally, identity checks at roadblocks signaled to minority groups in insurgent areas and Sunni Arabs in regime- and PYD-controlled areas that they were suspect or undesirable. Many Kurds were arrested north of Aleppo on suspicion of being PYD collaborators. For non-Sunnis, the mere presence of an Islamic State checkpoint *de facto* kept them from traveling on that road. In 2013, Islamic State combatants broadcast their slaughter of three Alawite truck drivers.[16]

Second, the strategic use of violence by political actors played a key role in redefining intercommunal relationships. The regime's bombing of Sunni districts in Latakia and Aleppo widened the gulf between Sunnis and Alawites. Similarly, the ISIL massacre of hundreds of Alawites north of Latakia and of Ismaelis near Salamiyah imposed a sectarian template on the war that made compromise impossible. Sacred sites were destroyed to further incite hatred. In March 2014, when ISIL strengthened its grip on Raqqa province, it destroyed the Uways al-Qarni tomb, an important Shia pilgrimage site.[17] Earlier, insurgents had destroyed the grave markers of saints in areas they controlled. In January 2013, we watched as a tomb in the old town was vandalized over the protests of

[14] I-120, in Afrin, January 2013.
[15] Personal observations in Aleppo, January 2013.
[16] "Islamic State in Iraq Executes Syrian Truck Drivers," www.youtube.com/watch?v=z F35a5E0uss, viewed October 4, 2014.
[17] "Shiite shrine bombed by ISIL in Syria's Raqqa," *ARA news*, May 16, 2014, http://aranews .net/2014/05/shiite-shrine-bombed-by-isil-in-syrias-raqqa/, consulted September 11, 2014.

both fighters and local residents. Even intervention by Liwa' Ahrar Suriya was not enough to save it.[18] In addition, the destruction, deliberate or otherwise, of religious places during the fighting heightened tensions, such as the regime's bombardment of the tomb of Sunni cleric Sheikh Muhammad Adib Hassun in October 2012, or the damage inflicted on the shrine of the Shia saint Sakina Bint Ali in Daraya in February 2013. In this context, protecting sacred sites (the Sunni mosque Khalid ibn al-Walid in Homs, and the Shia mausoleum of Sayyida Zaynab south of Damascus) represented a challenge separate from fighting the war.

Third, the categories used to frame events and actors played a role in exacerbating the crisis. The regime's designation of revolutionaries as "Sunni Islamists" or "terrorists affiliated with al-Qaida" became performative. On the other side, characterizing the regime as Alawite reinforced the sectarian reading of the conflict. During the summer of 2013, our interviewees often distinguished Alawites from Sunnis in videos based on phenotypes. The pejorative use of the term *nussayrin* to describe Alawites was part of the same trend. In the same vein, the term PKK was often used in insurgent areas to stigmatize Kurds. Jokes and stereotypes reinforced sectarian divisions. The violence practiced by the insurgents was simplistically attributed to Sunni Arab poverty and lack of education, while the insurgents often pointed to the supposedly questionable mores of the Alawites. The escalation of that hatred between our first visit to Aleppo and our second fieldwork was patently obvious to us. Alawites had never been the targets of revolutionary songs in the winter of 2012–2013, whereas by the summer of 2013, they were being systematically denigrated.

Rumors that reinforced negative stereotypes played an important role in this context. Starting in 2012, Alawites fled zones conquered by insurgents despite there having been no massacres yet and even though inclusive revolutionary discourse still dominated. The insurgents often interpreted their having fled as proof that they had links to the regime. Both sides traded accusations that sacred sites had been destroyed by the other. In the last months of the battle for Homs, the regime was accused of plotting to destroy the Khalid ibn al-Walid mosque.[19] Syrian journalists and the Arab media were complicit in the spread of these rumors, which exacerbated sectarian hostilities. More generally, the effects of violence and destruction were multiplied by being disseminated in the media and on social networks. Video played as significant a role in the civil war as it

---

[18] Observations in Aleppo, January 2013.
[19] "Les forces d'Assad détruisent le sanctuaire de Khalid ibn al-Walid à Homs," *Al Arabiya*, July 22, 2013, viewed October 4, 2014.

had during the peaceful phase of the protests. In many cases, broadcast strategies were unnecessary: Fighters or bystanders spontaneously took videos of violent scenes with their cell phones and shared them via YouTube and Facebook. Likewise, the regime, at the very minimum, turned a blind eye to the diffusion of videos showing torture and cruel treatment meted out by its soldiers or militiamen. Syrians had collections of extremely violent videos on their computers and telephones, which they would show at *a priori* inappropriate occasions, such as a family dinner.[20] This fascination with violent images, which was also widespread in Libya, Pakistan, and Iraq but not in Afghanistan, may be attributable to the coarsening induced by the brutal, rapid plunge into acute violence.

Complexity and Ambiguity of Identities

Amid these tensions, individuals confronted complex situations, especially in terms of movement, in which they tried to make the best of their multiple, often ambiguous identities. Many Syrians continued to travel between areas variously held by the regime, PYD, and insurgents. In Aleppo, a transit point between the government- and rebel-controlled parts of the city remained open. Despite the danger from regime snipers who would randomly target people crossing the no-man's-land, thousands of people passed through it every day to visit family or go to work. Similarly, buses linking Aleppo with Damascus travelled through successive regime- and insurgent-controlled zones. For instance, we met a Sunni Arab doctor who worked both at the hospital in PYD-controlled Afrin and in a hospital in Aleppo's insurgent controlled part. Commuters had to negotiate roadblocks where checks were erratic: sometimes purely visual, at other times an ID would be demanded. Often the name and the place of birth appearing on identity cards suggested religious affiliation. Many people therefore developed dissimulation strategies: fake documents, payoffs, or detours to avoid roadblocks. For instance, one revolutionary would hide his Palestinian origins so he could cross regularly from East to West Aleppo because the regime suspected Palestinians of collaborating with the insurgents.[21] An Alawite took advantage of her gender to take part in a documentary in insurgent areas, concealing her face under a veil and blending in with a group of Sunni friends.[22] Moreover, it was common to make local arrangements, including between villages of different religious denominations,

---

[20] Videos of decapitations and summary executions, under sometimes atrocious conditions, show violence against both the enemy and their own group. Victimization mentality does not seem to dominate.

[21] I-160, with a Palestinian living in Aleppo, in Aleppo, January 2013.

[22] I-139, in Gaziantep, September 2013.

which made movement possible. North of Latakia, for example, where there were no foreign fighters and elite regime troops, the militias tended to be more accommodating.[23]

Some individuals had heterogeneous identities, and made use of this ambiguity. The daughter of an Alawite-Sunni couple from Latakia managed to keep in touch with the revolutionary circles in Tripoli (Lebanon) as a Sunni, but also enter Latakia's Alawite districts. However, she skirted insurgent-held areas as dangerous.[24] Many Kurdish students at the University of Aleppo passed themselves off as Kurds in the PYD-controlled areas and as Sunnis in insurgent territories. Even when tensions between the PYD and the insurgency were at their height in the summer of 2013, they were able to commute between Aleppo and the Kurdish enclaves.

In addition, exile allowed more flexible treatment of identity. In Istanbul, a protester gave lessons to all children eager to learn without regard to their religious or ethnic origin. International organizations provided resources to Syrians willing to look beyond ethnic and sectarian divisions. Thus, the Beirut offices of the German Friedrich Ebert Foundation were directed by an Alawite female revolutionary; she took part in many documentary film and art collectives with both Sunnis and Christians.[25]

---

[23] I-75, in Antakya, September 2013.
[24] I-103, in Gaziantep, September 2013.
[25] I-139, in Gaziantep, September 2013.

Conclusions

The results of this Syria case study, despite being limited by difficulties in field access and the scarcity to this day of published works, confirms for us the interest inherent in our research agenda. In the first place, Syria at war meets our definition of civil wars: the regime, the insurgency, the PKK, and the Islamic State have installed competing social orders, each with its own administrative apparatus, economy, and differentiated identity regime. Moreover, the hypotheses we developed in our prefatory remarks did indeed guide our investigation through three inquiries: the passage to civil war, the territorialization and competition among armed groups, and the variability of the different species of capitals. In this respect, one of this work's limitations is our inability to validate the propositions we make for individual dispositions to act, competencies, and decision-making. While we take this dimension into account in the case of the 2011 mobilizations, the actual conditions on the ground prevented us from developing it as regards to other aspects of the civil war in a satisfactory manner. Moreover, while we tried to confine ourselves to answering the questions drawn from the prolegomena, we did not approach the Syrian case as a mechanical application of a model, which poses the problem of confronting the case study with the starting hypotheses. If Syria conforms to the model in most points, it also presents certain features that call for an *ad hoc* explanation.

In concluding this study, it may therefore be useful to review what it is in our results that validate or invalidate our hypotheses. Specifically, what could we have said about the probable evolution of the crisis at its different stages? Our model allows the identification of the sequence of situations already detected in other conflicts in a comparative, probabilistic, and non-nomological perspective. *A contrario*, also of interest is to show the sequences on which the general model is silent. As it turned out, some evolutions were indeed more probable than others, confirming previous works on Afghanistan.

The (Limited) Predictability of Syria's Path

What predictions can we draw from our model and how does the Syrian case confirm (or not) our hypotheses? Without going into great detail, we propose to exhibit two series of hypotheses, one that is specific to situations of going to war by acephalous mobilizations and another, more general, which takes into account the limited predictability of the Syrian trajectory.

In point of fact, Syria's path seems to correlate relatively well with three hypotheses that can be proposed to account for the passage to civil war specifically in a situation where there are no preexisting armed groups. *First, a social system marked by transversal role (present in the principal fields) of the security apparatus or the dominant party tends to favor a model of acephalous protest in the form of massive and rare demonstrations.* From this point of view, Syria represents almost a pure case of such mobilization without mobilizer, particularly comparable to the Iran of 1979, East Germany in 1989, and Libya in 2011. Second, *the regime's violence that touches off the entry into civil war presupposes its ability to hold on to the security institutions.* A large-scale repression is made all the easier if the security apparatus is incapable of separating from the regime (e.g., when it is fragmented or weakly institutionalized). *A contrario*, the Egyptian and Tunisian cases show the decisive impact of the security institutions defecting in the fall of the regime. Third, *the regime's withdrawal is marked by the practically immediate rebuilding of institutions that often are highly local.* This hypothesis is especially well validated in the Syrian case; however, it is specific due to the disconnection between civil institutions and armed groups. Indeed, in a number of mobilizations from below that lead to civil war, the groups very rapidly become politico-military structures. This Syrian peculiarity is explained by the action of militant networks that develop during the street demonstrations and in part remain distinct from the military groups.

In addition, the Syrian case allows validating certain hypotheses of a more general nature. For one, *the competition between armed groups tends to favor those that are adept at accumulating resources, which reflects their relative degree of bureaucratization.* In Syria, the less-structured groups were systematically eliminated in favor of organizations with leaders and strong discipline. The same logic tends to favor the unification of armed groups and the homogenization of political territories, whether by peaceful means or not. It also confirms that economic logics (sharing of indivisible goods and resources) lack the power to stop the fighting. The Syrian case is specific in the initial phase as the armed groups are not territorialized and as the fighters move from group to group. This peculiarity probably relates to the quasi-absence of parties or political groups sufficiently implanted to furnish the base for a military organization.

In the second place, *the international system tends to foster the stability of borders and thus to limit the chances of success for groups that challenge them.* In this sense, the Islamic State and the PKK are outsiders whose survival as territorialized entities in Syria collides with the question of international recognition. The constraints of the international system disadvantage actors whose project is incompatible with re-forming a state and the stability of borders. The conservative logic of the international system passes through legal categories such as terrorism, diplomatic support, or the action of international organizations, without these different actors necessarily having as their project participating in or maintaining the rules of the game. The strategies of the armed actors confirm this hypothesis. The regime and the insurgency have retained national goals and rejected any idea of partitioning. Jabhat al-Nusra and the PYD have progressively discarded their transnational ambitions, at least publicly, reaffirming as their aims, respectively, the overthrow of Bashar al-Assad and setting up a federal regime. The sole movement to have continually denied the national frontiers, the Islamic State, has federated the ensemble of local and international actors, including those, like the Kurdistan Regional Government of Iraq and Saudi Arabia, which had an interest in supporting it against the Iraqi regime. Its disappearance as a territorial entity appears as the direct corollary of its negation of the contemporary international order.

Finally, *the external actors (states, IOs, NGOs, transnational parties) have a major role in the models of governance.* The Syrian case validates this proposition, but it remains specific due to the importance of transnational groups that impose their governance models on a substantial part of the territory. In effect, the insurgency's governance model is very much linked to the external actors, from which it expects support and financing. Moreover, Russia's and Iran's growing importance and, even more so, Hezbollah's in the Syrian security apparatus profoundly alters the regime's nature, which, in part, is passing under foreign tutelage. However, the governance models of the PKK and the Islamic State are less influenced by the foreign actors to the conflict than by their history in the countries where they formed. Thus, the PKK's Autonomous Administration results foremost from its Turkish experience of the 1990s and 2000s, while the caliphate's institutions derive from the Islamic State's genesis during the American occupation of Iraq between 2003 and 2009.

Regarding the points detailed above, the Syrian trajectory therefore appears to be relatively predictable, contrary to the widespread perception that it is an exceptional war. Moreover, Syria is a good example of a particular chaining: protests without organizer, multiplicity of armed groups, progressive consolidation by eliminating the less well organized, high dependence on outside for resources. The comparison with Afghanistan and Libya therefore imposes itself, at least within the theoretical framework that we have chosen. The traits specific to Syria – initial disconnection between civilian and military institutions, fluidity among groups, importance of non-Syrian actors – reflect the absence beforehand of political parties, the importance of networks of peaceful protesters, and the regional context, including the American occupation of Iraq and the Kurdish issue.

Moments of Indetermination

The predictability that we assume runs directly counter to the tendency toward teleological argumentation, which particularly affects analysts in this type of situation. Such reinterpretation of data by working backward from the final results is most often manifested in the fact of detecting simple explanatory causes of the final result, in this case the sectarian variable. The risk then becomes one of ignoring the chronology and interpreting 2011 in the light of subsequent events. So, when some argue that *from the outset* the protesters were radical Islamists, this is a false analysis, but the error is a hallmark of extant work that seeks to impose a particular narrative on the civil war. The problem is magnified by the fact that the story of the first events is largely oral, meaning that the participants are reconstructing the past rapidly with omnipresent ideological stakes. In actuality, a precise analysis of the *turning points* in the crisis demonstrates a strong degree of unpredictability at different moments. Investigating the moments of *indetermination* helps to refute the idea of an inevitable situation and to underline the part played by contingency and chance – the interaction of a series of independent causes – in a war for which external forces are *critical*.

Where can we empirically show these zones of indetermination? They undoubtedly exist in certain strategic decisions and in the hazards of war, but, above all, the Syrian war presents the characteristic of a very strong international involvement. Iranian troops, Iraqi militias, Hezbollah, Turkey, and Russia fight in Syria; American advisors are present on the side of the PKK. Two of the conflict's principal actors, the PKK and the Islamic State, are transnational movements whose objectives are not specifically Syrian. The regime's advances are very largely linked to its foreign supporters, and the insurgency cannot survive without a sanctuary and outside financing. Thus, a series of *turning points* comes into focus:

Hezbollah's involvement in the war in 2013, the choice by the United States to refrain from bombing the regime in 2013, the confrontation between Saudi Arabia and Qatar in 2013, the collapse of the Iraqi security forces in Mosul in the summer of 2014, the war in Yemen that distracts the Gulf States' attention, the intervention by Russia in September 2015 or again the limiting of the Turkish intervention on its border in August 2016. For the most part, the war's dynamics are remarkably overdetermined by non-Syrian issues, multiplying the relevant causality chains.

Here the case of the American policy furnishes a good example, both because the sources are – comparatively – easier to access and because the decisions made in Washington probably were the determining factor. It shows the strong part played by contingency in decisions made out of complex considerations in which Syria probably had a marginal place. Thus, the shifts in American policy are decisive (without American support, the insurgency is for all intents and purposes doomed), but they are not the expression of very well defined strategic interests. By comparison, the actions by Iran, by Hezbollah, or by Turkey reflect more strategic coherence due to the major costs of a defeat in Syria, which makes their actions more predictable. Conversely, the power struggles in Washington to this day are impossible to model and, in any case, far outside our knowledge interests. In particular, the swing in the fall of 2013 appeared to be largely random, for the United States was ready to hit the regime for using chemical weapons against the population, but the negative vote in the British Parliament led to the strikes being aborted on the eve of the intended start date. Opponents of the Syrian insurgency, notably the US president's deputy national security advisor, Ben Rhodes, and the former head of the International Crisis Group think tank, Robert Malley, seized the moment to make their point of view prevail. They organized the liquidation of the Syrian insurgency, which accelerated with the emergence of the Islamic State a year later: freezing of the southern front, withholding of military assistance, calling on Russia, rendering support to the PKK. In this case at least, these actors anticipated accurately enough the consequences of their actions.

Annex

Interviews

Codes	Location of the interview	Date of the interview	Sex	Religion /ethnicity	Place of origin	Profession or status before 2011	Political activities and position at the time of the interview
I-1	Antakya	Sep-13	M	Arab Christian	Aleppo	Businessmen, member of a prominent family	Took part in the protests, continues trading
I-2	Maraa	Dec-12	M	Arab Sunni	Maraa	Former student, unemployed	Took part in the protests, fighter in an armed group in Maraa
I-3	al-Bab	Dec-12	M	Arab Sunni	al-Bab	Primary school teacher	Took part in the protests, head of al-Bab local council
I-4	Antakya, Ganziantep	Sep-13	F	Arab Sunni	Idlib	Self-employed dressmaker	Took part in the protests, activist in Idlib then member of Idlib Governorate Council
I-5	Erbil	Dec-12	M	Kurd	Qamishli	Professor of Political Science, university of Erbil	Took part in the protests, no political affiliation. In exile in Iraqi Kurdistan after 2004
I-6	Erbil	Jan-12	M	Kurd	Damascus	Shopkeeper, militant of the Patriotic Union of Kurdistan until 2004	took part in the protests in 2011, no political affiliation
I-7	Aleppo	Dec-12 Aug-13	M	Arab Sunni	Aleppo	Student	Took part in the protests, member of al-Sukari District Council in Aleppo
I-8	Maraa	Dec-12	M	Arab Sunni	Maraa	Student	Took part in the protests, in Maraa
I-9	Aleppo	Aug-13	M	Arab Sunni	Aleppo	Primary school teacher	Employee of the Aleppo City Council
I-10	Gaziantep	Sep-13	F	Arab Sunni	Damascus	Employed by an international organization	Employee in a Western NGO
I-11	Maraa	Dec-12	M	Arab Sunni	Maraa	Retired primary school teacher	Employee in the Maraa Local Council

I-12	Aleppo	Dec-12 Jan-13	M	Arab Sunni	Aleppo	Student in English	Took part in the protests, media activist in Aleppo
I-13	al-Bab	Dec-12	M	Arab Sunni	al-Bab	Unemployed	Took part in the protests in al-Bab
I-14	Istanbul	Sep-13	F	Arab Sunni	Damascus	Employee in a Western NGO	Took part in the protests, employee of a Western private company in Turkey
I-15	Istanbul	Sep-13	M	Arab Sunni	Homs	Manager in a large company in Homs	Took part in the protests, employee of a Western private company in Turkey
I-16	Aleppo	Aug-13	M	Arab Sunni	Aleppo	Student, day laborer	Took part in the protests, activist in Aleppo
I-17	Aleppo	Aug-13	M	Arab Sunni	Aleppo	IT employee in Aleppo	Took part in the protests, activist and member of Aleppo City Council
I-18	Aleppo, al-Bab	Jan-13	M	Arab Sunni	Aleppo	Student	Took part in the protests, member of the Revolutionary Security of Aleppo
I-19	Aleppo	Aug-13	F	Arab Sunni	Aleppo	Doctor	Took part in the protests, doctor
I-20	Istanbul	Jul-13	M	Arab Sunni	Damascus	Teacher of Arabic in Syria	Former communist militant, took part in the protests, in exile in Turkey, where he teaches Arabic
I-21	al-Bab	Dec-12	M	Arab Sunni	al-Bab	Day laborer	Took part in the protests
I-22	Aleppo	Dec-12	M	Arab Sunni	Aleppo	Shopkeeper	Took part in the protests in Aleppo, activist, participates in civil institutions in al-Sukari neighborhood (Aleppo)
I-23	Aleppo	Dec-12	M	Arab Sunni	Aleppo	Unknown	Took part in the protests
I-24	al-Bab	Dec-12	M	Arab Sunni	al-Bab	Shopkeeper	Took part in the protests, member of City Council in al-Bab
I-25	al-Bab	Dec-12	M	Arab Sunni	al-Bab	Unemployed	Activist, member of a police unit

(cont.)

Codes	Location of the interview	Date of the interview	Sex	Religion /ethnicity	Place of origin	Profession or status before 2011	Political activities and position at the time of the interview
I-26	Aleppo	Aug-13	M	Arab Sunni	Aleppo	Student	Took part in the protests, leader of an armed group in Aleppo
I-27	Urfa	Sep-13	M	Kurd	Raqqa	Shopkeeper	Took part in the protests in Raqqa, refugee in Turkey
I-28	Cairo	Jan-14	M	Arab Sunni	Damascus	Businessman	Took part in the protests, refugee in Egypt
I-29	Amman	Oct-13	M	Arab Sunni	Daraa	Civil servant, engineer	Took part in the protests in Daraa, Homs and Damas, then employee of a Western NGO in Jordan
I-30	Azaz	Dec-12	M	Arab Sunni	Azaz	English teacher	Did not take part in the protests
I-31	Azaz	Dec-12 Jan-13	M	Arab Sunni	Azaz	Imam and student of Islamic law	Took part in the protests, member of the Judicial Committee in Azaz
I-32	Erbil	Feb-12	M	Kurd	Qamishli	Unknown	PDKS militant, refugee in Erbil
I-33	Aleppo	Dec-12	M	Arab Sunni	Aleppo	Shopkeeper	Took part in the protests in Aleppo
I-34	Azaz	Dec-12	M	Arab Sunni	Aleppo	Civil servant	Took part in the protests in Aleppo
I-35	Amman	Oct-13	M	Arab Sunni	Daraa	Civil servant	Took part in the protests in Daraa, refugee in Jordan
I-36	Istanbul	Sep-13	M	Arab Sunni	Homs	Civil servant	Took part in the protests in Homs, refugee in Turkey, employee in a Western security company
I-37	Aleppo	Jan-13	M	Arab Sunni	Aleppo	Shopkeeper	Took part in the protests in Aleppo Participate in the activities of the Aleppo City Council
I-38	Aleppo	Jan-13	M	Arab Sunni	Aleppo	Student	Took part in the protests in Aleppo, leader of an armed group
I-39	Azaz	Dec-12	M	Arab Sunni	Azaz	Day laborer	Took part in the protests in Azaz, head of Azaz police force

I-40	Maraa	Dec-12	M	Arab Sunni	Maraa	Shopkeeper	Took part in the protests, combatant in armed group from Maraa Aleppo
I-41	Aleppo	Dec-12	M	Arab Sunni	Maraa	Policeman	Took part in the protests, leader of an armed group from Maraa, fighting in Aleppo
I-42	Maraa	Dec-12	M	Arab Sunni	Maraa	Shopkeeper	Took part in the protests, combatant in armed group from Maraa fighting in Aleppo
I-43	Azaz	Dec-12	M	Arab Sunni	Azaz	Student	Syrian army deserter
I-44	al-Bab	Dec-12	M	Arab Sunni	-	Non-commissioned officer in the Syrian Army	Defect in 2011, take charge of deserters in al-Bab
I-45	Aleppo	Jan-13	M	Arab Sunni	Aleppo	Unemployed	Took part in the protests in Aleppo, member of an armed group
I-46	Aleppo	Jan-13	M	Arab Sunni	Aleppo	Shopkeeper	Took part in the protests, leader of an armed group in Aleppo
I-47	Amman	Oct-13	M	Arab Sunni	Daraa	Employed in Western NGO in Damascus	Took part in the protests in Deraa, member of an armed group
I-48	al-Bab	Dec-12	M	Arab Sunni	al-Bab	Economics graduate, shopkeeper	Took part in the protests, manager of the administrative office in Liwa' al-Umawiyyin
I-49	Azaz	Dec-12	M	Arab Sunni	Azaz	Unemployed, military service	Took part in the protests, former combatant in Jabhat al-Nusra until 2012, join another armed group in Azaz
I-50	Aleppo	Aug-13	M	Arab Sunni	Aleppo	English literature student	Took part in the protests, combatant in Harakat Ahrar al-Sham al-Islamiyya, former combatant in Jabhat al-Nusra
I-51	Aleppo	Jan-13	M	Arab Sunni	Aleppo	Physiotherapist, bodybuilding champion	Took part in the protests, leader of armed group in Aleppo

(*cont.*)

Codes	Location of the interview	Date of the interview	Sex	Religion /ethnicity	Place of origin	Profession or status before 2011	Political activities and position at the time of the interview
I-52	Aleppo, al-Raʿi	Jan-13, Aug-13	M	Arab Sunni	Aleppo	Employee in a trading company	Took part in the protests, work in media center in the Revolutionary Security in Aleppo
I-53	Afrin	Jan-13	F	Kurd	–	Legal practitioner	Judge in Afrin
I-54	al-Bab	Dec-12	M	Arab Sunni	Al-Bab	Islamic law student	Took part in the protests, judge in al-Bab
I-55	al-Bab	Dec-12	M	Arab Sunni	Al-Bab	Islamic law student in Damascus, imam	Took part in the protests, judge in al-Bab
I-56	Azaz	Dec-12	M	Arab Sunni	Azaz	Lawyer	Took part in the protests, judge in Azaz
I-57	Gaziantep	Aug-13, Sep-13	M	Arab Sunni	Deir ez-Zor	Student	Took part in the protests in Deir ez-Zor
I-58	Azaz	Dec-12	M	Arab Sunni	Azaz	Imam, Ph.D. student in Islamic law	Took part in the protests, Judicial Committee judge in Azaz
I-59	Azaz	Dec-12	M	Arab Sunni	Azaz	Imam	Took part in the protests, Judicial Committee judge in Azaz
I-60	Aleppo	Jan-13	M	Arab Sunni	Aleppo	Police officer	Commander of the Free Police of Aleppo
I-61	Aleppo	Jan-13	M	Arab Sunni	Aleppo	Police officer	Second-in-command of the Free Police of Aleppo
I-62	Aleppo	Jan-13	M	Arab Sunni	Aleppo	Judge	Took part in the protests, judge at the Court of the United Judicial Council of Aleppo
I-63	Azaz	Dec-12	M	Arab Sunni	Azaz	Imam, unemployed	Took part in the protests, police commander in Azaz
I-64	Aleppo	Jan-13	M	Arab Sunni	Aleppo	Unemployed	Took part in the protests, leader of a security enforcement group in Salahaddin district in Aleppo

I-65	Aleppo	Jan-13	M	Arab Sunni	Aleppo	Private sector employee	Took part in the protests, head of administration of Free Police of Aleppo
I-66	Aleppo	Jan-13	M	Arab Sunni	Aleppo	Police officer	Free police commander in Aleppo
I-67	Cairo	Jan-14	M	Arab Druze	Suweida	Shopkeeper, communist militant	Took part in the protests, refugee in Cairo, representative of the Syrian National Coalition in Cairo
I-68	Cairo	Jan-14	M	Arab Sunni	Damascus	Shopkeeper, communist opponent	Took part in the protests in Damas, refugee in Cairo
I-69	Istanbul	April-13	M	Arab Sunni	Damascus	Executive in private company in Damascus	Took part in the protests in Damascus, refugee in Istanbul
I-70	Paris	Sep-12	M	Arab Sunni	Damascus	Civil servant	Took part in the protests in Damascus, refugee in France
I-71	Beirut	Jul-14	M	Arab Sunni	Damascus	Student, artist	Took part in the protests in Damascus, refugee in Lebanon
I-72	Cairo	Jan-14	M	Arab Sunni	Aleppo	Businessman	Took part in the protests in Aleppo, refugee in Cairo
I-73	Cairo	Dec-13	M	Arab Druze	Suweida	Businessman in Saudi Arabia	Expelled from Saudi Arabia in 2012, refugee in Egypt, employee in the Syrian National Coalition in Cairo
I-74	Aleppo	Aug-13	M	Arab Sunni	Aleppo	Primary school teacher	Head of education department in Aleppo City Council
I-75	Antakya, Gaziantep	Sep-13	M	Arab Sunni	Homs	Businessman	Took part in the protests, refuge in Turkey, director of an NGO
I-76	Ayn al-Arab	Jan-13	M	Kurd	Ayn al-Arab	Lawyer	Took part in the protests

(cont.)

Codes	Location of the interview	Date of the interview	Sex	Religion /ethnicity	Place of origin	Profession or status before 2011	Political activities and position at the time of the interview
I-77	Erbil	May-13	M	Kurd	Aleppo	Student at University of Aleppo	Took part in the protests, refugee in Erbil
I-78	Erbil	Jan-12	M	Kurd	Damascus	Shopkeeper	Took part in the protests, refugee in Erbil
I-79	Erbil	Dec-12	M	Kurd	Aleppo – Qamishli	Student	Took part in the protests, refugee in Erbil
I-80	Erbil	May-13	M	Kurd	Damascus	Shopkeeper	Took part in the protests, refugee in Erbil
I-81	Erbil	Dec-12	M	Kurd	Amuda	Civil servant	Took part in the protests, refugee in Erbil
I-82	Erbil	Jan-12	M	Kurd	Qamishli	Student	Militant of Avahi movement
I-83	al-Bab	Jan-13	M	Kurd	Aleppo	Unemployed	Took part in the protests, Kurdish FSA combatant
I-84	Ayn al-Arab	Dec-12	M	Kurd	Ayn al-Arab	Lawyer	Took part in the protests, refugee in Erbil, judge at the Ayn al-Arab tribunal
I-85	Ayn al-Arab	Dec-12	M	Kurd	Ayn al-Arab	Member of the PYD, shopkeeper	Asayish Commander in Ayn al-Arab
I-86	Ayn al-Arab	Dec-12	M	Kurd	Ayn al-Arab	Shopkeeper	Shopkeeper
I-87	Beirut	Jul-14	M	Kurd	Ayn al-Arab	Civil servant in Ayn al-Arab	Refugee in Lebanon
I-88	Gaziantep	Sep-13	M	Kurd	Qamishli	Lawyer from Qamishli	Refugee in Turkey
I-89	Erbil	May-13	M	Kurd	Aleppo	Student, active in black market	Took part in the protests, refugee in Erbil
I-90	Erbil	Sept-12	M	Kurd	Qamishli	Civil servant	Militant with the Kurdish Youth Movement, refugee in Iraqi Kurdistan

I-91	Erbil	Apr-13	F	Kurd	Afrin	Student	Took part in the protests, refugee in Erbil
I-92	Erbil	May-13	M	Kurd	Qamishli	Shopkeeper, leader of the PDKS	Militant with the PDKS, refugee in Erbil
I-93	Erbil	Apr-13	M	Kurd	Ayn al-Arab	Shopkeeper	Militant with the PDKS, refugee in Erbil
I-94	Gaziantep	Sep-13	M	Kurd	Aleppo	Shopkeeper	Commander of an armed group
I-95	al-Bab	Dec-12	M	Arab Sunni	al-Bab	Primary school teacher	Took part in the protests, mayor of al-Bab
I-96	Istanbul	Sept-13, April-14	M	Arab Sunni	-	Student, economic analyst in private sector	Took part in the protests, Muslim Brotherhood militant, refugee in Turkey
I-97	Aleppo	Aug-13	M	Arab Sunni	Aleppo	Shopkeeper	Took part in the protests, employee in the Aleppo City Council
I-98	Aleppo	Dec 12, Jan-13	M	Arab Sunni	Aleppo	Day laborer	Took part in the protests, combatant in an Aleppo armed group
I-99	Azaz	Dec-12	M	Arab Sunni	Azaz	Day laborer	Took part in the protests, combatant in an Azaz armed group
I-100	Aleppo	Jan-13	M	Arab Sunni	Aleppo	Private sector accountant	Took part in the protests, mayor of Aleppo
I-101	Antakya	Sep-13	M	Arab Sunni	Latakia	Imam, Ph.D. student in Islamic law in al-Azhar, in Cairo	Took part in the protests, active with funding armed groups, declared apostate by ISIS, refugee in Turkey
I-102	Bab al-Salam border post	Dec-12	M	Arab Sunni	Azaz	Student	Took part in the protests, media activist
I-103	Gaziantep	Sep-13	M	Arab Alawite	Latakia	Journalist	Took part in the protests, refugee and student in London

Codes	Location of the interview	Date of the interview	Sex	Religion /ethnicity	Place of origin	Profession or status before 2011	Political activities and position at the time of the interview
I-104	Ayn al-Arab	Dec-12	M	Kurd	Ayn al-Arab	Lawyer	Lawyer
I-105	Ayn al-Arab	Dec-12	F	Kurd	-	PKK leader	PKK leader
I-106	al-Bab	Dec-12	M	Arab Sunni	Al-Bab	Imam, teacher in a madrassa	Took part in the protests, judge in al-Bab
I-107	Afrin	Jan-13	M	Kurd	Afrin	Shopkeeper, PYD militant	Mayor of Afrin
I-108	Amman	Oct-13	M	Arab Druze	Suweida	Shopkeeper and civil servant	Took part in the protests, refugee in Jordan
I-109	Afrin	Jan-13	M	Kurd	Aleppo	Shopkeeper	Refugee in Afrin
I-110	Urfa	Sep-13	M	Kurd	Raqqa	Shopkeeper	Took part in the protests, refugee in Turkey
I-111	Amman	Oct-13	M	Arab Sunni	Daraa	Civil servant	Took part in the protests, refugee in Jordan
I-112	Aleppo	Jan-13	M	Arab Sunni	Aleppo	Imam	Took part in the protests, judge at the United Judicial Council in Aleppo
I-113	Akhtarin	Jan-13	M	Arab Sunni	Akhtarin	Imam	Took part in the protests, judge at village court
I-114	al-Bab	Jan-13	-	-	-	-	Foreign Doctor, working for Doctors without Borders
I-115	Ayn al-Arab	Dec-12	M	Kurd	Ayn al-Arab	Notable	Leader of the KDPS in Ayn al-Arab
I-116	Ayn al-Arab	Dec-12	M	Kurd	Ayn al-Arab	Employee in the private sector	YPG forced recruit
I-117	Afrin	Jan-13	M	Kurd	Afrin	Day laborer	PYD forest guard
I-118	Ayn al-Arab	Dec-12	M	Kurd	Ayn al-Arab	Shopkeeper	KDPS militant
I-119	Erbil	April-13	M	Kurd	Qamishli	Shopkeeper	Shopkeeper
I-120	Paris	Sep-12	M	Kurd	Afrin	Civil servant	KNCS militant, in exile in Paris

ID	Origin	Date	Sex	Ethnicity/sect	Location	Occupation	Notes
I-121	Azaz	Dec-12	M	Arab Sunni	Azaz	No information	Umma party militant
I-122	Antakya	Sep-13	M	Arab Sunni	Damascus	Civil servant	Took part in the protests, refugee in Turkey
I-123	Gaziantep	Sep-13	M	Arab Sunni	-	Engineer	Took part in the protests, Harakat Ahrar al-Sham al-Islamiyya militant
I-124	Aleppo	Jan-13	M	Arab Sunni	Aleppo	Unknown	Took part in the protests, activist, Jabhat al-Nusra ex-prisoner
I-125	Urfa	Sep-13	M	Arab Sunni	Raqqa	Shopkeeper	Took part in the protests
I-126	Kirkuk	Apr-13	M	Turkmen Shia	Kirkuk (Iraq)	Telephone operator employee in Iraq	Telephone operator employee in Iraq
I-127	Hawija	Apr-13	M	Arab Sunni	Hawija (Iraq)	No information	Close to the Sunni Iraqi insurrection
I-128	Aleppo	Aug-13	M	Arab Sunni	Aleppo	Student of English and management	Took part in the protests, human resources manager at Aleppo City Council
I-129	Gaziantep	Sep-13	M	Arab Sunni	Damascus	Notable	Took part in the protests, member of the Assistance Coordination Unit
I-130	Aleppo	Aug-13	F	Arab Sunni	Aleppo	Housewife, from a prominent family in Aleppo	Took part in the protest, Hamdaniyya district mayor, Aleppo
I-131	al-Bab	Dec-12	M	Arab Sunni	al-Bab	Unemployed	Took part in the protests
I-132	Aleppo	Jan-13	M	Arab Sunni	Aleppo	Son of a shopkeeper in Aleppo	Took part in the protests
I-133	Cairo	Jan-14	M	Arab Sunni	Aleppo	Syrian manufacturer	Refugee in Cairo
I-134	Aleppo	Jan-13	M	Arab Sunni	Aleppo	Electrician	Electrician
I-135	Gaziantep	Sep-13	M	Arab Sunni	Raqqa	Student	Took part in the protests, refugee in Turkey
I-136	Aleppo	Jan-13	M	Arab Sunni	Aleppo	Manager of an industrial bakery	Took part in the protests, manager of industrial bakery

(*cont.*)

Codes	Location of the interview	Date of the interview	Sex	Religion /ethnicity	Place of origin	Profession or status before 2011	Political activities and position at the time of the interview
I-137	Gaziantep	Sep-13	M	Arab Sunni	Aleppo	Civil servant	Activist, refugee in Turkey, works for an NGO
I-138	Aleppo	Jan-13	F	Arab Sunni	Aleppo	Anglo-Syrian student in London	Took part in the protests
I-139	Gaziantep	Sep-13	F	Arab Alawite	Damascus	Student, artist, activist	Director of the Beyrouth office of the Friedrich Ebert Foundation
I-140	Ayn al-Arab	Dec-12	M	Kurd	Ayn al-Arab	Employee in the private sector	PYD militant
I-141	Hawija	May-13	M	Arab Sunni	Hawija (Iraq)	major tribal notable	IDP
I-142	Kirkuk	Apr-12	M	Arab Sunni	Kirkuk (Iraq)	Director of the Water department in Kirkuk	Director of Water department in Kirkuk
I-143	Kirkuk	Jan-15	M/F	Arabs Sunni	Salaheddin and Nineveh province (Iraq)	Mukhtar, tradesmen	IDPs
I-144	Debaga	Jan-15	M	Arabs Sunni	Du-Azat, Sultan Abdullah, Talasheri, Tenta (Iraq)	Mukhtar, tradesmen, labors, imams, teachers	IDPs
I-145	Debaga	Jan-15	M	Arabs Sunni	Du-Azat, Sultan Abdullah, Talasheri, Tenta (Iraq)	Mukhtar, tradespeople, labors, imams, teachers	IDPs

ID	Location	Date	Sex	Ethnicity/Religion	Place of origin	Occupation	Role/Status
I-146	Khanakin	Jan-15	M	Sunni and Shia Arabs	Baji (Iraq)	Day laborers	IDPs
I-147	Khanakin	Jan-15	M F	Arabs Sunni	Surroundings of Muqdadiyah (Iraq)	Housewife, Day laborers	IDPs
I-148	Debaga	Feb-15	M	Arabs Sunni	Talarim, Duawad (Iraq)	Mukhtar, tradespeople, day laborers, imams, teachers	IDPs
I-149	Skype/Raqqa	Feb-15	M	Arab Sunni	Raqqa	Shopkeeper	Took part in the protests, clandestine opposition to IS in Raqqa
I-150	Skype/Tal Abyad	Feb-15, Mar-15	M	Sunni Arab	Aleppo	Textile entrepreneur	Shopkeeper
I-151	Skype/Germany	Feb-15	M	Arab Sunni	Raqqa	Student	Refugee in Germany
I-152	Skype/Latakia, Raqqa	Feb-15	M	Arab Sunni	Raqqa	Student	Took part in the protests, clandestine opposition to IS in Raqqa
I-153	Erbil Dohuk	March-15 May-15	M	Kurd	Dohuk	PDK Peshmerga	PDK Peshmerga
I-154	Skype/Turkey	Jun-15	M	Arab Sunni	Raqqa	Unknown	Took part in the protests, member of an armed group of Raqqa fighting against IS and the regime
I-155	Erbil	Mar-15	M	Arab Sunni	Tikrit (Iraq)	Unknown	IDP
I-156	Kirkuk	Feb-15	M	Turkmen Shia	Tal Afar (Iraq)	Unknown	IDP
I-157	Kirkuk	Mar-15	M	Arab Sunni	Kirkuk (Iraq)	Leader of the Iraqi Islamist Party in Kirkuk	Leader of the Iraqi Islamist Party in Kirkuk

(cont.)

Codes	Location of the interview	Date of the interview	Sex	Religion /ethnicity	Place of origin	Profession or status before 2011	Political activities and position at the time of the interview
I-158	Kirkuk	Mar-15	M	Arab Sunni	Kirkuk / Hawija (Iraq)	Notable	IDP
I-159	Aleppo	Aug-13	M	Arab Sunni	Aleppo	Shopkeeper	Took part in the protests, shopkeeper
I-160	Aleppo	January-13	M	Arab Sunni	Aleppo (Palestinian refugee)	Student	Took part in the protests
I-161	Hasaka	October-16	M	Arab Sunni	Hasaka	SDF fighter	Ex-FSA fighter, join the SDF in 2016
I-162	Qamishli	October-16	M	Kurd	Qamishli	Journalist	Took part in the 2011 protests, media activist

Slogans of Protest

The site, www.facebook.com/Syrian.Revolution, which had over 300,000 likes in September 2011 (940,000 at the end of 2014), posted the locations and instructions for the demonstration of March 15, 2011 in Damascus. The proportion of likes prior to May 2011 are unknown, but Adam Alqvist estimated that at the time 35 percent of fans were living in Syria, 50 percent were Syrians living outside of Syria, and 15 percent were Arabs from other countries in the region.[1] Management and doubts concerning voting procedures caused many debates between Internet users concerning the necessity of political and religious slogans. The choice of the slogan for Friday March 9, 2012, "Loyalty to the Martyrs of the Kurdish Uprising [of 2004]," was particularly controversial, as in this instance the page administrator imposed a slogan rather than acting on a vote. The SNC consequently intervened to put into place new voting methods on the page, via a specialized site, in order to ensure votes would be counted and there would be one vote per person. The page was an indicator of how the revolutionaries' discourse and aims evolved. A moral vocabulary was present from the very first weeks. Hope for military intervention, as in Libya, was apparent in the slogans from the summer of 2011. From January 2012, positions were taken in favor of the Free Syrian Army and armed combat, while the first Koranic quotes date from spring 2012 and remained rare.

2011

March 18	الكرامة	Dignity
March 25	العزة	Honor
April 1	الشهداء	Martyrs
April 8	الصمود	Steadfastness
April 15	الإصرار	Persistence
April 22	العظيمة	Great Friday
April 29	الغضب	Rage
May 6	التحدي	Defiance
May 13	الحرائر	Free Women
May 20	أزادي	Azadi
May 27	حماة الديار	Defenders of Homes
June 3	أطفال الحرية	Children of Freedom
June 10	العشائر	Tribes
June 17	الشرفاء صالح العلي	The Honorables – Saleh al-Ali
June 24	سقوط الشرعية	Fall of Legitimacy

[1] Adam Alqvist, "The Syrian Insurgency and the Transnational Sphere: Transforming the Conflict in Syria" in Carsten Wieland, Adam Almqvist and Helena Nassif, *The Syrian Insurgency: Dynamics of an Insurgency*, Boulder, Lynne Rienner, pp. 57–58.

(cont.)

Date	Arabic	English
July 1	ارحل	Leave!
July 8	لا للحوار	No to Dialogue
July 15	أسرى الحرّية	Prisoners of Freedom
July 22	أحفاد خالد	Descendants of Khalid
July 29	صمتكم يقتلنا	Your Silence Kills Us
August 5	الله معنا	Allah Is with Us
August 12	لن نركع	We Will not Kneel
August 19	بشائر النصر	Beginnings of Victory
August 26	الصبر والثبات	Patience and Determination
September 2	الموت ولا المذلّة	Death Rather than Humiliation
September 9	الحماية الدولية	International Protection
September 16	ماضون حتى اسقاط النظام	We Will Continue until the Fall of the Regime
September 23	وحدة المعارضة	Opposition Unity
September 30	النصر لشامنا ويمننا	Victory for Our Sham and Our Yemen
October 7	المجلس الوطني يمثّلني	The National Council Represents me
October 14	أحرار الجيش	Army Freemen
October 21	شهداء المهلة العربية	Martyrs of the Arab Deadline
October 28	الحظر الجوّي	No-Fly Zone
November 4	الله أكبر	Allah Is Great
November 11	تجميد العضوية مطلبنا	The Suspension of Membership Is Our Demand
November 18	جمعة طرد السفراء	Expelling the Ambassadors
November 25	الجيش الحر يحميني	The Free Army Protects Me
December 2	المنطقة العازلة مطلبنا	The Buffer Zone Is Our Demand
December 9	اضراب الكرامة	The Strike of Dignity
December 16	الجامعة العربية تقتلنا	The Arab League Is Killing Us
December 23	بروتوكول الموت	Protocol of Death
December 30	الزحف الى ساحات الحرية	March to the City Squares of Freedom

2012

Date	Arabic	English
January 6	إن تنصروا الله ينصركم	If You Support Allah, He Will Support You
January 13	دعم الجيش السوري الحر	Support of the Free Syrian Army
January 20	معتقلي الثورة	Revolution's Detainees
January 27	حق الدفاع عن النفس	Right to Self Defense
February 3	عذرا حماة سامحينا	Sorry Hama, Forgive Us
February 10	النفير العام – روسيا تقتل أطفالنا	General Mobilization – Russia Is Killing Our Children
February 17	المقاومة الشعبية	Popular Resistance
February 24	سننتفض لأجلك بابا عمرو	We Rise for You, Baba 'Amr
March 2	تسليح الجيش الحر	Arming the Free Army
March 9	الوفاء للإنتفاضة الكردية	Loyalty to the Kurdish Uprising
March 16	التدخل العسكري الفوري	Immediate Military Intervention
March 23	قادمون يا دمشق	We're Coming, Damascus
March 30	خذلنا العرب والمسلمون	Muslims and Arabs Failed Us
April 6	من جهز غازياً فقد غزا	He Who Has Equipped a Fighter Has Himself Fought

(*cont.*)

April 13	ثورة لكل السوريين	Revolution for All Syrians
April 20	سننتصر ويهزم الاسد	We Will Prevail and Defeat Assad
April 27	اتى امر الله فلا تستعجلوه	The Command of Allah Is Coming, So Be Not Impatient for It
May 4	اخلاصنا خلاصنا	Our Devotion Is Our Salvation
May 11	نصر من الله وفتح قريب	Help from Allah and a Close Victory
May 18	ابطال جامعة حلب	The University of Aleppo's Heroes
May 25	دمشق موعدنا القريب	Damascus, Our Time Is Near
June 1	أطفال الحولة . . . مشاعل النصر	The Children of Houla Are Torches of Triumph
June 8	ثوار وتجار يدا بيد حتى الانتصار	Revolutionaries and Merchants, Hand in Hand Until Victory
June 15	الاستعداد التام للنفير العام.. روسيا عدوة الشعب السوري	Full Preparation for Full Mobilization; Russia Is the Enemy of the Syrian People
June 22	إذا كان الحكام متخاذلين . . . فأين الشعوب ؟؟؟	If the Rulers Are Weak, Where is the People?
June 29	واثقون بنصر الله	We Trust in the Triumph of Allah
July 6	حرب التحرير الشعبية	People's Liberation War
July 13	إسقاط عنان خادم الأسد و إيران – الغضب لشهداء التريمسة	Toppling Annan, the Servant of Assad and Iran – Rage for The Martyrs of Tremseh
July 20	رمضان النصر سيكتب في دمشق	Ramadan Triumph Will Be Written in Damascus
July 27	انتفاضة العاصمتين	Uprising of the Two Capitals
August 3	دير الزور النصر قادم من الشرق	Deir Ez-Zor – Triumph Is Coming from the East
August 10	سلحونا الطيران	Arm Us with Anti-Aircraft
August 17	بوحدة جيشنا الحر يتحقق النصر	With the Union of Our Free Army, Triumph will be Achieved
August 24	لا تحزني درعا إن الله معنا	Do Not Grieve Daraa; Allah Is with Us
August 31	الوفاء لطرابلس الشام وأحرار لبنان	Loyalty to Tripoli and the Free People of Lebanon
September 7	حمص المحاصرة تناديكم	Besieged Homs Is Calling
September 14	إدلب مقبرة الطائرات ورمز الانتصارات	Idlib Is the Grave of the Air Force and the Symbol of Victories
September 21	أحباب رسول الله في سوريا يذبحون	The Lovers of the Messenger of Allah in Syria Are being Slaughtered
September 28	توحيد كتائب الجيش الحر	Unifying Free Army Battalions
October 5	نريد سلاحاً لا تصريحات	We Need Weapons, Not Statements
October 12	أحرار الساحل يصنعون النصر	The Freemen of the Coast Are Achieving the Triumph
October 19	أمريكا ألم يشبع حقدك من دمائنا	America, Is Your Animosity Not Satisfied with our Blood?
October 26	الله أكبر نصر عبده وأعزّ جنده وهزم الاحزاب وحده	Allah Is Great: He Supported his Worshippers, Made His Soldiers Mighty, and Defeated the Factions Alone
November 2	داريا أخوة العنب و الدم	Daraya Brotherhood of Grapes and Blood

(cont.)

November 9	آن أوان الزحف إلى دمشق	It's Time to March to Damascus
November 16	دعم الإئتلاف الوطني	Support the National Coalition
November 23	اقتربت الساعة وآن الانتصار	The Hour Has Drawn Close and It Is Time for Victory
November 30	ريف الشام أصابع النصر فوق القصر	The Damascus Countryside Is the Fingers of Triumph over The Palace
December 7	لا لقوات حفظ السلام على أرض الشام	No to Peacekeeping Forces in the Land of Sham
December 14	لا إرهاب في سوريا إلا إرهاب الأسد	There Is No Terrorism in Syria Except for The Terrorism of Assad
December 21	جمعة النصر انكتب غ بوابك يا حلب	The Triumph Was Written on Your Gates, Oh Aleppo
December 28	خبز الدم	Bloodied Bread

2013

January 4	حمص تنادي الأحرار لفك الحصار	Homs Calls for Liberals to Lift the Siege
January 4	لا للأخضر الابراهيمي كلنا جبهة النصرة	No for Lakhdar We Are all Jabhat Nusra
January 11	مخيمات الموت	The Camps of Death
January 18	جامعة الثورة.. هندسة الشهادة	Revolution University – Martyrdom Engineering
January 25	قائدنا للأبد سيدنا محمد	Our Leader Forever, Our Sayyed Muhammad
February 1	المجتمع الدولي شريك الأسد في مجازره	The International Community Is a Partner to al-Assad in His Massacres
February 8	و اعتصموا بحبل الله جميعاً	And Hold Fast, All of You Together, To The Rope of Allah
February 15	وكفى بالله نصيرا	And Allah Is Sufficient As A Supporter
February 22	الرقة الأبية على طريق الحرية	Proud Raqqa is on The Road of Freedom
March 1	أمة واحدة راية واحد حرب واحدة	One Nation, One Flag, One War
March 8	لن تمر دولتكم الطائفية	Your Sectarian State Will Never Come to Pass
March 15	عامان على الكفاح و نصر ثورتنا قد لاح	Two Years of the Struggle and the Triumph of our Revolution Has Drawn Near
March 22	أسلحتكم الكيميائية لن توقف مدّ الحرية	Your Chemical Weapons Will Not Stop the Tide of Freedom
March 29	و بشر الصّابرين	Give Glad Tidings to Those Who Patiently Persevere
April 5	لاجئون.. والشرف والكرامة عناوننا	Refugees . . . Honor and Dignity Is Still Our Motto
April 12	سوريا أقوى من أن تقسّم	Syria Is too Strong to Be Divided
April 19	إيران وحزب الشيطان: ستهزمون مع الأسد	Iran, Party of the Devil, You Will Be Defeated Along with al-Assad
April 26	حماية الأكثرية	Protection of the Majority
May 3	بخطوطكم الحمراء يقتل السوريون	By Your Red Lines Syrians Die

(cont.)

May 10	بانيـاس -إبادة طائفية و ا لغطاء اممي	Banyas – Sectarian Genocide and International Cover-Up
May 17	استقـلال القـرار السـوري	Independence of the Syrian Decision
May 24	دَجّالُ المقاومة.. القدس ليست في حمص	The "False Resistance," al-Quds Is Not in Homs
May 31	مبادئ الثورة خطوطنا الحمراء	The Principles of the Revolution Are Our Red Lines
June 7	جمعة الغوطة والقصير إرادة لا تنكسر	al-Ghouta and al-Qusayr, Unbreakable Will
June 14	المشروع الصفوي: تهديد للأمة	The Safavid Project: A Threat to the Umma
June 21	نصرة الشام بالأفعال لا بالأقوال	Support of Sham Is in Action Not Words
June 28	ثورة متوقدة ومعارضة مقعدة	Ardent Revolution and a Paralyzed Opposition
July 5	تنبهوا واستفيقوا أيتها الكتائب	Beware and Wake Up Oh Battalions
July 12	حتى نغير ما بأنفسنا	Until We Change Ourselves
July 19	رمضان شهر النصر والفتوحات	Ramadan Is the Month of Triumph and Conquests
July 26	سيف الله المسلول	The Drawn Sword of Allah
August 2	إن ينصركم الله فلا غالب لكم	Should Allah Support You, No One Can Overcome You
August 9	أبطال الساحل قادمون	The Heroes of the Coast Are Coming
August 16	دعم ثوار الساحل	Support the Revolutionaries of the Coast
August 23	الإرهابي بشار يقتل المدنيين بالكيماو ي، والعالم يتفرج	The Terrorist Bashar Kills Civilians with Chemicals While the World Watches
August 30	وما النصر إلا من عند الله	There Is No Triumph Except from Allah
September 6	ليس بالكيماوي وحده يقتل الأسد أطفالنا	Not With Chemicals Alone, Bashar Kills Our Children
September 13	القاتل بحماية المجتمع الدولي	The Murderer Is Protected by the International Community
September 20	وحدهم السوريون من سيحرر سوريا	Syrians Alone Will Liberate Syria
September 27	أسيرات بطهر الياسمين	Female Prisoners with Jasmine Purity
October 4	شكرًا تركيا	Thank You Turkey
October 11	سلاحنا للجبهات لا للمناطق المحررة	Our Weapons Are for the Fronts, Not for the Liberated Areas
October 18	أنقذوا المعضمية وجنوب دمشق	Save Moadamiyyah and Southern Damascus
October 25	الحل في لاهاي لا في جنيف	The Solution Is in the Hague, Not Geneva
November 1	الحصار جريمة إبادة مستمرة	The Siege Is a Continuous Genocide
November 8	لا للاحتلال الـإيراني لسوريا	"No" to the Iranian Occupation of Syria
November 15	انفروا خفافاً وثقالاً	Go Forth, Whether Light or Heavy
November 22	دم الشهيد عبد القادر الصالح يوحدنا	The Blood of the Martyr Abdel-Qader Saleh Unites Us
November 29	يد الله مع الجماعة	God's Hand Is with the Community
December 6	كسر الحصار	Breaking the Siege
December 13	نقل المعركة لمناطق الاحتلال الاسدي	Moving the Battle to the Areas of the Assad Occupation

Chronology

1920 – 1946: Syria is administered by France under a League of Nations mandate

1946 – 1949: Syrian Republic with a parliamentary system

March 1949: General Shishackly coup d'Etat

February 1954: Popular uprising, restoration of parliamentary system

1958 – 1961: United Arab Republic between Egypt and Syria

8 March 1963: Coup d'Etat by the Syrian branch of the Baath party

November 1970: Hafez al-Assad, defense minister, seizes power

March 1971: Hafez al-Assad declares himself President

February 1982: Hama massacre by the regime, end of the popular uprising led by the Muslim Brotherhood (between 10,000 and 40,000 deaths)

July 2000: death of Hafez al-Assad, his son Bashar al-Assad succeeds him

17 December 2010: Start of the Tunisian Revolution

25 January 2011: Start of the Egyptian Revolution

15 February 2011: Start of the Libyan Revolution

13 March 2011: Fifteen teenagers from Daraa are tortured, arrested for having written graffiti against the regime

25 April 2011: Daraa besieged by Syrian army

4 June 2011: First setback for the army at Jisr al-Shughur, near the Turkish border

29 July 2011: A group of deserter officers announces the formation of the Free Syrian Army

13 August 2011: Sunni districts in south of the town of Latakia are bombed

2 October 2011: The Syrian National Council (SNC) is formed in Istanbul

26 October 2011: The Syrian Kurdish National Council (KNCS) is formed in Erbil

11 July 2012: The Erbil agreements between the Syrian branch of the PKK, the PYD and the KNCS

15 July 2012: Rebel offensive in Damascus

19 July 2012: Rebel offensive in Aleppo

July 2012: The Syrian regime hands over power to the PYD, which takes control of territories with a Kurdish majority

April 2013: Jabhat al-Nusra splits from Islamic State in Iraq and the Levant (ISIL)

21 August 2013: Chemical attack against Ghouta

January 2014: Generalized FSA offensive against ISIS

January – February 2014: Geneva II negotiations between the regime and the opposition

10 June 2014: Mosul falls at the hands of Islamic State and the Iraqi rebels

29 June 2014: ISIS announces the inauguration of a caliphate; Abu Bakr al-Baghdadi is proclaimed caliph

July 2014: Islamic State offensive in eastern Syria and Ayn al-Arab

August 2014: Islamic State offensive in Iraqi Kurdistan

22 September 2014: Aerial intervention from international coalition led by the United States against the Islamic State in Syria and in Iraq

March 2015: Idlib and Jisr al-Shughur falls at the hand of the insurgency

May 2015: Islamic State takes Palmyra

30 September 2015: Russia intervenes in support of the regime

December 2015: Regime captures Homs

August 2016: Turkey intervenes in northern Syria

December 2016: Eastern Aleppo falls to the regime

Bibliography

Ababsa, Myriam, "Agrarian Counter-Reform in Syria," in Hinnenbusch, Raymond (ed.), *Agriculture and Reform in Syria*, Boulder, Lynne Rienner, 2011, pp. 83–107.

Ababsa, Myriam, "Contre-réforme agraire et conflits fonciers en Jazîra syrienne (2000–2005)," *Revue d'études des mondes musulmans et de la Méditerranée* 115–116, 2007, 211–230.

Ababsa, Myriam, "La recomposition des allégeances tribales dans le Moyen-Euphrate syrien (1958–2007)," *Etudes rurales* 184, 2009, 65–78.

Ababsa, Myriam, "Le démantèlement des fermes d'Etat syriennes: une contre-réforme agraire (2000–2005)," in Dupret, B., Ghazzal, Z., Courbage, Y., and al-Dbiyat, M. (eds.), *La Syrie au présent. Reflets d'une société*, Paris, Actes Sud, 2007, pp. 739–745.

Ababsa, Myriam, Dupret, Baudouin, and Denis, Eric (eds.), *Popular Housing and Urban Land Tenure in the Middle East*, Cairo, The American University in Cairo Press, 2012.

Ababsa, Myriam, Roussel, Cyril, and al-Dbiyat, Mohammed, "Le territoire syrien entre intégration nationale et métropolisation renforcée," in Dupret, B., Ghazzal, Z., Mujahidin, Y., and al-Dbiyat, M., *La Syrie au présent. Reflets d'une société*, Paris, Actes Sud, 2007, pp. 37–78.

Abboud, Cha'ban, "Les quartiers informels de Damas: une ceinture de misère," in Dupret, B., Ghazzal, Z., Mujahidin, Y., and al-Dbiyat, M., (eds.), *La Syrie au présent. Reflets d'une société*, Paris, Actes Sud, 2007, pp. 169–176.

Abboud, Samer, *Syria*, Cambridge, Polity Press, 2016.

Abdullah, Ibrahim, "Man Does Not Live by Bread Alone," *African Review of Books* 2 (1), 2006, 12–13.

Acemoglu, Daron, Ticchi, Davide, and Vindigni, Andrea, "Persistence of civil wars," *Journal of the European Economic Association* 8, 2010.

Adang, Camilla, Ansari, Hassan, Fierro, Maribel, and Schmidtke, Sabine (eds.), *Accusations of Unbelief in Islam: A Diachronic Perspective on Takfir*, Leiden, Brill, 2015.

Adelman, Howard, "Why Refugee Warriors Are Threats," *Journal of Conflict Studies* 18 (1), 1989, 49–70.

Ahmad, Balsam, "Neighbourhood and Health Inequalities in Formal and Informal Neighbourhoods in Aleppo," in Ahmad, B. and Sudermann, Y. (eds.), *Syria's Contrasting Neighbourhoods: Gentrification and Informal Settlements Juxtaposed*, Boulder, Lynne Rienner, 2012.

Aita, Samir, "L'économie de la Syrie peut-elle devenir sociale? Vous avez dit: 'économie sociale de marché'?" in Dupret, B., Ghazzal, Z., Courbage, Y., and al-Dbiyat, M. (eds.), *La Syrie au présent. Reflets d'une société*, Paris, Actes Sud, 2007, pp. 541–580.

Al-Dik, Majd, *A l'est de Damas, au bout du monde: Témoignage d'un révolutionnaire Syrien*, Paris, Editions Don Quichotte, 2016. Emile Hokayem, *Syria's Uprising and the Fracturing of the Levant, Adelphi Papers 438*, 2013.

Allal, Amin, "'Revolutionary' trajectories in Tunisia : Processes of political radicalization 2007-2011," *Revue française de science politique* 62 (5), 2012, 821–841.

Allison, Roy, "Russia and Syria: Explaining Alignment with a Regime in Crisis," *International Affairs* 89 (4), 2013, 795–823.

Allsopp, Harriet *The Kurds of Syria: Political Parties and Identity in the Middle East*, London, I.B. Tauris, 2014.

Alqvist, Adam, "The Syrian Insurgency and the Transnational Sphere: Transforming the Conflict in Syria," in Wieland, Carsten, Almqvist, Adam, and Nassif, Helena (eds.), *The Syrian Insurgency: Dynamics of an Insurgency*, Boulder, Lynne Rienner, pp. 57–58.

Alshesh, Eli, "The Doctrinal Crisis Within the Salafi-Jihadi Ranks and the Emergence of Neo-Takfirism: A Historical and Doctrinal Analysis," *Islamic Law and Society* 21, 2014, 419–452.

Anderson, Paul, "The Politics of Scorn in Syria and the Agency of Narrated Involvement," *Journal of the Royal Anthropological Institute* 19, 2013, 463–481.

Arjona, Ana and Kalyvas, Stathis, "Recruitment into Armed Groups in Colombia: A Survey of Demobilized Fighters," in Guichaoua, Yvan (ed.), *Understanding Collective Political Violence: Conflict, Inequality and Ethnicity*, New York, Palgrave-Macmillan, 2011, pp. 143–171.

Arjona, Ana, Mampilly, Zachariah, and Kasfir, Nelson, *Rebel Governance in Civil War*, Cambridge, Cambridge University Press, 2015.

Atzili, Boaz, "When Good Fences Make Bad Neighbors: Fixed Borders, State Weakness, and International Conflict," *International Security* 31 (3), 2006/2007, 139–173.

Audoin-Rouzeau, Stéphane, *Combattre: une anthropologie historique de la guerre moderne (XIXe-XXe siècle)*, Paris, Seuil, 2008.

Autesserre, Séverine, *The Trouble with Congo: Local Violence and the Failure of International Peacebuilding*, Cambridge, Cambridge University Press, 2010.

Baczko, Adam, "Judging in the Midst of Civil War: The Taliban Courts in Afghanistan (2001–2013)," *Politix* 104 (4), 2013, 25–46.

Baczko, Adam, "Legal Rule and Tribal Politics: The US Army and the Taliban in Afghanistan (2001–2013)," *Development and Change* 47 (6), 2016, 24–35.

Baczko, Adam, Dorronsoro, Gilles, "Pour une approche sociologique des guerres civiles," *Revue française de science politique* 63 (5), 2013, 309–327.

Baczko, Adam, Dorronsoro, Gilles, and Quesnay, Arthur, "Le capital révolutionnaire," *Actes de la recherche en sciences sociales* 211–212, 2016, 24–35.

Baczko, Adam, Dorronsoro, Gilles, and Quesnay, Arthur, "Mobilisations as a Result of Deliberation and Polarising Crisis: The Peaceful Protests in Syria (2011)," *Revue française de science politique* 63 (5), 2013, 815–839.

Baczko, Adam, Dorronsoro, Gilles, Quesnay, Arthur, and Youssef, Maaï, "The Rationality of an Eschatological Movement: The Islamist State in Iraq and Syria," *The Program on Governance and Local Development Working Paper* 7, 2016.

Balanche, Fabrice, "Clientélisme, communautarisme et fragmentation territoriale en Syrie," *A contrario* 11, 2009, 122–150.

Balanche, Fabrice, "Communautarisme en Syrie: lorsque le mythe devient réalité," *Confluences Méditerranée* 89, 2014, 29–44.

Balanche, Fabrice, "Géographie de la révolte syrienne," *Outre-terre* 29 (3), 2011, 437–458.

Balanche, Fabrice, "L'habitat illégal dans l'agglomération de Damas et les carences de l'Etat," *Revue géographique de l'Est* 49 (4), 2009.

Balanche, Fabrice, "La région côtière: d'une périphérie délaissée à une périphérie assistée," in Dupret, B., Ghazzal, Z., Mujahidin, Y., and al-Dbiyat, M. (eds.), *La Syrie au présent. Reflets d'une société*, Paris, Actes Sud, 2007, pp. 87–98.

Balanche, Fabrice, "La Syrie entre révolution, guerre civile et statut quo," in Gardelle, L., *Un "printemps arabe"?* Paris, L'Harmattan, 2013, pp. 103–132.

Balanche, Fabrice, "Transports et espace syrien," *Annales de Géographie* 112 (630), 2003, 146–166.

Balanche, Fabrice, *La région alaouite et le pouvoir syrien*, Paris, Karthala, 2006.

Barkey, Karen, *Bandits and Bureaucrats: The Ottoman Route to State Centralization*, Ithaca, Cornell University Press, 1994.

Barnes, John A., "Class and Committees in a Norwegian Island Parish," *Human Relations* 7, 1954, 39–58.

Barth, Fredrik, *Ethnic Groups and Boundaries: The Social Organization of Culture Difference*, Long Grove, Waveland Press, 1969.

Batatu, Hanna, *Syria's Peasantry, the Descendants of its Lesser Rural Notables, and their Politics*, Princeton, Princeton University Press, 1999.

Bates, Robert, "Letter from the President: Area Studies and the Discipline," *APSA-CP: Newsletter of the APSA Organized Section in Comparative Politics* 7 (1), 1996, 1–2.

Bayart, Jean-François, Ellis, Stephen, and Hibou, Béatrice, *The Criminalization of the State in Africa*, Bloomington, Indiana University Press, 1999.

Beath, Andrew, Christia, Fotini, and Enikolopov, Ruben, "Winning Hearts and Minds Through Development: Evidence from a Field Experiment in Afghanistan," *Policy Research Working Papers* 6129, 2012.

Beath, Andrew, Christia, Fotini, and Enikolopov, Ruben, "Direct Democracy and Resource Allocation: Experimental Evidence from Afghanistan," *Policy Research Working Papers* 6133, 2012.

Beath, Andrew, Christia, Fotini, and Enikolopov, Ruben, "Empowering Women through Development Aid: Evidence from a Field Experiment in Afghanistan," *American Political Science Review* 107 (3), 2013, 540–557.

Beaud, Stéphane, "L'usage de l'entretien en sciences sociales: plaidoyer pour l'"entretien ethnographique'," *Politix* 9 (35), 1996, 226–257.

Beaugrand, Claire, "L'engagement des monarchies du Golfe contre le régime de Bachar al-Assad," in Burgat, F. and Paoli, B. (eds.), *Pas de Printemps pour la Syrie, Les clés pour comprendre les acteurs et les défis de la crise (2011–2013)*, Paris, La Découverte, 2013, pp. 310–321.

Becker, Annette, *La guerre et la foi: de la mort à la mémoire, 1914–1930*, Paris, Armand Colin, 1994.

Beinin, Joel, "Introduction: The Middle East and North Africa Beyond Classical Social Movement Theory," in Beinin, J. and Vairel, F. (eds.), *Social Movements, Mobilization, and Contestation in the Middle East and North Africa, Second Edition*, Stanford, Stanford University Press, 2013, pp. 1–31.

Belhadj, Souhaïl, "L'appareil sécuritaire syrien, socle d'un régime miné par la guerre civile," *Confluences Méditerranée* 89 (2), 2014, pp. 15–27.

Belhadj, Souhail, *La Syrie de Bashar al-Assad: anatomie d'un système autoritaire*, Paris, Belin, 2013.

Bennani-Chraïbi, Mounia and Fillieule, Olivier, "Pour une sociologie des situations révolutionnaires," *Revue française de science politique* 62 (5), 2012, 767–796.

Bennett, Andrew and Checkel, Jeffrey, *Process Tracing: From Metaphor to Analytic Tool*, Cambridge, Cambridge University Press, 2015.

Berger, Peter and Luckmann, Thomas, *The Social Construction of Reality: a Treatise in the Sociology of Knowledge*, Garden City, Anchor Books, 1966.

Berman, Bruce, and Lonsdale, John, *Unhappy Valley: Conflict in Kenya and Africa*, Volume 1: *State and Class*, London, James Currey, 1992.

Berman, Eli, Callen, Michael, Felter, Joseph, and Shapiro, Jacob, "Do Working Men Rebel? Insurgency and Unemployment in Afghanistan, Iraq, and the Philippines," *Journal of Conflict Resolution* 55 (4), 2011, 496–528.

Bizeul, Daniel, "Faire avec les déconvenues: une enquête en milieu nomade," *Sociétés contemporaines* 33–34, 1999, 111–137.

Bizeul, Daniel, "Que faire des expériences d'enquête? Apports et fragilité de l'observation directe," *Revue française de science politique* 57 (1), 2007, 69–89.

Blazquez, Adèle, "Négocier dans une marge criminalisée. L'application de la loi agraire de 1992 dans la sierra de Badiraguato (Sinaloa, Mexique)," *Cahiers des Amériques latines* 81 (1), 2016, 73–91.

Blom, Amélie, "Do Jihadist 'Martyrs' Really Want to Die? An Emic Approach to Self-Sacrificial Radicalization in Pakistan," *Revue française de science politique* 61 (5), 2011, 867–891.

Boëx, Cécile, "La vidéo comme outil de l'action collective et de la lutte armée," in Burgat, F. and Paoli, B. (eds.), *Pas de Printemps pour la Syrie, Les clés pour comprendre les acteurs et les défis de la crise (2011–2013)*, Paris, La Découverte, 2013, pp. 172–184.

Boëx, Cécile, "Ce que la révolution fait à la création cinématographique en Syrie," *Revue des mondes musulmans et de la Méditerranée* 133, 2013, 145–156.

Boëx, Cécile, "Mobilisations d'artistes dans le mouvement de révolte en Syrie: modes d'action et limites de l'engagement," in Allal, A. and Pierret, T., *Au cœur des révolutions arabes: devenir révolutionnaire*, Paris, Armand Colin, 2013, pp. 87–112.

Boëx, Cécile, "The End of the State Monopoly over Culture: Toward the Commodification of Cultural and Artistic Production," *Middle East Critique* 20 (2), 2011, 139–155.

Boissière, Thierry, "L'anthropologie face au conflit syrien: replacer la société au coeur de l'analyse," *Revue d'étude des mondes musulmans et de la Méditerranée* 138, 2015, 117–130.

Bou Nassif, Hicham, "'Second-Class': The Grievances of Sunni Officers in the Syrian Armed Forces," *Journal of Strategic Studies* 38 (5), 2015, 626–649.

Boudon, Raymond, *Raison, bonnes raisons*, Paris, Presses Universitaires de France, 2003.

Bougarel, Xavier, *Bosnie, anatomie d'un conflit*, Paris, La Découverte, 1996.

Bourdieu, Pierre *On the State: Lectures at the College de France, 1989–1992*, Polity Press, Cambridge, 2015.

Bourdieu, Pierre *The Logic of Practice*, Stanford, Stanford University Press, 1990.

Bourdieu, Pierre, "Le capital social", *Actes de la recherche en sciences sociales*, January 31 1980, p. 2–3.

Bourdieu, Pierre, "The Forms of Capital," in Richardson, J. (ed.), *Handbook of Theory and Research for the Sociology of Education*, New York, Greenwood, 1986, pp. 241–259.

Bourdieu, Pierre, *Homo academicus*, Stanford, Stanford University, 1988.

Bourdieu, Pierre, *Sociologie générale, Volume 1: Cours au Collège de France 1981–1983*, Paris, Seuil, 2015.

Bourgois, Philippe, "La violence en temps de guerre et en temps de paix," *Cultures & Conflits* 47, 2002, 81–116.

Brubaker, Rogers and Cooper, Frederick, "Beyond 'Identity'," *Theory and Society* 29 (1), 2000, 1–47.

Burgat, François, "La stratégie al-Assad: diviser pour survivre," in Burgat, F. and Paoli, B. (eds.), *Pas de Printemps pour la Syrie, Les clés pour comprendre les acteurs et les défis de la crise (2011–2013)*, Paris, La Découverte, 2013, pp. 17–32.

Burgat, François, *Face to Face with Political Islam*, New York, I.B. Tauris, 2002.

Burgat, François and Caillet, Romain, "Une guérilla islamiste ? Les composantes idéologiques de la révolte armée," in Burgat, F. and Paoli, B. (eds.), *Pas de Printemps pour la Syrie, Les clés pour comprendre les acteurs et les défis de la crise (2011–2013)*, Paris, La Découverte, 2013, pp. 55–83.

Burgat, François and Paoli, Bruno (eds.), *Pas de Printemps pour la Syrie, Les clés pour comprendre les acteurs et les défis de la crise (2011–2013)*, Paris, La Découverte, 2013.

Camau, Michel, "L'exception autoritaire ou l'improbable point d'Archimède de la politique dans le monde arabe," in Picard, E. (ed.), *La politique dans le monde arabe*, Paris, Armand Colin, 2006, pp. 29–54.

Camau, Michel, "Un printemps arabe? L'émulation protestataire et ses limites," *L'année du Maghreb* 8, 2012, 27–47.

Cattedra, Raffaele and Idrissi-Janati, M'hammed, "Espace sacré, espace de citadinité, espace de mouvement. Les territoires des mosquées au Maroc," in

Bennani-Chraïbi, M. and Fillieule O. (eds.), *Résistances et protestations dans les sociétés musulmanes*, Presses de Sciences Po, Paris, 2003, pp. 127–175.

Cederman, Lars-Erik, Gleditsch, Kirstian Skrede, and Buhaug, Halvard, *Inequalities, Grievances and Civil Wars*, Cambridge, Cambridge University Press, 2013.

Centlivres, Pierre, "Les trois pôles de l'identité afghane au Pakistan," *L'Homme* 28 (108), 1988, 134–146.

Centlivres, Pierre, "The Controversy over the Buddhas of Bamiyan," *South Asia Multidisciplinary Academic Journal* 2, 2008.

Centlivres, Pierre, "Violence illégitime et violence légitime: à propos des pratiques et des représentations dans la crise afghane," *L'Homme* 144, 1997, 51–67.

Centlivres, Pierre and Centlivres-Demont, Micheline, "The Afghan Refugee in Pakistan: An Ambiguous Identity," *Journal of Refugee Studies* 1 (2), 1988 141–152.

Chabal, Pascal and Daloz, Jean-Pascal, *Africa Works: Disorder as a Political Instrument*, Oxford, James Currey, 1999.

Chakrabarty, Dipesh, *Provincializing Europe: Postcolonial Thought and Historical Difference*, Princeton, Princeton University Press, 2000.

Charap, Samuel, "Russia, Syria and the doctrine of intervention," *Survival* 55 (1), 2013, 35–41.

Chassang, Sylvain and Padro i Miquel, Gerard, "Economic Shocks and Civil War," *Quarterly Journal of Political Science* 4 (3), 2009.

Checkel, Jeffrey, "Socialization and Violence: A Framework Essay," *Simons Papers in Security and Development* 48, 2015.

Checkel, Jeffrey, *Transnational Dynamics of Civil War*, Cambridge, Cambridge University Press, 2015.

Chiffoleau, Sylvia, "Fête et procession de Maaloula: une mise en scène des identités dans l'espace d'un village chrétien," *Revue d'études des mondes musulmans et de la Méditerranée* 115–116, 2006, 176–189.

Chiffoleau, Sylvia (ed.), "La Syrie au quotidien: cultures et pratiques du changement," *Revue des mondes musulmans et de la Méditerranée* 115–116, 2006.

Clark, Janine, *Islam, Charity and Activism: Middle-class Networks and Social Welfare in Egypt, Jordan Yemen*, Bloomington, Indiana University Press, 2004.

Coleman, James, "Social Capital in the Creation of Human Capital," *American Journal of Sociology* 94, 1988, 95–120.

Collier, Paul and Hoeffler, Anke, "Greed and Grievance in Civil War," *The World Bank Policy Research Working Paper* 2355, 2000.

Collier, Paul and Hoeffler, Anke, "On the Economic Causes of Civil War," *Oxford Economic Papers* 50, 1998, 563–573.

Colliot-Thélène, Catherine, "La fin du monopole de la violence légitime? " *Revue d'études comparatives Est-Ouest*, 34 (1), 2003, 5–31.

Courbage, Youssef, "La population de la Syrie: des réticences à la transition (démographique)," in Dupret, B., Ghazzal, Z., Mujahidin, Y., and al-Dbiyat, M. (eds.), *La Syrie au présent. Reflets d'une société*, Paris, Actes Sud, 2007, pp. 177–213.

Cousin, Bruno and Chauvin, Sébastien, "L'économie symbolique du capital social," *Actes de la recherche en sciences sociales* 193 (3), 2012, 96–103.

Cramer, Christopher, "Homo Economicus Goes to War: Methodological Individualism, Rational Choice and the Political Economy of War," *World Development* 30 (11), 2002, 1845–1864.

Cramer, Christopher and Richards, Paul, "Violence and War in Agrarian Perspective," *Journal of Agrarian Change* 11 (3), 2011.

Daher, Aurélie, "In the Wake of the Islamic State Threat: Repercussions on Sunni-Shi'i Competition in Lebanon," *Journal of Shi'a Islamic Studies* 8 (2), 2015, 209–235.

Daher, Aurélie, "Un chiisme combattant face au monde: La politique étrangère du Hezbollah," in Adraoui, M.-A. (ed.), *Les islamistes et le monde. Islam politique et relations internationales*, Paris, L'Harmattan, 2015, pp. 147–164.

Davenport, Christian and Ball, Patrick, "Views to a Kill: Exploring the Implications of Source Selection in the Case of Guatemalan State Terror, 1977–1995," *The Journal of Conflict Resolution* 46 (3), 2002, 427–450.

De Châtel, Francesca, "The Role of Drought and Climate Change in the Syrian Insurgency: Untangling the Triggers of the Revolution," *Middle Eastern Studies* 50 (4), 2014, 1–15.

De Sardan, Jean-Pierre Olivier, "La politique du terrain," *Enquête* 1, 1995.

De Swaan, Abram, *The Killing Compartments: The Mentality of Mass Murder*, New Haven, Yale University Press, 2015.

De Vaumas, Etienne, "La population de la Syrie," *Annales de Géographie* 64 (341), 1955, 74–80.

De Waal, Alex, "Mission Without End: Peacekeeping in the African Political Marketplace," *International Affairs* 85 (1), 2009, 99–113.

Debos, Marielle, *Living by the Gun in Chad: Governing Africa's Inter-Wars*, London, Zed Books 2016.

Della Porta, Donatella, *Mobilizing for Democracy: Comparing 1989 and 2011*, Oxford, Oxford University Press, 2014.

Derluguian, Georgi, *Bourdieu's Secret Admirer in the Caucasus*, Chicago, University of Chicago Press, 2005.

Dobry, Michel, *Sociologie des crises politiques: la dynamique des crises multisectorielles*, Paris, Presses de Sciences Po, 2009.

Donati, Caroline, "The Economics of Authoritarian Upgrading in Syria: Liberalization and the Reconfiguration of Economic Networks," in Heydemann S. and Leenders, R. (eds.), *Middle East Authoritarianisms: Governance, Contestation, and Regime Resilience in Syria and Iran*, Stanford, Stanford University Press, 2013, pp. 35–60.

Donati, Caroline, *L'exception syrienne: entre marchandisation et résistance*, Paris, La Découverte, 2011.

Dorronsoro, Gilles, "Dynamiques entre champs religieux et politique. Le cas de l'Afghanistan," *Purusārtha* 30, 2012

Dorronsoro, Gilles, "La torture discrète: capital social, radicalisation et désengagement militant dans un régime sécuritaire," *European Journal of Turkish Studies* 8, 2008, https://ejts.revues.org/2223.

Dorronsoro, Gilles, *Que veut la Turquie?*, Paris, Autrement, 2008.

Dorronsoro, Gilles, *Revolution Unending: Afghanistan, 1979 to the Present*, New York, Columbia University Press, 2005.

Dorronsoro, Gilles, "The Transformation of the Afghanistan-Pakistan Border," in Bashir S. and Crews R. (eds.), *Under the Drones: Modern Lives in the Afghanistan-Pakistan Borderlands*, Cambridge, Harvard University Press, 2012, pp. 30–44.

Dorronsoro, Gilles and Gourisse, Benjamin, "Une clé de lecture du politique en Turquie: les rapports État-Partis," *Politix* 107 (1), 2015, 195–218.

Dorronsoro, Gilles and Grojean, Olivier (eds.), *Identity, Conflict and Politics in Turkey, Iran and Pakistan*, Hurst, London, 2017.

Dorronsoro, Gilles and Watts, Nicole, "The Collective Production of Challenge: Civil Society, Parties, and pro-Kurdish Politics in Diyarbakir," in Massicard, Elise and Watts, Nicole (eds.), *Negotiating Political Power in Turkey: Breaking up the Party*, London, Routledge, 2013.

Dot-Pouillard, Nicolas, "Le mouvement national palestinien et la crise syrienne: une division contenue," in Burgat, F. and Paoli, B. (eds.), *Pas de Printemps pour la Syrie, Les clés pour comprendre les acteurs et les défis de la crise (2011–2013)*, Paris, La Découverte, 2013, pp. 264–275.

Dot-Pouillard, Nicolas, "Les divisions stratégiques des oppositions syriennes: un leadership impossible?" in Burgat, F. and Paoli, B. (eds.), *Pas de Printemps pour la Syrie, Les clés pour comprendre les acteurs et les défis de la crise (2011–2013)*, Paris, La Découverte, 2013, pp. 115–218.

Druckman James, Green, Donald, Kuklinski, James, and Lupia, Arthur (eds.), *Cambridge Handbook of Experimental Political Science*, Cambridge, Cambridge University Press, 2011.

Drysdale, Alasdair, *Center and Periphery in Syria: A Political Geographic Study*, Thesis, University of Michigan, 1977.

Dupret-Schepens, Catherine, "Les populations syriennes sont-elles homogènes?" in Dupret, B., Ghazzal, Z., Mujahidin, Y., and al-Dbiyat, M. (eds.), *La Syrie au présent. Reflets d'une société*, Paris, Actes Sud, 2007, pp. 115–233.

Dupret, Baudouin, Belhadj, Souhail, and Ferrié, Jean-Noël, "Démocratie, famille et procédure. Ethnométhodologie d'un débat parlementaire syrien," *Revue européenne des sciences sociales* 65 (139), 2007, 5–44.

Dupret, Baudouin, Ghazzal, Zouhair, Courbage, Youssef, and al-Dbiyat, Mohammed (eds.), *La Syrie au présent. Reflets d'une société*, Paris, Actes Sud, 2007.

El Salah, Ali, "Les bourgeoisies syrienne," in Dupret, B., Ghazzal, Courbage, Y., and al-Dbiyat, M. (eds.), *La Syrie au présent. Reflets d'une société*, Paris, Actes Sud, 2007, pp. 771–778.

El-Chazli, Youssef, "On the road to revolution : How did 'depoliticised' Egyptians become revolutionaries?" *Revue française de science politique* 62 (5), 2012.

Elias, Norbert, *The Civilizing Process, Vol. II. State Formation and Civilization*, Oxford, Blackwell, 1982.

Elwert, Georg, "Market of Violence," in Elwert, G., Feuchtwang, S. and Neuvert D. (eds.), *Dynamics of Violence. Processes of Escalation and De-Escalation in Violent Group Conflicts*, Berlin, Duncker & Humblot, 1999, pp. 85–102.

Esteban, Joan and Schneider, Gerald, "Polarization and Conflict: Theoretical and Empirical Issues," *Journal of Peace Resolution* 45 (2), 2008.

Fearon, James, "Rationalist Explanations for War," *International Organization* 49 (3), 1995, 379–414.

Ferwerda, Jeremy and Miller, Nicholas L., "Political Devolution and Resistance to Foreign Rule: A Natural Experiment," *American Political Science Review* 108 (03), 642–660.

Festinger, Leon, Riecken, Henry, and Schachter, Stanley, *When Prophecy Fails: A Social and Psychological Study of a Modern Group That Predicted the Destruction of the World*, New York, Harper-Torchbooks, 1964.

Fillieule, Olivier, "Requiem pour un concept. Vie et mort de la notion de structure des opportunités politiques," in Dorronsoro G. (ed.), *La Turquie conteste*, Paris, Presses du CNRS, 2006, pp. 201–218.

Finnström, Sverker, *Living with Bad Surroundings: War, History and Everyday Moment in Northern Uganda*, Durham, Duke University Press, 2008.

Flach, Anja, Ayboga, Ercan, and Knapp, Michael, *Revolution in Rojava: Democratic Autonomy and Women's Liberation in the Syrian Kurdistan*, Chicago, University of Chicago Press, 2016.

Flugerud, Øivind, *Life on the Outside: Tamil Diaspora and Long Distance Nationalism*, London, Pluto Press, 1999.

Foucault, Michel, *The Courage of the Truth (The Government of Self and Others II): Lectures at the Collège de France, 1983–1984*, Basingstoke, Palgrave Macmillan, 2011.

Foucault, Michel, "The Political Function of the Intellectual," *Radical Philosophy* 17, 1977, 12–15.

Frisch, Hillel (ed.), "The Role of the Military in the Arab Tumult," *Journal of Strategic Studies* 36 (2), 2012.

Gayer, Laurent, "Faire l'amour et la guerre: le problème des 'relations physiques' au sein de la People's Liberation Army (PLA) du Népal," *Politix* 107 (3), 2014, 85–115.

Gayer, Laurent, *Karachi: Ordered Disorder and the Struggle for the City*, London, Hurst, 2014.

Geffray, Christian, *La cause des armes au Mozambique: anthropologie d'une guerre civile*, Paris, Karthala, 1990.

Geisser, Vincent, "Le Liban, au coeur de la crise syrienne, en marge des révolutions arabes?," in Burgat, F. and Paoli, B. (eds.), *Pas de Printemps pour la Syrie, Les clés pour comprendre les acteurs et les défis de la crise (2011–2013)*, Paris, La Découverte, 2013, pp. 219–237.

Georgeon, François, *Abdülhamit le Sultan calife (1976–1909)*, Paris, Fayard, 2003.

Ghazzal, Zouhair, "Shared Social and Juridical Meanings in Aleppo Neighborhood," in Ababsa, M., Dupret B., and Denis, E. (eds.), *Popular housing and urban land tenure in the Middle East*, Cairo, The American University in Cairo Press, 2012, pp. 169–202.

Glasman, Wladimir, "Les ressources sécuritaires du regime," in Burgat, F. and Paoli, B. (eds.), *Pas de Printemps pour la Syrie, Les clés pour comprendre les acteurs et les défis de la crise (2011–2013)*, Paris, La Découverte, 2013, pp. 33–53.

Goffman, Erving, *Asylums: Essays on the Social Situation of Mental Patients and Other Inmates*, Garden City, Anchor Books, 1961.

Goulden, Robert, "Housing, Inequality, and Economic Change in Syria," *British Journal of Middle Eastern Studies* 38 (2), 2011, 187–202.

Granovetter, Mark, "The Strength of Weak Ties," *American Journal of Sociology*, 78 (6), 1973, 1360–1380.

Granovetter, Mark, "Threshold Models of Collective Behavior," *American Journal of Sociology* 83 (6), 1978, 1420–1443.

Grawert, Elke, "Cross-Border Dynamics of Violent Conflict: The Case of Sudan and Chad," *Journal of Asian and African Studies* 43 (6), 2008, 595–614.

Green, Donald P. and Shapiro, Ian, *Pathologies of Rational Choice Theory: A Critique of Applications in Political Science*, New Haven, Yale University Press, 1994.

Green, Linda, *Fear as a Way of Life: Mayan Widow in Rural Guatemala*, New York, Columbia University Press, 1999.

Grojean, Olivier, "La production de l'Homme nouveau au sein du PKK," *European Journal of Turkish Studies*, 8, 2008.

Grojean, Olivier, *La révolution kurde: enquête sur une utopie en actes*, Paris, La Découverte, 2017.

Grojean, Olivier, "Les aléas d'un terrain comme révélateurs de sa structuration: gestion et objectivation d'une relation d'enquête sur une mouvance radicale et transnationale," *Revue internationale de politique comparée* 17 (4), 2010, 63–76.

Gunter, Michael *Out of Nowhere: The Kurds of Syria in Peace and War*, Oxford, Oxford University Press, 2014.

Gurr, Ted, *Why Men Rebel?* Princeton, Princeton University Press, 1970.

Gutiérrez Sanín, Francisco and Wood, Elisabeth, "Ideology in Civil War: Instrumental Adoption and Beyond," *Journal of Peace Research* 51 (2), 2014, 213–226.

Haddad, Bassam, *Business Networks in Syria: The Political Economy of Authoritarian Resilience*, Stanford, Stanford University Press, 2012.

Haddad, Bassam, "Syria's State Bourgeoisie: An Organic Backbone for the Regime," *Middle East Critique* 21 (3), 2012, 231–257.

Haddad, Bassam, "The Formation and Development of Economic Network in Syria: Implications for Economic and Fiscal Reforms, 1986–2000," in Heydemann, S. (ed.), *Networks of Privilege in the Middle East: The Politics of Economic Reform Revisited*, New York, Palgrave Macmillan, 2004, pp. 53–66.

Haenni, Patrick, *L'ordre des caïds. Conjurer la dissidence urbaine au Caire*, Paris, Karthala, 2005.

Hammal, Fadi, Mock, Jeremiah, Ward, Kenneth, Fouad, Fouad, Beech, Bettina, and Maziak, Wasim, "Settling with Danger: Conditions and Health Problems in Peri-Urban Neighbourhoods in Aleppo, Syria," *Environment and Urbanization* 17 (2), 2005, 113–125.

Harpviken, Kristian Berg, *Social Networks and Migration in Wartime Afghanistan*, London, Palgrave Macmillan, 2009.

Hashemi, Nader and Postel, Daniel (eds.), *The Syrian Dilemma*, Cambridge, MIT Press, 2013.

Hassine, Jonathan, *Les réfugiés et déplacés de Syrie: Une reconstruction nationale en question*, Paris, L'Harmattan, 2016.

Hegghammer, Thomas and Nesser, Petter, "Assessing the Islamic State's Commitment to Attacking the West," *Perspectives on Terrorism* 9 (4), 2015, 14–30.

Herrera, Yoshiko and Kapur, Devesh, "Improving Data Quality: Actors, Incentives, and Capabilities," *Political Analysis* 15 (4), 2007, 365–386.

Heydemann, Steven, *Upgrading Authoritarianism in the Arab World*, Washington, Brooking's Institute, 2007.

Heydemann, Steven and Leenders, Reinoud (eds.), *Middle East Authoritarianisms: Governance, Contestation, and Regime Resilience in Syria and Iran*, Stanford, Stanford University Press, 2013.

Heydemann, Steven and Leenders, Reinoud, *Resilient Authoritarianism in the Middle East: Lessons from Syria and Iran & Implications for Democracy Promotion*, La Hague, Hivos, 2011.

Hibou, Béatrice, *Anatomie politique de la domination*, Paris, La Découverte, 2011.

Hibou, Béatrice, "Retrait ou redéploiement de l'Etat," *Critique internationale* 1, 1998, 128–129.

Hibou, Béatrice, "The Political Economy of the World Bank's Discourse: from Economic Catechism to Missionary Deeds (and Misdeeds)," *Etudes du CERI* 39, 2000.

Hinnenbusch, Raymond A. and Zintl, Tina (eds.), *Syria from Reform to Revolt: Volume 1, Political Economy and International Relations*, Syracuse, Syracuse University Press, 2015.

Hinnenbusch, Raymond A., "Local Politics in Syria: Organization and Mobilization in Four Village Cases," *Middle East Journal* 30 (1), 1976, 1–24.

Hinnenbusch, Raymond A., *Revolution From Above*, New York, Routledge, 2002.

Hinnenbusch, Raymond A., "Syria: From Authoritarian Upgrading to Revolution?" *International Affairs* 88 (1), 2012, 95–113.

Hinnenbusch, Raymond A., "Syria: The Politics of Economic Liberalization," *Third World Quarterly* 18 (2), 1997, 249–265.

Hinnenbusch, Raymond A., "The Political Economy of Economic Liberalization in Syria," *International Journal of Middle East Studies* 27 (3) 1995, 305–310.

Hokayem, Emile, "Iran, the Gulf States and the Syrian Civil War," *Survival* 56 (6), 2014, 59–86.

Hokayem, Emile, "Syria's Uprising and the Fracturing of the Levant," *Adelphi Papers* 438, 2013.

Honneth, Axel, *The Struggle for Recognition: The Moral Grammar of Social Conflicts*, New York, Polity Press, 1995.

Hourcade, Bernard, "L'Iran contre l'encerclement sunnite'," in Burgat, F. and Paoli, B. (eds.), *Pas de Printemps pour la Syrie, Les clés pour comprendre les acteurs et les défis de la crise (2011–2013)*, Paris, La Découverte, 2013, pp. 276–281.

Hudson, Leila, "Le voile et le portable: l'adolescence sous Bachar al-Assad," in Dupret, B., Ghazzal, Z., Mujahidin, Y., and al-Dbiyat, M. (eds.), *La Syrie au présent. Reflets d'une société*, Paris, Actes Sud, 2007, pp. 303–312.

Humphreys, Macartan and Weinstein, Jeremy, "Field Experiments and the Political Economy of Development," *Annual Review of Political Science* 12, 2009, 367–378.

Humphreys, Macartan and Weinstein, Jeremy, "Who Fights? The Determinants of Participation in Civil War," *American Journal of Political Science* 52 (2) (2008), 436–455.

Ismail, Salwa, "The Syrian Insurgency: Imagining and Performing the Nation," *Studies in Ethnicity and Nationalism* 11 (3), 2011, 538–549.

James, Fearon and Laitin, David, "Ethnicity, Insurgency, and Civil War," *American Political Science Review* 97 (1), 2003, 75–90.

Jasper, James, *The Art of Moral Protest*, Chicago, The University of Chicago Press, 1997.

Jervis, Robert, *Perception and Misperception in International Politics*, Princeton Princeton University Press, 1978.

Kalyvas, Stathis, *The Logic of Violence in Civil War*, Cambridge, Cambridge University Press, 2006.

Karabet, Aram, *Treize ans dans les prisons syriennes. Voyage vers l'inconnu*, Paris, Actes Sud, 2013.

Karmer, Martin, "Syria's Alawis and Shi'ism," in Karmer, M. (ed.), *Shi'ism, Resistance and Revolution*, Boulder, Westview Press, 1987, pp. 246–249.

Khalifé, Moustafa, *La Coquille. Prisonnier politique en Syrie*, Paris, Actes Sud, 2007.

Kienle, Eberhard, "Entre jamaa et classe: le pouvoir politique en Syrie contemporaine," *Revue des mondes musulmans et de la Méditerranée* 59–60, 1991, 211–239.

Kocher, Matthew, and Monteiro, Nuno, "What's in a line? Natural Experiments and the Line of Demarcation in WWII Occupied France (July 31, 2015)." Available at SSRN: http://ssrn.com/abstract=2555716.

Koloma Beck, Teresa *The Normality of Civil War: Armed Groups and Everyday Life in Angola*, Frankfurt, Campus Verlag, 2012.

Kooning, Kee and Kruijts, Dirk (eds.), *Societies of Fear: The Legacy of Civil War, Violence and Terror in Latin America*, London, Zed Books, 1999.

Koopmans, Ruud, Duyvendak, Jan W., "The Political Construction of the Nuclear Energy Issue and its Impact on the Mobilization of Anti-Nuclear Movements in Western Europe," *Social Problems* 42 (2), 1995, 235–251.

Kuran, Timur, *Private Truths, Public Lies: The Social Consequences of Preference Falsification*, Cambridge, Harvard University Press, 1997.

Kurzman, Charles, *The Unthinkable Revolution in Iran*, Cambridge, Harvard University Press, 2005.

Lagroye, Jacques (ed.), *La politisation*, Paris, Belin, 2003.

Lahire, Bernard, *Monde pluriel: penser l'unité des sciences sociales*, Paris, Seuil, 2012, p. 63.

Lahire, Bernard, *Portraits sociologiques: Dispositions et variations individuelles*, Paris, Nathan, 2002.

Laue, Franziska, "Vertical Versus Horizontal: Constraints of Modern Living Conditions in Informal Settlements and the Reality of Construction," in Ababsa, M., Dupret, B., and Denis, E. (eds.), *Popular Housing and Urban Land Tenure in the Middle East*, Cairo, The American University in Cairo Press, 2012, pp. 111–135.

Lavergne, Marc, "L'urbanisation contemporaine de la Syrie du Nord," *Revue des mondes musulmans et de la Méditerranée* 62, 1991, 195–208.

Lawson, Fred H., *Demystifying Syria*, London, Saqi Books, 2010.

Le Caisne, Garance, *Opération César: Au cœur de la machine de mort syrienne*, Paris, Editions Stock, 2015.

Le Saux, Mathieu, "Les dynamiques contradictoires du Champ associatif syrien," *Revue d'études des mondes musulmans et de la Méditerranée* 115–116, 2006, 193–209.

Leenders, Reinoud, "Collective Action and Mobilization in Dar'a: an anatomy of the onset of Syria's popular insurgency," *Mobilization* 17 (4), 2012, 419–434.

Leenders, Reinoud, "Iraqi Refugees in Syria: Causing a Spill-over of the Iraqi Conflict," *Third World Quarterly* 29 (8), 2008, 1563–1584.

Leenders, Reinoud, "'Oh Buthaina, Oh Sha'ban – The Hawrani Is Not Hungry, We Want Freedom!': Revolutionary Framing and Mobilization at the Onset of the Syrian Insurgency," in Beinin, J. and Vairel, F. (eds), *Social movements, Mobilization, and Contestation in the Middle East and North Africa, Second Edition*, Stanford, Stanford University Press, 2013, pp. 246–261.

Leenders, Reinoud, and Heydemann, Steven, "Popular Mobilization in Syria: Opportunity and Threat, and the Social Networks of the Early Risers," *Mediterranean Politics* 17 (2), 2011, 139–159.

Lefevre, Raphaël, *Ashes of Hama: The Muslim Brotherhood in Syria*, London, Hurst, 2013.

Lischer, Sarah, "Collateral Damage: Humanitarian Assistance as a Cause of Conflict," *International Security* 28 (1), 2003, 79–109.

Lister, Charles, *The Syrian Jihad: Al-Qaeda, the Islamic State and the Evolution of an Insurgency*, Oxford, Oxford University Press, 2016.

Lohmann, Susanne, "The Dynamics of Informational Cascade: The Monday Demonstrations in Leipzig, East Germany, 1989–1991," *World Politics* 47 (1), 1994, 42–101.

Lubkemann, Stephen C., *Culture in Chaos: An Anthropology of the Social Condition in War*, Chicago, Chicago University Press, 2008.

Lund, Aron, *Struggling to Adapt: The Muslim Brotherhood in a New Syria*, Washington, Carnegie Endowment for International Peace, 2013.

Lyall, Jason, Blair, Graeme, and Imai, Kosuke, "Explaining Support for Combatants During Wartime: A Survey Experiment in Afghanistan," *American Political Science Review* 107 (4), 2013, 679–705.

Macek, Ivana, *Sarajevo Under Siege: Anthropology in Wartime*, Philadelphia, University of Pennsylvania Press, 2009.

Majed, Ziad, *Syrie, la révolution orpheline*, Paris, Actes Sud, 2014.

Mampilly, Zachariah, *Rebel Rulers: Insurgent Governance and Civilian Life During War*, Ithaca, Cornell University Press, 2011.

Marchal, Roland and Messiant, Christine, "De l'avidité des rebelles: l'analyse économique de la guerre civile selon Paul Collier," *Critique internationale* 16, 2002, 58–69

Martinez, Luis, *The Algerian Civil War 1990–1998*, New York, Columbia University Press, 2000.

Martinez, Luis, *The Libyan Paradox*, New York, Columbia Press, 2007.

Massey, Douglas, Espana, Felipe, "The Social Process of International Migration," *Science* 237, 1987, 733–738.

Mauss, Marcel "Techniques of the body," *Economy and Society* 2 (1), 1973, 70–88.

McDowall, David, *The Kurds of Syria*, London: KHRP, 1998.

McGovern, Mike, "Popular Development Economics – An Anthropologist Among the Mandarins," *Perspectives on Politics* 9 (2), 2011, 345–355.

Menkhaus, Ken, "Governance without Government in Somalia: Spoiler, State-Building and the Politics of Coping," *International Security* 31 (3), 2006/7, 74–106.

Méouchy, Nadine, "Les mobilisations urbaines et rurales à l'époque mandataire. Remarques préliminaires," in Méouchy, N. (ed.), *France, Syrie et Liban, 1918–1946: les ambiguïtés et les dynamiques de la relation mandataire*, Damas, IFEAD, 2002, pp. 315–323.

Mervin, Sabrina, "Des nosayris aux ja'farites: le processus de 'chiitisation' des alaouites," in Dupret, B., Ghazzal, Z., Mujahidin, Y., and al-Dbiyat, M. (eds.), *La Syrie au présent. Reflets d'une société*, Paris, Actes Sud, 2007, pp. 359–364.

Mikaïl, Barah (ed.), "La tragédie syrienne," *Confluences Méditerranée* 89 (2), 2014.

Mildner, Stormy-Annika, Lauster, Gitta, and Wodni, Wiebke "Scarcity and Abundance Revisited: A Literature Review on Natural Resources and Conflict," *International Journal of Conflict and Violence* 5 (1), 2011.

Mohtadi, Shahrzad, "Climate Change and the Syrian Uprising," *Bulletin of the Atomic Scientists*, 2012.

Monsutti, Alessandro "Fuzzy Sovereignty: Rural Reconstruction in Afghanistan, between Democracy Promotion and Power Games," *Comparative Studies in Society and History* 54 (3), 2012, 563–591.

Monsutti, Alessandro, *War and Migration: Social Networks and Economic Strategies of the Hazaras of Afghanistan*, London, Routledge, 2005.

Montgomery, Harriet, *The Kurds of Syria: An Existence Denied*, Berlin, Europäisches Zentrum für Kurdische Studien, 2005.

Moussaoui, Abderrahmane, "Du danger et du terrain en Algérie," *Ethnologie française* 37 (2), 2001, 51–59.

Nordstrom, Carolyn, *A Different Kind of War Story*, Philadelphia, University of Pennsylvania Press, 1997.

Nordstrom, Carolyn, *Girls and Warzones: Troubling Questions*, Uppsala, Life and Peace Institute, 1997.

Nordstrom, Carolyn, and Robben, Antonius, *Fieldwork Under Fire*, Oakland, University of California Press, 1996.

North, Douglass, Wallis, John, and Weingast, Barry, *Violence and Social Orders: A Conceptual Framework for Interpreting Recorded Human History*, Cambridge, Cambridge University Press, 2009.

O'Dell, Emily J., "Waging War on the Dead: The Necropolitics of Sufi Shrine Destruction in Mali," *Archaeologies* 9 (3), 2013, 506–525.

Olson, Mancur, *The Logic of Collective Action: Public Goods and The Theory of Groups*, Cambridge, Harvard University Press, 1971.

Opp, Karl-Dieter, Gem, Christiane, and Voss, Peter, *Origins of a Spontaneous Revolution: East Germany, 1989*, Ann Arbor, University of Michigan Press, 1996.

Paoli, Bruno, "Et maintenant, on va où? Les alaouites à la croisée des destins," in Burgat, F. and Paoli, B. (eds.), *Pas de Printemps pour la Syrie, Les clés pour comprendre les acteurs et les défis de la crise (2011–2013)*, Paris, La Découverte, 2013, pp. 124–143.

Pearlman, Wendy, "Moral Identity and Protest Cascades in Syria," *British Journal of Political Science*, Published online November 10, 2016.

Pérouse, Jean-François (ed.), "Les tribulations du terme gecekondu (1947–2004): une lente perte de substance. Pour une clarification terminologique," *European Journal of Turkish Studies* 1, 2004.

Perthes, Volker, *The Political Economy of Syria under Asad*, London, I.B. Tauris, 1995.

Petersen, Roger *Understanding Ethnic Violence: Fear, Hatred, Resentment in Twentieth Century Eastern Europe*, Cambridge, Cambridge University Press, 2002.

Pfaff, Steven, "Collective Identity and Informal Groups in Revolutionary Mobilizations: East Germany in 1989," *Social Forces* 75 (1), 1996, 91–117.

Picard, Elizabeth, "Fin de partie en Syrie," *Revue des mondes musulmans et de la Méditerranée* 81–82, 1996, 207–229.

Picard, Elizabeth, "Syrie: la coalition autoritaire fait de la résistance," *Politique étrangère* 4, 2005, 755–768.

Pierret, Thomas, *Baas et islam en Syrie: la dynastie Assad face aux oulémas*, Paris, Presses Universitaires de France, 2011.

Pierret, Thomas, "Crise et déradicalisation: les rebelles syriens d'Ahrar al-Sham," *Confluences Méditerranée* 94 (3), 2015, 43–49.

Pierret, Thomas, "Fragmentation et consolidation de l'opposition armée," *Confluences méditerranéennes* 89 (2), 2014, 45–51.

Pierret, Thomas, "L'islam dans la révolution syrienne," *Politique étrangère* 4, 2011, 884–888.

Pierret, Thomas, *Les oulémas syriens aux XXe-XXIe siècles*, Thesis, Sciences Po Paris – UCL, 2009.

Pierret, Thomas, "Les oulémas: une hégémonie religieuse ébranlée par la revolution," in Burgat, F. and Paoli, B.(eds.), *Pas de Printemps pour la Syrie, Les clés pour comprendre les acteurs et les défis de la crise (2011–2013)*, Paris, La Découverte, 2013, pp. 92–106.

Pierret, Thomas, "Les salafismes dans l'insurrection syrienne: des réseaux transnationaux à l'épreuve des réalités locales," *Outre-Terre* 44 (3), 2015, 196–215.

Pierret, Thomas, *Religion and State in Syria: The Sunni Ulama from Coup to Revolution*, Cambridge, Cambridge University Press, 2013.

Pierret, Thomas, "Salafis at War in Syria: Logics of Fragmentation and Realignment," in Cavatorta, Francesco and Merone, Fabio (eds.), *Salafism After the Arab Awakening: Salafism After the Arab Awakening Contending with People's Power*, London, Hurst, 2015.

Pierret, Thomas, "The State Management of Religion in Syria," in Heydemann S. and Leenders, R. (eds.), *Middle East Authoritarianisms: Governance, Contestation, and Regime Resilience in Syria and Iran*, Stanford, Stanford University Press, 2013, pp. 83–106.

Pierret, Thomas and Cheikh, Mériam, "'I Am Very Happy Here': Female Jihad in Syria as Self-Accomplishment," *Journal of Women of the Middle East and the Islamic World* 13, 2015, 241–269.

Pierret, Thomas and Selvik, Kjetil, "Limits of 'Authoritarian Upgrading' in Syria: Private Welfare, Islamic charities, and the Rise of the Zayd Movement", *International Journal Middle Eastern Studies* 41, 2009, pp. 595–614.

Poirier, Marine, "De la place de la Libération (al-Tahrir) à la place du Changement (al-Taghyir): Recompositions des espaces et expressions du politique au Yémen," in Allal A. and Pierret T. (eds.), *Au cœur des révolutions arabes: devenir révolutionnaire*, Paris, Armand Colin, 2013, pp. 31–51.

Polletta, Francesca and Amenta, Edwin, "Second That Emotion? Lessons from Once-Novel Concepts in Social Movement Research," in Goodwin, J., Jasper, J.M., and Polletta, F. (eds.), *Passionate Politics: Emotions and Social Movements*, Chicago, The University of Chicago Press, 2001, pp. 303–316.

Quesnay, Arthur and Roussel, Cyril, "Avec qui se battre ? Le dilemme kurde," in Burgat, F. and Paoli, B. (eds.), *Pas de Printemps pour la Syrie, Les clés pour comprendre les acteurs et les défis de la crise (2011–2013)*, Paris, La Découverte, 2013, pp. 144–157.

Rabo, Annika, "Affective, Parochial or Innovative? Aleppo Traders on the Margin of Global Capitalism," *Revue des mondes musulmans et de la Méditerranée* 115–116, 2006, 43–58.

Raymond, Candice, *Réécrire l'histoire au Liban. Une génération d'historiens face à la période ottomane, de la fin des années 1960 à nos jours*, Thesis, EHESS, 2013.

Revel, Jean-François, *The Flight from Truth: The Reign of Deceit in the Age of Information*, New York, Random House, 1992.

Richards, Paul, *Fighting for the Rain Forest: War, Youth and Resources in Sierra Leone*, Portsmouth, Heinemann, 1996.

Richmond, Anthony, "Sociological Theories of International Migrations: The Case of Refugees," *Current Sociology* 36 (2), 1988, 7–26.

Roberts, David B., "Understanding Qatar's Foreign Policy Objectives," *Mediterranean Politics* 17 (2), 2012, 233–239.

Robinson, Glenn, "Elite Cohesion, Regime Succession and Political Instability in Syria," *Middle East Policy* 5 (4), 1998, 159–179.

Rodgers, Dennis, *Making Danger a Calling: Anthropology, Violence and the Dilemmas of Participant Observation*, London, LES Development Research Centre, 2001.

Rougier, Bernard, *L'oumma en fragments*, Paris, Presses Universitaires de France, 2011.

Roussel, Cyril, "La construction d'un territoire kurde en Syrie: un processus en cours," *Maghreb-Machrek* 213 (3), 2012, 83–98.

Roussel, Cyril, *Les Druzes du Liban et de Syrie*, Gallimard, Paris, forthcoming.

Roussel, Cyril, *Les Druzes de Syrie. Territoire et mobilité*, Beirut, Presses de l'Ifpo, 2011.

Roussel, Cyril, "Les grandes familles druzes entre local et national," *Revue des Mondes Musulmans et de la Méditerranée* 115–116, 2006, 135–153.

Roussel, Cyril "Les Kurdes de Syrie et le projet du Rojava: rêve éphémère ou espoir durable ?" *Maghreb-Machrek* 222 (4), 2014, 75–97.

Rowell, Jay, *Le totalitarisme au concret. Les politiques du logement en RDA*, Paris, Economica, 2006.

Rufin, Jean-Christophe and Jean, François (eds.), *L'économie des guerres civiles*, Paris, Hachette, 1996.

Ruiz de Elvira Carrascal, Laura, "State/Charities Relation in Syria: Between Reinforcement, Control and Coercion," in Ruiz de Elvira Carrascal, L. and Zintl, T. *Civil Society and the State in Syria: The Outsourcing of Social Responsibility*, Boulder, Lynne Rienner, 2012, pp. 5–29.

Ruiz de Elvira, Laura and Tina, Zintl, "The End of the Ba'thist Social Contract in Bashar al-Asad's Syria: Reading Sociopolitical Transformations Through Charities and Broader Benevolent Activism," *International Journal of Middle Eastern Studies* 46, 2014, 329–349.

Salamandra, Christa and Stenberg, Leif (eds.), *Syria from Reform to Revolt, Volume 2, Culture, Society, and Religion*, Syracuse, Syracuse University Press, 2015.

Salehyan, Idean, "Transnational Rebels: Neighboring States as Sanctuary for Rebel Groups," *World Politics* 59 (2), 2007, 217–242.

Salehyan, Idean and Gleditsch, Kristian Skrede, "Refugees and the Spread of Civil War," *International Organization* 60 (2), 2006, 335–366.

Salibi, Kemal S., *Crossroads to Civil War: Lebanon, 1958–1976*, New York, Caravan Books, 1976.

Sambanis, Nicholas, "What Is Civil War," *Journal of Conflict Resolution* 48 (6), 2004.

Sanín, Francisco Gutiérrez and Wood, Elisabeth, "Ideology in Civil War: Instrumental Adoption and Beyond," *Journal of Peace Research* 51 (2), 2014, pp. 213–226.

Schlichte, Klaus, *In the Shadow of Violence. The Politics of Armed Groups*, Campus Verlag, Frankfurt/New York, 2009.

Scott, James, *Domination and the Arts of Resistance: Hidden Transcripts*, New Haven, Yale University Press, 1990.

Seurat, Michel, "Les populations, l'Etat et la société," in Raymond, André (ed.), *La Syrie d'aujourd'hui*, Paris, Editions du CNRS, 1980, pp. 87–141.

Seurat, Michel, *L'Etat de Barbarie*, Paris, Presses Universitaires de France, 2012.

Sewell Jr., William H., "A Theory of Structure: Duality, Agency, and Transformation," *The American Journal of Sociology* 98 (1), 1992, 1–29.

Shapiro, Jacob and Weidmann, Nils, "Is the Phone Mightier than the Sword? Cellphones and Insurgent Violence in Iraq," *International Organization* 69 (2), 2015, 247–274.

Shelling, Thomas C., "Hockey Helmets, Concealed Weapons, and Daylight Saving: A Study of Binary Choices with Externalities," *The Journal of Conflict Resolution* 17 (3), 1973, 381–428.

Shesterinina, Anastasia, "Collective Threat Framing and Mobilization in Civil War," *American Political Science Review* 110 (3), 2016, 411–427.

Sluka, Jeffrey, "Participant Observation in Violent Social Contexts," *Human Organization* 49 (2), 1990, 114–126.

Sluka, Jeffrey, "Reflections on Managing Danger in Fieldwork: Dangerous Anthropology in Belfast," in Sluka, J. and Robben, A. (eds.), *Ethnographic Fieldwork: An Anthropological Reader*, Hoboken, Wiley-Blackwell, 2012, pp. 283–296.

Staniland, Paul, *Networks of Rebellion: Explaining Insurgent Cohesion and Collapse*, Ithaca, Cornell University Press, 2014.

Staniland, Paul, "States, Insurgents, and Wartime Political Orders," *Perspectives on Politics* 10 (2), 2012, 243–264.

Stoner, James A., *A Comparison of Individual and Group Decisions Involving Risk*, unpublished master's dissertation, Cambridge, MIT, 1961.

Sunayama, Sonoko, *Syria and Saudi Arabia: Collaboration and Conflicts in the Oil Era*, London, I.B. Tauris, 2007.

Tarrow, Sydney, "Inside Insurgencies: Politics and Violence in an Age of Civil War," *Perspective on Politics* 5 (3), 2007.

Tarrow, Sydney, *Power in Movement: Social Movements, Collective Action and Politics*, Cambridge, Cambridge University Press, 1994.

Tejel, Jordi, "La jeunesse kurde entre rupture et engagement militant," in Dupret, B., Ghazzal, Z., Mujahidin, Y., and al-Dbiyat, M. (eds.), *La Syrie au présent. Reflets d'une société*, Paris, Actes Sud, 2007, pp. 269–276.

Tejel, Jordi, "Les Kurdes de Syrie, de la 'dissimulation' à la 'visibilité'?" *Revue d'études des mondes musulmans et de la Méditerranée* 115–116, 2006, 117–133.

Tejel, Jordi, *Syria's Kurds, History, Politics and Society*, London, Routledge, 2009.

Tejel, Jordi and Savelsberg, Eva, "The Syrian Kurds in Transition to Somewhere," in Gunter, Michael and Mohammed, Ahmed (eds.), *The Kurdish Spring: Geopolitical Changes and the Kurds*, Costa Mesa, Mazda Publishers, 2013, pp. 189, 2017.

Terray, Emmanuel, "Le climatiseur et la véranda," in Adler, Alfred (ed.), *Afrique plurielle, Afrique actuelle: hommage à Georges Balandier*, Paris, Karthala, 1986, pp. 37–44.

Theodoropoulou, A. M. Kastrinou, "A Different Struggle for Syria: Becoming Young in the Middle East," *Mediterranean Politics* 17 (1), 2012, 68–73.

Tilly, Charles, "War-Making and State-Making as Organized Crime," in Evans, P.B., Rueschmeyer, D., and Skocpol, T. *Bringing the State Back in*, Cambridge, Cambridge University Press, 1985, pp. 169–191.

Traïni, Christophe, "From Feelings to Emotions (and Back Again): How Does One Become an Animal Rights Activist?" *Revue française de science politique* 60 (2), 2010, 335–338.

Turner, Lewis "Explaining the (Non-)Encampment of Syrian Refugees: Security, Class and the Labour Market in Lebanon and Jordan," *Mediterranean Politics* 20 (3), 386–404.

Valter, Stéphane (ed.), "La crise syrienne," *Maghreb-Machreq*, 213 (3), 2013, 5–8.

Vigh, Henrik, *Navigating Terrains of War: Youth and Soldiering in Guinea-Bissau*, New York, Berghahn, 2006.

Vignal, Leila, "Destruction-in-Progress: Revolution, Repression and War Planning in Syria (2011 Onwards)," *Built Environment* 40 (3), 2014, 326–341.

Vignal, Leïla, "Jours tranquilles à Damas. Aperçus de la révolte syrienne," *Esprit* 6, 2011, 94–102.

Vignal, Leïla, "La 'nouvelle consommation' et les transformations des paysages urbains à la lumière de l'ouverture économique: l'exemple de Damas," *Revue des mondes musulmans et de la Méditerranée* 115–116, 2006, 21–41.

Vlassenroot, Koen "Societal View on Violence and War: Conflict & Militia Formation in Eastern Congo," in Kaarsholm, Preben (ed.), *Violence, Political, Culture & Development in Africa*, Oxford, James Currey, 2006, pp. 49–65.

Vlassenroot, Koen, "War and Social Research: The Limits of Empirical Methodologies in War-Torn Environments," *Civilisations* 54, 2006, 191–198.

Vlassenroot, Koen and Raymaekers, Timothy, *Conflict and Social Transformation in Eastern DR Congo*, Gent, Academia Press, 2004.

Vlassenroot, Koen, and Raeymaekers, Timothy, "New Political Order in the D.R. Congo? The Transformation of Regulation," *Afrika Focus* 21 (2), 2008, 39–52.

Vlassentroot, Koen, Menkhaus, Ken, and Rayemaekers, Timothy "State and Non-State Regulation in African Protracted Crises: Governance Without Government," *Afrika Focus* 21 (2), 2008, 7–21.

Volker, Perthes, *Syria under Bachar al-Asad: Modernisation and the Limits of Change*, Adelphi Series (Book 366), 2004.

Walt, Stephen, "Rigor or Rigor Mortis: Rational Choice and Security Studies," *International Security* 23 (4), 1999, 5–48.

Walter, Barbara, "Bargaining Failures and Civil War," *Annual Review of Political Science*, 12, 2009, 243–261.

Walter, Barbara, *Reputation and Civil War: Why Separatist Conflicts Are so Violent*, Cambridge, Cambridge University Press, 2009.

Weber, Max, *Weber's Rationalism and Modern Society*, New York: Palgrave Macmillan, 2015.

Weber, Max, *Economy and Society: An Outline to Interpretative Sociology*, Berkeley, University of California Press, 1978.

Weber, Max, *From Max Weber: Essays in Sociology*, New York, Oxford University Press, 1946.

Wedeen, Lisa, "Ideology and Humor in Dark Times: Notes from Syria," *Critical Inquiries* 39, 2013, 841–873.

Wedeen, Lisa, "Reflections on Ethnographic Work in Political Science," *Annual Review of Political Science* 13, 2010, 255–272.

Wedeen, Lisa, *The Ambiguities of Domination: Politics, Rhetoric, and Symbols in Contemporary Syria*, Chicago, Chicago University Press, 1999.

Wehrey, Frederic, *Sectarian Politics in the Gulf: From the Iraq War to the Arab Uprisings*, New York, Columbia University Press, 2016.

Weinstein, Jeremy, *Inside Rebellion: The Politics of Insurgent Violence*, Cambridge, Cambridge University Press, 2007.

Weiss, Max, "Who Laughs Last: Literary Transformation of Syrian Authoritarianism," in Heydemann S. and Leenders, R. (eds.), *Middle East Authoritarianisms: Governance, Contestation, and Regime Resilience in Syria and Iran*, Stanford, Stanford University Press, 2013, 143–167.

Weiss, Michael and Hassan, Hassan, *ISIS: Inside the Army of Terror*, New York, Regan Arts, 2016.

Werrell, Caitlin and Femia, Francesco, "Climate Change Before and After the Arab Awakening: The Cases of Syria and Libya," in Werrell, Caitlin, Femia, Francesco, and Slaughter, Anne-Marie (eds.), *The Arab Spring and Climate Change*, Center for American Progress, Stimson, The Center for Climate and Security, pp. 23–32.

Wieland, Carsten, "Asad's Decade of Lost Chances," in Wieland, C., Almqvist, A., and Nassif, H. *The Syrian Uprising: Dynamics of an Insurgency*, Boulder, Lynne Rienner, 2013.

Wiktorowicz, Quintan, (ed.), *Islamic Activism: A Social Movement Theory Approach*, Bloomington, Indiana University Press, 2003.

Wolfinger, Raymond, "The Rational Citizen Faces Election Day, or What Rational Choice Theories Don't Tell You About American Elections," in Jennings, M. Kent and Mann, Thomas E. (eds.), *Elections at Home and Abroad: Essays in Honor of Warren E. Miller*, Ann Arbor, University of Michigan Press, 1993.

Wood, Elisabeth, "The Ethical Challenges of Field Research in Conflict Zones," *Qualitative Sociology* 29 (3), 2006, 373–386.

Wood, Elisabeth, *Insurgent Collective Action and Civil War in El Salvador*, Cambridge, Cambridge University Press, 2003.

Yazbek, Samar, *The Crossing: My Journey to the Shattered Heart of Syria*, London, Ebury Publishing, 2016.

Zacher, Mark, "The Territorial Integrity Norm: International Boundaries and the Use of Force," *International Organization* 55 (2), 2001, 215–250.

Zolberg, Aristide R., Suhrke, Astrin, and Aguayo, Sergio, *Escape from Violence, Conflict and the Refugee Crisis in the Developing World*, Oxford, Oxford University Press, 1989.

Index